COMMUNICATE!

A Workbook for Interpersonal Communication

Fifth Edition

Communication Research Associates

KENDALL/HUNT PUBLISHING COMPANY
4050 Westmark Drive   Dubuque, Iowa 52002

———— ACKNOWLEDGEMENTS ————

Editor-in Chief
Linda A. Joesting

Authors-Editors

Richard D. Carroll
Dianne Faieta
Gregg Florence
Linda A. Joesting
Betty Martin
Jim Ostach
Dianne G. Van Hook
Roger E. Van Hook
M. James Warnemuende

Special Credits

Relational Communication Chapter: Kat Carroll

FROM US
TO YOU AND YOUR SELF

We,
with our thoughts of today,
wish you the words of tomorrow.

We
want you
to be you,
to smile and to cry,
to touch the sensations of each day,
of each new way
you grow in your self.

We
need you
to reach beyond our limitations,
to willingly open
your eyes to laughter,
your ears to the song,
your hands to feel your world
and your voice to speak
the greatness of the small.

We
want and need you now
to communicate today
the sounds of Your valuable Self
and the value of Others,
that you might be the words
of solidarity,
blending the breaks of Humankind.

LAJ

TABLE OF CONTENTS

GETTING ACQUAINTED | 1

DEFINITIONS

Getting acquainted is the first step of any relationship. Below are some terms which you will find useful as you proceed through this chapter.

Dyad

A dyad is a group of two individuals.

Triad

A triad is a group of three individuals.

Ice Breaker

An ice breaker is an activity, strategy or game used to facilitate getting acquainted/getting to know someone.

THE IMPORTANCE OF GETTING ACQUAINTED

People often react very differently to the act of getting acquainted, of getting to know someone else. Some people seem to be able to hit it off very easily with people they have never met. Other people seem to get sweaty palms, heart palpitations, nervous stomachs at the very thought of having to meet another person for the first time. Why? We are all human, aren't we? Of course we are, but the answer goes way beyond that.

It is true that in many respects we are all alike; however, as the following boxed selection indicates, we are all unique individuals with different personalities and needs, as well as different levels of socialization skills. The purpose of this chapter is to help you develop and expand these skills.

BARRIERS TO GETTING ACQUAINTED

Many people have barriers toward classes such as speech and interpersonal communication. These barriers may have to do with our self-image and with our perceptions of other people.

Self-Image

Self-image barriers include poor self-esteem, shy behavior, lack of social skills and anxiety over how others may view us. For example, if we have not had a lot of experience in interacting with others in classes, clubs, families, etc., we may be afraid to try. We may be afraid of saying the wrong thing or if we do speak up, people may not like what we say and thus reject us. Therefore, classes such as this one must start with the requirement that we all

1

The Person Next to You

Who is the person sitting next to you?

What is the person's name? How tall is the person? I clearly see the color of my neighbor's hair and eyes, but I wonder what kind of clothes this individual likes? Where do you think the person lives? Does this person believe in evolution or creation? I wonder if my new neighbor will trust me? I wonder if we will enjoy talking about the same types of things? Is the person married . . . single . . . committed to another person . . .?

Do these questions define who the person next to you is?

Not really; you see the person next to you has a life story of extraordinary fullness. This living soul is a unique world of experience—a cluster of past memories, current actions, and expectations for the future. That person is a whole colony of people and events that have passed in and out of the person's life—parents, guardians, teachers, friends, enemies, jobs, schools, vacations, parties, problems, dreams, hobbies.

Much of the person next to you cannot be known immediately. How does the person make choices, accept responsibility, solve problems, perceive the world, work to capacity? How may I bring out the person's character as quickly as the photographer's chemicals bring out the forms latent in the negative?

How much does this person like himself or herself? How well does this person know and accept both his or her strengths as well as weaknesses? Is this person aware of how he/she fits into the scheme of things?

The person next to you is happy and sad, fearful and sure, content and wondering, shy and outgoing, asking questions and knowing answers—looking for respect, looking for love, looking for acceptance, looking for you . . . to reach out and care . . .

How much is this person like you? You probably will never know until you reach out, reach out to meet that unique person sitting next to you.

Who knows—you might even discover that even though the two of you are very different, you are in many ways very much the same. It is this seeming contradiction of "uniqueness" and "sameness" which can turn the person next to you into a close acquaintance, into your next best friend . . .

respect each other, support one another and refrain from rejecting or judging others.

Prejudging Others

Our perception of others can create barriers such as misjudging people, not giving others a chance, and/or stereotyping. For example, if we see someone sitting next to us who has a different hair style or who is from a different racial or ethnic background, we may not want to get to know him or her because of preconceived ideas or beliefs—i.e., long hairs take drugs; blacks don't take school seriously; football players are dumb; Asians are unfriendly, etc. These stereotypes have no basis in fact—the only thing they do is keep us from getting to know one another. When we get past these barriers and accept people individually, we find that each individual is unique and does not fit these preconceived notions.

Take a Risk

So, we challenge you to risk in this class. Risk getting to know others. Stay open to others and their ideas. Do not prejudge others. Remember to separate people from their ideas or behaviors. For example, others may wear their hair differently from you or have different ideas and values from your own but that does not mean that they are not worth knowing. Again, take risks, keep an open mind, get to know one another and make new friends in this course.

NAME GAME

PURPOSE:

To reduce the number of strangers in the class and to give you a chance to meet your classmates.

PROCEDURE:

1. Form a class circle so that everyone can see each other easily.
2. One person (perhaps the instructor) begins by stating his name to the whole group, using a word beginning with the same letter for association: "I am John and I feel jovial," or however he feels.
3. The person seated to the left of the first speaker will go next, first giving the name of whomever preceded and that person's feeling word: "You are John and you feel jovial. I am Susie and I feel silly." The third person then begins with the first speaker, progressing through everyone preceding him. Continue this procedure until the last person names everyone.
4. Things to watch out for:
   a. Don't worry if you forget a name; that person will help you out if necessary.
   b. Ask for a repeat of any name which you do not hear or understand.
   c. Keep the atmosphere informal; as you may know, humor and individual comments lessen tension.

ALTERNATE
PROCEDURE:

1. If statements of feelings seem too risky for you, a phrase such as, "I'm John and I *like* joking," using the same initial sound principle, could be used. Thus, either a statement of feeling or interest can be made.
2. Continue this procedure as explained above but make sure you use positive associations.

DISCUSSION:

You're well on your way now that you at least know one another's name.

1. What patterns of remembering/forgetting emerged?
2. What were some individual reactions of those whose names were forgotten?
3. How did you feel/react when your own name was forgotten?
4. In how many classes that you have attended did you know the other people's names? Discuss the implications. ❏

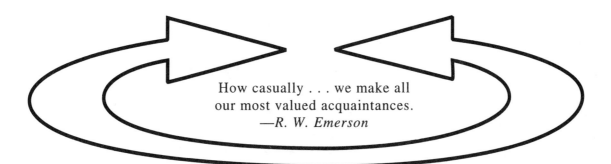

How casually . . . we make all
our most valued acquaintances.
—*R. W. Emerson*

FILL IN A FRIEND

PURPOSE: To aid class members in getting acquainted.

PROCEDURE:
1. Class mills around collecting signatures based on the list below.
2. Before he/she signs his/her name, ask each person, "Can you honestly sign your name by this statement?"
3. The first person to complete the list will be declared the winner.

_____ I use mouthwash regularly.

_____ I lie about my age.

_____ I have a hole in my sock right now.

_____ I read Peanuts.

_____ I was born over 1,000 miles from here.

_____ I cry at movies.

_____ I believe in equal rights for women.

_____ I squeeze the toothpaste tube in the middle.

_____ I refuse to walk under a ladder.

_____ I often have lint on my belly button.

_____ I love classical music.

_____ I have a warm relationship with both my parents.

_____ I eat raw oysters.

_____ I watch Sesame Street.

_____ I use roll-on deodorant.

_____ I like to play chess.

_____ I have never changed a diaper.

_____ I can wiggle my ears.

_____ I can recite the books of the Bible.

_____ I have used an outhouse.

DISCUSSION: 1.   Did this activity aid in helping you to feel comfortable with new class members? Explain.
2.   Did certain questions seem to fit certain stereotypes? Discuss.   ❏

APPLE ACTIVITY ——————————————————————

PURPOSE: To identify behavior you most often utilize as a means of self-introduction.

PROCEDURE: 1.   Choose one apple from among the many that have been brought to class.
2.   Take three minutes to study your apple. How is your apple different from every other apple? Notice the shape, size, characteristic markings, etc. Study it carefully as you'll soon be asked to reclaim it from its original pile. (This is possible and easier than it sounds.)
3.   Return the apples to the original pile. Mix up the apples.
4.   Reclaim your apple.
5.   Now imagine that you were placing this apple in a display case. Which side would you put forward? Consider shine, redness, imperfections, texture and shape. Which side would you turn under? Consider bruises, scrapes, dents, etc. In what ways are you similar to this apple in presenting your public self? What qualities do you put forward? Which qualities do you turn under or minimize? Form a dyad where each of you describes the ways in which you are like and unlike your apple. Take about five minutes each.
6.   Introduce your partner to the class with a sentence that describes how she relates to her apple.

DISCUSSION: 1.   What can be learned about people from this activity?
2.   What behaviors do you see as most effective for you in meeting people?
3.   Below are ways we may think about apples or people. Discuss the various viewpoints and indicate which one(s) you agree with:
a.   All apples are alike.
b.   All apples should be like my apple.
c.   All apples should be like the super apple.
d.   Apples are apples and they'll always be apples, so what are you going to do?
e.   I'll show this apple that it could have been a peach.
f.   Each apple is unique, different and capable of contributing something.   ❏

TO SEE ME IS TO KNOW ME ————————————

PURPOSE: To utilize feedback in discovering how accurate your judgments are about people. To identify the behaviors which contribute to this process.

PROCEDURE: 1. Silently choose a person you do not know and sit together. Do not speak.
        2. Complete one form based on guesses you make about your partner from observation only. Do not signal each other in any way.
        3. Complete the second form estimating what you suppose your partner has written about you.

ABOUT OTHER

This sheet to be used for nonverbal observation of partner.

	None	Little	Moderate	Much
Willingness to participate sincerely in this exercise:				
Degree of anxiety about participating in this exercise:				

Estimated age: _____ Place of birth: _____ Month of birth: _____

Marital status:
Married _____ Separated _____ Divorced _____ Single _____ Widowed _____

Children: Yes _____ No _____ Estimated Number _____

Estimated Maximum Education: _____

Nationality: _____

Occupation: First guess _____ Second guess _____

Economic Status: Lower _____ Low middle _____ Upper middle _____ Upper _____

Interests:

_____ Dancing	_____ Participation in membership organizations
_____ Civic activities	_____ TV
_____ Spectator sports	_____ Writing
_____ Participant sports	_____ Camping, hiking
_____ Music, type	_____ Travel
_____ Movies, type	_____ Politics
_____ Reading, type	_____ Gambling
_____ Artistic and creative, type	_____ Sewing, cooking
_____ Gourmet foods and drinks	_____ Other

Personality Traits:

	None	Little	Moderate	Much
Flexibility				
Receptivity to change				
Degree of personal warmth				
Degree of openness about self				
Generosity				
Self-confidence				
Sense of humor				
Ability to receive				
Concern for others				
Openness to consider new ideas				
Ease of establishing friendships				

This Person Is:

_____ Leader	_____ Follower	_____ Impatient	_____ Insightful
_____ Aggressive	_____ Assertive	_____ Rigid	_____ Extrovert
_____ Passive	_____ Patient	_____ Shy	_____ Introvert

Is this the kind of person with whom you would like to establish an ongoing relationship?

Yes _____ No _____ Explain answer: _____

_____

ABOUT SELF

This sheet to be used for your estimate of partner's observation of you.

	None	Little	Moderate	Much
Willingness to participate sincerely in this exercise:				
Degree of anxiety about participating in this exercise:				

Age: _____ Place of birth: _____ Month of birth: _____

Marital status:
Married _____ Separated _____ Divorced _____ Single _____ Widowed _____

Children: Yes _____ No _____ Number _____

Maximum Education: _____

Nationality: _____

Occupation: _____

Economic Status: Lower _____ Low middle _____ Upper middle _____ Upper _____

Interests:

_____ Dancing

_____ Civic activities

_____ Spectator sports

_____ Participant sports

_____ Music, type

_____ Movies, type

_____ Reading, type

_____ Artistic and creative, type

_____ Gourmet foods and drinks

_____ Participation in membership organizations

_____ TV

_____ Writing

_____ Camping, hiking

_____ Travel

_____ Politics

_____ Gambling

_____ Sewing, cooking

_____ Other

Personality Traits:

	None	Little	Moderate	Much
Flexibility				
Receptivity to change				
Degree of personal warmth				
Degree of openness about self				
Generosity				
Self-confidence				
Sense of humor				
Ability to receive				
Concern for others				
Openness to consider new ideas				
Ease of establishing friendships				

I Am:

_____ Leader   _____ Follower   _____ Impatient   _____ Insightful

_____ Aggressive   _____ Assertive   _____ Rigid   _____ Extrovert

_____ Passive   _____ Patient   _____ Shy   _____ Introvert

Am I the kind of person with whom you would like to establish an ongoing relationship?

Yes _____ No _____ Explain answer: _____

_____

DISCUSSION:
1. Discuss the accuracy of your judgments.
2. Were there any surprises, good guesses, or accurate perceptions?
3. How easy/difficult was this activity for you?
4. How does this apply to your everyday interactions? ❏

BILLFOLD SCAVENGER HUNT

PURPOSE: To get acquainted by sharing items from your billfold or purse.

PROCEDURE: 1. Take four items from your billfold or purse that fit into the following four categories:
        a. The most worthless item
        b. The most priceless item
        c. The most revealing item
        d. The most memorable item
      2. Form dyads or triads and share your four items.

DISCUSSION: 1. What did you learn about the other person from this sharing?
      2. What did you learn about the person's values?
      3. How can you personally grow from this sharing? ❏

MAKE YOURSELF KNOWN

PURPOSE: To introduce yourself and to get to know others.

PROCEDURE: 1. On a blank piece of paper, print in large letters across the top: *Who Am I?* or *What I'm Like.*
      2. Below your heading, make a list of eight separate words that help answer the question printed across the top of your paper. You might include words like *student, humorous, dismayed, willing, afraid, forceful, confident, husband, brother,* etc. Be sure to print legibly so that others are able to read your sign from some distance.
      3. Now pin the list to your front and circulate throughout the class. Do not talk. Using just your eyes, take in the information offered by the signs and appearances of the class members. Take enough time to let the words become meaningful to you. Remember, too, others need time to study your list.
      4. When the instructor calls time, pick two other class members that you would like to know more about.
      5. In your triad, explain the words on your list to the other two members. These explanations may lead to further questions. Feel free to take this time to get to know one another better.
      6. Now join another triad and form a group of six.
      7. In your new group, introduce one member of your triad to the rest of the group. Do this in round-robin fashion so that everyone has a chance to participate.
      8. As you are introduced, try to analyze your feelings so that you can describe them during discussion later.
      9. When all the group members have been introduced, tell each other how you felt while you were being introduced. Remember to describe your *feelings* rather than your *thoughts.* Can you distinguish between them?

DISCUSSION: 1. Did you notice any similarities in the words used by all members in your original triad? Give examples.
2. How did you feel when you were introduced? Why?
3. How easy/difficult was it to reveal your feelings to your group members? Why?   ❏

CIRCLE-TO-CIRCLE ICE BREAKER ——————————————

PURPOSE: To get to know many class members, to experience three parts of an encounter (greeting, conversation, parting), and to examine both verbal and nonverbal communication.

PROCEDURE: 1. This activity requires an even number of participants. In the case of an extra person, she can be an observer. Divide into two groups, with both men and women in each group.
2. One group will form a circle in the center of the room, facing outward.
3. The other group will form an outer circle around the first group, facing them, so that each person has a partner.
4. The inner circle will remain stationary throughout the activity; the outer circle will rotate to the right, one person at a time for each part of the activity, until outer circle people have gone completely around the inner circle people and have rejoined their original partner.
5. Be sure to greet each new partner, using as many different ways as possible—both verbal and nonverbal. The conversation part of the encounter will vary each time according to the list below, which your instructor will read. After completing the sentence which your instructor begins, say goodbye to your partner verbally or nonverbally and the person in the outer circle will move one person to the right.

ALTERNATE
PROCEDURE: 1. You may go through this list of sentence completions with just one partner rather than in the circle-to-circle format.
2. Each partner responds to each statement before continuing to the next.
3. You may decline to answer any question asked by your partner.
4. Feel free to stop the activity when either partner becomes obviously uncomfortable.

THE
CONVERSATION: (Your instructor may add or delete items as necessary.)

1. Take your partner's hands, make eye contact, communicate something nonverbally and then say goodbye nonverbally.
2. Each partner complete this statement: "Right now I feel _____ ."
3. Each partner complete this statement: "What I want you to know right now is _____ ."
4. Each partner complete this statement: "When I'm in a new situation, I _____ ."

5. Each partner complete this statement: "One of the things I like best about myself is _____ ."
6. Each partner complete this statement: "When I'm feeling anxious in a new group, I _____ ."
7. Give your partner a verbal or nonverbal "stroke." (positive response)
8. Those in the inner circle turn around so that your back is to your partner. Outer circle give your partner a gentle neck massage. Inner circle turn back around after you've received your massage.
9. Outer circle people turn around and reverse the process you just completed.
10. Each partner complete this statement: "When I look at you, I see _____ ."
11. Each partner complete this statement: "What I want to say right now is _____ ."
12. Each partner complete this statement: "I believe in _____ ."
13. Each partner complete this statement: "Communication is _____ ."
14. Each partner complete this statement: "My friends _____ ."
15. Each partner complete this statement: "This class _____ ."
16. Each partner complete this statement: "The topic I know most about is _____ ."
17. Each partner complete this statement: "Women are _____ ."
18. Each partner complete this statement: "Men are _____ ."
19. Each partner complete this statement: "The main quality I look for in people is _____ ."
20. Each partner complete this statement: "I am happiest when _____ ."
21. Each partner complete this statement: "The thing that turns me on the most is _____ ."
22. Each partner complete this statement: "When I'm alone, I usually _____ ."
23. Each partner complete this statement: "My weakest point is _____ ."
24. Each partner complete this statement: "I love _____ ."
25. Each partner complete this statement: "I am afraid of _____ ."

DISCUSSION:
1. How did your feelings change throughout the activity?
2. Which questions seemed most meaningful to you? Why?
3. Which questions seemed most difficult to answer? Why?
4. During which part of the encounter did you feel most comfortable? The greeting? The conversation? The parting?
5. How did you react to the nonverbal communication? Why?
6. What can a brief encounter like this communicate about someone?
7. If there was an observer, she should contribute both specific and general observations. ❏

FAVORITE OBJECT

PURPOSE:
To let you display a concrete object that explains something about you and what you value.

PROCEDURE:
1. Bring in some object that you value highly because of the idea or activity it represents for you.
2. Objects will be displayed in front of the whole class for 10 minutes so that everyone may freely browse.
3. Claim your object when you are ready to discuss it, and tell what value it has for you. Class questions are optional.
4. As students explain their object, the audience should write down the name of the presenter and what values they think the person has, based on that object.
5. Form small groups for discussion.

DISCUSSION:
1. How did you get interested in this object or come to value it?
2. How much value did the object have for you three years ago?
3. Do you think you will still value this object three years from now? Why/why not?   ❏

DYADIC INTERVIEWS

PURPOSE:
To interview another person in order to get to know that person well enough to introduce him to others.

INTRODUCTION:
Each of us is the center of our own world. Since I cannot transport myself completely into your world, nor can you transport yourself into mine, if we are to communicate at all we must establish a mutual world. Even within this mutual world, my responses to you are dictated by my perceptions of myself. When I talk to you, I am actually talking to an image I have of you, which is probably not the same as your image of you. How, then, do I find out about the real you? I ask questions. Yet, because the questions are based on my perceptions, they cannot give me an accurate picture of how you see yourself. What questions should I ask you in order to obtain an accurate perception of you?

PROCEDURE:
1. On a separate sheet of paper, make a list of 10 questions that you would like someone to ask you.
2. Choose a partner and exchange your lists of questions with that person.
3. During the 30 minutes you have in which to interview each other, write out your partner's answers as you ask him his questions. Your partner should also write down your answers as he asks you your questions.
4. Then you and your partner form a group of six with two other couples. Introduce your partner to the rest of the group using the information you received in your interview. Each partner may correct or modify

the impressions created by his interview as he is introduced to the group.

DISCUSSION: When each person has introduced her partner, discuss the following questions:

1. During the interview, your interaction with your partner was on the spur of the moment. Describe the obstacles this created in your ability to communicate. How did you feel? Why?
2. What problems were caused by the time limits? Why?
3. Did you encounter a situation in which conversation was one-sided? Was it an equal exchange of information? Why?
4. How is an interview different from an ordinary conversation?
5. Now that you have spent several minutes with another class member, how do you feel about him? Do you know him?
6. Do you think the impression you have gained from the person you have interviewed is accurate? Why?
7. The information your partner received by interviewing you is only as accurate and revealing as your questions. Were your questions honest? Carefully edited? Did you purposely list questions that would avoid or conceal an important aspect of your life? How open do you feel your partner's questions were? ❑

ENERGIZERS: GROUP STARTERS ——————————

Listed below are several brief activities that can be used at the beginning of a group session to prepare participants for the meeting. An "energizer" should be nonthreatening, be fun, involve physical movement, stimulate breathing and provide a shared experience. It is important for the facilitator to indicate that persons with physical impairments need not participate.

1. *The Scream.* Participants stand and close their eyes. They are told to breathe slowly and deeply. Then all members of the group breathe in unison. Continuing to breathe together, they reach up and then reach higher and higher. They are instructed to jump up and down together and then to scream as loudly as they can.
2. *Songs.* Participants stand on their tiptoes and walk about while they sing together "Tiptoe Through the Tulips." The song and movement are then changed to "Walking Through the Tulips," "Running Through the Tulips," and finally "Stomping Through the Tulips." (Other "activity" songs can be used, such as "Itsy Bitsy Spider," "Bunny Hop," and "Head and Shoulders, Knees and Toes.")
3. *Whoosh.* Participants stand, reach up, and breathe deeply in unison. Then they are told to bend forward quickly at the waist, dropping their arms as if they were going to touch their toes, while exhaling all the air in their lungs. This is repeated several times.
4. *Machine.* One person goes to the center of the room and acts out the repetitive motion and sound of a part of a machine. Others add parts to the machine, one by one, until the entire

Reproduced from J. William Pfeiffer and John E. Jones (eds.), *A Handbook of Structural Experiences for Human Relations Training*, Volume V. La Jolla, Calif.: University Associates, 1975. Used with permission.

group is involved. Variation: Subgroups can be formed to devise or to act out (as in charades) machines that would manufacture concepts such as love, empathy, competition, etc.

5. *Computers.* Subgroups of four or five members each are designated to be "computers." They stand in semicircles, facing the facilitator. The facilitator inserts a "card" into one of the computers by saying the first word of a sentence ("Life . . .," "Bosses . . .," "Women . . .," etc.). The "components" of the computer respond by creating the rest of the sentence, one word per person. The sentence is ended by one "component" saying "period," "question mark," or "exclamation point." The process is repeated with each of the other computers. Then the computers take turns asking questions of the other computers, e.g., "What is the meaning of life?" "Who will be the next president?" Finally, the computers are linked together to build a sentence about the experience, with at least one word contributed by each component part.

6. *Nerf.* Participants stand in a circle and bounce a Nerf Ball (a soft, spongy ball distributed by Parker Brothers) or a balloon in the air as long as possible. Ground rules are as follows: (1) no person may hit the ball twice in a row; (2) the ball must not touch the floor; (3) before the ball can be hit randomly, it must be bounced at least once by each person around the complete circle; (4) the person who makes a bad pass must share something about himself with the group; and (5) the group makes binding decisions about "bad passes." (Allan G. Dorn.)

7. *Playground.* The facilitator announces that the group room is a playground. Participants act out swinging, climbing, sliding, etc.

8. *Elephant and Giraffe.* Participants stand in a circle, and one person volunteers to be "it." The volunteer stands in the center of the circle, points to one member, and says either "Elephant" or "Giraffe." The person pointed to and the participant on each side of him have to pantomime some part of the designated animal (nose, ears, neck, eyes, etc.) before the volunteer counts to three. If a person fails to respond in time, he becomes "it."

9. *Congo Line.* Participants line up, placing their hands on the waist of the person in front of them. Various rhythmic patterns can be used as the group moves about the room. "Serpent" variation: Members line up and hold hands; the person at the head of the line leads it through the room, coiling and winding like a snake.

10. *Hum.* The facilitator announces that on his signal the group will begin humming. Each participant hums any song that occurs to him. Members are encouraged to "interpret" their spontaneous choices of songs. ❏

It's great to be great, but it's greater to be human.—*W. Rogers*

GETTING ACQUAINTED DYADS

PURPOSE: To get to know another class member and experience important communication skills.

PROCEDURE:
1. Form a dyad.
2. "Interview" each other with purpose of getting to know each other. Try to interview in such a way that you get beyond the general information.
3. After 5 to 7 minutes of interaction, each person will answer, on paper, the following questions about her partner. (If the information is not known as a result of the interview, partners may answer what they *perceive* the answer might be.)
   a. If money were no object, where would your partner choose to go on a vacation?
   b. If money were no object, what kind of car would your partner prefer?
   c. What would your partner order to drink?
   d. What is your partner's favorite sport?
   e. Is your partner a Democrat, Republican, Independent?
   f. What kind of music does your partner prefer?
   g. What do you perceive to be your partner's opinion about television?
   h. What kind of pet would your partner have?
   i. If you gave a costume party, describe the costume your partner would wear.
   j. In what TV or movie role would you cast your partner?
4. Share your answers with your partner.

DISCUSSION:
1. How much information was based on what was heard in the pre-discussion, and what was the basis for perceptions drawn during the exercise?
2. Discuss the role of listening in information gathering.
3. What other observations do you have? ❑

The applause of a single human being is of great consequence. —*S. Johnson*

REACTIONS

1. What initial behaviors do you look for when meeting someone else for the first time?

2. What positive attributes do you look for in others?

3. What good things did you learn about yourself as you participated in some of these getting acquainted activities?

4. What does it take for you to open up and disclose yourself to others?

WHAT IS COMMUNICATION? | 2

Definitions

Following are some important definitions of communication, the three major types of communication and a definition of the term "process" as it specifically relates to the study of communication.

Communication

General Definitions:

Communication is the process of shared meaning through symbolic interaction.
—D. Fabun

Communication is the process by which we understand others and in turn are understood by them. (It is dynamic, constantly changing in response to the total situation.) —M. Anderson

Communication involves the conveyance of something to someone else—our ideas, our aims, our wants, our values, our very personalities.
—Robinson and Lee

Intrapersonal Communication

Definition: Intrapersonal communication is the process of communicating with oneself, our self-talk; when we daydream, reflect on what we have done, what is presently going on, or what we will do in the future, we are engaging in intrapersonal communication.

Example: As we consider buying a car, we weigh the pros and cons of one model versus another model in our head before making an overt decision.

Interpersonal Communication

Definition: Interpersonal communication is the process of communicating and interacting with other people.

Example: As we are buying a car, we interact with the salesperson, discussing equipment, pricing, financing. We try to work out a deal that is acceptable to both parties.

Extrapersonal Communication

Definition: Extrapersonal communication is the process of interacting with beings or articles which are nonhuman.

Example: We can talk to a dog, a plant, or even yell at our car when it will not start.

Process

Definition: When we speak of communication as a process, we are referring to the ongoing, continuous, dynamic sense of relationships existing in all communication. Communication has no beginning and no end.

Example: As I communicate with someone, I send a message to that person. The other person then receives my message and speaks back. As he/she speaks back to me, that person becomes the source and I now become the receiver of his/her message. Throughout the entire communication process, we are constantly changing—changing our roles, changing our language, changing our presentation, changing our attitudes and perceptions.

THE IMPORTANCE OF COMMUNICATION

Human beings are constantly communicating. In both sending and receiving messages, adults spend almost half of their total verbal communication time as listeners. We spend over one-third of our communication time as speakers.

Communication is a skill.

Because we spend so much time in oral communication, effective communication skills are vital to all of us. Indeed, you may be enrolled in this communication course to improve your communication skills and to become a more knowledgeable communicator. Employers look for employees who are effective communicators. Generally, the most successful people in our society are those who have strong communication skills. In his autobiography, Lee Iacocca, the head of Chrysler Corporation, stresses how important both speaking and listening skills are to success in motivating people. *A course in speech communication can help you gain these skills.*

Communication links people.

During any given day, you may talk to your friends, listen to members of your family, receive correspondence, observe and react to others' gestures and facial expressions, and even carry on conversations with yourself. You, like all humans, are a communicating being. "Communication is the way relationships are created, maintained and destroyed," observed one communication specialist. Every day, we depend on our abilities to speak, listen, write, read, think and interpret nonverbal messages. *Without these abilities, we would lose much of what makes us human,* and trying to be human in this very complex world requires all the help we can get. This chapter will show you just how vital communication is to our survival.

BARRIERS TO UNDERSTANDING COMMUNICATION

Communication as a natural process

The major barrier to studying intrapersonal, interpersonal and extrapersonal communication is that most people have a tendency to see communication as a **natural process**, requiring little effort or training. After all, we can all talk to a person sitting next to us in this room—can't we? And we seem to make it through life (childhood, adolescence, marriage, relationships, adulthood) interacting with others at each stage—don't we?

The answer to both of these questions is "yes." But wait. True, we may have made it this far in our communicating with others and could make it the rest of the way through life continuing as we are. The point here is not whether we are "communicating" or not. The real point is whether we are **communicating with maximum effectiveness** or not. This effective communication is the major concern of this book.

As you study the principles and strategies presented in the following pages, you will begin to see that effective communication is not as simple as most believe. Each chapter presents different barriers that can interfere with or prevent effective communication from taking place. You may find, for example, that we do not always really listen to others. Or perhaps we may not describe what we perceive all that accurately. Also, we might not be as aware of ourselves—our values and attitudes or the way we think others see us—as we think. Finally, we might not be handling conflict or our personal relationships as effectively as we could.

Overall, communication requires a great deal of effort to overcome the many barriers that confront us. Our hope is that as you study this essential life skill, the barriers become easier to handle and your relationships with others become more meaningful.

 There is nothing permanent except change. —*Heraclitus*

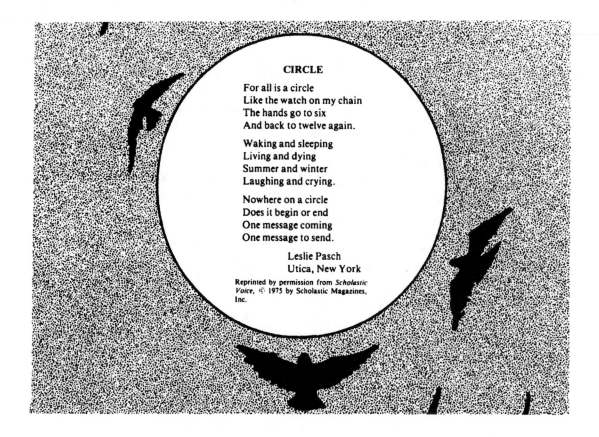

CIRCLE

For all is a circle
Like the watch on my chain
The hands go to six
And back to twelve again.

Waking and sleeping
Living and dying
Summer and winter
Laughing and crying.

Nowhere on a circle
Does it begin or end
One message coming
One message to send.

Leslie Pasch
Utica, New York

Reprinted by permission from *Scholastic Voice*, © 1975 by Scholastic Magazines, Inc.

COMMUNICATION QUIZ

PURPOSE: To consider some basic concepts about speech communication and to begin thinking about the communication process.

PROCEDURE: Indicate your response to each of the following statements by circling either **T (True)** or **F (False)**.

T ~~F~~   1. How you communicate has very little impact on what you communicate.

T F   2. Communication is a natural, human process requiring little or no effort.

T ~~F~~   3. When communication is good, both people will understand each other totally.

T ~~F~~   4. Dictionaries give us the meanings for most of our words.

~~T~~ F   5. We learn who we are from others.

T ~~F~~   6. People who talk to themselves are in need of psychiatric help.

T ~~F~~   7. Your past experiences and future expectations do not greatly influence your present communication.

T ~~F~~   8. Communication basically involves getting our ideas across to others.

T ~~F~~   9. Listening and hearing are the same thing.

~~T~~ F   10. We can't not communicate.

T ~~F~~   11. Most of us perceive the world accurately.

~~T~~ F   12. Once we communicate a message, we have no control over what will be done with it.

DISCUSSION: As a class, discuss each question and its implications. ❏

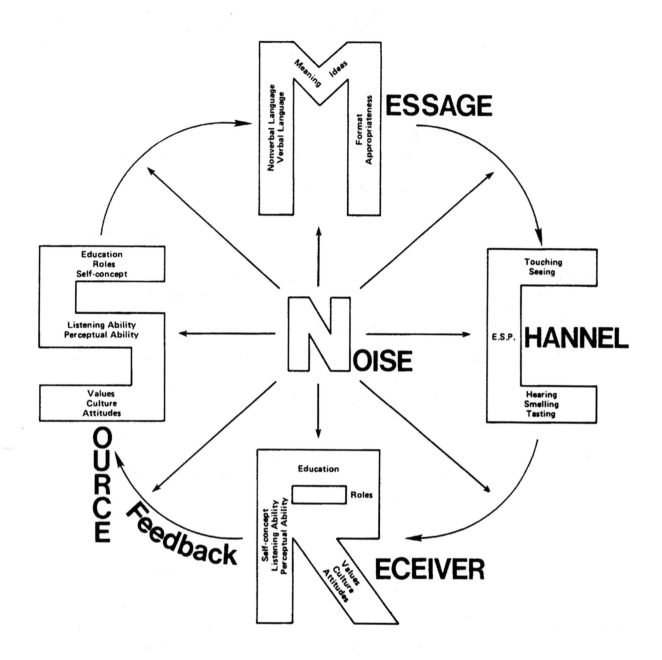

BASIC TERMS

Following are some important terms related to understanding the process of communication.

SOURCE: One who begins the communication through verbal or nonverbal means. Other names for source include encoder and speaker.

SOURCE EXAMPLES

1. Pianist   2. Instructor.

RECEIVER: One to whom the source's verbal/nonverbal communication is directed. Other names for receiver include decoder, listener, audience.

RECEIVER EXAMPLES

1. Audience.

2. Students.

MESSAGE: That information or product of the source's purpose which is coded into symbols/language and expressed through verbal/nonverbal means.

MESSAGE EXAMPLES

1. Music by Elton John.

2. Lecture-discussion, with visual aids, on why/how we communicate.

CHANNEL: That sense-related medium by which a message is transmitted. Light-waves, sound, and airwaves are considered as channels.

CHANNEL EXAMPLES

1. Sound/airwaves— sense of hearing, lightwaves—sense of sight.

2. Sound waves—sense of hearing, lightwaves—sense of sight.

FEEDBACK: The receiver's response to the source's message. Feedback indicates how well the source is doing in communicating his message.

FEEDBACK EXAMPLES

1. Screams, applause, restlessness at performances; letters afterwards.

2. Wandering eyes, nervousness, questions, attentive faces during lecture-discussion; good answers on exam afterward.

ENCODING: A process involving (1) selecting a means of expression and (2) transforming ideas into those means through appropriate selection of symbols/language.

ENCODING EXAMPLES

1. Notes on paper are transformed into music as Elton John plays the piano.

2. The instructor selects appropriate language to effectively communicate his ideas.

DECODING: The receiver's interpretation of the message based on background, education and future expectations.

1. Audience interprets the music according to their capacity.

2. Students interpret information according to their interest and educational background.

NONVERBAL: The use of hand gestures, posture, eye contact, vocal tone, personal distance, to emphasize or complement oral communication.

NONVERBAL EXAMPLES

1. At the end of each song, the singer raises his arms, stands, faces audience and bows.

2. On having two students talking in the back row, the instructor stops talking, puts hands on hips and glares in their direction.

FIDELITY: High fidelity is the ultimate goal of communication.

FIDELITY EXAMPLES

1. The audience understands the singer's song and begins to identify with its message.

2. The students understand the instructor's assignment and complete it to everyone's satisfaction.

MECHANICAL (External) NOISE: Any external interference in the environment that prevents the message from being accurately encoded or decoded.

MECHANICAL NOISE EXAMPLES

1. A defective microphone screeches through the auditorium.

2. A loud group walks down the hall. A police siren blares outside.

SEMANTIC (Internal) NOISE: Any internal interference in one's mind that prevents the message from being accurately encoded or decoded.

SEMANTIC NOISE EXAMPLES

1. The audience has never heard rock music and has difficulty understanding what it means.

2. The instructor refers to concepts the student does not understand.

❏

DEFINING COMMUNICATION

PURPOSE: To start you thinking about communication and to determine how much you and the rest of the class already know.

PROCEDURE: The class will be divided into groups and will be asked to discuss the following questions for approximately 30 minutes. Each group should try to reach general agreement on each of the questions. Everyone in the group should be afforded equal opportunities to contribute ideas.

1. What are the major elements of any communication event? (See note below.)
2. Why do you think communication is called a process?
3. What is communication? Describe what you think communication is. Try to arrive at a definition that the group will accept. (Be sure to include the concept of *effective* communication.)
4. What communication barriers did you perceive as your group discussed the above three questions?

DISCUSSION: Record the responses of your group and be prepared to discuss the conclusion in class.

NOTE: Which of these terms are *absolutely necessary* for communication to occur? These are the elements of communication.

Decoding	Intent	Stimulus
Noise	Understanding	Sender
Listening	Message	Response
Emotions	Process	Encoding
Context	Receiver	Channel
Feedback	Hearing	Transmission
Symbols	Trust	Environment ❑

VETERANS/ROOKIES ——————————————

PURPOSE: To analyze and evaluate a variety of definitions of communication.

PROCEDURE: 1. Rank the following definitions from 1 to 10, with 1 being your opinion of the "best" definition and 10 the worst.
2. In small groups compare your decisions with the other members. Explain why you ranked the definitions the way you did. Listen to the other members and see if you understand why they chose their rankings.
3. Your instructor will then show you how a group of 100 speech "experts" (professionals in the communication field) ranked the 10 definitions at a recent convention.

_____   A.   "In its broadest perspective, communication occurs whenever an individual assigns significance or meaning to an internal or external stimulus."

_____   B.   "A communicates B through channel C to D with effect E. Each of these letters is to some extent an unknown and the process can be solved for any one of them or any combination."

_2.__   C.   "Communication means that information is passed from one place to another."

_____   D.   "All communication proceeds by means of signs, with which one organism affects the behavior of another (or more generally the state of another)."

_1.X_   E.   "The word communication will be used here in a very broad sense to include all of the procedures by which one mind may affect another. This, of course, involves not only written and oral speech but also music, the pictorial arts, the theater, the ballet, and in fact, all behavior."

_____   F.   ". . . the intuitive interpretation of the relatively unconscious assimilation of the ideas and behaviors of one's culture."

_____   G.   ". . . The process by which an individual (the communicator) transmits stimuli (usually verbal symbols) to modify the behavior of other individuals (communicatees)."

_3.__   H.   "Communication does not refer to verbal, explicit, and intentional transmission of messages alone . . . The concept of communication would include all those processes by which people influence one another . . . This definition is based upon the premise that all actions and events have communicative aspects, as soon as they are perceived by a human being; it implies, furthermore, that such perception changes the information which an individual possesses and, therefore, influences him."

_____   I.   "This definition (communication is the discriminatory response of an organism to a stimulus) says that communication occurs when some environmental disturbance (the stimulus) impinges on an organism and does something about it (makes a discriminatory response). If the stimulus is ignored by the organism, there has been no communication."

_____ J. "Communication is the assignation of meaningfulness or significance to one's perception of an arbitrary sign."

DISCUSSION:
1. Were you surprised by any of the "expert" rankings? Why?
2. Did your group agree that some (or one) definitions were better than others?
3. What did the definitions that were ranked near the top have in common?
4. What critical aspects of communication did the bottom ranked definitions lack?
5. Would it be possible to write a definition of communication that would please everyone who studies it? Why or why not?
6. As you listened to the other group members, could you understand why they ranked the definitions as they did? Why or why not? ❏

COMMUNICATION DIAGRAMS ————————————

PURPOSE: To create your own diagram based on how you perceive the process of communication.

PROCEDURE:
1. Create *your own* diagram of communication. Include elements that you consider important and present the model in your own way. Your model might be one of the following: a drawing, a collage, a three-dimensional model, etc.
2. Share your diagram with the class.

DISCUSSION:
1. Discuss the similarities and differences among the illustrations.
2. How might the similarities and differences in the way we perceive communication help or hinder our communication? ❏

JULIE AND MR. CONROY

PURPOSE: To examine a communication breakdown and analyze how it could have been prevented.

PROCEDURE: 1.   Read the following situation.
2.   In groups of five to six, answer the questions that follow.
3.   Try to achieve consensus as you discuss each item.

"I only figured that any kid who was messing around like that deserved some kind of punishment."

John and Patricia Conroy were apparently no more, no less perplexed by the generation gap than any other parents of a teen-age girl. Julie, their 16-year-old daughter, was a good student, reliable, known for her quick smile and friendly manner. She never caused her parents any great problems, though they had long since given up trying to make sense out of the exuberant and slang-filled speech she constantly used.

Julie was an only child and her parents were often quite restrictive as to where she went and whom she went with. Julie naturally complained occasionally, but there were never any major problems until one warm June evening.

School had just been dismissed for the summer and Julie was given the family car for the evening to go to a girlfriend's party. She was given careful instructions that she was to be home by 12 o'clock.

The all-girl party was a success, and the happy teenagers were so engrossed in talk that hours slipped by quickly. Someone finally pointed out that it was almost 1 a.m. Julie gasped with surprise and quickly told her hostess that she had to leave. Several of her friends quickly asked for rides home. Julie knew she was already late so why would a few extra minutes matter?

As she drove down the street toward the first girl's house, one of the other girls in the car spotted two boys she knew walking down the street and asked Julie to stop to give them a ride. Julie knew neither of them but stopped anyway to pick them up. At the next intersection Julie's car was hit broadside by a man who failed to stop at the traffic light. No one was hurt, but the car was inoperable. Police, after questioning all of them, took Julie home in a squad car. Both worried parents came running out of the house to see what happened. In the turmoil of Julie's excited efforts to explain, all her father heard was, "We were riding around with a couple of guys and some old man hit us." Visions of his daughter roaming the streets late at night in a car with boys she didn't even know combined with his built-up tensions and Mr. Conroy vented his anger by slapping Julie so hard she fell to the pavement. The patrolman attempted to intervene and Mr. Conroy hit him, breaking his nose.

Julie spent 10 days in the hospital with a concussion, the officer needed emergency treatment, and Mr. Conroy was fined $500 and given a suspended sentence for striking an officer of the law. It was months before father and daughter could even begin to talk to each other without anger and years later, there is still bitterness between them.

DISCUSSION: 1.   Who was the sender and the receiver of the fateful communication?
2.   What effect did the time, place and circumstances have on Mr. Conroy's action?
3.   Did Julie's choice of words have any effect on Mr. Conroy's actions?
4.   What effects did the emotions of both Julie and her father have?
5.   Were both Julie and her father attempting to communicate? Were they listening to each other?

6. What roles do values play in this incident? What are the possible differences in orientation for Mr. Conroy and Julie?
7. Was the "punishment" by Mr. Conroy related more to what Julie did or what she said?
8. Did Mr. Conroy show any sensitivity to Julie's needs?
9. How could this incident have been prevented?
10. What sort of interference was there in this communication event?

Speech is a civilization itself.
The word, even the most contradictory word,
preserves contact.—It is silence which isolates.
—*T. Mann*

REACTIONS

1. What is your personal definition of effective communication?

2. Give three reasons why communication is vital to your survival.

   a.

   b.

   c.

3. Many people feel that communication is an effortless, natural process, requiring little or no work. Do you agree or disagree? Why or why not?

4. Some authorities believe that all communication breakdowns are the fault of the sender. Do you agree or disagree? Why or why not? *disagree* .

LISTENING | 3

Definitions

Are you a good listener? Listening is a very important communication skill, yet we seldom receive special training for it in school. People often confuse listening with hearing. Some people play the game of listening by putting on a rubber reaction face along with occasional head nods and verbal sounds.

Listening requires time and effort. It involves much more than hearing. The purpose of this chapter is to provide information about listening and activities which will help you learn about this most frequently used element of communication. You must have a desire to apply what you learn if you wish to improve as a receiver.

First, let us understand four very important terms:

Hearing

Definition: Hearing is necessary for listening, but is a separate process involving the reception of sound waves by the ear and brain.

Example: You may hear sounds but not necessarily pay any attention to them. Have you ever been guilty of staring at the speaker when she says, "You're not listening to me"?

Listening

Definition: A mental process of interpreting sound waves in the brain. We focus our hearing upon the stimuli we wish to attend to. Listening isn't passive. You must interpret this stimuli into meaning and action.

Example: Mother, in the kitchen, may be slightly aware of children's laughter and noise coming from the next room, yet can still concentrate on a meaningful task without distraction. But let some unusual sounds occur; they are then interpreted as being significant danger signals.

Feedback

Definition: Those verbal and nonverbal responses that affect the speaker in either a positive or negative way. Feedback may either strengthen or weaken communication. Feedback should express clearly what we want the speaker to know of our understanding about the message.

Example: A student speaker in a public speaking class would be more encouraged upon seeing affirmative head nods regarding a proposal than if he read anger, negative body language, and glances at the clock.

Empathic Listening

Definition: Listening to discover the sender's point of view. The speaker is encouraged to selfdisclose. Establishing trust, the listener enters into that person's world and attempts to imagine the thoughts and feelings of the speaker. Empathic listening responses should be a willingness to understand, but not give advice.

Example: Let us imagine that a fellow student is sharing with a classmate that Professor Jones hates him, is out to get him and will certainly fail him no matter how hard the student tries. An empathic response might be: "You don't feel Professor Jones is being fair with you?" To suggest that this person is irrational and should "talk-it-out" with Professor Jones is being judgmental and giving advice.

THE IMPORTANCE OF LISTENING

Most of us have, at one time or another, had the experience of talking with someone and getting the feeling that we weren't being listened to. At such times we may have felt frustrated or perhaps even angry. At other times we may have been in the role of the listener and experienced the embarrassment of being caught not listening. At these times, whether we have been the speaker or the listener, we may have become acutely aware that listening skills, whether someone else's or our own, were not as good as they could or should be. How many times have you made, or heard someone else make, the accusation, "You're not listening to me?" In trying to understand why we are not the listeners we could be, let's consider five questions essential to that understanding. How important is listening? How good are we as listeners? What are the various types of listening? What are the major barriers to listening effectively? How can we become better listeners?

Listening as a Basic Activity

How important is listening? Beyond our own awareness that it is important to have others listening to us when we are talking, research has indicated that listening is the most used basic communicating activity in our day-to-day lives. On the average, we spend about 70–80 percent of our time awake in some kind of communicating. Of that time, we spend approximately 9 percent writing, 16 percent reading, 30 percent speaking and 45 percent listening. Furthermore, of all the information we come to know during our lifetime, we learn over 90 percent of it through our eyes and ears. In fact, some people have even suggested that the causes of some of the major disasters in history were due to poor listening.

In addition to being the most frequent communicating task that we perform, the importance of listening is further amplified when we consider that listening to someone is a form of recognizing and validating that person's worth. This is probably why we get angry, frustrated or simply feel rejected when we are not being listened to. How often have you heard, or said, during an argument, "You're not listening to me." Good, effective listening is a way of reducing hostility while poor, or withheld listening, is a way of creating hostility. In fact, intentionally withheld listening has been used as a form of punishment during Victorian times and by primitive tribes. Withholding listening is also a major element in brainwashing techniques. Obviously then, being listened to is a very real need we all have!

Listening as a Skill

Finally, when looking at how important listening is, consider your attitude about people you know who are good listeners. You probably like them more than others who you feel are poor listeners. Research has revealed that being a good listener is considered the most important management skill. So it seems that listening is very important—it's the most used communicating skill. We depend on it heavily for most of the information we come to know. It's important for our success in school, on the job, and in relationships, as well as being vital to our own psychological wellbeing and it's a key to having more friends.

How good are we as listeners? Listening ability is one communication skill that is relatively easy to measure and when researchers have measured it, the results have been astounding. Studies have found that the average listening efficiency, in this culture, is 25 percent. This dismal figure was first discovered in research with college students listening to a 10 minute lecture. While we may wish that the percentage was higher or even feel that we aren't as bad at listening as other people, the facts suggest that there is a great deal of room for improvement. To test out your own listening efficiency, ask yourself how often you repeat questions that have just previously been answered, ask someone to repeat something she said, write down the wrong information, or try to listen to someone while reading or watching television at the same time. None of us is perfect but when it comes to being a good listener, most of us don't even come close! The logical question to ask is, "Well, if we're such poor listeners, how did we get that way and what's keeping us from being better?" Before dealing with these two questions, let's consider the different kinds of listening that are possible.

Types of Listening

Listening is not just a single activity, rather it is a series of steps relating to a specific goal—what we wish to pay attention to. Just as there is more than one thing to which we can pay attention, there is more than one type of listening. For our purposes, listening can be classified into the following five types:

1. Listening for enjoyment
2. Listening for details
3. Listening for main ideas
4. Listening for overall understanding
5. Listening for emotional undertones

Listening for enjoyment is probably the easiest type of listening we are involved with because, rather than paying attention to someone else, we simply tune into our own emotional response to what we are listening to. This is the type of listening we do when we listen to our favorite radio station or a favorite tune. We enjoy the music for what it does to us, how it makes us feel.

Listening for details is one of the types most closely associated with school. This is the type we use when we are listening for the detailed information in a teacher's lecture. Here we are trying to pay attention to specific factual information which the speaker is trying to relate.

Listening for main ideas is also closely allied with the classroom. However, in this situation we are trying to identify the speaker's main point. What is he driving at? What is the point he is attempting to make? In this type of listening, we must pay more attention and attempt to tune in to the general main ideas.

Listening for overall understanding is even more difficult than the types previously mentioned. In this situation we are trying to piece together all of the speaker's information in an effort to get at the overall meaning in the message. What is the bottom line? In order to do this type of listening, we must attend to much more of the message and try to assemble it in much the same way that a child might assemble a puzzle in order to see the entire picture.

Yet another type of listening is **listening for emotional undertones**. This is probably the most difficult of all because it requires the most attention and effort. In this type of listening, we shift our focus from what is being said to how the speaker is *feeling*. We are attempting to understand what is going on inside of her. Unlike listening for enjoyment where we were concerned with tuning in to our emotions, in this situation we are concerned with the emotions of the other person. This is particularly difficult since emotions are often hidden beneath layer upon layer of verbal camouflage. Often the speaker may not be in touch with her own feelings. Here, great attentiveness to the emotion-laden words is vital along with the discipline to keep our own thoughts and comments quiet.

These, then, are the major types of listening. As we can see, this seemingly simple task is far more complicated than may have previously been thought. But why are we such bad listeners on the average? What keeps us from achieving our goal?

The word "listen" contains the same letters as the word "silent." —*A. Brendel*

BARRIERS TO LISTENING

What are the major causes of the problem? While there are probably many causes to poor listening, four major factors can be identified which contribute in large part to the problem.

Physiological Factors

The first major factor is physiological in nature and, as such, is one we must learn to live with. That is the difference between the thinking and speaking rates. In essence, the brain works much faster than the mouth. Although the average speaking rate in our culture is about 125 words per minute, the brain processes language at the rate of approximately 800 words per minute. Since we can't slow the brain down, this gives us approximately 675 words per minute "free time" in our brain. So how do we use this "free time?" Well, we could use it to reinforce the message we are listening to, or we could use it to identify and organize the speaker's main points and supporting ideas. Unfortunately, most of us don't do this. Instead, we use this time to evaluate or criticize the speaker or message, prepare our rebuttal or just daydream about a million things totally unrelated to the message. In short, we tune in to our own internal dialogue rather than tuning in to the speaker's message.

Some researchers have approached this problem from the other side. If we can't slow down the brain, perhaps we can speed up the message. Speech "compressors," which increase the rate without distorting the tone, have been developed and tested on subjects. Results have shown that it is possible to listen to rates two to three times normal without significant loss of comprehension. In fact, in some instances comprehension has been improved. Perhaps this is due to having less "free time" to allow distractions to creep in and divert the listener's attention. However, even though it sounds promising, "speed listening" is not practical in our day to day lives, so we must develop skill that enables us to use this "free time" constructively or we will surely continue to use it destructively.

Psychological Factors

The second major factor for poor listening is psychological. This is the tendency to treat listening as a passive, automatic activity. In other words, we confuse listening with hearing. Hearing is a physical process involving the reception of sound waves. It is passive and automatic. Listening, on the other hand, is an extremely active psychological process requiring attention and interpretation and involving skills which must be learned. As we have seen, there is more than one kind of listening and each involves a different set of skills suited to different needs or situations.

When we are actively involved in listening, our blood pressure and pulse rate increase and our palms tend to perspire. We actually burn more calories when we listen. (It might even be possible, but not too practical, to go on a listening diet.) Obviously, therefore, if listening takes work, it is important that we get our bodies ready to work in order to be better listeners and that we employ the proper skills.

Educational Factors

The third major factor causing poor listening is educational. To understand this factor we must remember two concepts mentioned earlier: listening is the largest part of our daily communication and listening is an active process. Yet in all the formal education which we have received, we have spent major amounts of time learning how to read and write, two skills which total only 25 percent of our daily communication, little if any time learning how to speak in a formal way and, for the vast majority of us, no time learning how to listen effectively. This is not to suggest reading and writing should not be taught, but when you consider the lack of emphasis which listening skills have received in our formal education, it is no wonder why our average listening efficiency is only 25 percent.

Some private corporations have come to realize the importance of teaching listening skills and have developed their own listening programs. As the educational community increases its focus on the importance of listening education and more of us are taught proper listening skills, we will hope to see improvement in that 25 percent efficiency rate.

The last major factor relates to the previous one. Since we have not been taught how to listen effectively, *we often choose the wrong type of listening to do.* Have you ever found yourself tuning in to your own internal dialogue or emotions rather than trying to understand the meaning or emotion in the other person? Have you ever found yourself getting nice and comfortable, as if you were listening for enjoyment, when you were about to listen to a classroom lecture? Clearly, you may have wanted to listen, but you were doing the wrong type of listening.

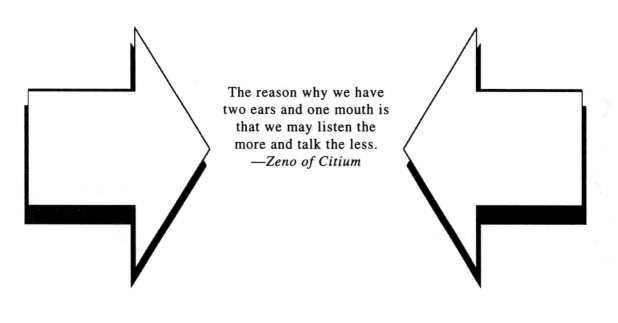

The reason why we have two ears and one mouth is that we may listen the more and talk the less.
—*Zeno of Citium*

STEPS TO BETTER LISTENING

How then can we overcome these barriers and improve our listening? As was mentioned earlier, listening actually consists of sets of skills which can be employed in different situations to meet different needs. However, there are six steps which actually underlie all the different types of listening skills.

1. Decide to listen. Obviously the commitment to listen is at the heart of being a better listener.
2. Get your body ready to work. Remember that listening is work. So it's important to get ready to do work by having an erect posture, being located close to the speaker and creating some inner tension to combat the tendency to relax and daydream.
3. Create a supportive climate. Reduce or eliminate environmental distractions. Avoid statements or actions likely to create defensiveness.
4. Put the other person first. Focus on understanding what he/she has to say and use your brain's "free time" to that end.
5. Select the appropriate type of listening. Determine what your goal should be and focus on the appropriate part of the other person's message. Is the most important element your own feelings, the other person's details, main ideas, overall meaning or underlying emotions?
6. Communicate that you are listening. Being a better listener is only half the job; you must also let the other person know that you are listening through eye contact, facial expressions, body posture and feedback.

Since listening is a learned skill, changes won't occur overnight. As with any skill, "practice makes perfect." With the desire to become a better listener, knowledge of listening skills and a willingness to work, major improvements can be made. Then, no one will say to you, "You never listen to me!"

LISTENING QUIZ

PURPOSE: This quiz is designed to get you thinking about the topic of listening and to expose popular conceptions and misconceptions about listening. To the left of each statement indicate whether you think that the statement is true or false by placing a T or F in the blank. Please answer honestly and don't try to "psych-out" the quiz.

1. Most people are pretty good listeners.
2. Listening is an easy, natural, passive behavior.
3. While listening, it is possible to learn how to pay attention to some other idea, person, event, etc. in our environment at the same time.
4. There is no way you can "make" someone listen to you.
5. To be an effective listener we must focus only on what the other person is saying and avoid being distracted by nonverbal cues.
6. There is basically only one type of listening we can utilize in our day to day lives.
7. When listening to someone with a problem, it's a good idea to offer sympathy or advice when possible.

T.   8. Good listeners are better liked than bad listeners.

F.   9. Hearing and listening are essentially the same thing.

F. 10. Good listeners are born not made.

F. 11. Being a better listener simply means taking in more information from the other person.

T. 12. When we are listening, we are also communicating to the other person at the same time.

F. 13. To be a really good listener, you have to be a mindreader.

T. 14. Using feedback is an important part of listening.

T. 15. Sometimes when listening, the words get in the way.

T. 16. The single most neglected communication skill is listening.

T. 17. There are ways to tell when a person is probably not listening.

F. 18. We spend about 25 percent of our awake time listening.

T. 19. No matter how good a listener a person may be, he/she will always misunderstand part of what is being communicated.

F. 20. When people listen to each other more, there is less chance that they will disagree.

F. 21. The average listening efficiency of this culture is about 60 percent.

T. 22. Pretending to listen is better than admitting that we're not interested or don't have the time.

F. 23. The major cause of poor listening is physical rather than psychological.

T. 24. Good listeners get sweaty palms.

T. 25. Most people are more interested in "telling their own story" than in listening to anyone else.

DISCUSSION: As a class (or in small groups) discuss each question and its implications. ❏

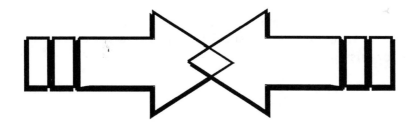

One of the best ways to persuade others
is with your ears—by listening . . . —D. Rusk

LISTENING QUESTIONNAIRE ————————————

1. Think about 3 people whom you consider to be good listeners.

   a. What is it about them that makes them good listeners? How do they act, what do they do, what do they say?—Be as specific as possible.

   b. What is your attitude about these people?

2. Do you consider yourself a good listener? Why/why not?

   a. When do you have the greatest difficulty listening?

   b. When do you have the least?

3. Why would you want to improve your listening?

   a. When do you consider it important for you to listen?

   b. What do you want to gain from studying listening techniques? In what ways do you want to improve your listening? (Be as specific as possible since these will be your personal objectives for this unit.)

❏

LISTENING SKILLS SELF-INVENTORY

This self-inventory is designed to enable you to assess your skills and behaviors as an effective listener.

PART 1—INITIAL JUDGMENT OF OVERALL LISTENING EFFECTIVENESS

Circle the term below which you feel most closely approximates your overall listening effectiveness:

POOR	FAIR	AVERAGE	GOOD	EXCELLENT
(0)	(38)	(76)	(114)	(152)

PART 2—ASSESSMENT

For each item below, indicate the frequency with which you exhibit that particular behavior according to the following scale:

0	1	2	3	4	5
never					always

Place the appropriate number on the blank to the left of each statement. Be honest in your responses and avoid "psyching-out" the questionnaire.

FRAME OF MIND

	I understand that listening is one of the most important managerial skills.
	I understand that listening is a major way of "validating" the worth of others.
	I am willing to indicate when I don't have the time to listen productively.
	I recognize that the goal of effective listening is to understand the other person and his/her communication as fully as possible.
	I treat listening as an "active" skill.
	I am willing to listen intently to the other person even though I may disagree with what I think he/she is about to say.
	I desire to be empathetic to a person with a problem rather than directing or giving advice.
	I recognize that the person with a personal problem is the best one to solve it.

STRATEGIES AND VERBAL BEHAVIORS

	I ask questions to clarify confusion.
	I paraphrase what is said to ensure my understanding in vague or especially important areas.
	I listen to opposing viewpoints without arguing or defending my own position.
	I avoid being distracted by my surroundings or the appearance or mannerisms of the other person.
	I begin my conversations with questions rather than statements.
	I avoid "analyzing" the other person while he/she is speaking.
	I avoid interrupting the other person.
	While listening, I maintain my focus on the other person and what he/she means by what he/she says.
	I encourage the other person to continue communicating.
	I focus my responses on what is said rather than directly on the other person.
	I admit that I am confused or unsure when I am.
	I try to reduce defensiveness if I perceive that the other person is hostile or angry.
	I avoid "invalidating" the other person's emotions and feelings. If he/she is angry, I acknowledge that he/she has a right to feel angry.
	I avoid asking probing or personal questions.
	I avoid giving advice, preaching or moralizing when listening to someone with a problem.
	I avoid collecting "ammunition" for later arguments.
	I give honest and assertive responses when they are asked for and when appropriate.
	I avoid giving "you should" responses.
	I close conversations with a "positive" statement.
	I use "I think" or "I feel" when responding about my own reactions.

	I appear interested by maintaining a pleasant expression on my face.
	I look at the other person when he/she is speaking.
	I appear unrushed by avoiding "fidgeting," carrying on "standing" conversations or looking at the clock.
	I maintain an "open" posture and level body position.
	I appear energetic by using a comfortable but erect and slightly forward-leaning posture.
	I maintain appropriate conversational distance by avoiding talking over my desk.
	I demonstrate interest, responsiveness and "connectedness" by using head-nods, smiles and vocal responses such as "um hum," "oh," and "yes" or "yeah."
	I "read" the other person's nonverbal cues such as his/her tone of voice, eye contact and posture to enhance my understanding of what he/she means along with how he/she feels about what he/she is saying.
	I avoid a relaxed posture which would undercut the effort necessary for effective listening.
	I continually monitor the tension in my body which is present when I am working at listening effectively.
	TOTAL POINTS FROM PART 2. Compare your total points with the number beneath the word you circled in Part 1. How does your original estimate compare with your actual score? Have you discovered any areas you would like to work on?

DILBERT by Scott Adams

I HEAR YOU NEED A CARPOOL URGENTLY.

NO, I NEED "CARPAL TUNNEL SURGERY."

THE REPETITIVE MOTION OF TYPING HAS CAUSED PERMANENT DAMAGE I HAVE TO WEAR BRACES UNTIL THE SURGERY.

THERE'S NO ROOM IN MY CARPOOL.

ANALYSIS OF MY LISTENING EFFECTIVENESS ———————

This form is designed to give you an opportunity to evaluate my listening effectiveness. Please complete it when you are alone and return it to me within two days. The information you provide will enable me to gain some important insight into my strengths and areas for improvement as a listener.

PART 1—OVERALL ESTIMATE OF MY LISTENING ABILITY

Please rate my overall ability as a listener according to the following scale:

POOR   FAIR   AVERAGE   GOOD   EXCELLENT

PART 2—ASSESSMENT OF SPECIFIC LISTENING SKILLS

Section A—For each of the following items, please indicate to the left of each item the frequency with which I demonstrate, to you, the behaviors indicated based upon the following scale:

0	1	2	3	4
never				always

_____ 1. Appear interested and concerned about what I have to say.

_____ 2. Appear energetic and anxious to listen.

_____ 3. Encourage me to continue communicating.

_____ 4. Indicate if you are confused or don't understand what I am saying.

_____ 5. Respond to what I am saying in a non-evaluative and non-judgmental way.

_____ 6. Avoid interrupting me while I am speaking.

_____ 7. Look at me when I am speaking to you.

_____ 8. Don't try to change my mind when it's your turn to speak.

Section B—In your own words complete the following two items:

1. My main strength as a listener is:

2. The area I most need to work on as a listener is:

❏

"THE SOUNDS OF SILENCE" LISTENING ACTIVITY ———

PURPOSE: To evaluate your listening behavior and to distinguish among different types of listening.

PROCEDURE:
1. Your instructor will play Simon and Garfunkel's "The Sounds of Silence." Simply listen for enjoyment.
2. In order to see how well you pick up details when listening for enjoyment, your instructor will ask you seven fact questions. Write your answers below:
   a.
   b.
   c.
   d.
   e.
   f.
   g.
3. Your instructor will play the same song again. This time listen for the same seven facts.
4. As your instructor reads you the same seven questions as in Step 2, write your answer below:
   a.
   b.
   c.
   d.
   e.
   f.
   g.
5. Now that you have experienced the differences between listening for enjoyment and listening for facts, try this: As your instructor plays "The Sounds of Silence" for the third time, try to put all the details together in your mind as you listen for the theme or central idea of the song. To illustrate how watching helps you listen, your instructor will provide you with a copy of the lyrics. Follow along as you listen.

DISCUSSION:
1. Discuss the song verse by verse.
   a. What is the singer doing in the first verse?
   b. What has happened to the singer by the second verse?
   c. What does the third verse mean to you?
   d. What does the singer want to do in the fourth verse?
   e. What is the fifth verse about?
2. How would you state the central idea or theme of the song in one sentence?
3. You may want to discuss or write about one of the following:
   a. What would you add in a sixth verse?
   b. Describe how the writer feels.
   c. Discuss one of the problems mentioned in the song. ❏

TEST FOR LISTENING POWER ———————————

PURPOSE: To carefully examine your listening habits and identify those that might be improved.

PROCEDURE: Imagine yourself in a classroom or meeting where you are not the most important individual, but a participating member. Score yourself on these 10 worst listening habits: always guilty, 1; almost always, 2; frequently, 4; infrequently, 6; almost never, 8; never, 10.

Score

_____ 1. Calling the subject uninteresting. When the subject is a little remote, do you take the first opportunity to "tune out"?

_____ 2. Reacting to externals. Do you let the speaker's facial expression, accent or dress interfere?

_____ 3. Getting overstimulated. Are you easily aroused to anger or unbridled enthusiasm?

_____ 4. Listening for specifics only. Do you listen to words rather than for themes?

_____ 5. Writing too little or too much. Do you think you will remember everything without abbreviated notes? Or, equally bad, are you a compulsive note taker?

_____ 6. Faking attention. Do you smile and nod your head in the speaker's direction? (No extra points for doing it because you think it's polite.)

_____ 7. Tolerating or creating distractions. Do you let noises outside the room interfere? Do you chat, doodle, play with paper?

_____ 8. Avoiding difficult material. Are you only attracted to material of general interest?

_____ 9. Letting personal prejudice or bias interfere. Do personal biases clog your listening?

_____ 10. Wasting the thought-speech ratio. Do you tell yourself you can follow the speech and still do some private blue-skying?

_____ Total Score

TESTING SCORE: If you scored more than 90, you are a very superior listener. (A psychiatrist or personnel interviewer might score this high.) Other scores are ranked as: 80–90, excellent; 70–80, good; below 70, improvement needed.

DISCUSSION: 1. Were you surprised by your score? Identify your worst habits and how to improve them. ❑

SUGGESTIONS ABOUT LISTENING HABITS

10 Bad Listening Habits	**10 Good Listening Habits**
1. Calling subject "uninteresting."	1. Tuning in the speaker to see if there is anything you can use.
2. Criticizing speaker's delivery, personal appearance, etc.	2. Getting the speaker's message which is probably more important.
3. Getting over excited and preparing rebuttal.	3. Hearing the person out before you judge her.
4. Listening only for facts.	4. Listening also for main ideas, principles and concepts.
5. Trying to make an outline of everything you hear.	5. Listening a couple of minutes before taking notes.
6. Faking attention to the speaker.	6. Good listening is not totally relaxed. There is a collection of tensions inside.
7. Tolerating distractions.	7. Doing something about the distractions, closing a door, requesting a person to speak louder, etc.
8. Avoiding difficult material.	8. Learning to listen to difficult material.
9. Letting emotion-laden words affect listening.	9. Trying to understand your reaction to emotion-laden words which might cause barriers.
10. Wasting difference between speech speed (words per minute) and thought speed (words per minute).	10. Making thought speed an asset instead of a liability by: a. Anticipating the next point to be made. b. Mentally summarizing.

DISCUSSION:
1. Which habits do you plan to improve?
2. Specifically, what will you do to improve each one?

By permission, Ralph Nichols and Leonard Stevens; *Are You Listening?*

"LISTENING IS A LOST ART UNTIL SOMEONE NEEDS YOU": AT WIT'S END

Erma Bombeck

It was one of those days when I wanted my own apartment . . . unlisted. My son was telling me in complete detail about a movie he had just seen, punctuated by 3,000 "You know's?" My teeth were falling asleep. There were three phone calls—strike that—three monologues that could have been answered by a recording. I fought the urge to say, "It's been nice listening to you."

In the cab from home to the airport, I got another assault on my ear, this time by a cab driver who was rambling on about his son whom he supported in college, and was in his last year, who put a P.S. on his letter saying "I got married. Her name is Diane." He asked me, "What do you think of that?" and proceeded to answer the question himself.

There were 30 whole beautiful minutes before my plane took off . . . time for me to be alone with my own thoughts, to open a book and let my mind wander. A voice next to me belonging to an elderly woman said, "I'll bet it's cold in Chicago."

Stone-faced I answered. "It's likely."

"I haven't been to Chicago in nearly three years," she persisted. "My son lives there."

"That's nice," I said, my eyes intent on the printed page of the book.

"My husband's body is on this plane. We've been married for 53 years. I don't drive, you know and when he died a nun drove me from the hospital. We aren't even Catholic. The funeral director let me come to the airport with him."

I don't think I have ever detested myself more than I did at that moment. Another human being was screaming to be heard and in desperation had turned to a cold stranger who was more interested in a novel than the real-life drama at her elbow.

All she needed was a listener . . . no advice, wisdom, experience, money, assistance, expertise or even compassion . . . but just a minute or two to listen.

It seemed rather incongruous that in a society of super-sophisticated communication, we often suffer from a shortage of listeners. She talked numbly and steadily until we boarded the plane, then found her seat in another section. As I hung up my coat, I heard her plaintive voice say to her companion, "I'll bet it's cold in Chicago."

I prayed, "Please God, let her listen."

Why am I telling you this? To make me feel better. It won't help, though.

By permission, Erma Bombeck, *At Wit's End;* Field Newspaper Syndicate.

WHERE ARE YOU?

PURPOSE: To improve listening skills and become more aware of conversational habits.

PROCEDURE:
1. Divide into pairs.
2. Hold a conversation without using these pronouns: "me," "I," "we." When one individual uses "me," "I," or "we," he is eliminated. The last two persons left go to the front of the room to have the last conversation. Award some small token or have the group simply applaud the "winner." You'd be surprised how difficult it is not to talk about yourself.

DISCUSSION:
1. The word "you" is said to be the most important word in our language. Why don't we use it more often?
2. Why do we find it so awkward or difficult to lessen the "I's, me's, mine, etc." in daily conversations?
3. Are there ways we can persuade ourselves to rely more on the "you" part of conversation? ❏

LISTENING CITATION
(Because I Care)

I have noticed you:

_____ Talking too much

_____ Responding to what you *wanted* to hear

_____ Faking attention

_____ Not responding at all

_____ Looking like "the lights are on but no one is home"

_____ Seeming bored

_____ Listening only to what you agree with

_____ Other: _____

Place: _____

Date: _____ Time: _____

Remember, poor listening may cause loss of friends, job and money!

SIMPLE LINE DRAWINGS: A FEEDBACK EXERCISE

PURPOSE: To better understand the value of feedback in the communication process.

PROCEDURE:
1. Break into dyads.
2. Devise two simple line drawings, such as geometric designs or sketches of familiar objects, that are of about the same complexity. Do *not* show them to your partner.
3. Sit back to back. Have your partner try to duplicate one of your drawings with only your verbal assistance. Note: Tell your partner how to draw it, not what it is. She is *not* to communicate with you in any way and you are not to see what she is doing.
4. Sit facing each other. Have your partner try to duplicate the second drawing. This time feedback is allowed.
5. When you've finished, compare her drawings with yours.
6. Now reverse the process so that you both have a chance to play both roles.

DISCUSSION:
1. What differences did you note in the rate of accomplishment with and without feedback?
2. What differences did you notice in the accuracy of the final product?
3. As the direction-giver, how did you feel each time?
4. As the "artist," how did you feel each time?
5. Which method of instruction yielded greater satisfaction? How?
6. After discussing the above questions, attempt to write a definition of feedback. Compare yours with your partner's. ❏

LISTENING LOG

PURPOSE:
To see how much time you personally spend on each of these activities by logging your behavior for one entire day.

PROCEDURE:
Record your communication activities from the time you get up until the time you go to bed. Set up your work sheet on about one-hour intervals, with six columns. See the example below:

Time	Speaking	Listening	Writing	Reading	Remarks
6:30–7:30	20% (thinking to myself, talking to my family)	80% (radio, my roommates)	0%	0%	none
8:00–9:00	5% (talking to my friends before class)	80% (listening to history teacher)	10% (filling out questionnaires)	5% (looking over book)	WOW! I feel like I've been watching T.V.

DISCUSSION:
1. How do your findings compare with the findings mentioned in the previous article?
2. How do your findings compare with those of other students? Why?
3. Why do similarities and differences exist?
4. How would your findings differ if you were in a role other than that of a student? Why?
5. How might your findings differ if you were a member of another culture? Why? ❏

COMMUNICATION: ITS BLOCKING AND ITS FACILITATION

Carl R. Rogers

It may seem curious that a person whose whole professional effort is devoted to psychotherapy should be interested in problems of communication. What relationship is there between providing therapeutic help to individuals with emotional maladjustments and the concern of people today with obstacles to communication? Actually the relationship is very close indeed. The whole task of psychotherapy is the task of dealing with a failure in communication. The emotionally maladjusted person, the "neurotic," is in difficulty first because communication within himself has broken down, and second because as a result of this, his communication with others has been damaged. If this sounds somewhat strange, then let me put it in other terms. In the neurotic individual, parts of himself which have been termed unconscious, or repressed, or denied to awareness, become blocked off so that they no longer communicate themselves to the conscious or managing part of himself. As long as this is true, there are distortions in the way he communicates himself to others, and so he suffers both within himself, and in his interpersonal relations. The task of psychotherapy is to help the person achieve, through a special relationship with a therapist, good communication within himself. Once this is achieved he can communicate more freely and more effectively with others. We may say then that psychotherapy is good communication, within and between men. We may also turn that statement around and it will still be true. Good communication, free communication, within or between men, is always therapeutic.

It is, then, from a background of experience with communication in counseling and psychotherapy that I want to present here two ideas. I wish to state what I believe is one of the major factors in or impeding communication, and then I wish to present what in our experience has proven to be a very important way of improving or facilitating communication.

I would like to propose, as a hypothesis for consideration, that the major barrier to mutual interpersonal communication is our very natural tendency to judge, to evaluate, to approve or disapprove, the statement of the other person, or the other group. Let me illustrate my meaning with some very simple examples. As you leave a lecture meeting, one of the statements you are likely to hear is, "I didn't like that man's talk." Now what do you respond? Almost invariably your reply will be either approval or disapproval of the attitude expressed. Either you respond, "I didn't either. I thought it was terrible," or else you tend to reply, "Oh, I thought it was really good." In other words, your primary reaction is to evaluate what has just been said to you, to evaluate it from your point of view, your own frame of reference.

Or take another example. Suppose I say with some feeling, "I think the Republicans are behaving in ways that show a lot of good sound sense these days." What is the response that arises in your mind as you listen? The overwhelming likelihood is that it will be evaluative. You will find yourself agreeing, or disagreeing, or making some judgment about me such as "He must be a conservative," or "He seems solid in his thinking." Or let us take an illustration from the inter-

By permission, Carl R. Rogers, *Northwestern University Information*, 1952, 20, 9–15.

national scene. Russia says vehemently, "The treaty with Japan is a war plot on the part of the United States." We rise as one person to say, "That's a lie!"

This last illustration brings in another element connected with my hypothesis. Although the tendency to make evaluations is common in almost all interchange of language, it is very much heightened in those situations where feelings and emotions are deeply involved. So the stronger our feelings, the more likely it is that there will be no mutual element in the communication. There will be just two ideas, two feelings, two judgments, missing each other in psychological space. I'm sure you recognize this from your own experience. When you have not been emotionally involved yourself, and have listened to a heated discussion, you often go away thinking, "Well, they actually weren't talking about the same thing." And they were not. Each was making a judgment, an evaluation, from his own frame of reference. There was really nothing which could be called communication in any genuine sense. This tendency to react to any emotionally meaningful statement by forming an evaluation of it from our own point of view is, I repeat, the major barrier to interpersonal communication.

But is there any way of solving this problem, of avoiding this barrier? I feel that we are making exciting progress toward this goal and I would like to present it as simply as I can. Real communication occurs, and this evaluative tendency is avoided, when we listen with understanding. What does this mean? It means to *see the expressed idea and attitude from the other person's point of view, to sense how it feels to him, to achieve his frame of reference in regard to the thing he is talking about.*

Stated so briefly, this may sound absurdly simple, but it is not. It is an approach which we have found extremely potent in the field of psychotherapy. It is the most effective agent we know for altering the basic personality structure of an individual and improving his relationships and his communications with others. If I can listen to what he can tell me, if I can understand how it seems to him, if I can see its personal meaning for him, if I can sense the emotional flavor which it has for him, then I will be releasing potent forces of change in him. If I can really understand how he hates his father, or hates the university, or hates communists—if I can catch the flavor of his fear of insanity, or his fear of atom bombs, or of Russia—it will be of the greatest help to him in altering those very hatreds and fears, and in establishing realistic and harmonious relationships with the very people and situations toward which he has felt hatred and fear. We know from our research that such empathic understanding—understanding *with* a person, not *about* him—is such an effective approach that it can bring about major changes in personality.

Some of you may be feeling that you listen well to people, and that you have never seen such results. The chances are very great indeed that your listening has not been of the type I have described. Fortunately, I can suggest a little laboratory experiment which you can try to test the quality of your understanding. The next time you get into an argument with your wife, or your friend, or with a small group of friends, just stop the discussion a moment and for an experiment, institute this test. Each person can speak up for himself only when he has first restated the ideas and feelings of the previous speaker accurately, and to that speaker's satisfaction. You see what this would mean. It would simply mean that before presenting your own point of view, it would be necessary for you to really achieve the other speaker's frame of reference—to understand his thoughts and feelings so well that you could summarize them for him. Sounds simple, doesn't it? But if you try it you will discover it is one of the most difficult things you have ever tried to do. However, once you have been able to see the other's point of view, your own comments will have to be drastically revised. You will also find the emotion going out of the discussion, the differences being reduced, and those differences which remain being of a rational and understandable sort.

Can you imagine what this kind of an approach would mean if it were projected into larger areas? What would happen to a labor-management dispute if it was conducted in such a way that labor, without necessarily agreeing, could accurately state management's point of view in a way that management could accept; and management, without approving labor's stand, could state labor's case in a way that labor agreed was accurate? It would mean that real communication was established, and one could practically guarantee that some reasonable solution would be reached.

If then this way of approach is an effective avenue to good communication and good relationships, as I am quite sure you will agree if you try the experiment I have mentioned, why is it not more widely tried and used? I will try to list the difficulties which keep it from being utilized.

In the first place it takes courage, a quality which is not too widespread. I am indebted to Dr. S. I. Hayakawa, the semanticist, for pointing out that to carry on psychotherapy in this fashion is to take a very real risk, and that courage is required. If you really understand another person in this way, if you are willing to enter his private world and see the way life appears to him without any attempt to make evaluative judgments, you run the risk of being changed yourself. You might see it his way, you might find yourself influenced in your attitudes or your personality. This risk of being changed is one of the most frightening prospects most of us can face. If I enter, as fully as I am able, into the private world of a neurotic or psychotic individual, isn't there a risk that I might become lost in that world? Most of us are afraid to take that risk. Or if we had a Russian communist speaker here tonight, or Senator Joe McCarthy, how many of us would dare to try to see the world from each of these points of view? The great majority of us could not *listen*; we would find ourselves compelled to *evaluate*, because listening would seem too dangerous. So the first requirement is courage, and we do not always have it.

But there is a second obstacle. It is just when emotions are strongest that it is most difficult to achieve the frame of reference of the other person or group. Yet it is the time the attitude is most needed, if communication is to be established. We have not found this to be an insuperable obstacle in our experience in psychotherapy. A third party, who is able to lay aside his own feelings and evaluations, can assist greatly by listening with understanding to each person or group and clarifying the views and attitudes each holds. We have found this very effective in small groups in which contradictory or antagonistic attitudes exist. When the parties to a dispute realize that they are being understood, that someone sees how the situation seems to them, the statements grow less exaggerated and less defensive, and it is no longer necessary to maintain the attitude, "I am 100 percent right and you are 100 percent wrong." The influence of such an understanding catalyst in the group permits the members to come closer and closer to the objective truth involved in the relationship. In this way mutual communication is established and some type of agreement becomes much more possible. So we may say that though heightened emotions make it much more difficult to understand *with* an opponent, our experience makes it clear that a neutral, understanding, catalyst type of leader or therapist can overcome this obstacle in a small group.

This last phrase, however, suggests another obstacle to utilizing the approach I have described. Thus far all our experience has been with small face-to-face groups— groups exhibiting industrial tensions, religious tensions, racial tensions, and therapy groups in which many personal tensions are present. In these small groups our experience, confirmed by a limited amount of research, shows that this basic approach leads to improved communication, to greater acceptance of others and by others, and to attitudes which are more positive and more problem-solving in nature. There is a decrease in defensiveness, in exaggerated statements, in evaluative and critical behavior. But these findings are from small groups. What about trying to achieve understanding between larger groups that are geographically remote? Or between face-to-face groups who are not speaking for themselves, but simply as representatives of others, like the delegates at Kaesong? Frankly, we do not know the answers to these questions. I believe the situation might be put this way. As social scientists we have a tentative test-tube solution of the problem of breakdown in communication. But to confirm the validity of this test-tube solution, and to adapt it to the enormous problems of communication breakdown between classes, groups and nations, would involve additional funds, much more research and creative thinking of a high order.

Even with our present limited knowledge we can see some steps which might be taken, even in large groups, to increase the amount of listening *with*, and to decrease the amount of evaluation *about*. To be imaginative for a moment, let us suppose that a therapeutically oriented international group went to the Russian leaders and said, "We want to achieve a genuine understanding of your views and even more important, of your attitudes and feelings, toward the United States. We will summarize and resummarize these views and feelings if necessary, until you agree that our description represents the situation as it seems to you." Then suppose they did the same thing with the leaders in our own country. If they then gave the widest possible distribution to these two views, with the feelings clearly described but not expressed in name calling, might not the effect be very great? It would not guarantee the type of understanding I have been describing, but it would make it much more possible. We can understand the feelings of a person who hates us much more readily when his attitudes are accurately described to us by a neutral third party, than we can when he is shaking his fist at us.

But even to describe such a first step is to suggest another obstacle to this approach of understanding. Our civilization does not yet have enough faith in the social sciences to utilize their findings. The opposite is true of the physical sciences. During the war when a test-tube solution was found to the problem of synthetic rubber, millions of dollars and an army of talent were loosed on the problem of using that finding. If synthetic rubber could be made in milligrams, it could and would be made in the thousands of tons. And it was. But in the social science realm, if a way is found of facilitating communication and mutual understanding in small groups, there is no guarantee that the findings will be utilized. It may be a generation or more before the money and the brains will be turned loose to exploit that finding.

In closing, I would like to summarize this small-scale solution to the problem of barriers in communication, and to point out certain of its characteristics.

I have said that our research and experience to date would make it appear that breakdowns in communication, and the evaluative tendency which is the major barrier to communication, can be avoided. The solution is provided by creating a situation in which each of the different parties comes to understand the other from the *other's* point of view. This has been achieved, in practice, even when feelings run high, by the influence of a person who is willing to understand each point of view empathically, and who thus acts as a catalyst to precipitate further understanding.

This procedure has important characteristics. It can be initiated by one party, without waiting for the other to be ready. It can even be initiated by a neutral person, providing he can gain a minimum of cooperation from one of the parties.

This procedure can deal with the insincerities, the defensive exaggerations, the lies, the "false fronts" which characterize almost every failure in communication. These defensive distortions drop away with astonishing speed as people find that the only intent is to understand, not judge.

This approach leads steadily and rapidly toward the discovery of the truth, toward a realistic appraisal of the objective barriers to communication. The dropping of some defensiveness by one party leads to further dropping of defensiveness by the other party, and truth is thus approached.

This procedure gradually achieves mutual communication. Mutual communication tends to be pointed toward solving a problem rather than toward attacking a person or group. It leads to a situation in which I see how the problem appears to you, as well as to me, and you see how it appears to me, as well as to you. Thus accurately and realistically defined, the problem is almost certain to yield to intelligent attack, or if it is in part insoluble, it will be comfortably accepted as such.

This then appears to be a test-tube solution to the breakdown of communication as it occurs in small groups. Can we take this small-scale answer, investigate it further, refine it, develop it and apply it to the tragic and well-nigh fatal failures of communication which threaten the very existence of our modern world? It seems to me that this is a possibility and a challenge which we should explore.

LISTENING SKILL EXERCISE

PURPOSE: To practice the "Rogerian" Listening Technique in order to improve listening skills.

PROCEDURE:
1. Form listening triads and designate each participant A, B, or C. In each group, one person will act as referee (observer) and the other two will have a discussion, each alternating between being the listener and the speaker.
2. The discussion is to be unstructured, except that before each participant speaks she must summarize, in her own words and without notes, what has been said previously. If the summary is thought to be incorrect, the others are free to interrupt and clarify the misunderstanding. After about seven minutes, the participants switch roles and continue the process. The following topics may be used:

   a. nuclear energy
   b. fad fashions
   c. male liberation
   d. smoker's vs. nonsmoker's rights
   e. pollution
   f. energy crisis
   g. death penalty
   h. crime/criminals
   i. gun control
   j. drug abuse
   k. marijuana
   l. abortion
   m. women's liberation
   n. draft
   o. political parties

DISCUSSION:
1. Do we usually listen to all that the other person is saying?
2. Did you find that you had difficulty formulating your own thoughts and listening at the same time?
3. Were you forgetting what you were going to say? Not listening to others? Rehearsing your response?
4. When others paraphrased your remarks, did they do it in a more concise way?
5. How important is it to *check out* with the other person what you thought you heard her say?
6. Was the other's manner of presentation affecting your listening ability?

7. Does the way another person listens to you affect *your* self-concept? How?

8. Does the way a person listens to you affect your perception of *that person's* intelligence and personality? How?

9. What are some guidelines for good listening?

    a.

    b.

    c.

    d. ❏

NOTE: The preceding article entitled "Communication: Its Blocking and Facilitation" by Carl Rogers explains Rogers' feelings about the value of the above method.

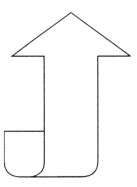

It is the providence of knowledge to
speak and it is the privilege of wisdom to listen. —*O. W. Holmes*

LISTEN

(anonymous)

When I ask you to listen to me and you start giving advice,

you have not done what I asked.

When I ask you to listen to me and you begin to tell me

why I shouldn't feel that way,

you are trampling my feelings.

When I ask you to listen to me and you feel you have to

do something to solve my problems, you have failed me,

strange as that may seem.

So please, just listen and hear me. And if you want to talk,

wait a few minutes for your turn and I promise I'll listen

to you.

ACTIVE/EMPATHIC LISTENING ——————————

PURPOSE: To increase your active/empathic listening skills.

PROCEDURE:
1. The first part is based on programmed instruction. Simply read and follow each step.
2. After completing the programmed section, role play the situations suggested in the "Active Listening Exercise."
3. Try to determine the extent to which empathic/active listening is used in each of these situations.

Cover all sections, except 1, with a sheet of paper.

---

1. This program is designed to help improve communication between people. You should be covering all of this page so that only this first instruction is exposed. Each printed instruction is called a frame. A black line, like the one below, means the end of a frame. After you have finished reading this frame, move the cover down to the black line below the next frame.

---

2. There are several reasons for attempting to improve communication. For one thing, in any relationship which the partners want to develop, situations will appear in which one person wants to talk about a problem and the other wants to listen. This session focuses on an approach to listening.

---

3. Experience has shown that people who work with others in solving problems typically go through specific stages of relating. At each stage they require new, more useful ways of looking at their problems which leads them to better understanding and to new approaches to solutions. These new approaches come from changes in their awareness, thinking, feeling and doing.

---

4. This program focuses on the first stage of relating to one another, that is, actively listening to the other so he can freely explore with you what is on HIS mind.

---

5. This is a step-by-step learning program. You will be learning from a series of brief exercises which involve YOU in DOING something. You will be learning from *your own experience*.

---

6. Now we can begin. I am going to describe an incident to you which involves you and another person in conversation. It ends with the other replying to you and waiting for your response. I will then give five possible responses. Imagine you are listening to the responses. Then read below and pick the ONE which is *most likely to encourage the other to keep telling you what's on HIS mind and to help you both explore the problem as HE sees it.*

---

7. Here's the situation: A person in your class is telling you about how hard it has been lately for him to do the homework. You ask him why and he replies, "I don't know why, I just can't get to it. Frankly, I don't have any enthusiasm for doing it. I've lost interest in the class. I just stall around and then rush like mad to even get here on time every day."

---

8. Which of the following responses is most likely to encourage the other to keep talking about what's on his mind and what he is feeling?
   a. Don't you know that you are not going to get anything out of the class if you don't do your homework?
   b. You've just got to get it done or you'll flunk.
   c. What's happening? You been playing around too much?
   d. You shouldn't be late so much. It's not fair to the rest of us.
   e. It sounds as though you've lost your enthusiasm and interest in the class.

9. Write your answer here

10. Now let's continue. We will go through more steps before I tell you the answer I would give. It is not important whether your answer and mine agree; however, it IS important that you understand my answer. The purpose of the next few steps is to develop that understanding.

11. Now let's look at what the other is feeling. Pretend to be the other and speak his words aloud and with feeling. How do you feel as you speak the other's words? "I don't know why. I just can't get to it. Frankly, I don't have any enthusiasm for doing it. I've lost interest in the class. I just stall around and then rush like mad to even get here on time every day."

12. Write down some of your feelings as you spoke. Were you happy or sad? Were you angry? Write your feelings in the next frame.

13. I felt:

14. Many people report feeling discouraged, depressed, down, bummed out, dull, bored, listless, aimless, etc. Were the feelings you had generally the same or were they different? (If your feelings were quite different, listen to the words again and try to feel them as having a discouraged, aimless feeling. The fact that you felt differently does not mean you were wrong, but that you just felt differently.)

15. The first possible response was: "Don't you know that you are not going to get anything out of the class if you don't do your homework?" Imagine that you are the other and are lacking in enthusiasm and have lost interest in your class. How do you feel when you hear this response? Write some of your feelings in the space below.

16. I felt:

_____

17. Some people feel blamed, punished, criticized, resentful, misunderstood, annoyed, angry, etc. Other people feel blamed, regretful, bad, hurt, apologetic, sorry, etc. Were your feelings close to any of those?

_____

18. Now react to each of the other responses as if you are the other. Remember that you have said: "I don't know why. I just can't get to it. Frankly, I don't have any enthusiasm for doing it. I've lost interest in the class. I just stall around and rush like mad to even get here on time every day."

_____

19. Speaker's response to you: Your reaction to the speaker:

   a.   a.
   b.   b.
   c.   c.
   d.   d.
   e.   e.

_____

20. In looking back over your reaction, remember that *what a speaker intends or means* to say does not necessarily affect a listener's feelings. The listener's feelings are affected by what he **hears** the speaker saying. With that point in mind, revise what you have written if you want to.

_____

21. In our incident, the **other's** personal feelings are probably strong during the early part of this conversation and almost any response will move him AWAY from expressing what's on HIS mind. He may move away because he feels you are blaming, criticizing, or analyzing him. Even if you are supporting or approving, he is likely to move away from freely exploring what's on HIS mind because he wants to keep getting the good feeling of your support and approval.

_____

22. Now let's think about some different ways of responding to another person. The ones given in the exercise are evaluating, forcing, probing, directing and accepting.

_____

23. Each of the five responses you were given earlier is an example of a different way of responding by the respondent (R) to the speaker (S).

_____

Response "a" says: "Don't you know that you are not going to get anything out of this class if you don't do your homework?"
These words are FORCING. They begin with "Don't you . . ." and the rest of the words express R's opinion about what S is doing. Look at the words again. The question FORCES

S into agreeing with R's opinion and leaves S free only to admit that he "knows" or "doesn't know" that he's "letting himself down." The question shifts S's attention to what is on R's mind.

Response "b" says: "You've just got to get it done or you'll flunk."

These words are DIRECTING. They *tell* the other to *do* something. They also shift S's attention on what R considers important or interesting.

Response "c" says: "What's happening? You been playing around too much?"

These words are PROBING. They *ask for information* about a hunch the responder has. They focus S's attention on what R considers important or interesting.

Response "d" says: "You shouldn't be late so much. It's not fair to the rest of us."

These words are EVALUATING. They place blame on the other for the practice of unfairness.

Response "e" says: "It sounds as though you've lost your enthusiasm and interest in the class."

These words are ACCEPTING. They repeat the other's *key words* back to him without judging him. S knows that he has been heard and he is free to keep talking about what's on his mind.

---

24. In my experience, the response that is most likely to encourage the OTHER to keep telling you what's on HIS mind and to help you both explore the problem as HE sees it is the **accepting** response(e).

---

25. Later in a conversation, other kinds of responses can be helpful in (1) exploring the facts and feelings that are not at the surface of the other's mind, (2) in creating alternative solutions, (3) in evaluating alternatives, (4) in deciding, and (5) in motivating action.

---

26. Until the other gets **his feelings** off his chest and really feels you have understood and accepted his feelings, his communication will contain facts distorted by his feelings. Until you actively show your understanding and acceptance of his feelings, it is too soon for you to explore facts, create alternative solutions, or suggest action.

---

27. There is a logical sequence in working with another person to solve a problem.

ACCEPTING and UNDERSTANDING the other's way of seeing and feeling about things as being HIS then . . .

EXPLORING and PROBING for facts and feelings then . . .

CREATING alternative solutions then . . .

DECIDING on one solution then . . .

ACTING then . . .

FOLLOWING UP to see what is happening . . . ETC.

This session focuses on the first step—developing your ability to respond in an ACCEPTING way when you feel it is appropriate.

---

28. Now we will look at another incident. A student in your class seems to be unable to do the work and tells you,

"I just can't seem to get the hang of things. I try to find out what I'm supposed to do but none of you tell me. No one pays attention to me and I can't learn anything by just watching. Maybe I ought to quit."

---

29. Which of these responses is *accepting?*
    a. "Why don't you try harder? No one gets ahead without hard work."
    b. "If I were you, I'd ask the other people to help you."
    c. "Do you have any ideas why the others won't help you?"
    d. "Don't feel too bad. All of us have problems."
    e. "You feel that the others don't pay attention to you?"

---

30. Answer "e" is *accepting*. It reflects the other's main thinking and feelings.

---

31. Here's another incident. A student tells you, "That teacher. I've been here three years and no one ever told me before that I did a lousy job. So I made a few mistakes: but why does she blame me for everything?"

---

32. Which response is *accepting?*
    a. "All she wanted to do was to get you to be more thorough."
    b. "You think she expects too much of you?"
    c. "She really doesn't blame you for everything. She just wanted you to do it over again."
    d. "You feel she blames you for everything."
    e. "Are you really sure it's not all in your mind?"

---

33. Response "D" is *accepting*. It reflects the other's main thinking and feelings.

---

34. This time, you do the responding yourself. I'm going to say something to you and you will then write down an *accepting* response in the following frame.

---

35. I say, "I don't usually admit it, but I often have feelings of inadequacy when I'm asked to speak before a group of people. I'm sure they think I don't know what I'm talking about because I get so shaky and lose my train of thought."

---

36. You respond:

---

37. Now imagine that you are the person speaking. You have just said, "I don't usually admit it, but I often have feelings of inadequacy when I'm asked to speak before a group of people. I'm sure they think I don't know what I'm talking about because I get so shaky and lose my train of thought." Now listen to 10 possible responses. Put a check in front of the responses that are **accepting** to you.
    a. ____ "You get shaky when you speak before a group?"
    b. ____ "How do you know what the group thinks about you?"
    c. ____ "Don't you realize that even the best speakers get a little shaky?"
    d. ____ "When did this kind of thing first happen to you?"
    e. ____ "Why are you afraid to admit to such a minor neurosis?"
    f. ____ "You feel inadequate and lose your train of thought?"
    g. ____ "I've had the experience many times. Have you tried taking deep breaths?"
    h. ____ "Do you think this inferiority complex stems from your early childhood?"
    i. ____ "Don't you think that this will hurt you in your activities as a leader?"
    j. ____ "Wouldn't you like to sit in on the 'Speaking in Meetings' course I'm taking?"

---

38. Responses "a" and "f" are **accepting.**

---

39. Take a minute to look back at the responses you wrote down. Do they still seem accepting?

---

40. Now listen to a series of expressions. In the right hand column, write an *accepting* response.

Others say: *You say:*

"I don't think you understand some of the problems with this assignment."

"Sure I want to improve, but I think I'm doing all I can right now. After all, if I take time out to go to the lab sessions, my job will suffer."

"Do you really think I don't take enough initiative? I've always prided my-self on my ability to really plunge into an assignment."

"I think you've got a fine idea there, however, I really doubt that the teacher will buy it."

(ANGRY) . . . "Most of the people in this class don't give a damn about it, so why should I?"

---

41. Some *accepting* responses that I might give to the aforementioned expressions are:

a. ____ "I don't understand some of the problems with this assignment." (And yet, I might say this with a tone of voice that says, "That's what YOU think, but I really DO understand." If I do say it this way, however, the other still won't feel understood or accepted.)

b. ____ "You want to improve but your work will suffer if you go to the study sessions."

c. ____ "You feel that you really plunge into an assignment but I think you don't take enough initiative." (I would need to reassure him that I didn't see him. However, if I do reassure him, then I stop his talking about what is on HIS Mind.)

d. ____ "You doubt that the teacher will buy it." (I would feel a need to start telling him how he could get the teacher to buy it. It might be that this is not the *main thing* on his mind. I won't find THAT out, though, unless I hear him out.)

e. ____ "Why should YOU care when most of the people in this class don't give a damn about it." (I am just repeating his idea—not asking a question.)

---

42. Review your responses in frame 40 and revise them if you want to. As you revise them, think about the tone of voice in which you would say them. Think about how the other would react to your tone.

---

43. Experiment with ACCEPTING responses in your encounters with people for the next few days and try to sense how people react. The only way to develop the skill of **accepting** is through practice. When you are really tuned into the other's world, you will find (if your experience is like mine) that the other becomes noticeably more interested in talking to you. YOU will enjoy it more, too.

---

44. a. As you listen, your main purpose is to ACTIVELY show the other that you are "with him," "in tune," "understanding him," and "caring about what he is trying to communicate to you." (If you don't honestly care, that will show through and the **accepting** responses will sound phony.)

b. You can show that you are "in tune" in other ways than accepting words. For example, there are times when the most helpful thing you can do is to be **quietly attentive.** Nodding your head to let the other know you are with him can help, too.

c. As the other continues talking to you, do more than just parrot his words. Try to capture the flavor of his ideas and his feelings—i.e., try to be a mirror. If you are a clear mirror (and not a "judge" or a "critic"), he will feel free to change with you and in front of you. (And, if your experience is like mine, that can be a very satisfying experience.)

---

45. The next frame lists several statements. Try thinking of responses that catch the flavor or spirit of what the other is saying without just being repetitive of his words. Write your responses in the right hand column of the next frame.

---

46. *Others say:*   *You say:*

"It really gripes me when people say that. Ever since I was a kid in elementary school people have said I was stubborn. I'll be damned if I can see how being a 'wet mop' will help me to do a better job!"

(INCREDULOUSLY) . . . "You mean somebody said that about me?"

(ANGRY) . . . "One trouble with people in our class is that they never can see that we need answers now. I think too many of you have been concentrating on theories that still need to be proved."

"I doubt that it will work. I don't think you understand our problem. Our situation is completely different from anyone else's."

"It's hard to say where I would like to be five years from now. I certainly would like, gee . . . I don't know. I feel I could be doing a lot more than I am . . .; but, somehow, it doesn't seem worth it. Why bother trying?"

---

47. Answers I might give are:
   a. ____ "It really gripes you when people call you stubborn."
   b. ____ "You are surprised to hear that."
   c. ____ "You are angry that we don't get answers for you right away."
   d. ____ "You feel that I don't understand your situation."
   e. ____ "Are you saying that life seems pretty overwhelming to you? That you feel like
           you'd like to do something—but why bother?"

---

48. As you practice using accepting responses you may feel discomfort. If you do, remember that a new way of behaving is usually uncomfortable at first.

---

49. As you listen actively by using **accepting** responses, remember that your **purpose** is to **help** the other **help himself**. If you are like me, this will probably be difficult, particularly if the other has a problem and you have a solution. I feel a very strong desire to give the other my solution—even if I have to force it down his throat.

---

50. I find I am most helpful, in most situations, when I help the other **release** his feelings, **explore** the facts (including his feelings), and create alternatives. Then I leave HIM with the responsibility for deciding on what HE wants. I have a strong desire to help the other decide, too; but I have found that if I let the other know the alternative I would choose, he tends to be influenced by my choice. I do not want the other to be influenced by my choice for two reasons. First, my choice is likely to be misleading because my "world" is not his. Second, the more completely the other accepts responsibility for his own decisions, the more he will feel responsibility for doing whatever is necessary to carry out his decisions. ❑

ACTIVE LISTENING EXERCISE

PURPOSE: To practice deciding what kind of statements can be responded to with the empathic/active listening skills.

PROCEDURE: In small groups, discuss each of the following statements. What responses should be made? Why?

1. I wonder if I ought to start looking for another job. They're reorganizing the company, and what with drop in business and all maybe this is one of the jobs they'll cut back on. But if my boss finds out I'm looking around, maybe he'll think I don't like it here and let me go anyway.
2. I said I'd do the collecting for him, but I sure don't feel like it. But I owe him a favor, so I guess I'll have to do it.
3. I've got a report due tomorrow, an exam the next day, rehearsals every night this week, and now a meeting this afternoon. I don't think I can even fit in eating and this has been going on all month.
4. Sure she gets better grades than I do. She's a housewife, takes only two classes, and all she has to do is study. I have to work a job and go to school too. And I don't have anyone to support me.
5. I can't understand why they haven't written. They've never been gone this long without at least a card, and I don't even know how to get in touch with them.
6. My daughter got straight A's this year and the high school has a reputation for being very hard. She's a natural student. But sometimes I wonder if she isn't all books. I wish I could help her get interested in something besides studying.
7. I worked up that whole study—did all the surveying, the compiling, the writing. It was my idea in the first place. But he turned it into the head office, with his name on it, and he got the credit.
8. Boy, the teacher tells us he'll mark us off on our grade every time we're late, but it doesn't seem to bother him when he comes in late. He must figure it's his privilege.

9. I don't know whether I'm doing a good job or not. She never tells me if I'm doing well or need to work harder. I sure hope she likes my work.
10. She believed everything he said about me. She wouldn't even listen to my side; she just started yelling at me.
11. Look, we've gone over and over this. The meeting could have been over an hour ago if we hadn't gotten hung up on this one point. If we can't make a decision let's table it and move on.
12. Look, I know I acted like a rat. I apologized, and I'm trying to make up for it. I can't do anymore, can I? So drop it!

DISCUSSION: What are five reasons why empathic/active listening is important in maximizing communication efforts?

1.
2.
3.
4.
5.   ❏

LISTENING ACTIVITY ————————————————————

PURPOSE: To demonstrate how vital listening is to memorization.

PROCEDURE: 1. Break into dyads.
                2. Have one person in each pair read the following list to the other. The reader should first read item one, then items one and two, and so on through ten. The listener should try to repeat what she heard after each reading.
                3. Read the following as directed:
                   One pig.
                   Two jaws.
                   Three orange VWs.
                   Four lively pacifiers.
                   Five squelching jackasses.
                   Six marinated chicks, prepared to perfection.
                   Seven fox-trotters from Amazon County, New Delhi.
                   Eight rusty outhouse seats unearthed from the tomb of King Tut.
                   Nine dirty men, wearing purple tennis shoes, jogging to Lucretia's massage parlor in back of Mr. Yee's gas station.
                   Ten amphibious, blubbery octopi legs from the northeast corner of the westernmost island of Mungula-Stikwee, two-stepping to "I Wanna Hug You All Night Long."
                4. Get into a circle and see how many can repeat all ten lines.

DISCUSSION: 1. What problems did you encounter as you got into this activity? Why?
                2. How important is concentration to effective listening?
                3. What part can verbal repetition play in acquiring good listening-memory skills?
                4. Does the quality of the source's message affect receiver listening?   ❏

REACTIONS

1. Why is listening such an important communicating skill?

2. Listen to a recording of your favorite ballad.

   a. What is the main idea in the song?

   b. Focus your attention on sounds of the musical instruments. List the instruments you are able to hear.

3. Why is it that we have a tendency to evaluate what a person says rather than listening with understanding?

4. Explain why we don't need training to hear, but we do need training to become better listeners.

5. What kinds of verbal and nonverbal feedback can we use to let a person know we are listening?

6. Select a specific listening experience where you blocked out what the person was saying. What are some ways you plan to overcome this bad listening habit?

7. Where do you plan to practice empathic or active listening? How do you expect it to improve your communication?

PERCEPTION | 4

————————————————————

We spend our entire lives communicating our perceptions of what we think our world is like, what is happening in it and what we are doing about it.

Thus, what and how we perceive constitutes a critical element in our study of communication.

Perception

DEFINITIONS:

1. the manner in which we assign meaning, value, significance and usefulness to elements in our environment;
2. the sensing, processing, organizing and interpreting of our reality.

EXAMPLES:

Consider the following situations. Your *perception of* the central figure in each will determine your *reaction to* it.

Example A:

As you are casually strolling through your own neighborhood, you observe a female black kitten on the sidewalk in front of you. Do you:

1. want to lift, cuddle and talk to her because she is soft, loving and vulnerable?
2. step around but otherwise ignore her because you are simply not interested in cats?
3. avoid even looking at her, crossing to the other side of the street, because in your mind she is associated with the devil and bad luck?

Example B:

Upon entering the room for your morning Communication class you observe a + sign on the chalkboard. Do you:

1. regard it positively as a symbol of Christianity, thus salvation, and gently touch the one around your neck?

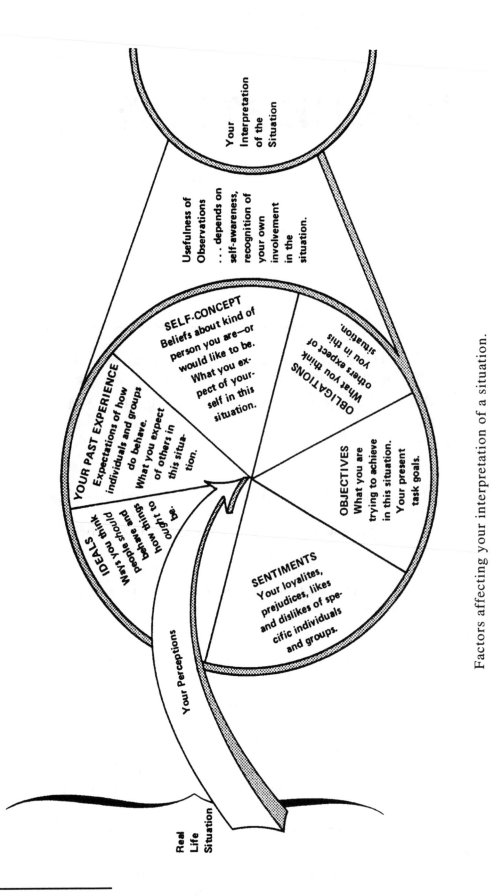

Factors affecting your interpretation of a situation.

By permission, Dr. Robert L. Holz, *Developing Human Skill*; © 1955, Amos Tuck School of Business Administration, Dartmouth College.

72

2. disregard its presence because two randomly intersecting lines obviously have no consequence to your study of Communication?
3. feel irritated and distracted because mathematics has always been very difficult for you, and any representation of a mathematical function reminds you of how stressful every one of your math classes has been?

As you continue through this chapter, you will become more aware of the importance of perception in every day communication.

THE IMPORTANCE OF PERCEPTION
The P's and Cues of Perception

Frank C. Faieta

Not unlike the individual stamp of a person's fingerprints or the unique sound of one's voice print, a person's perception likewise carries a unique code. If continual disagreements and differences of opinion are not enough to convince most of us that we all simply do not perceive the world the same way, then let's consider some reasons for the selectivity of perception. But first it is helpful to establish that *perception involves selecting, organizing and interpreting into a meaningful picture the world around us.* It is no secret that effective communication skills can help us bridge our innate differences. We can, in fact, share similar perceptions only in so far as the verbal/nonverbal mergings made possible by our established and re-established meanings allow. When we communicate we share our perception of the world, not the "truth." Some reasons for the differences in the perceptual process and for further consideration include: (1) physiological, (2) psychological, (3) position in space, and (4) past experience. Taking each of the four in turn, it is likewise interesting to consider the implications for effective interpersonal communication, or simply the odds against it.

(1) **Physiological factors** include what we are able to perceive, i.e., what capacity we possess with our senses of sight, touch, hearing, taste and smell. My perception is most certainly a function of my individual optical power. Yours is different, even if only by slight degree. Expanding this difference to any large population, countless millions of onlookers with varying degrees of visual acuity see a myriad of stimuli—the numeric variables become incomprehensible. Enter the next modality, hearing. I personally have suffered no loss of hearing, at least according to commonly accepted routine tests, though I'm quite my-

opic. Now take the end effect of just these two variables and multiply them times the number of people I or any given person interacts with in a lifetime and already the implications for the odds of agreement/disagreement about events in the extrinsic world become awesome.

(2) The **psychological factors** might most simply be said to encompass what we need to perceive and therefore do. We all differ in immediate needs, desires, interests and motives, and perceive accordingly. Thus, we tend to pay attention to only or especially those things which interest us. The continual barrage of external stimuli necessitates, of course, that we attend to limited aspects of our environment; however, we choose not randomly but with our psychological drives as a primary motive. For example, two friends are riding together in a car. If one is looking for entertainment or a good time, he is more likely to see the theaters and bars, etc. while the other who happens to be tired after a long day at work fails to see or blocks these entirely. The less energetic of the two may in fact tend to see peaceful and relaxation-oriented stimuli. Most of us are so good at paying attention to only what interests us that we even distort external events and things so they will fit what we want to perceive. The need for beauty can be strong enough to find it in rubble. An intense need for security will sense trouble where it does not exist. An unsatisfied need for love or interest in friendship or companionship can attribute its existence where it probably does not really merit this perception. We may even go so far as to deceive ourselves according to the intensity of our needs, motives, interests, desires, etc.

(3) A person's **position in space** certainly adjusts what can be seen. We are able to see according to angle, height, location in time and

space, and so on. Our very physics of body motion and resulting intentional or unintentional location at any given second prescribes what will be perceived. Like the physiological factors discussed above, we can voluntarily control this factor by simply moving or adjusting position via body kinesics. Take the split second timing of a nearby automobile accident where no adjustment is possible. It simply happens too fast. The resulting reports of several onlookers are just what we could expect in the light of the perceptual position in space of each: different by varying degree, a function of an incredible complexity of each witness's perceptual totality.

(4) **Past experience** is our last stop in this sequence of P's. People tend to perceive according to what they've learned to perceive. Call it expectation or even anticipation, but regardless of terminology, it is the knee jerk of familiarity. An individual's vocabulary is one way of understanding this final reason for selectivity. We have, figuratively speaking, a blind spot for words we don't know; in fact, we sometimes don't even hear them. Once a new word is learned, we fill in using perceptual closure to attribute contextual meaning and the sense of the whole statement tends toward clarity—no guarantees of course. Another way of viewing this area of past experience is that we can explain our world only in so far as we have learned it—values included. Our very language directs and causes us to know the world within its parameters—vast as that may at first seem, until another language is learned and even new thought possibilities emerge.

Benjamin Lee Whorf's theory of linguistic relativity might lend one additional explanation here. The so-called Whorf-Sapir Hypothesis explains in its most fundamental tenets that: (1) Thought is determined by language, (2) Human behavior is determined by language, (3) Language is culture-bound and shapes reality, and (4) Language is a filtering system—a given language, especially its grammar, provides its speakers with habitual grooves of expression which predispose them to see the world in ready-made patterns. Since language is indeed a learned skill, one's past language experience can do no less than have an all-pervasive effect on individual percep-

tion. Thus, in a simple statement, our familiarity with something helps us to accept as well as recognize it. Our past experience accompanies us in each perception we have and thus in the act selecting it by the very nature of what we are like, who we are, where we've been and so on.

The P's of perception are four in number; the cues are innumerable. Cue sensitivity is still another way of understanding the selectivity of perception in keeping with the earlier stated definition. The cues are external to oneself, out there in the world of stimuli; the sensitivity is internal and quite individualized. The sensitivity or lack of it on the part of the individual is not uniform or equivalent by any stretch of the imagination. As mentioned above, the four P's will have the effect of sorting the perceptual deck each time with consistent randomness, rendering no event perceived exactly the same for any two or more individuals. The associated reasons are most interesting from a heuristic as well as an interpersonal standpoint.

The process of cue sensitivity, to begin, is best defined as paying attention to important signals in our environment. The voluntary omission of those cues we choose to ignore is beyond the scope of consideration here. The ones we would like to become more attentive to, hence the cues we want to learn to attend to as adults but can't or won't, bring us to an interesting crossroads. What can we know about ourselves as adult learners based on this issue of perception as opposed to the path of conceptual aspects alone? We can first realize that we miss many important cues for various reasons:

1. *Familiarity*—We often ignore what we take for granted. The "a's" and "the's" on this page were probably not even seen by you, yet they are indeed printed. A gate passed through daily is not there consciously. A frequently heard sound disappears, but only in your perception. A spouse's repeated question is simply not heard. Such cues may not seem important until demand or change forces recognition bringing with it a degree of consequence, too often negative in nature.

2. *Complacency*—Our very contentment can serve to disarm us and render lessened degrees of sensitivity. A relaxed state of body and/or mind can diminish our awareness. Certainly trained states of relaxed awareness such as meditation can overcome this; however, on a daily scale of activity we become numb with our contentments as needs are satisfied.

3. *Lack of experience or knowledge*—If something is not familiar at all, a signal for danger for example, no capacity for sensitivity is yet developed for one's own protection. The child soon learns the hazard of a hot stove. Any noise, smell, sight is likewise not an understood cue for the untried perceiver. New ideas or values could be included here also.

4. *Problem Paralysis*—The person who is experiencing problem overload or sensory overkill and is so burdened from within is likely to miss that which is outside. There simply is no room not even for one more thing.

5. *Singularity*—Thoughts or concerns which are near-obsessive tend to override other stimuli. The task-oriented, Type A personality attempting to succeed in a given assignment may block not only distractions but also helpful cues as well. Many generals have indeed won the battle but lost the war.

Other related reasons might include lack of practice, self-focus, habitual patterns, failure to recognize relationships, and automatic reactions or responses.

Having examined cue sensitivity from the standpoint of reasons for overlooking important cues, a brief summary of why we see particular cues might be illuminating. Our degree of awareness, our internal sensitivity stems from: knowledge, sensing selectively, vigilance, vocabulary, topic interest, openmindedness, experience and even practice. That these items might be construed as the converse of the previous list is a potential mnemonic for internalizing both sides of the issue.

What is offered is not intended as a simplified "how to" list for improving perception and winning friends in 10 easy steps. But rather, the usefulness of recognizing one's level of sensitivity or lack of it in any problem environment is a realistic springboard for change. From recognition an individualized action plan charged from self-motivated and subsequently heightened interest can lead to results. Useful steps include: (1) Describe situations for yourself; (2) Look for good examples, role models to observe and from whom to draw inspiration; (3) Look for the cues and when found or realized, write, log, report, or sequence pertinent information. Try to realize and then remember that pitfalls and obstacles to a plan for cue sensitivity exist. Often important cues are hidden, or buried in others. Latent cues are the challenge since the test of any new powers of perception, and a true test of your action plan will be consistent discoveries—those which illuminate as well as inspire. Another obstacle lies in the response we ourselves attempt after recognizing a cue. Old patterns are apt to emerge. For example, upon discovering that subordinates on the job are dropping hints, (clues) that fell on previously deaf ears will be heard. A person may get angry, defensive, or even threaten when the cues surface unwelcomed information. The attitude of open-mindedness will likewise need to be learned and practiced if intrapersonal balance is to be maintained.

The choice to select, organize and interpret a greater and broader spectrum of possibilities carries an added burden of responsibility. The challenge to the emerging perceiver is to open the attitudes as well. The P's and cues may engender many why's; after all biases and predispositions were also chosen or selected.

New modes of knowing, expanded awareness can foster the greatest reward expected, an enhanced capacity for humanity and the concomitant actualization of self-growth.

BARRIERS TO PERCEPTION

Let's summarize some of the problems we have communicating to others what we perceive. We tend to perceive the world in terms of our own needs, wants, experiences, culture, expectations and physical abilities or limitations regardless of what external reality might really be. Since our perception process is unique to each of us, we often perceive the world very differently from those around us.

We perceive the external world through our senses (an internal process) and we can be fooled. Even the symbols (both verbal and non-verbal) we use to communicate our perceptions to others may have meanings which are considerably different from what we intend our receiver to understand. Your ability to perceive is learned. Like any other complex skill, you can learn to do it better.

PERCEPTION: AGREE/DISAGREE

PURPOSE: To test your understanding of basic perception principles.

PROCEDURE:
1. Read each statement carefully.
2. If you believe it to be true, check the A column under Individual.

   If you believe it, or any part of it, to be false, check the D column under Individual.
3. For each of the following statements, record (A) if you agree or (D) if you disagree.

Individual			Group	
A	D		A	D
		1. The perception of a physical object or event depends more upon the object or event than upon the mind of the observer.		
		2. Perception is primarily an interpersonal phenomenon.		
		3. The fact that hallucinations and dreams may seem as real as waking perception indicates that perception depends very little upon external reality.		
		4. The reaction we have to what we see generally depends upon learning and culture.		
		5. We tend to see what we wish to see or are expecting to see regardless of what reality is.		
		6. We can eliminate all distortion in our perception by careful, scientific observation.		

Individual			Group	
A	D		A	D
		7. Scientific instruments, though they extend the limits of our perception, do not make perception any more real.		
		8. What we perceive is no more than a representation of what is.		
		9. Perception is a physical response to a physical reality. It is only when we begin talking about our perceptions that we begin to distort them.		
		10. If we are careful, we can see the world as it really is.		
		11. We react to our environment on the basis of what we perceive that environment to be like and not on what the environment is really like.		
DISCUSSION:		Your instructor will lead a discussion, comparing Individual and Group responses.		

THE ISSUES IN PERSON PERCEPTION

Albert H. Hastorf, David J. Schneider, and Judith Polefka

The Perceptual Process

Both philosophers and psychologists have long been intrigued with the nature of the human perceptual process. One explanation for their interest is that man is naturally curious about his contact with the outside world and wonders how his experiences are caused and to what degree they reflect the world accurately. Beyond general curiosity, the reason for the interest stems from an apparent paradox, the basis of which lies in the difference between the nature of our experiences and our knowledge of how those experiences are caused.

. . . The world appears to be given to us in experience. Yet a causal analysis of these events indicates a very different state of affairs.

You have opened your eyes and you experience a blue vase about six inches high situated on a table. The vase appears to be at a certain distance, and its shape and color are equally clear. Let us remind ourselves of the causal events that are involved. Light waves of a certain wavelength are reflected off the vase. Some of them impinge on the retina of your eye, and if enough retinal cells are irritated, some visual nerves will fire and a series of electrical impulses will be carried through the sensory apparatus, including the subcortical centers, and will finally arrive at the cortex. This description paints a picture of a very indirect contact with the world: light waves to retinal events to sensory nerve events to subcortical events and finally to cortical events, from which visual experiences result. What is especially important is that this causal description reveals a very different picture than does our naive description of experience. (This causal description led a famous German physiologist to remark that "we are aware of our nerves, not of objects.") Thus we have a conflict between our everyday-life experiences of objects together with their properties and an analysis of how these experiences come to exist. How *does* the human being create a coherent perceptual world out of chaotic physical impingements?

Our world of experience has structure.

Let us begin with this fact of experience and explore how the structure may be achieved. First of all, we know that our experiences are ultimately dependent on our sensory apparatus, which for visual experiences would include both the retina of the eye and the sensory neurons connecting the retina to the visual areas of the cortex. This apparatus plays, in a manner of speaking, the role of translator. Light waves impinge on the eyes and we experience color. Sound waves impinge on the ear and we experience pitch. Without the sensory apparatus we would have no contact with the external world. There remains, however, the question of the nature of this translation.

A number of philosophers and psychologists have conceived of the translation process as an essentially passive one, completely determined by the physical properties of the stimulus and by the structure of the receptors and sensory nervous system. They conceive of our sensory apparatus as working somewhat like a high-speed translation device. . . . This conception has led to arguments as to how much

By permission, Albert H. Hastorb, David J. Schneider, Judith Polefka, *Person Perception*, 1970, Addison-Wesley, Reading, Mass.

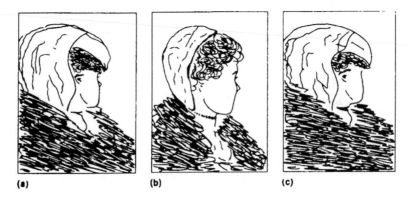

Figure 4.1.

of this dictionary is present at birth and how much is the product of our learning history. One reason for the popularity of the passive recording view of perception is the immediacy and "giveness" of our experience. Our experiences are immediate and they feel direct. These feelings led to the belief that the translation process must be automatic and built in.

The primary argument against that position stems from the fact that our experience of the world is highly selective. If we passively translated and recorded stimuli, our world would be a jumble of experiences: while you were reading a book, you would also be aware of the pressure of your clothes on your body and of all the sounds around you. Actually, from a myriad of impinging stimuli, we are aware of only certain objects and certain attributes of the objects. Anyone who has asked two different persons to describe the same scene has been struck by the fact that they often describe it very differently; each selects different events and different attributes of the events. Given this phenomenon, we must be more than passive translators. In fact, we must be active processors of information. The world is not merely revealed to us; rather, we play an active role in the creation of our experiences.

Let us take an example from the research of Robert W. Leeper to illustrate our point. The stimulus he used was an ambiguous picture which can be seen as either an old hag or an attractive young woman (Fig. 4.1). Continued inspection of the picture usually permits an observer to see first one and then the other. Leeper had the original picture redrawn so that one version emphasized the young woman (b)

and another emphasized the old hag (c). Subjects who had been exposed to one or the other of these redrawings found themselves "locked in" on that view when the original ambiguous picture was presented. One hundred percent of the subjects who had had prior experience with the version emphasizing the hag saw the hag and only the hag in their first look at the ambiguous picture; ninety-five percent of the subjects who had had prior experience with the version emphasizing the young woman saw only the young woman when first looking at the same ambiguous picture. The subjects had been given a set to process the input stimuli in a certain way, and they created a structure consistent with that set. Although our experiences are both immediate and structured, extremely complex participation by the organism, including the active selection and processing of stimulus impingements, is involved in their creation.

One of the most salient features of the person's participation in structuring his experiential world can be described as a categorizing process. He extracts stimuli from the world and forces them into a set of categories. We have here a powerful example of the effects of linguistic coding on the structuring of experience. The subjects in Leeper's experiment did not see a complex pattern of light and dark nor even "a person" (a possible category); they saw an old hag or a young woman. The categories we use are derived from our past history and are dependent on our language and our cultural background. . . . Whatever the nature of the categories we use, they play an important role in the processing of information.

We have begun with the experiential fact that our perceptions are both structured and organized. This structure is immediate and appears to be given by the world of objects. . . . These structured perceptions are the outcome of the organism's engaging in active processing of information, which includes the translation of physical impingements to nerve impulses and the active selection and categorizing of the inputs.

Our world of experience has stability.

When we open our eyes and look at a scene, we are not overwhelmed with constant shifts in the picture as our eyes and our attention wander. There is a certain enduring aspect to our experience. We select certain facets of the situation and stick with them. Check this statement against your own experience with the ambiguous picture in Fig. 4.1. If it was like the experience of most people, the first organization of the picture, whether it was the old hag or the young woman, continued to demand your attention. It was hard to "find" the other one. You made various attempts to shift the focus of attention by blinking your eyes or by concentrating on a certain part of the picture, but those stratagems did not always work. Although stability in a case of this kind may frustrate us to such an extent that it deserves to be given a different and more pejorative label—rigidity—the example demonstrates that we do *not* experience a world of chaotic instability.

The most obvious example of the maintenance of stability in our experience has been termed *the constancies* in perception. . . . Let us consider an example. You are sitting in a chair in your living room. Another person walks into the room, moves over to a table by the window, picks up a magazine, and then goes across the room to sit down and read it. What are the successive visual-stimulus events impinging on your retina and your successive experiences? Every time the person moves closer to you, the impingement, or *proximal stimulus,* gets larger; in fact, if he moves from 20 feet away to 10 feet away, the height of the image on your eye doubles in size. The oppo-

site occurs as he moves away from you because the size of the retinal image is inversely proportional to the distance of the object from you. Furthermore, when the person moves near the window, more light is available and more light is reflected to the retina. Yet your perception does not fit this description of the stimulus events. While the person is moving about the room, you experience him as remaining relatively constant in size and brightness. In spite of dramatic alterations in the proximal stimulus, you experience a stable world. Given this discrepancy between proximal-stimulus events and experience, the organism must actively process information to produce the stability in his world of experience. . . .

Let us think of the perceptual act as a complex form of problem-solving, the goal of which is to create a stability in which our perceptions bear some relationship to external events. We can then draw an analogy between perceptual problem-solving and scientific problem-solving. Just as the scientist attempts to reduce a complex jumble of events to a small set of variables which serve as a set of determining conditions for a particular event, so we search out the invariant aspects of a situation to produce stable perceptions. The scientist searches for invariance in order to understand and to predict the world; we as perceivers also seek to understand and to predict the world in order that we may behave in it to our advantage. In other words, the perceptual act can be said to generate a prediction that we can use as a basis for action. The goal in both cases is predictably of the environment, and the means to the goal is the specification of causal relationships.

Our world of experience is meaningful.

The connotation of "meaningful" here is that structured and stable events are not isolated from one another but appear to be related in some orderly fashion over time. . . . It is so common for the world of experience to make sense to us that the most powerful way to point out the importance of the phenomenon is to suggest trying to conceive of a world that does not make sense. Events would follow each other with no apparent causal relationships. Almost every event would entail surprise. Nothing would seem familiar. The general experience would be one of chaos. Such a state of affairs is so alien to our everyday-life experience that it is extremely difficult to imagine. Our experiences usually *are* meaningful in that they are structured and they are stable; they are related in the sense that they seem familiar, but particularly in the sense that events have implications for one another. . . .

We could cite innumerable studies demonstrating the influence on perception of either the individual's past learning or his present motivational state. Leeper's experiment on the young woman-old hag picture is an example of the former. An experiment by Schafer and Murphy provides an example of the effects of motivational state on perception. They presented subjects with a simple ambiguous drawing (Fig. 4.2) and gave them a small monetary reward when they indicated that they saw one of the profiles but took money away when they indicated that they saw the other. The results indicated that, over time, positive consequences associated with a given perception increased the likelihood of that perception. . . .

In summary, our past experiences and purposes play an absolutely necessary role in providing us with knowledge of the world that has structure, stability, and meaning. Without them, events would not make sense. With them, our perceptions define a predictable world, an orderly stage for us to act on.

Figure 4.2.

Rorschach ink-blot
What do you perceive?

"Black Signature" by Magritte
What do you perceive?

What do you perceive?

CHECK YOUR PERCEPTION

PURPOSE: To give you a chance to check your perception.

PROCEDURE: 1.   Read the following aloud.

Paris
in the
the Springtime

Bird
in the
the Hand

Once
in a
a lifetime

2.   How many times does the letter F appear in the box below?

> Finished Files are the Result
> of Years of Scientific Study
> Combined with the Experience
> of Many Years

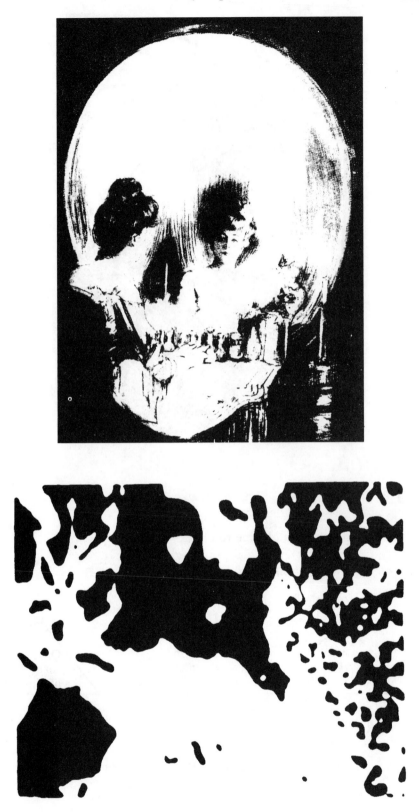

Do you see the face of Christ?

QUIZ—COMMON PERCEPTION

PURPOSE: To understand how accurately we perceive our commonplace world.

PROCEDURE: This is a timed test (10 minutes). Place your answer to the left of the number; you are encouraged to guess.

_____   1. On a standard traffic light, is the green on top or bottom?

_____   2. The stripes of a man's tie usually slant down in what direction from the wearer's view (left, right, both)?

_____   3. In which hand is the Statue of Liberty's torch?

_____   4. Name the six colors in the Campbell's soup label.

_____   5. What two letters of the alphabet do not appear on a telephone dial?

_____   6. What two digits on a telephone dial are not accompanied by letters?

_____   7. When you walk, does your right arm swing with your right leg or your left leg?

_____   8. How many matches are in a standard pack?

_____   9. On the American flag, is the upper-most stripe red or white?

_____   10. What is the lowest <u>number</u> on an FM radio dial?

_____   11. On a standard typewriter, over which number is the "%" symbol? (percent)

_____   12. Which way does the red diagonal slash go in the international "no parking" or "no smoking" signs?

_____   13. How many channels on a standard VHF television dial?

_____   14. Which side of a woman's blouse has the button holes?

_____   15. On the California license plate, is the state name at the top or the bottom?

_____   16. Which direction do the blades on a fan rotate?

_____   17. Whose face is on a dime?

_____ 18. How many sides does a stop sign have?

_____ 19. Do books have their even-numbered pages on the left or the right?

_____ 20. How many lug nuts are on a standard American car wheel?

_____ 21. How many sides are there on a standard pencil?

_____ 22. Sleepy, Happy, Sneezy, Grumpy, Dopey and Doc. Name the seventh dwarf.

_____ 23. How many hot dog buns are in a standard package?

_____ 25. On which card in the deck is the cardmaker's trademark?

_____ 26. On which side of a standard venetian-blind is the cord that adjusts the opening between the slats?

_____ 27. On the back of a $5 bill is the Lincoln Memorial. What's in the center of the backside of a $1 bill?

_____ 28. There are 12 buttons on a touch-tone telephone. What symbols are on the two buttons that bear no digits?

_____ 29. How many curves in a standard paper clip?

_____ 30. Does a merry-go-round turn clockwise or counterclockwise?

Scoring: 28–30 Excellent
            25–27 Good
            20–24 Okay
            16–19 Fair

DISCUSSION: 1. What are some reasons you may fail to perceive, or perceive incorrectly, your commonplace world?
               2. How much of our perception comes from experiences stored in our subconscious (those items at which you guessed)?
               3. Is it important to perceive our immediate environment/surroundings accurately? Objectively? Why? Why not?   ❏

What disturbs men's minds is not events
but their judgments on events. —*Epictetus*

Applicable Quotes for PERCEPTION

Warning

Jenny Joseph

When I am an old woman I shall wear purple
With a red hat which doesn't go, and doesn't suit me.
And I shall spend my pension on brandy and summer gloves
And satin sandals, and say we've no money for butter.
I shall sit down on the pavement when I'm tired
And gobble up samples in shops and press alarm bells
And run my stick along the public railings
And make up for the sobriety of my youth.
I shall go out in my slippers in the rain
And pick the flowers in other people's gardens
And learn to spit.

You can wear terrible shirts and grow more fat
And eat three pounds of sausages at a go
Or only bread and pickle for a week
And hoard pens and pencils and beermats and things in boxes.

But now we must have clothes that keep us dry
And pay our rent and not swear in the street
And set a good example for the children.
We must have friends to dinner and read the papers.

But maybe I ought to practise a little now?
So people who know me are not too shocked and surprised
When suddenly I am old, and start to wear purple.

Lyn Cowan, Ruby at the Fair

From SELECTED POEMS published by Bloodaxe Books Ltd.,
New Castle-upon-Tyne. Copyright © Jenny Joseph 1992.

Two battleships assigned to the training squadron had been at sea on maneuvers in heavy weather for several days. I was serving on the lead battleship and was on watch on the bridge as night fell. The visibility was poor with patchy fog, so the captain remained on the bridge keeping an eye on all activities.

Shortly after dark, the lookout on the wing of the bridge reported, "Light, bearing on the starboard bow."

"Is it steady or moving astern?" the captain called out.

Lookout replied, "Steady, captain," which meant we were on a dangerous collision course with that ship.

The captain then called to the signalman, "Signal that ship: We are on a collision course, advise you change course 20 degrees."

Back came the signal, "Advisable for you to change course 20 degrees."

The captain said, "Send, I'm a captain, change course 20 degrees."

"I'm a seaman second class," came the reply. "You had better change course 20 degrees."

By that time, the captain was furious. He spat out, "Send, I'm a battleship. Change course 20 degrees."

Back came the flashing light, "I'm a lighthouse."

We changed course.

THE WAY I SEE THINGS ——————————————————

PURPOSE: To help you understand that recent events in your life affect the way you perceive the world.

PROCEDURE: 1. In the space below, write about an event which has occurred within a recent time period which has affected the way you perceive the present and, thus, your intra/interpersonal communication with others. For example, it might be a new job, a change of schools, a birth or death, a relationship, experience, accomplishment, decision, etc. Be very specific in your description.

                2. Describe the ways this event has affected your perception, your communication, your opinion about yourself and your values.
                3. In what ways has this event caused you to alter your behavior? Explain.
                4. Form small groups and discuss what each has written. Also discuss the following questions.

DISCUSSION: 1. How does the way you see the world affect your communication on both the intrapersonal and interpersonal levels?
                2. How can you relate this knowledge and insight to your personal, professional, and social lives?
                3. Are you likely to let this event have a lasting effect or will you soon forget it?   ❏

A CASE STUDY FOR PERCEPTION

The following communication interaction took place at an information desk in the college center between Ndegwa, a student from Nigeria, and Jane, a Midwestern student who was in charge of the information service. Ndegwa, who approached the desk in an effort to get to know Jane, engaged her in a conversation, and began telling her about life in Nigeria. The girl appeared quite interested as she nodded her head and leaned on the desk closer to Ndegwa.

He described the Ibo People of Nigeria as being more advanced in education, commerce, the professions, and other walks of life than the other ethnic groups of Nigeria. He explained that these other groups of Nigeria treated the Ibos unjustly and that at one time 30,000 innocent Ibo civilians were massacred by Nigerian soldiers. "After this," he said, "the Ibos seceded from Nigeria and formed the nation of Biafra. Nigeria then unleashed a savage war, aided by two world powers, against the Ibos to force them back to Nigeria." At this point in the conversation the telephone rang and the girl had to answer the call. That done, the girl directed her attention to Ndegwa and asked, "But don't you think the Ibo people were wrong to secede?" Ndegwa responded, "How dare you ask that question? Thirty thousand of us were massacred and the government which should protect its citizens raised no voice against the atrocities." Jane replied, "Are you mad?"

With this Ndegwa slammed his books on the desk and shouted, "My heavens! You say I'm mad? You call me a mad man? That is to say I am insane?"

As the girl tried to explain that she had used this word "mad" in the American meaning "angry," Ndegwa stormed out of the room.

DISCUSSION:
1. Identify the (a) source, (b) message, (c) channel, and (d) receiver in this communication situation.
2. Incorporate these terms and others like encoding, decoding, feedback, and interference into a communication model which (a) shows the process of communication between Ndegwa and Jane at a particular time in the conversation, and (b) shows the interference that occurred in this specific situation.
3. Identify two different types of interference that occurred in the case study and explain their causes. ❏

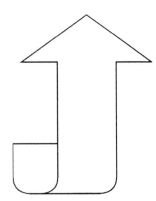

What you believe the universe to be and how you react to that belief, in everything you do, depends on what you know. And when that knowledge changes, for you, the universe changes. —*J. Burke*

COUNT THE SQUARES

PURPOSE: To compare your perception with the perception of others and to see how others can teach you to perceive.

PROCEDURE: 1.   Count the number of squares in the diagram below. How many squares are there?

2.   Join a triad, recount the squares and enter the total number of squares you see.

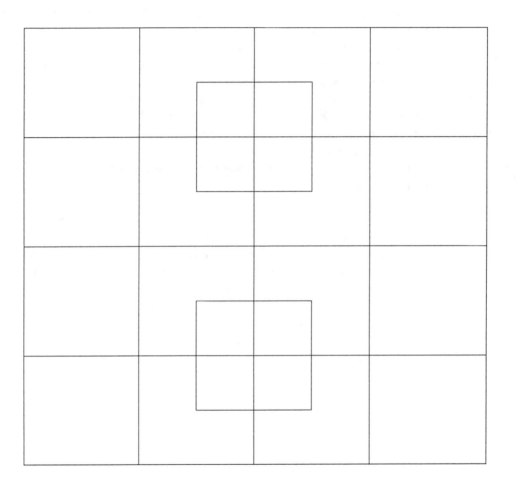

DISCUSSION: How does communicating with others affect our perception?   ❏

OBJECT PERCEPTION

PURPOSE:
To allow you to experience the process of perception and the factors which affect communication.

PROCEDURE:
1. Divide into groups of 10. Each of the groups will be allowed to examine a number of objects for a period of two minutes. You may examine the items by sight, touch, taste, etc. YOU MAY NOT TALK TO ANYONE NOR TAKE NOTES.
2. After the two minutes of examination time, return to your desk and begin to list the items in the order in which you remember them. Include in this list as precise a description of each item as you can.
3. You will have a total of 10 minutes to complete your list and description.

DISCUSSION:
Upon completion of the above phase, join a small group and discuss the following questions.

1. How did the lists differ?
   a. In length (number of objects)?
   b. Detail (description of objects)?
   c. Order in which things were remembered?
2. Why were the lists and descriptions different or alike?
3. What object was most commonly remembered and why?
4. What does the word *perception* mean?
5. What part do the five senses play in perception?
6. Is it desirable in a communication situation for people to perceive as much alike as possible? Why/Why not?
7. How can a person go about improving her perceptions? Make a list of suggestions. ❏

REACTIONS

1. List at least five reasons you perceive differently from everyone else.

2. Why do we study perception in a Speech Communication class?

3. How will your new knowledge of perception help you to be a better communicator? Give an example using a specific person from your job, family, friends, or other relationships.

4. What are at least four things we can do to increase fidelity when we find that the persons with whom we are communicating have perceptions different from our own?

NONVERBAL COMMUNICATION | 5

Definitions

Nonverbal communication consists of relaying message units to augment, contradict, or replace verbal communication. In other words, nonverbal communication:

Nonverbal Communication

GENERAL DEFINITIONS

Relays messages from individual to individual or from object to individual.

Example: Husband smiles at his wife.
Red light signals vehicles to stop.

Can augment verbal communication.

Example: A mother can shout at her child and simultaneously stamp her foot. Both her vocal utterance and physical gesture convey similar meanings.

Can contradict verbal communication.

Example: A man can tell a woman that he loves her while unconsciously he is backing away from her.

Can replace verbal communication.

Example: Visitors in foreign countries have often asked for and received directions through gesture.

THE IMPORTANCE OF NONVERBAL COMMUNICATION

Most of us already know a great deal about nonverbal communication. After all, we've been doing it since the instant we were born. We already know (or think we do) when someone's verbal message is contradicted by the nonverbal signals. And we almost always subconsciously choose the nonverbal message over the verbal!

Depending on which set of definitions we use, from 75–95 percent of all the communication that we do is nonverbal. With these two facts in mind (we already know much about nonverbal communi-

nication and we do an enormous amount about it), let's ask one more question: How good are we at communicating nonverbally?

If we are honest with ourselves, we may have to admit that we are not very effective at it. Many of our misunderstandings and our communication failures result from the errors we make in "reading" nonverbal communication.

And that is what this chapter is all about. Taking the knowledge you already have, let's learn how to make our own nonverbal communication more effective and how to do a better job of interpreting the nonverbal language of others.

Some very basic definitions follow and are in the articles by Gelman. Reasons that nonverbal communication is really important are in the next five articles.

BARRIERS TO NONVERBAL COMMUNICATION

Since nonverbal communication is so important, you would think that people would be more aware of how to make effective use of it in their conversations but they don't. Why don't they? We think that at least three barriers get in the way: 1. A lack of awareness of our own nonverbal messages. 2. A lack of knowledge and training about nonverbal communication. 3. A tendency to assume that we understand each other's nonverbal communication.

Lack of Awareness

A lack of awareness of our own nonverbal messages. Most of us tend to be unaware that we are always communicating nonverbally with everyone who can see or hear us. As soon as other persons notice us, they attach some meaning to what they see or hear. If they like what they hear or see, they attach positive value to us. If we seem similar to someone they like, they think well of us. The opposite can also occur if they don't like what they see. Much of our talking is an attempt to make sure that others see us as we want them to, not as they do.

In addition to the passive messages that we send to others, we also actively send messages to others about how we feel about them every time that we communicate with them. For example, when I tell the person behind the ice cream counter that I want a vanilla ice cream cone, my nonverbal message will let the person know how I feel about her. Are we equal as people or is she my servant for the moment?

We may spend a lot of time carefully planning the words that we are going to say but our nonverbal messages may totally invalidate everything that we had intended.

Lack of Knowledge and Training

A lack of knowledge and training about nonverbal communication. The elocutionists of the 18th and 19th centuries were very much aware of the impact that their gestures, posture and use of their voices had on audiences and they received careful training to perfect those skills. With the more conversational style of modern speakers, we left behind the grand style of earlier speakers and we also forgot the understanding on which it was all built. Recently, communication experts have popularized nonverbal communication as a way of learning about others' behavior. Few, however, have indicated the need to be aware of and to understand our own nonverbal actions.

Although many courses are available for teaching how to speak and fewer courses and seminars are designed to help people to listen better, there is still little opportunity to learn how to more effectively use nonverbal communication.

Our Tendency to Assume

A tendency to assume that we understand each others' nonverbal communication. If you have already read about verbal communication (sending audio messages), you should be able to see the similar pattern with nonverbal communication. When others send messages, whether they are sent verbally or nonverbally, our tendency is to respond to them from our frame of reference. That means that we guess what they are saying and respond based on our guesses. For example, if we guess correctly that our friend's crossed arms mean that she is upset, we would respond correctly by quietly talking about what is bothering her. However, those symbols of crossed arms may merely mean that she is cold.

It is difficult not to see others as we see ourselves. Yet to be effective communicators, we need to know that we are all very different from each other and that the purpose of communication is to discover our differences and similarities.

YOU DON'T SAY

Alex Gelman, J. D.

You arrive at work and a message awaits you at your desk. The boss wants to see you. You enter the grey walled office of your boss. He stands . . . arms folded, behind a large rectangular desk. He motions you to sit. He peers at you with a direct, unwavering stare.

The term "nonverbal" is commonly used to describe human and animal communication excepting those of spoken or written words. Our "nonverbal" communication, which is our manner of speaking without words, is partly taught, partly imitative and partly instinctive. These "nonverbal" messages may repeat, contradict, compliment, accent or regulate that which we actually "say."

Let us look at the fact situation above. What would be your reaction? "Why is he staring at me?" "His arms are folded, why is he angry?" The direct stare is seen by many in this culture as a form of threat. However, while not unique, this is characteristic of our culture specifi-cally. Staring, in addition, is considered a threat in many species of animals. Now, let us change slightly the fact situation above. Now, your boss stares, but also smiles and nods suggestively. What does he mean now? He may be expressing emotion, a possible raise, even sexual interest by the same stare when coupled by other nonverbal messages.

Nonverbal communication is quite possibly the most important part of the communicative process, for researchers now know that our actual words carry far less meaning than nonverbal cues. For example, repeat many times the following sentence, emphasizing different words in the sentence each time you do so: "I beat my spouse last night." Does not the meaning of the sentence change? The words themselves carry many meanings depending upon nonverbal cues, in this case, inflection. Essentially, the study of nonverbal communication is broken down to (1) environmental clues; (2)

NONVERBAL ASPECTS OF COMMUNICATION: NOTABLE QUOTES

"Americans are characteristically illiterate in the area of gesture language."
Weston LaBarre

"Watch out for the man whose stomach doesn't move when he laughs."
Cantonese Proverb

"The eyes of men converse as much as their tongues, with the advantage that the ocular dialect needs no dictionary, but is understood the world over."
Ralph Waldo Emerson

"Man is a multisensorial being. Obviously he verbalizes."
Ray Birdwhistell

"Silence, the instrument of isolation, can create community."
J. Vernon Jensen

"Words can mean that I want to make you into a friend and silence can mean that I accept you already being one."
Hugh Prather

spatial study; (3) physical appearance; (4) behavioral cues; (5) vocal qualities; and (6) body motion or kinesics.

Kinesics—Eye Contact and Facial Expression

A great deal is conveyed through our eyes and facial expression. However, we cannot isolate this study without considering all other bodily and environmental cues. Facial expression is probably the most communicative of our body. Researchers have only recently discovered that the facial expressions made are extremely rapid and may not be consciously noticed in normal communication. They are, however, picked up by our subconscious or faculties in giving meaning to the words used. By careful study, one can learn to notice expressions of affective states and be accurate in identifying facial expressions.

Of all facial cues, eye contact has found the most interest by researchers. Years of study have gone into characterizing and identifying pupil dilation. We know, for instance, that continued eye contact may signal arousal, interest or attentiveness. However, we do not as yet know the full extent of cultural aspects of such eye contact. As an example, in our culture when we feel physically uncomfortable due to the proximity of others, we lower our eyes traditionally though not always. We feel awkward or somehow invaded if someone stares intently at us. It is deemed a threat. Eye contact may differ from age to age and between sexes. Researchers are, however, not sure to what degree. It remains an open field for research and investigation.

The Environment

There is little doubt that the environment in which one speaks may contribute to the overall communicative process. Ponder for a moment how the size of the room, furniture arrangements, temperature, lighting, color of the walls and even the space between persons may affect our desire to communicate or the openness of the communication.

High in the study of environmental clues is the study of "proxemics," or the investigation of how space between individuals may affect the communicative process between them. It appears that we culturally and instinctively maintain a protective perimeter of space between us and the outside world. While this space may differ from culture to culture, it may have its base in the protective instincts of our animalistic past. Researchers have isolated several distances and attached to them levels of communication. Between zero and 18 inches, we traditionally allow our most intimate friends. We communicate on a "personal" level with those persons within 18 inches to four feet. This personal level is usually reserved to classmates or other persons at a party or meeting. A "social" distance is considered somewhere between four feet and twelve feet, this level being reserved to guests in living rooms, etc. Finally, there appears a "public" distance, which does not seem to generate communication. These distances are not hard and fast but seem to differ with cultural, even physical differences between individuals.

Kinesics—Behavior and Gestures

When we speak of gestures and body language, we deal with the heart of the study of nonverbal behavior. As in all nonverbal study, we note that such behavior is contextual and must not be isolated from the study of other "cues." We also note that the field of body language or kinesics is still ripe for eager and youthful research.

For the most part, body language seems to reinforce facial communication. For instance, while our face may indicate what emotion we feel, the body gestures may indicate the intensity of that emotion. Think of the small child that frowns and stamps her foot. This body gesture study and body language itself seems to parallel elementary spoken language without the complexity of grammar, punctuation or the like. Consider the way other individuals and ourselves stand. Do we point our body, so to speak, toward the source of a verbal message, or do we seem to lean away from the source? Do we cross both our arms and legs when faced with unwished vocality?

What message is portrayed by an individual who slouches in his chair? Generally, he appears to lack interest in the conversation. He may, in fact, be intensely interested but his body language contradicts his motivation. Those communicating with him perceive this lack of interest and adjust accordingly, many times negatively to the communicative process. However, what message is portrayed by an individual who leans forward, nodding occasionally?

When we speak of gestures, we usually speak of hand gestures, although other body parts may, in fact, gesture equally as well. In fact, some hand gestures may be used instead of words such as the language of the deaf. Hand gestures may also indicate the intensity of the emotion felt.

Physical Appearance and Dress

Here, as in most of the nonverbal communication studies, while researchers are aware of the power of physical appearance and dress on communication, they are yet unsure of the full role it plays. We know, for example, that appearance plays a part in the process as it influences responses to vocal messages. Appearance can be the determinative feature of our message and may signal messages to others as to our own personality. To deny this importance is to deny the millions of dollars spent each year on perfumes, creams, oils, hair ornaments, contact lenses, beards, eye shadow, suits, clothes, toothpaste, mouthwash, deodorant. These physical messages we give are many times called "Thing Communication" or "Object Language."

Our clothing often determines the credibility of our message as does our physical make-up. If we are going to speak to a business group, we dress conservatively, less comfortably to show confidence and personality. For example, how do we perceive the personality or individual who is dressed in a military uniform? How is that military person perceived differently from the judge in a black robe? Consider the length of someone's hair, whether the beard or hair is unkempt or neatly trimmed.

Paralanguage (Vocal Cues)

The last nonverbal cue to be discussed here, while certainly not the end of the study of nonverbal messages, is the area of vocal cues or paralanguage. These vocal cues play a major role in assisting the listener in determining meaning. A vocal cue can be defined as an audible stimuli to a message that, while not using actual words, conveys a type of meaning. For example, consider the nervous man who speaks too fast . . . the angry person who begins speaking louder and louder. As we discussed before, the simple inflection in a sentence can greatly change the meaning of the message.

Nonverbal Communication

The most important aspect of message delivery is still wide open for scrutiny and research. Investigators have only reached the surface of a vastly interesting and meaningful study.

BODY LANGUAGE LOUD AND CLEAR

S. I. Hayakawa

Two American men talk together comfortably at a distance of three or more feet from each other, unless, of course, they are forced closer by having adjacent seats in an airplane. Latin/Americans are accustomed to shorter interaction distances—two feet or less.

Therefore when an American and a Latin converse, the Latin tries to get closer in order to feel more comfortable. The American backs away—for the same reason.

"I have observed an American backing up the entire length of a long corridor while a foreigner whom he considers pushy tries to catch up with him," writes the anthropologist Edward T. Hall of Northwestern University in "The Silent Language" (1959), a pioneer study of the differences between modes of nonverbal communication from one culture to another.

Studies of this kind also were much advanced by another anthropologist. Ray L. Birdwhistell of Philadelphia, whose book "Kinesics and Context: Essays on Body Motion Communication" (University of Pennsylvania Press, 1970) brings together the results of his years of study of how people communicate—with eyes, facial expressions and gestures of arms or legs or head—their unstated wishes, their hidden hostilities, their unspoken appeals for attention or love.

I especially remember an evening with Birdwhistell and other friends in San Francisco many years ago, when he began expounding his theories about body communication, using as his example a pretty young English professor who was also a guest at the party.

He had her figured out very well—why she was silent, why she crossed her legs and held her arms and shoulders as she did. He didn't miss very much about her, except the fact that by the time he had finished his analysis she was so angry that she would gladly have killed him!

Why, in our culture, is it impolite to stare? When you meet the eyes of a stranger in the street or on a bus, you are supposed to look quickly away. If your gaze lasts too long, it is likely to become embarrassing or annoying to the other person.

In America if you look at a girl whom you do not know, she promptly averts her eyes. It was both a surprise and a pleasure to me when I visited Norway to find that when I looked at a pretty girl in the street, she would look right back—not provocatively or impudently, but simply in friendly curiosity, like a child.

In a crowded New York subway people read newspapers, stare out at the darkness, close their eyes. They don't look at each other. Nevertheless, the eyes are our primary instrument of nonverbal communication. By gazing into each other's eyes, lovers assess the interpersonal climate—and if the gazes are sincere and tender enough, they fling themselves into each other's arms.

We are suspicious of people who don't look you in the eye. We can tell by the movements of another's eyes whether he is happy, afraid or just not listening. We avert our eyes to shield ourselves from an uncomfortable thought.

Eyes can be aggressively impudent: "He undressed her with his eyes." They can be penetrating: "She saw right through me." They can be secretive, like those of a good poker player. Eyes narrowed and lowered can be seductive.

Wide-open eyes express pleasure, surprise, disbelief.

"Contact: The First Four Minutes," by Leonard Zunin with Natalie Zunin, says that much, if not most, of what happens between people is determined by the first four minutes of interchange, and that, while there are many kinds of verbal exchange by means of which people establish contact, the nonverbal interchanges are of enormous importance, both in giving meaning to what you say and in communicating that which you are not ready to put into words.

A tilted head communicates curiosity—but with raised eyebrows or narrowed eyes signifies disbelief. Arms folded communicate a closed attitude while spontaneous movements of the arms show openness. The shoulders reveal self-confidence or the lack of it.

Then, on top of all the nonverbal communication that we apprehend by sight, there is the huge area of communication by touch—something we all understood when we were babies in mother's arms but that, after a long intellectualized education, most of them have to learn over again.

Many of us learn through love and lovemaking. Some learn through self-conscious training in tactile experience, as in the modern encounter group.

Psychologist Sidney Jourard of the University of Florida, the Zunins tell us, observed couples in cafes in four different cities.

"In Paris the average couple came into physical contact 110 times during an hour. In San Juan, Puerto Rico, couples patted, tickled and caressed 180 times during the same interval. But the typical London couple never touched at all, and Americans patted once or twice in an hour's conversation."

Are we in the Anglo-American culture missing something?

POLICEMEN'S 'BODY LANGUAGE' SPEAKS LOUDER THAN WORDS

Doug Smith

If you should be stopped by a policeman and go away thinking him rude, impersonal and hostile but unable to say exactly why, Lt. Ken Hickman, community relations officer for the West Los Angeles Division, has an answer.

He's just hit you with an assault of policeman's "body language."

Policemen, like everyone else, have an unconscious silent language, says Hickman, but the nature of it, unfortunately, rubs against deeply ingrained social standards of dignity, privacy and territorial security.

In a research report prepared for a public administration class at USC, Hickman describes how policemen use visual and body intrusion under stress conditions to gain physical and psychological superiority over subjects who might be dangerous.

After patroling for a month on his off-time with fellow policemen to watch them at work, Hickman has compiled a statistical composite of how policemen acted in 123 one-to-one contacts with persons under stress and nonstress conditions.

In effect it shows the policeman zeroing in on the subject, looking him over like an inanimate object, moving with hands in a ready position, stepping up to what behavioralists describe as an intimate distance and then leaning even a little closer.

The aggressive "body language" subsides as soon as the policeman feels that the subject does not represent a threat to him, but not before that person has suffered a decidedly negative experience with the police.

In this conflict between the citizen's right to privacy and dignity and the policeman's need to protect himself, Hickman feels that the use of aggressive "body language" is justified when it is necessary and effective, but that "the frightening aspect of 'body language' and its impact on police-citizen relationships is the fact that neither party is usually aware of what is happening."

Hickman got into his research to test a theory he developed over 10 years with the Los Angeles Police Department.

"As one who has had considerable experience as a police officer and who has spent several years listening to citizen complaints against police officers," Hickman wrote, "I am convinced that much of the negative response voiced by citizens stems from nonverbal sources and that during in-field stress contacts with citizens, police officers unconsciously use body movements, body space violations and visual intrusion to effect psychological and physical control over the subject."

His findings, after one month of watching West Los Angeles policemen in action, clearly support that theory, he said.

The following is a summary of what he saw: In most of the 82 stress encounters, Hickman noted that the officers' "heads were tilted back slightly, causing their chins to tilt upward somewhat," and that "once the officers exited their vehicles and assumed their basic approach posture, the head, neck, and trunk did not change position appreciably."

This conveyed the impression that the officer had zeroed in on a target by sighting down his nose and was making a deliberate and unwavering approach toward contact.

Zeroed In

"There was often an apparent build-up of anxiety on the part of the citizen as he watched the officer approach. This was even observable on the part of some citizens who had called for police assistance and were not, themselves, the subject of police inquiry."

In making contact it was almost always the officer who established the conversation distance by stepping to within 18 inches of the citizen and maintaining that distance even when the citizen backed off. In 36 specific cases the officer closed that distance to as little as eight inches.

"The significance of those 36 instances is that relations between the officers and the citizens more often than not remained strained through the encounter," said Hickman. "Two of these contacts ended in minor altercations and a total of 12 with the arrest of the citizen."

Strained Relations

While approaching the subjects, "not one officer walked with his arms swinging naturally at his side. Every officer had at least one hand resting somewhere along the front portion of his equipment belt," a gesture that suggests defensive readiness, Hickman said.

In all "negative" contacts, the officer's arms and hands moved considerably but "never hung at the sides or moved away from the front portion of his body," and in "positive" contacts only when the original tension subsided.

Finally, Hickman said, "policemen observed during stress contacts did not 'look at' the citizens to whom they spoke; they 'watched' them, 'measured' them and visually digested them."

The eye intrusion was of the type normally reserved for someone who is looking at an inanimate object such as a statue or painting, showing, "purposeful but casual watching rather than eye to eye confrontation."

Although Hickman's observations all took place within the West Los Angeles Division, the stress encounters included almost all the major or possibilities. Thirty-six occurred during the daytime, 42 at night.

Of 34 contacts in which the officer stopped a pedestrian to investigate suspicious conduct, 12 were blacks, 6 Mexican-American and 16 Anglo, ranging from teenage to middle-age. The suspicions included curfew violations, narcotics, burglary, robbery and theft.

Persons Involved

The 17 vehicle stops in stress conditions involved 13 males and four females suspected of car theft, intoxicated driving and robbery. By contrast, Hickman noted only four cases out of 41 nonstress encounters in the Police Station and at Basic Car Plan meetings in which an officer changed from a casual and polite demeanor.

Three times he noticed an officer "assume a greater degree of muscle tone around the torso" when talking to exceptionally attractive females and once, when a middle-aged woman abruptly asked an officer "when are you going to do something about the speeders in Beverly Glen?" the officer "moved from a relaxed posture to the common stress mode of back-tilted head, raised chin and vertical trunk."

Characteristically in these encounters it was the citizens who set the conversation distance by moving up closer after the officer was standing still.

The significance of the intrusive police conduct Hickman observed under stress is immediately obvious, but becomes even more so in the context of the research that has recently been conducted on the effects of "body language."

Body Zone

"Researchers in the field of proxemics (body space) have generally concluded that the average American maintains an invisible bubble, or body zone, of about two and a half feet around his body," Hickman said.

Dr. August F. Kinzel of the New York Psychiatric Institute has found that people tend to react in quite negative fashions when unwanted intrusions of this personal body zone occur. The reactions may range from an attempt to move away from the intruder as unobtrusively as possible to violent physical attack.

Other studies have concluded that one of the most common methods used by one person to dominate another is to covertly signal an aggressive readiness by leaning toward the person and moving into an intimacy distance of about 13 inches.

Visual Intrusion

It is the prolonged visual intrusion which Hickman found the most dehumanizing aspect of nonverbal police communication, however.

As a result of his research, Hickman believes that the need for greater research into the nature of police body language is clear and that police basic training in Los Angeles should certainly include far greater emphasis on nonverbal communication and its effects both for the safety of officers and for the improvement of community relations.

The Los Angeles Police Academy does not teach recruits anything about the significance of body zones or nonverbal communication in stress situations, Hickman said.

Little Training

Ironically, the academy teaches them to maintain slightly more than the suspect's arm reach to avoid being grabbed, a practice which policemen obviously teach themselves not to follow.

"It is commonly accepted by lawmen, criminologists and legal experts all over the world that 'reading' people is the key to successful interrogation, investigation and police community relations," Hickman said. "Yet, there is little training given to police officers in this country to teach them this skill.

"It is generally left to the individual policeman to develop these skills in the field. While he is learning, if he ever does, who can guess how many cases he loses or how many confessions he does not get or how many people he angers, all because he hasn't learned the significance of body language.

"Even those officers who excel in the ability to read nonverbal messages cannot usually describe their observations. They refer vaguely to a 'hunch' or, as the courts have recently called it, 'a policeman's sixth sense.'"

"Unfortunately, too many cases are lost in court today because officers have seemed to rely on hunches and sixth senses, abstract terms that fail to meet constitutional requirements," says Hickman.

Because the aggressive investigation of unusual or suspicious conduct is accepted as a superior method of crime prevention, Hickman does not propose that policemen discard the use of intrusive "body language," which generally provides the protection for which it is developed.

What he suggests is greater training so that policemen will be aware of their body intrusions and know when to use them and when to avoid them.

PLEASE TOUCH! HOW TO COMBAT SKIN HUNGER IN OUR SCHOOLS

Sidney B. Simon

You can see them in any junior high school. They're the ones who shove and push. They knock one another down the stairwell and slam the locker door on each other's head. And behind every push and shove, they are crying out their skin-hunger needs.

The shovers and trippers aren't your disruptive discipline problems. They're not the window breakers, either. The ones I have in mind are your nice kids from nice families. They abound in those suburban orthodontia belts ringing our major cities.

They are kids with a severe form of malnutrition—a malnutrition of the skin. Their disease is called skin hunger, and it has reached almost epidemic proportions in all of our schools.

It is shocking that we have allowed this disease to persist despite research which shows that infants who weren't touched and handled and fondled when they were fed by their orphanage attendants simply withered up and died. Today, no orphanage or child-care agency would think of putting a baby down with a bottle propped up to work on gravity feed.

There are dozens of animal studies which support what so many of us instinctively know. Researchers found that laboratory rats from the cages of certain keepers were smarter than other rats. What was the difference? The smarter rats had keepers who fondled them, stroked them, or touched them when they cleaned their cages or fed them. Not only were the rats smarter, they were less vicious, had larger and healthier litters, and took care of their young with much more tenderness and warmth. The research was overwhelmingly clear: when we touch and caress and stroke, life is better for *rats*.

There are enormous implications here for people: Touch! But don't do it in school. No way. There, the rules are clear. *No* one touches anyone else. No hand holding. No hugging. No recognition that touching and being touched are vital to the well-being of all of us.

Woe to the teacher who should dare break the icebound tradition. You can predict the responses—"Say, what are you? A dirty old woman?" (Or a dirty old man?) "Hey, aren't you getting enough at home?" Schools have people memorize research but act as if they don't believe that research since they don't apply it.

Oh, there are exceptions to the no-touch rule. Kindergarten children can be touched. And some first grade teachers might still hold kids on their laps and read to them. But by the end of the third grade, touching has just about dried up in most of our schools, replaced by the onward push of the college-entrance curriculum.

We have conveyed the message very clearly: Don't touch! There are some kids who even flinch when you reach out to them. They somehow have read us to say, "Touch is very dangerous. It can lead to sex." And in our schools, dominated by minds which are somehow third-sex neuters, we can't have any of that.

So, instead, we have the shovers and the pushers and the trippers. For some of these kids, violence becomes a way of getting the touching they need. Sometimes I think contact sports were invented to provide what a saner society would have supplied in a saner way. One wrestling coach told me, "My wrestlers don't have skin hunger. They get lots of touching, every day." In some ways, the coach is right. They do. But it is underground, not owned for what it is—a rather convoluted way of getting what we need naturally, daily and with open recognition of our need.

As you read this, you may be thinking: "What's all the furor about? I didn't need touching when I was in school, and these kids don't need it either. We've got other more important work to be done."

Well, I certainly hope you did get the touching you needed when you were younger and that because you did, you don't recall needing it in school. I do hope you came from a family which routinely gave each other back rubs and that hugging each other warmly and at some length was also a part of your family pattern. Clearly, there are thousands of adults roaming this pornographic society who were not touched by their families, and so they don't touch their own children, who will not touch their own children—and so on. Adults spread and dump onto children their own confusion and conflict about love and sex, touch and caring, and the difference between hands which touch to heal and hands which touch to turn someone on.

In this slightly cockeyed world, there doesn't seem to be provision for someone to get touched without having to go to bed with whomever does the touching. Think about that. We have mixed up simple, healing, warm touching with sexual advances. So much so, that there seems to be no middle road between, "Don't you dare touch me!" and, "Okay, you touched me, now let's make love."

Some of this confusion shows up in our high school kids today. In the spirit of the new freedom, many of them are experiencing intercourse years before they really are ready for it. Lovemaking involves such complex feelings and responses, requires so much more than merely being stroked; it's no wonder some youngsters remain baffled with the question, "You mean, that's all it is?" Of course it's a whole lot more. What many of these young kids really, truly want is simply to be held and rocked and stroked. They are suffering from skin hunger. And it is a need as strong as the need for water or food—and quite different from the need for sex. If touching were permitted—even tolerated—in our schools, how much less grief and anxiety and deep feelings of inadequacy we would find in our young people. How much less jumping into bed with the first person who strokes them gently.

I feel the schools should face this problem and begin to find ways to deal with the skin-hunger needs of the youth they serve. It is that simple. We are deeply involved these days in providing students with all kinds of help. We have budgets for helping students gain college entrance. We pour enormous resources into fostering athletic programs, preventing drug abuse, and aiding disabled children. But there is little attention paid to the children who are starving from skin malnutrition.

Since their skin-hunger needs are not being met in other ways, some students get pregnant, or cruise the highways at diabolical speeds—indifferent to life or start trafficking in drugs. Many of these cases are skin hunger related. The loss of human joy and potential is just too great for us to sit by and remain quiet while our students wither and die from skin starvation.

Obviously, I feel strongly about this. If you are still with me and willing to try something to deal with your own students' skin-hunger needs, I'd like to share with you some strategies I have developed in my own work.

I teach a course called Education of the Self at the University of Massachusetts. The course was originally developed by Gerald Weinstein, but several of us have evolved our unique ways of carrying out Weinstein's original, brilliantly conceived scheme.

I'm fully aware that working with college students is a different cup of tea from working with your students in a typical public school setting, but that is an interesting issue in itself. What magic transforms your students so that I am permitted to do in a September college class what you couldn't do the previous June in high school? I guess that's still another discussion, best saved for a future article.

In my Education of the Self class I work from the following premises:

1. Every human being comes into this world needing to be touched, and the need for skin contact persists until death, despite society's efforts to convince us otherwise.

2. Being touched in ways which are aware, respectful, tender and full of caring can be therapeutic—one of the most healing things a person can experience. (Wise hospital workers have long known that the alcohol back rub does more than merely prevent bedsores.) Even animals lick and cuddle their injured young. Yet, we slap a Band-Aid on our kids and tell them to quit crying and grow up, to act like a big person. Consistent denial of skin-hunger needs often means smoking too much, drinking too much, or being depressed too often. People who get their skin-hunger needs met are healthier.

3. For some, there is a confusion between touches. A caring touch, comforting touch, soothing touch and healing touch are all somewhat alike, but still quite different from being touched or touching for sexual arousal. Admittedly, the line is a very fine one and sexuality can spill over almost instantly. But all of us have given our own children back rubs and toussled their hair and kissed them all over when they were babies. We have given body comfort to friends who have fallen and hurt themselves. We have held people in our arms while they cried in grief over the loss of a loved one. We have done all that and have also touched for sexual arousal. We know the difference.

4. In many homes, children are fortunate enough to have their skin-hunger cravings satisfied. But there are thousands of other homes where children rarely, if ever, get touched. For them, touching takes the form of a spanking or a rough washcloth searching for dirt. Some of us believe that there are kids who deliberately misbehave just for a chance at skin contact, even in the form of a beating.

When you teach, you can see the difference. Children from homes which are well aware of skin-hunger needs tend to be more open and warm and less frenetic. Children at the other end of the continuum, those who rarely get touched at home, often seem more withdrawn, more fantasy ridden, or more aggressively hostile. I feel they tend to have a lesser sense of their own worth and beauty. In children who are getting lots of skin-hunger care and comfort, you can see clear eyes and energy which seems to flow effortlessly throughout their bodies. I feel I can always tell a child who is well-touched—the one with more brilliant eyes, looking out less afraid. Then there are the furtive eyes of those who don't get touched at all. Or the more glassy eyes of the ones who get touched a lot, but only for sex. The difference is marked.

Working from these four premises, I take my students through the following strategies in an effort to provide skin-hunger care, usually at the start of each class. It is amazing how much more work we get done when we care for skin-hunger needs first.

Skin Strategies

Massage Train

The group forms a large circle. Even with chairs bolted to the floor, you can make a large circle round the room's perimeter. People turn to the right and put their hands on the shoulders of the person they find there. Someone has his or her hands on your shoulders and you have your hands on someone else's shoulders. My instructions are, "Bring some comfort to the tired shoulders of the person you are touching. Make your hands healing, comforting, soothing and full of caring."

There will be some verbal discharge of anxiety, but firmly insist that they let their hands do their talking. They will settle down. Some of the more embarrassed ones may show their momentary distress by massaging too hard or tickling. You will have to stay on top of that and restate the notion that their hands must be healing and comforting.

I usually inject an idea which I think is funny. I often say, "This is the way we're going to begin all school board meetings from now on." Then I add, "The trick is to divide your mind between the giving and the taking. Half of your mind on your own shoulders and half on the shoulders of the person you are comforting."

I try not to let the exercise run so long that people get tired reaching out, and then I say, "Slowly, let your hands come to a rest, but don't take them away, yet. Cradle that person's shoulders in your caring hands. And then, very, very slowly take your hands away, so gradually that the person won't know they are gone."

If you have held your group together this far, you are home free. They will have told you that they trust you as a teacher and will be looking forward to what you plan to do next. Skin-hunger caring will have been brought home to them. You will see a noticeable quiet and tenderness in the group. And it will grow, I have never seen anything which has more potential for building community than skin-hunger work. It is almost magical.

The next direction is, "Now turn to the person who gave to you and give that person a caring and comforting shoulder massage, too." They will get right to it, and with much less embarrassment than on the first round. They will be telling you, nonverbally, that this is something they have been wanting and needing for a long, long time.

I usually add some ideas that seem important to me at the moment, like, "If you learn anything new from the person caring for your back, try it on the person in front of you." Or, I might say, "You probably can get an idea about what the person you are touching likes by what they gave to you when you were receiving from them." People laugh at that, but it is a laugh of insight. They are getting the hang of skin-hunger care.

At this point, you probably can go right into your standard subject matter. The total exercise has taken about eight to 10 minutes.

Temple Caring

This strategy comes after you've done a couple of days of massage trains. Divide the class in some way. My preference is to have people quickly pick partners and then measure heights. Two groups are formed, shorties and longies. However, anyone who has always been a shortie, can ask permission to be a longie. Then you say, "Shorties, sit down in a chair. Longies stand up. Shorties, close your eyes and keep them closed until I tell you to open them. Longies, go stand behind a shortie and touch him or her gently on the top of the head." I always add an important concept when I say, "Help each other find the people who aren't covered yet." I teach my students to snap their fingers if they are standing next to

a shortie who hasn't been found yet. And the "cricket" noises guide people who are still looking for a partner. I have done this in a gym with 500 people and it is simply incredible to see how quickly people will rally to help each other find a partner. Live crickets never sounded so sweet.

If there is an even number of students, I don't participate. If there is an odd number, I always take a partner—which, incidentally, is my preference. I don't like taking students through something which I am not willing to do myself.

I then say, "Now, longie, stand behind the chair your shortie is sitting in and get ready. Shortie, keep your eyes closed. Later on, you'll find out who your secret partner is.

"Longie, lean your shortie's head gently against your body and begin to give him or her one of the most gentle, caring, aware temple strokings you have ever given anyone." And they do. You will see some of your roughest kids caring tenderly for some other students.

Something important needs to be said here. One of the advantages of the shortie and longie pairing is that it is almost always men who are longies and women who are shorties. Caring for people of the same sex is still so taboo in our culture that you would be wise to avoid it in the beginning, but inevitably there will be some pairing, as in the massage train, in which a guy gives to a guy and a woman gives to a woman. I usually defuse the situation with something direct and yet light. I usually say, "Now, listen, it's okay if you are a guy with a guy. No one is going to accuse you of being a homosexual. Later on you might even learn more about the genuine, sexless nature of this kind of comforting and caring."

Give about three minutes to the temple rubbing and then say, "Let your hands slowly come to a rest and cradle that head, ever so lightly, between your hands. Let your partner feel safe there with the warmth and tenderness and healing quality of your good hands." Then tell them to "very lingeringly, take your hands away and come around the front and let your shorties see who was there for them." Usually, there is an energetic roar of delight and surprise when the shorties discover who comforted them so much. Then I quickly say,

"Okay, shorties, you get a second one." Whereupon every shortie cheers. They are told to close their eyes again and settle down, and the longies are instructed to go off and find a new partner and repeat the sequence. Finally, the longies get to sit in a chair and receive two temple rubs from two different shorties.

When this is over, the class would really profit from a chance to share what they experienced. I think you will be delighted with the kind of talking they do. I think you will get tremendous satisfaction from the awareness of some kids you'd least expect to have it. You will also see the calming, soothing effect that skin-hunger caring has for all of your students. The class work you have to do next will go more easily, and I predict you will have fewer discipline or disorder problems, even in that single class period.

However, because of our culture and its ground rule that any touching is sex, you would have more difficulty if you were to repeat these exercises the next day. People will have had overnight to get back to feeling uptight and they will have had 24 hours to get their guilt feelings back in force. "All of that pleasure must be immoral," many of them will think. Consequently, you're going to have to do a little theory work with your students. You'll have to quote the studies about the orphanages and about the laboratory rats as I did earlier. You'll have to lead a discussion about the kinds of problems in our society which result from its use of only two modes: no touch at all or let's go to bed, baby.

If you, yourself, are free from such hangups, you will find the kids open to this kind of theoretical input. And if they are open, you can move on to the next strategy.

Head and Body Tapping

It's important for you to demonstrate this strategy with a partner. Stand behind your partner, curve your fingers and tap gently on the person's head, like raindrops falling. Check with the person receiving the raindrops to learn if they are too hard or too soft. This is important. No one should suffer discomfort. When everyone has a partner, encourage the whole room to get into the same rhythm. Have them increase the speed more and more. Sud-

denly, you say, "Take your hands away, at once." Everyone will laugh—the receivers because their scalps tingle and the givers because their fingertips feel so alive.

Then you say, "Okay, once again. Tap, tap, tap. Now faster and faster and faster and zoom—take your hands away. Make your hands flat and let's start gentle body slapping on the shoulders. Slap, slap, slap. Increase the speed and a little of the strength, but don't hurt your partner in any way. Now take your hands away."

Ask the receivers how they feel. You will find they feel more alive and energetic.

Next: "Flatten your hands and start on your partner's shoulders; go down the arms, over the hands, and back up again. Slap, slap, slap more and more rapidly until you reach the shoulders, then take your hands away—zoom.

"For the last body tap, start on the shoulders and do the whole back, never hurting but stimulating the blood and the energy flow. Take your hands away suddenly. Now partners, change places. Givers become receivers, and so on."

Back Massages

Here you need a room where the chairs are movable, but nothing more. I use a typical university room. We pile the chairs up or push them off to the side. People then get their jackets or sweaters and lie down on the floor. I encourage them to relax and give their weight up to the floor. I get them to think about their day—what it's been like. Those who seem to be having a somewhat tougher day usually get to be the first takers. Those students who are experiencing a more gentle day give first. Eventually, though, everyone takes and gives. Reciprocity is very important.

Back rubs are almost always given anonymously, although students soon learn to recognize hands and styles of massages. I feel the anonymity demonstrates that 30 different people can be there to meet skin-hunger needs, not only the ones who are cute or prestigious. That's an important point and it seems to work for my own students. Dozens of students who were full of self-putdowns on the first day of class now know that they are important and special to almost everyone else in the class.

The real lesson is learning how to give and how to receive.

Lots more could be written about back massages, but suffice it to say that it is one of the most important strategies a school system can employ. And it's free. I can't think of another group effort which does more to build a feeling of community and belonging than the effort to set up opportunities for students to be able to ask for a back massage when they are feeling down or tired.

Perhaps you've been made to feel more cynical by what you have read here. Maybe you still feel that your students don't have skin hunger and that this whole idea is a Communist plot or something. I'd just like you to think about what happens in your school cafeteria when a kid drops a tray and the dishes break and the food goes sloshing across the floor. In most schools, the students shout and hoot and whistle and stomp their feet and clap their hands and pound on the tables. They do everything they possibly can to increase the humiliation of a student who is already embarrassed to the point of tears—which he or she wouldn't dare trust crying in that unsafe place.

When I hear that hooting and hollering, I know I am in a school where there is rampant skin hunger.

In a school which meets students' skin-hunger needs and where comfort and caring go on throughout the school day, this is what would happen if someone dropped a tray of food. Two kids would get up out of their seats and help clean up the mess. A third would go back in line and get another tray of food. A fourth would stand behind the student who dropped the tray and give a most gentle back rub until the new tray of food arrived.

I hope you have been touched by the people in your life, and I hope you touch your students. If not, it's never too late to start.

To communicate through silence is a link between the thoughts of man. —*M. Marceau*

TALK TO ME BABY

Teryl Zarnow

Listen carefully to the cues your child gives: Even the littlest infant is trying to communicate. Your baby is chortling with delight the first few times you tickle her toes. Then, she starts to turn away and suck her thumb. She glances at you and then looks away again.

Your baby hasn't spoken a word, but as research is showing, she has said a lot.

Her message: Let me have a little time out; this is too stimulating for me right now. In a few moments, when she gives a bright-eyed smile, then she's ready to go again.

The mother who understands her baby's message and waits to resume the game also is sending her child a message.

"The baby is getting the sense she can correct the situation; she feels she can be effective," says Dr. Edward Tronick, who heads the Infant-Parent Communication Lab at the University of Massachusetts.

"But if the parent consistently responds wrongly, continues to overstimulate the baby, then the baby will use her resources to shut herself off from the environment," Tronick says. "She won't learn to overcome stress and correct it. She will begin to feel helpless."

Experts such as psychologist Tronick say they believe babies make conversation shortly after birth using face, body and voice. And much of the time many parents instinctively speak their language. But new research is assigning more importance to early infant-adult communication and the consequences of prolonged misunderstandings.

Starting in the first few weeks of life, a baby's cries carry specific meanings, says Tim Healey, an infant and child developmental specialist in Santa Ana, Calif.

There is the traditional baby cry that peaks in intensity and indicates a physical need such as hunger, he says, or the soft repetitive cry of a child who is ill. Those should be answered with parent intervention.

But with the cry that goes up and down, reaching the same peak, intervention not always is the answer. It can be a baby's way of unwinding and calming himself.

Parents also need to learn to recognize a baby's state of alertness, Healey says. These states range from deep sleep to total alertness.

"It seems simple that parents would recognize when an infant is in light sleep and not intervene," Healey explains, "but this also can be when they coo and talk." Parents who continue to play with such a baby can overstimulate him.

A baby's posture also communicates. A baby who flexes up and pulls his arms into his mid-body or brings his hands to his mouth is expressing enjoyment. A baby making fists, moving his arms backward and extending his head is not.

"If a mother recognizes these signals early on, she can prevent full-blown crying and arrest it," Healey says. He specializes in helping parents handle and calm premature babies who tend to be overstimulated by the high-tech environment of a neonatal unit and whose cues are less easily spotted.

Tronick has developed a guide to infant communication, "Small Talk," sponsored by Ultra Pampers Plus diapers. It provides an illustrated glossary of the language a baby uses to communicate.

But researchers also are studying the messages mommy sends to her infant.

"The way adults express anger is not unlike the way babies express anger," Tronick says. "We have the system in infancy and keep it."

Thus, at 3 or 4 months a baby can respond to tone of voice, the rhythm of intonation, eye contact and whether an adult is crowding them physically by getting too close. By 5 or 6 months a baby understands facial expressions.

"Babies look at their mother's face, listen to her voice, and they can respond to the tensions in the mother's arms when they are being held," says Dr. Justin Call, chief of child and adolescent psychiatry at the University of California, Irvine Medical Center. "They put it all together in responding to the mother's feeling state. This is one of the ways in which negative feelings, depression and anxiety are transmitted from parent to infant."

The "experts," of course, may be telling an experienced mother nothing new.

"Of course mothers have recognized many of the things we can recognize scientifically," Call says. "If you're a scientist you need to study it; if you're a mother you don't. . . . But sometimes you don't know what you know—and then you can make errors."

A mother responding to a child might react to the tension in a child's voice and interpret it as anger directed against her, Call illustrates. Instead of realizing the baby simply is upset, she might take it personally.

"The majority of the time parents are very sensitive to an infant's cues," Healey says, "but because of fatigue, stress and lack of education, we can miss cues. . . . We can become so concerned with doing it 'right' that we ignore the situation."

Parents comparing notes in his waiting room, he adds, can learn more from each other than he would be able to teach them.

Information on parent-infant communication is not necessarily new, Healey says. But only now are researchers beginning to realize how important that communication is during the first 15 months of life.

During the critical early months, Healey says, a child is developing the relationship of trust. If his needs are met, the infant realizes he has some control over his environment and he develops trust and optimism.

"If parents ignore a baby's cues, the child realizes what he gives his parents doesn't mat-

ter. . . . He sees the world as randomized. The mistrust leads to apathy, and that's for life."

Inevitably, parents will misread some of a baby's cues—usually without any long-term adverse consequences. But drug and alcohol abuse, depression or marital difficulties consistently can impair communication—and have severe consequences for the baby.

By age 4 weeks, babies whose mothers are not responsive appear passive, don't hold their heads up well, or don't follow objects with their eyes, Call says. Such babies might hear poorly and grow slowly.

Knowing that babies can communicate, researchers also want to know how they cope with the stimulation of that interaction.

For a long time babies used to be viewed as fragile with few abilities to deal with stress and overstimulation, Tronick explains. Now we know babies can take in information and respond to it.

How do they manage not to be overwhelmed? Tronick's new research will focus on the "timeout" message a baby can send when things aren't going quite right or get to be too much. Some babies comfort themselves by sucking on their hands; others listen to sounds. And others appeal to parents for help.

The nature of how much stress an infant undergoes and how he copes has a real effect on his development, Tronick says.

The experts are saying, in short, do not underestimate the tiny infant you bring home from the hospital. He is ready to talk and respond.

As Healey puts it:

"I still am surprised at how powerful an impact we have on our child—to see that relationship day in and day out, and how important it is to be sensitive to what he is trying to tell you. I'm surprised he can communicate so much with us. I'm also surprised at times when people don't feel they have an impact on their child—when they feel the child is just there. The parent of an infant is not in a caretaker role; it is a reciprocal role from day one."

I learn a great deal by merely observing you, and letting you talk as long as you please, and taking note of what you do not say. —*T. S. Eliot*

BODY POLITICS

Mills' law: Men and women in American culture speak a different body language. Corollary: Observable sex differences in nonverbal behavior influence male-female relations.

Gwen Rubinstein

Professor Janet Mills has transformed the great urban pastime—and her great love—of people watching into a career. Primarily, she has observed, men speak a body language that is high in status, power and dominance, while women speak a language of submission, affiliation and passivity. These differences often create chaos in the workplace.

By realizing their differences and striving more toward blending the best of masculine and feminine traits, however, men and women can improve their organizations and themselves, Mills has contended in presentations to countless civic, professional and business groups, including the Ohio Hospital Association, Columbus, Altrusa International, Chicago and the Chamber of Commerce of the United States, Washington, D.C. On leave from her position as a professor of human relations at the University of Oklahoma, Norman, Mills has been a visiting professor of management at Northern Arizona University, Flagstaff, since last August.

Men and women learn their body languages unconsciously as they grow up, she says. So by the time they reach adulthood, they send and receive their signals relatively unconsciously. Only when

someone breaks the unspoken rules do the differences—and the discord—rise to the surface of relationships.

Managerial and professional women face a particularly difficult struggle in their everyday communication, according to Mills. Expected to be feminine as women and powerful as managers, women simultaneously play two roles with different sets of often-contradictory rules.

Managerial and professional men are not exempt from the confusion, Mills adds. Expected to be the dominant and powerful protectors of women, many find themselves reporting to women executives and competing with women peers—the very women they were raised to protect.

Because one picture is supposed to be worth 1,000 words, Association Management offers this photographic essay for your education—and amusement. **Warning: By seeing traditional sex roles reversed in these poses, differences between men's and women's nonverbal behavior may become shockingly apparent.**

Women learn to sit with legs together, crossed at the ankles or knees, toes pointed in the same direction, feet tucked under the chair, as Mills demonstrates. Women also hold their arms close to their bodies, their hands together in their lap.

What's wrong with this picture? Volunteer model William D. Coughlan, CAE, executive vice president of the American Physical Therapy Association, Alexandria, Virginia, offers a man's interpretation of how a woman sits.

In what Mills calls the "power spread," men sit with legs in "broken four"—at a 5- to 15-degree angle and crossed ankle to knee—with their hands behind their head and their elbows away from the body.

How would you feel sitting across from this woman at a conference table, over lunch, or in your office? Notice that Mills leans back into the chair in her interpretation of this classic male pose.

In a typical office scene, ASAE Foundation Manager Eric Johnson portrays the dominant man—feet shoulder-width apart, hands in pockets, weight shifting side to side or back and forth, indirect gaze straight ahead.

In reverse, it's easy to notice how a man posing as a woman balances his weight on one hip, lowers his shoulders, and stands in a "bashful knee bend," with his hands "placed gingerly together."

In a typical scene from a convention general session: Between two men, a woman sits at attention, looking straight ahead, constricting her body and yielding her space to those around her.

In a mirror pose, Mills spreads out and intrudes on the space the two men have yielded to her. Notice the men have leaned their bodies tensely to the side; she is relaxed, "laid back," and comfortable.

Expected to be feminine as women and powerful as managers,
women play two roles with often-contradictory rules.

In an ordinary conversation with men or other women, whether in the workplace or somewhere else, women smile, open their eyes wide, arch their brows, lift and lower their heads, and nod more often than men.

Acting out a man's role in a one-on-one conversation, Mills sits back in her chair, sets her shoulders square, stares directly ahead, keeps her head erect and gestures forcefully.

To pick something up from the floor "femininely," women keep their knees together, their back straight, their arms close to their body and approach the object from the side.

To pick an object up from the floor "masculinely," men generally squat, keep their back flexible, extend their arms from their body and approach the object from the front.

NONVERBAL EXERCISE "55,000 B.C."

PURPOSE: To demonstrate the complexity of our written language and the limits of nonverbal communication.

PROCEDURE: From now on (until told otherwise) there will be *no* talking or writing. Situation: 55,000 BC. There is no language—you must rely totally upon gestures, facial expressions, signals and drawings.

1. You will be given a slip of paper with a message on it. Your group must decide *who* will convey the message to the class and at the same time assist that person in preparation for delivering the message. *No Talking!*

2. The sender will (when called) step before the class and *nonverbally* deliver the message. He may use drawings as long as he uses his *nontrained* hand—i.e., right handers draw with their left hand.

3. While in your groups, it will be necessary for you to help the chosen sender. Suggestions of pictures or gestures that the class will understand are recommended. The sender will have approximately two minutes to convey the message. At the end of the time limit, the class will write down what the message was and later we will check the accuracy.

4. Because of the incredible difficulty involved in this activity, your instructor will allow at *appropriate moments* in group discussion, a *few seconds* of language usage.

So, the activity should progress like this:
1. Read this page.
2. Go to groups.
3. Choose sender (nonverbally).
4. Help sender prepare message.
5. Use language breaks to clarify.
6. At time signal, turn chairs around.
7. Sender from group 1 will deliver message to rest of class. Other members of group 1 will remain calm, collected and quiet.
8. Class will, at end of 2 minutes, write down what the message was. *No Talking!*
9. Repeat 7 and 8 with groups 2, 3, 4, 5 and 6.
10. Try to figure out exactly *what* happened.

DISCUSSION: 1. What nonverbal messages were easy to communicate?
2. What nonverbal messages were difficult to communicate?
3. Why was it difficult to communicate nonverbally such words as "another," "tomorrow," "when" and "soon"? ❏

NONVERBAL CAFETERIA EXERCISE ——————

PURPOSE: To demonstrate that nonverbal communication sends "clues, not facts."

PROCEDURE: 1. With the following worksheet, select an interesting looking individual (whom you do not know) to observe. Try to pick someone who does not seem ready to move on and station yourself far enough away so that you can *see* your subject but *not hear* what she is saying.
2. Observe the individual for as long as possible, remembering to be discrete, and record your impressions.
3. When the person looks as though she is getting ready to leave, approach her with a smile, confess your "spying" and check your observations. You'll be surprised how friendly a stranger can be when she discovers she's helping you with classwork.
4. When you return to class, compare your observations with your classmates. ❏

Nonverbal Cafeteria Observation Form

BASIC DESCRIPTION	APPEARANCE	ACTUAL
Sex FEMALE	Female	=
Age 21	21-22	23
Major	acting or drama	Art
Income	—	
Political Party	Republican	None
Sports	softball	Tennis
Activities	Parting	traveling
Veteran of military service	N/A	
Children	maybe 1	None
Brothers, sisters	yes	Isis // Brother
Relationship to others at table	yes (good)	yes.
Mood	hyper (happy)	happy
From out of state	NO	Mexico
Type of car	HonDA Civic	Bi.
Name	Jennefer	Alegria
Religion	Cathlic	Cathlic

120

NAME THAT FACE

PURPOSE: To discuss and notice the importance of facial expressions in the overall communicative process.

PROCEDURE:
1. Take out a slip of paper.
2. For each of the faces, describe on your paper the emotion or feeling the person portrays. Describe the factual situation you feel this individual is in. Be creative.
3. Form groups and share your ideas.

DISCUSSION:
1. Did all of you receive about the same messages?
2. How do you account for any differences some of you may have received from the faces?
3. How could other bodily clues have affected how you "read" these facial messages? ❏

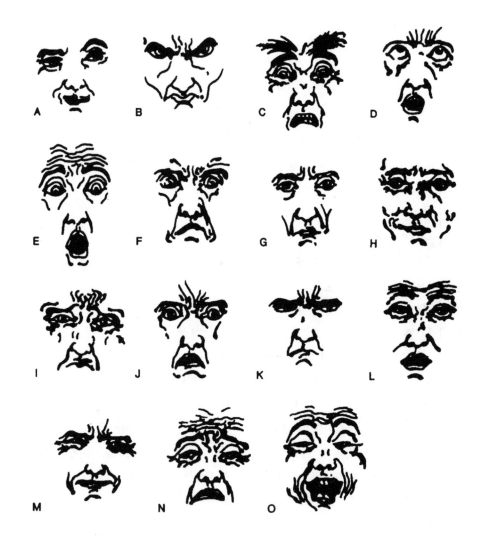

By permission, Joseph Luft, Mayfield Publishing Company; © 1969, National Press.

BACK RUBS

PURPOSE: To explore the effect of touch on communication.

PROCEDURE:
1. Each person is to give or to receive back rubs according to the following list.
2. Each person must follow these rules:
   a. You may receive a back rub only after you have given one.
   b. The giver will be scored by the receiver on a scale of 1 to 10 with 10 being best.
   c. On your sheet, the score is automatically 5 points for any back rub received by you.
   d. You will receive a score from 1 to 10 only on back rubs which you give. The receiver will judge your back rub.
   e. No score is valid without the initials of the other person (giver or receiver).
   f. You may not refuse to give or receive a back rub if someone asks you.
   g. The same person may be used only twice, once giving and once receiving.
   h. The highest score at the end of the time limit wins.

	THE BACK RUBS	SCORE	INITIAL
1.	Give to someone young.		
2.	Receive from someone older.		
3.	Give to someone who goes to the same school you do.		
4.	Receive from someone whose eyes are a different color than yours.		
5.	Give to someone whose first initial is before yours in the alphabet.		
6.	Receive from someone whose first initial is after yours in the alphabet.		
7.	Give to someone who would kiss on the first date.		
8.	Receive from someone who would go on a blind date.		
9.	Give to someone who would eat when worried.		
10.	Receive from someone who is afraid to be alone in the dark.		
11.	Give to someone who could be satisfied without a college degree.		
12.	Receive from someone who would order a new dish in a restaurant.		
13.	Give to someone who likes to stay up all night when friends visit.		
14.	Receive from someone who likes to take leadership responsibilities.		
15.	Give to someone who is not easily swayed by the latest fads and commercials.		
16.	Receive from someone who is against abortion.		
17.	Give to someone who is not interested in getting married.		
18.	Receive from someone who watches soap operas.		
19.	Give to someone who is for premarital interdigitation.		
20.	Receive from someone who is against premarital interdigitation.		

122

DISCUSSION:
1. Who was the easiest person for you to approach? Why?
2. Who was the most difficult person for you to approach? Why?
3. What are different types of touch you experienced during this activity?
4. Compare the difference you experienced in giving and receiving back rubs.
5. What effect did touching have on the verbal interaction?
6. What does our culture say about touching?
7. How did permission to touch affect this activity? ❑

PERSONAL SPACE (PROXEMICS)

PURPOSE:
To determine what your personal space is and to explore your feelings about your personal space when it is invaded.

PROCEDURE:
1. With your partners, perform the following exercise. As you perform the exercise, examine your "feelings" or emotional responses.
2. Have a person of the same sex approach you from each of the given directions. Stop the partner when the distance between you is comfortable. Measure the approximate distance.
   a. Directly from the front.
   b. Directly from the left.
   c. Directly from the right.
   d. From a 45 degree angle from the left.
   e. From a 45 degree angle from the right.
   f. From the rear.

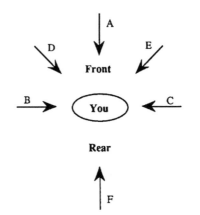

3. Repeat the same exercises with a person of the opposite sex.
4. From the front position allow the person to come too close. At this distance, engage the person in a conversation for at least one minute.
5. Again, take time to examine your feelings or emotional responses.

DISCUSSION:
1. What differences in your body space and in your emotional responses did direction make?
2. What difference did the sex of your partner make?
3. What other factors could influence the size of your "body bubble"?
4. How did you feel when your personal space was invaded? ❑

PROXEMICS

PURPOSE: To determine the effect when personal space is intruded upon. To prepare, please reread "You Don't Say" at the beginning of this chapter, especially the section concerning **The Environment**.

PROCEDURE: Choose a partner who will serve as an observer. Go to an area in which other people are congregated. Deliberately seat yourself extremely close to a stranger, intruding on the personal space of the individual. Observe whether he chooses to move away from you or stand his ground. Try this several times.

DISCUSSION:
1. How did you feel as you intruded on someone's space?
2. Did you also feel that your space had been invaded?
3. What messages did you get concerning the other's feelings by his actions?
4. What situations in life tend to intrude on our space?
5. How important is personal space?   ❑

EFFECTS OF ENVIRONMENT

PURPOSE: To demonstrate the effects that environmental factors have on us.

PROCEDURE: Note the physical arrangements of the following on the chart below.
Note the "messages" transmitted to you by the environmental factors.

	COLOR	LIGHTING	ARRANGEMENT	COMFORT	MESSAGES
Doctor's office					
Teacher's office					
Restaurant					
Supermarket					
Classroom					
Library					

DISCUSSION:
1. What differences in color, lighting, arrangement and comfort did you note?
2. How did these affect you?   ❑

NONVERBAL OBSERVATION EXERCISE

PURPOSE:
1. To become familiar with the various symbols in nonverbal communication.
2. To place those symbols of nonverbal communication in a specific context by applying them to a person.

PROCEDURE:
1. Your teacher will give you the name of a person in your class. You are to observe the nonverbal language of this person for the number of class sessions assigned by the teacher. Using the worksheet below, try to make at least one observation of the nonverbal language of your "observee" for each item. (Your teacher may ask you to keep the name of your "observee" secret.)
2. At the conclusion of the specified class period, write a report on the nonverbal language you observed and what you think that language communicated.

NONVERBAL WORKSHEET

Be sure that you understand each of the forms of nonverbal communication listed below:

KINESICS (Body Language)

1. Eye Movement
2. Eye Contact
3. Pupillometrics
4. Posture
5. Body Position
6. Gestures
7. Facial Expressions
8. Touch
9. Proxemics
10. Nervous Mannerisms
11. Uncontrolled Body Responses
12. Gait (walk)

OBJECT (environmental) LANGUAGE

13. Use of Time
14. Choice of Environment
15. Choice of Colors
16. Grooming
17. Choice of Associates
18. Choice of Clothing
19. Artifacts
20. Accessories
21. Olfactions (natural and artificial)

PARALANGUAGE

22. Vocal Intonations
23. Suggestive Sounds
24. Silences, Pauses
25. Vocal Rate
26. Conversational Initiative

1. How much does a person communicate with nonverbal language?
2. What are some specific things you learned about nonverbal communication when you did this exercise?
3. Why must nonverbal language be examined in context?   ❑

NONVERBAL INCONGRUITY ACTIVITY ——————————

PURPOSE: To learn how our nonverbal behavior might contradict or impede our verbal messages.

PROCEDURE: The class is divided into groups of four people according to the following diagram. A and B will discuss such a question as "What is my favorite restaurant?" C and D will observe as indicated. Then C and D will discuss a similar topic and A and B will observe as indicated.

The observers will note the ways in which the observee's behavior denies or impairs the verbal message which was intended.

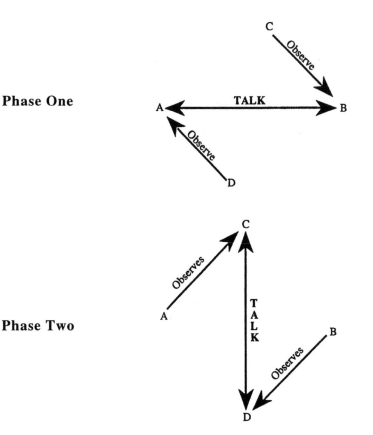

DISCUSSION: The observers will share with the observees the results of their observation with the sole purpose of helping the observee to be more aware of inconsistencies between her nonverbal and verbal communication.   ❑

REACTIONS

1. Why is an understanding of nonverbal communication absolutely essential to high fidelity communication?

2. Which generally tells the truth of a message, verbal or nonverbal communication? Why?

3. What might be some of the reasons that a nonverbal signal might have different meanings for people in different situations?

USING LANGUAGE | 6

LANGUAGE—A WORKING DEFINITION

As you have seen so far, our concern is to help you improve your interpersonal communication. This chapter shows the role that language plays in those encounters. Do you always understand what others are saying to you? Are you always understood by others? If you're like most of us, the answer to these two questions is an emphatic "No." When two people speak the same language, share the culture and experience similar incidents in their lives, why is it that one person can walk away confident that she has clearly communicated and the other stand in bewilderment wondering what was just said? In order to understand the problems that arise from taking our language abilities for granted, it will be necessary for us to first define a few concepts.

Language

An established and accepted set of symbols and structure used for the transfer of meaning. (English, Spanish, Navajo, Farsi)

Denotation

The commonly accepted definition of a word, as in the dictionary definition. (House = Dwelling)

Connotation

The feeling and emotions that we associate with a word. (House = "Home")

Linguistics

The study of language.

Semantics

The study of meaning.

General Semantics

The field of study that says language influences behavior.

THE IMPORTANCE OF USING LANGUAGE EFFECTIVELY

Language is Power

The study of how people have used language must certainly bring us to the conclusion that the "pen is mightier than the sword." Books, newspapers and pamphlets have been so powerful that dictators waste no time banning and burning them and imprisoning those who seek freedom of the press.

What happens to you as you read, "The green, vile-looking puss oozed from the cut on the victim's arm?" How do you feel when someone calls you a dirty name? If you're like most of us, you can't help but react negatively and strongly.

We speak to be heard, to be listened to, to be understood. Our energies in sending symbols are spent in the presence of someone who can hear the results. We want something. Over 2,000 years ago the philosopher Aristotle said, "All speech is persuasive in nature." And so it is. We communicate to get our needs met. Whether that is strengthening a relationship, asking directions or arguing with a friend, sending information through symbols to another is a way of persuading, thus we say that language is purposeful.

It is difficult to deny the power of language. In this chapter, we will examine how we can use language intrapersonally and interpersonally. Additionally, we will examine the extent to which language influences and is influenced by our culture.

Intrapersonal Use of Language

Think for a moment about the last vacation that you took, the party that you attended or success that you had. What came to your mind? Did you close your eyes and see the entire experience played back as if you had just begun your video cassette player? A few people may have answered yes to those questions. For most of us, however, we probably began by saying to ourselves, "Let's see—that was when . . ." Whether you then actually saw pictures or continued to recall the experience based on words, your thinking was either in part or wholly influenced by your manipulation of language.

Thinking is dependent, for most of us, on the use of language. The more successful we are in using language, the more successful we are going to be in thinking.

One of the important aspects of thinking that requires effective use of language is our ability to reason. Reasoning involves at least two steps: observation and inference. When we begin our reasoning process, we begin with an observation or with a statement (assumption) based on someone else's observation. These observations can also be called facts and are subject to errors that we have already described in the chapter on perception.

The second step in reasoning is inferring. In this step, we use language to connect the observable fact to the unobservable conclusion. For example, you see your friend on April 15. You know that he went to see a tax advisor today. He looks sad and you hear him say that he doesn't know where he is going to come up with that much money. So far you have had a number of observable facts to deal with. You may infer that he has to pay more money for his income taxes. How did you come to that conclusion? You used language to relate the observable facts with outcomes related to each of those facts until you narrowed the probable outcomes to your best guess.

Our ability to use language gives us more choice in the number of outcomes we can match with the facts that we observe. It also gives us a way of discounting or eliminating outcomes which are not appropriate. In other words, the power of reasoning depends on effective use of language.

Language is Symbolic

While this may seem to be quite apparent, it is of astonishing importance. Words do not have any meaning in and of themselves. They are void of meaning. The symbols D-O-G are not the animal that barks and answers to the name "Rover." The letters (symbols) represent the animal only when our culture/society agrees that they represent the reality. There is no living, breathing thing in the symbols themselves. There is only the meaning that we attach to them. This is why we say, "Words don't mean, people mean." Indeed, if we simply reverse the symbols D-O-G, we must form an entirely new concept in our minds. But notice, it isn't the word that has meaning, it's us. Some of our exercises in this chapter will point out the dangers of forgetting this important lesson.

Language is Learned

It is also important to realize that language is learned. Words, as symbols, must be learned in a context. While some are easily stored in our memory for future use (book, mother, day, food) many are so complex as to defy simply defining (is, to, be, the) and when you compound this with the idea that language (thus, words) is always changing, (bad, cool, gay, hip) it's no wonder that we often misunderstand another's intended "meaning." To further complicate matters, we have to consider the importance of how we learned the word. If you had a pleasurable experience when you learned the word "cat" (soft, purring, cute), your image of "cat" will be forever influenced by that experience. However, if your experience was negative (scratches, biting, fleas, catbox), think how differently the symbol "cat" will affect you. Can a word that you assign meaning to affect you? For an answer to this question your instructor will have you participate in an exercise designed to show the difference between Connotation and Denotation.

General Semantics

Perhaps there is a need to clarify General Semantics. Too often we hear, "Oh, we're only arguing semantics." Or, "Let's not get hung up on semantics." The implication is that the problem is a small one, but matters of meaning can have far reaching implication. Those of us who study language will be the first to tell you that words affect behavior. For instance, would you care to stop by my house for a slice of dead cow? Probably not, but most of you have enjoyed a barbecued steak. Do the words make a difference? You bet they do. This is no small matter, this "semantics." It can determine our entire perception of "reality" and that leads us to a definition that will not only help us to understand General Semantics, but will set the stage for you to learn the importance of language in our daily communication. What I call something can cause you to perceive it differently. Semanticists carry this idea to the word to associate with it. Is it a thing without a name? This argument will be further developed in the chapter as you study the power of words.

BARRIERS TO USING LANGUAGE

Some people consider barriers to communication as roadblocks. That is, some obstacle that gets between what we intend to say and what is understood by the receiver. Language is much more complicated than the roadblock analogy. Many of the language barriers occur in our minds as we consider what we intend to say. These main barriers are described below:

Confusion Between Language and the Real World

If I write that I plan to scratch my finger nails along the chalk board and you immediately feel a cold shiver down your spine, it is because you confused what I said for the reality of my doing it. Now such a reaction is not necessarily bad. As a matter of fact, if you were unable to react in such a manner, you probably would not enjoy reading a good book.

However, when we assume that the word we hear is exactly the same as the real-world counterpart that it describes, we are in trouble. To understand what we mean here, pretend that you are planning to hike up a mountain and have a trail map in front of you. You note that there is a moderate elevation gain and a small stream that you will have to ford. You consider that these representations on the map are exactly the way it will be and feel that you will have no difficulty on the hike. Once you set forth into the real world, however, you soon learn that the temperature is 92 degrees and the stream is 10 feet wide, five feet deep and is raging down the mountain. We very often make the same mistakes in the use of our language to describe the world around us.

An example of such confusion is found in the word "is." When you say, "He *is* a professional football player," what do you mean? To most people, the word "is" takes the place of "equals." Therefore, the meaning in the sentence is that "He equals professional football player." He is therefore not a father, brother, husband, student or anything else at the moment. Additionally, he "equals" professional football player as *you* see it to mean, which may be different from professional football player as *I* see it to mean.

Our language should be considered as a description of the real world the way maps are a description of the real world. Maps only tell us a small part of what really exists. Our language has the same limitation.

Allness Attitude

Just as maps are incapable of telling everything that there is to tell about the territory, language is incapable of telling everything that there is to tell about the way you feel about someone or how to do something that you have learned over many years of practice and effort. You can give us an idea through language of the broad boundaries. However, it is not possible for you to fill in every possible detail.

When people have an allness attitude, they act as though they have communicated everything that there is to say to another about a topic and then they expect that the other person will have exactly the same reaction to that topic that they have. When the other person fails to see it as they do, they blame the other person rather than recognizing that the other person only got part of the picture.

Frozen Evaluation

When we think about something the way that it was and describe it now as though it had never changed, we are guilty of frozen evaluation. Because language describes things, ideas and feelings, we often get hooked on the description and forget that everything in the real world constantly changes. So we run around with a lot of out-dated descriptions in our heads that we haven't recently checked out with reality.

People who are constantly talking about the way things should be (as in the "good old days") are unwilling to give up the old descriptions and look at what is happening now. If you think of the boy who was the eighth-grade clown as the same person you knew six or 10 years ago, you are going to have problems talking to someone about him who sees him as he is today.

Labeling

Labeling is where the sender of a message stereotypes someone and rather than describe the behaviors, she merely takes the easy path and says "Oh, he's a _____." When the receiver hears this label, he becomes the victim of the sender's laziness. Rather than let the receiver find out for himself what the other person is like, the sender, by labeling, has already placed in the receiver's mind the idea of the label. Let's take the label "jock" for an example. As soon as you hear, "That new kid in my class is a jock," you've begun to form an image. This prejudging is extremely dangerous because even before you've met the new student, you've probably created an image that could well be wrong. He must be big, athletic, in school only for sports, doesn't care about classes and may not be too bright. What a terrible judgment to form based only on someone's careless use of language. You know full well that all athletes are not big. Look at wrestlers in the lightweight division or gymnasts or archers or golfers even. ChiChi Rodrigues is 5'6". You also know that all athletes are not in school just for sports. Many are involved in several extracurricular activities. Sports may be only one of several. You also know that many student athletes are outstanding scholars, earning excellent grades in even the most difficult classes. Many end up on the Dean's List for academic excellence and many receive scholastic scholarships. Pat Hayden (exprofessional football player) was a Rhodes Scholar. And did we say "he"? How careless of us, because student athletes can, of course, be women. Do you see what can happen when labels are used? They are convenient, handy and easy to use, but they are real road blocks to being an accurate communicator. In addition to labels, your instructor will show you the dangers inherent in confusing assumptions and judgments as "facts." Some of the activities that she may assign are: For Sexists Only, The Semantics of Prejudice, Hidden Assumptions Test and The Uncritical Inference Test.

Polarization

This barrier occurs because of the nature of our language, English. Over the years English has evolved to a point where we have been forced to speak and think in extremes. The "middle ground" has been taken from us because we have few words to express the ideas that fall in the middle. Example: What word is the opposite of leader? Now, tell us what word is in-between? More difficult isn't it? Your instructor will have you participate in a brief activity called Polarization to further explain this barrier.

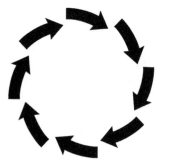

Language is the dress of thought. —*S. Johnson*

FOR SEXISTS ONLY

Why are forceful males referred to as charismatic while females are domineering?

When speaking about people who are talkative, why are men called articulate and women gabby?

Why are men who are forgetful called absentminded, when forgetful women are called scatterbrained?

Why are men who are interested in everything referred to as curious, but women are called nosy?

Why are angry men called outraged, while angry women are called hysterical?

Why are women who are ironic called bitter, while ironic men are called humorous?

Why are lighthearted men called easygoing, but the same type of women are called frivolous?

Why are devious men considered shrewd, when devious women are scheming?

Why are men who are thoughtful called considerate, while thoughtful women are called oversensitive?

Why are women who are dauntless considered brazen, when dauntless men are considered fearless?

Why is it that men of ordinary appearance are called pleasant looking, while ordinary women are homely?

Because of Sexism in Language:

> I know you believe you understand what you think I said, but I'm not sure you realize that what you heard is not what I meant.

SYD'S ANTICS WITH SEMANTICS

Sydney Harris

- My witticism was "a well-turned phrase;" yours was a "wisecrack;" his was "a smart-aleck remark."
- My proposal is "some fresh thinking on the subject;" your alternative proposal is an "untried innovation."
- An "awful" man is one a woman has just met and is interested in; a "sweet" man is one she has known a long time and is no longer interested in.
- Readers complain about "sensationalism" in the newspaper, but they won't change to the opposition paper because it's "dull."
- He refuses to take a lie-detector test because "he must have something to hide;" I refuse to take one because "it has no legal status, and the machine violates my protection against self-incrimination."
- The extroverted club member I happen to like is "jolly and open;" the extroverted one I happen to dislike is "loud and pushy."
- He "goofed;" you made a "boo-boo;" but all I had was "a mental block."
- Male chauvinism reveals itself semantically even in the use of little prepositions: a promiscuous and unattached male is amiably referred to as a "man *about* town," but a woman of the same status and inclinations is disparagingly referred to as "*on* the town."
- The nations we currently favor have "governments;" the nations we are quarreling with have "regimes." (Notice how quickly after detente "Red China" turned into the "People's Republic.")
- I answered the awkward question with "polite evasion;" you answered with "double-talk," he answered it with a "whopping lie."

"There's glory for you!"

"I don't know what you mean by 'glory,'" Alice said.

Humpty Dumpty smiled contemptuously. "Of course you don't—till I tell you. I meant, 'there's a nice knock-down argument for you!'"

"But 'glory' doesn't mean 'a nice, knock-down argument,'" Alice objected.

"When I use a word," Humpty Dumpty said, in rather a scornful tone, "it means just what I choose it to mean—neither more nor less."

"The question is," said Alice, "whether you *can* make words mean so many different things."

"The question is," said Humpty Dumpty, "who is to be master—that's all."

From *Alice in Wonderland* by Lewis Carroll.

By permission, *Long Beach Press Telegram*.

MEANING LIFT

The more specific your word choice, the more accurately others will receive your message.

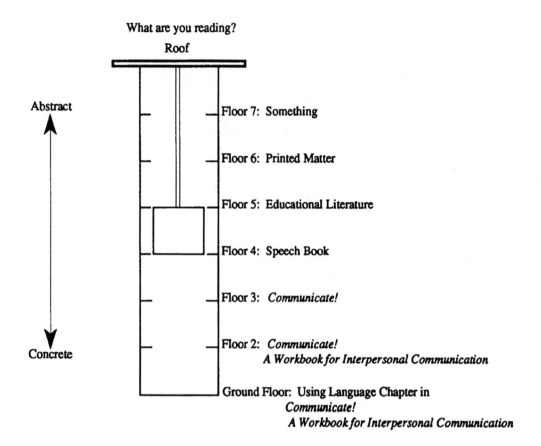

What are you reading?

Roof

Abstract

Concrete

Floor 7: Something

Floor 6: Printed Matter

Floor 5: Educational Literature

Floor 4: Speech Book

Floor 3: *Communicate!*

Floor 2: *Communicate!*
       A Workbook for Interpersonal Communication

Ground Floor: Using Language Chapter in
       Communicate!
       A Workbook for Interpersonal Communication

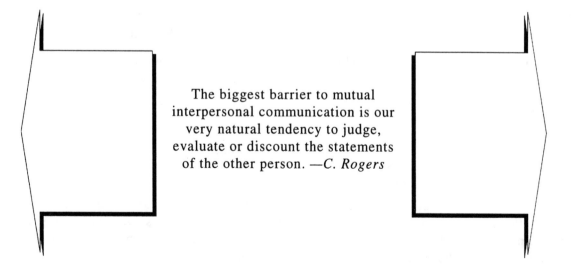

The biggest barrier to mutual interpersonal communication is our very natural tendency to judge, evaluate or discount the statements of the other person. —*C. Rogers*

THE SEMANTICS OF PREJUDICE

In the following analysis Dr. Cohen, an expert in semantics, analyzes the "language of prejudice." He shows that by choosing one word rather than another, we often structure the world into ingroups and outgroups and create unfavorable attitudes toward those we designate as "they."

Almost any human characteristic may be described either in honorific, favorable and approving, or in pejorative (unfavorable and disapproving) terms. If we examine the words used to describe particular human traits, we see that some are noncommittal and neutral, some favorable and *upgrading,* and others unfavorable or *downgrading.* For example, if we take a fairly neutral attitude toward a young man, we call him simply *young.* If we have an unfavorable attitude toward him and wish to *downgrade* him in the eyes of others, we say that he is *immature.* On the other hand, if we want to emphasize his vigor and freshness, we call the same person *youthful.* What word we use often depends upon some implicit value judgment we have made of a person and upon our desire to arouse the same attitude in others. The following list of some of the adjectives used to describe human traits shows how easy it is to create favorable or unfavorable attitudes toward the same behavior simply by a judicious use of language:

Favorable, Upgrading	In-between, Neutral	Unfavorable, Downgrading
Discrete	Cautious	Cowardly
Loyal	Obedient	Slavish
Careful	Meticulous	Fussy
Devoted	Self-subordinating	Fanatical
Kind	Soft	Mawkish
Warmhearted	Sentimental	Mushy
Tolerant	Nondiscriminating	Nigger-lover, Indian-lover
Generous	Liberal	Spendthrift
Courageous	Bold	Reckless, foolhardy
Mature	Old	Decayed
Youthful	Young	Immature
Sound	Conservative	Reactionary
Open-minded	Liberal	Unsound
Practical	Aware of material factors	Mercenary
Realistic	Suspicious	Cynical
Humanitarian	Idealist	Do-gooder

In the eyes of the satisfied employer, the servant is loyal and therefore possessed of an important virtue. In the eyes of the social critic, the same servant may be slavish, implying that her relationship to her employer is to be condemned. The same person may be called "generous" by those who approve of her and a *spendthrift* by those who do not.

Not only adjectives but nouns as well are used to express attitudes of approval and disapproval and to create them in others. Consider, for example, the varying connotations of respect or disrespect involved in choosing among the following ways of describing the position of a given individual:

Favorable, Upgrading	In-between, Neutral	Unfavorable, Downgrading
Official	Office-holder	Bureaucrat
Statesman	Policy-maker	Politician
Officer	Policeman	Cop
Investigator	Detective	Flatfoot
Governess	Nursemaid	Servant
Business executive	Employer	Boss
Financial leader	Banker	Moneylender
Pilgrim	Migrant, refugee, immigrant	Alien
Orator	Influential speaker	Rabble rouser

In her own language the nursemaid may be a governess but to her employer she may be a servant. Early Puritan refugees are praised as pilgrims but later refugees are aliens. Statesmen are always orators, while politicians are usually rabble rousers.

Verbs, too, fall on a value scale. The following list covers only a few of the key word-choices that, when applied to any controversial issue, may help us to identify the moral or political standpoint of the word-user and the direction in which he wishes to influence opinion, attitude and policy:

Favorable, Upgrading	In-between, Neutral	Unfavorable, Downgrading
Discern	Think	Theorize
Demonstrate	Assert	Allege
Cooperate	Act in concert	Conspire
Assist	Aid	Abet
Clarify	Retract	Admit error
Advise	Urge	Behest
Serve	Control	Interfere
Administer	Manage	Manipulate
Enlighten	Report	Propagandize
Inspire	Motivate	Inflame

So we find that, as a rule, majorities are inspired but minorities are inflamed and where the former cooperate with each other, the latter conspire.

Generally speaking, words of the first column in the three lists may be classed as "we" words. They are words we customarily apply to ourselves and our ingroups. Words of the third column, on the other hand, are "they" words, used to describe the actions of those outgroups from whom we are inclined to separate ourselves. Sometimes the relation between "we" words and "they" words involves no more than the addition of the three-letter pejorative suffix, "ism." We and our friends are for peace, or psychology, or social progress, or isolation. But our enemies are for pacifism, psychologism, socialism, progressivism, or isolationism.

The use of downgrading words helps to establish others as *they*. At the same time, the use of *they* words often serves to encourage unfavorable, downgrading attitudes. When a white judge refers to a defendant as a Negro, Indian, or savage, he is using an outgrouping line of demarcation that separates himself from the defendant. On the other hand, a judge who refers to the same defendant as a citizen, taxpayer, father, husband, or veteran is using an ingrouping delineation that includes himself or honored friends. Perhaps the most significant effort of attorneys on opposite sides of a case is to persuade the judge or jury or both to think of the defendant in *we* terms or *they* terms. Many American newspapers refer to arrested or suspected criminals as Negro or alien if they are either; on the other hand, they do not use words like whites or "seventh-generation American" or Protestant or freckled. This technique helps to build popular impressions as to the criminality of Negroes or aliens which are often very far removed from the facts. What may be called the technique of the irrelevant adjective is a smear technique that is difficult to answer. When a New York congressman objected to being referred to as a "Jewish congressman from New York," the answer was, in effect, "Well, you are Jewish, aren't you? Why be ashamed of it?"

The real issue here is not whether a radical or religious adjective is accurately descriptive of an individual but whether the adjective is properly relevant to the context in which it is used. The adjective Negro may be entirely relevant to a discussion of the medical effects of sunburn, and the adjective Jewish may be entirely relevant to a discussion of religious ritual. Those adjectives are irrelevant to a court trial in a report of a crime wave except upon the unstated premise that Negroes or Jews, Indians or immigrants, are especially disposed to criminal activity. Such unstated premises make the difference between sympathetic or unsympathetic accounts of the same event and bear upon the possibility of reaching a just judgment based on the merits of the individual case.

For evil, then, as well as for good, words make us the human beings we actually are. Deprived of language, we should be dogs or monkeys. Possessing language, we are men and women able to persevere in crime no less than in heroic virtue, capable of intellectual achievements beyond the scope of any animal, but at the same time capable of systematic silliness and stupidity such as no dumb beast could ever dream of. —A. Huxley

REVOLUTIONARY RUDENESS REFORMS RUSSIAN LANGUAGE

Michael Specter

MOSCOW—The man wanted to buy some perfume, and he seemed to be in a hurry.

"Girl!" he shouted at the young woman behind the cosmetics counter at Petrovsky Passage, one of the city's swankier malls. She didn't budge.

Undeterred, he shouted, "Girl!" a couple more times, before switching to a coarser form of address. "Woman!" he screeched, using a word that comes across as a vulgar variant of "Hey, broad!" "Woman," he bellowed, until she finally noticed him. "Woman, come here!"

This display made absolutely no impression on any of the other customers waiting for service. How could it? In Russia—a place where verbal niceties and polite address have gone the way of the Romanovs—rudeness, while not exactly new, has become as common as cheap vodka.

Fast, Abrupt, Dismissive

It is not as if the language of the Soviets was endearing, or that profanity appeared with democracy. Always brusque and irritatingly egalitarian, Soviet speech has nevertheless yielded to the sharp sounds of a new nation—fast, abrupt and dismissive.

Unsettling as it is, the linguistic confusion is understandable. Nobody wants to rely on the offensive euphemisms of communism. And while some pre-revolutionary phrases have returned, most seem so archaic that they too have found few users.

That leaves slang, curses and a seemingly endless string of foreign words—gangstery, biznesmeny (and for women, biznesmenka), kottedzhi (from "cottages," places where gangstery and other rich folks relax) and of course, kreditniye karty.

Labor camp slang, once used defiantly as a badge of contempt for the Soviets, has provided a vocabulary aptly suited to current Russian realities. When a guy drives by in a new Mercedes with smoked windows and three antennas on the roof, people don't say, "Wow, there goes a rich guy."

They don't even say he must be a gang member. They call him a "krutoy chelovek," a tough guy, a cool guy, a guy they'll never be.

"What is happening now is similar to what happened in the 20s after the revolution," said Irina Prokhorova, editor of *New Literary Review*, which is becoming something like a Russian version of *The New York Review of Books*. "The language is struggling to find its place. It is not easy. People who emigrated five years ago tell me they have trouble understanding the newspapers. Most of the time our speech lacks a certain decency."

She said she had just returned from her first visit to New York, where she was astonished to see that "even homeless people would say 'excuse me' when they bump into you on the street. I had never seen anything like it. You certainly don't see that here."

It has been years since there has been a suitable way to address a stranger in Russian.

The old greeting—comrade (tovarishch)—is about as welcome as a free membership in the Communist Party. Citizen (grazhdanin) was once in vogue but many years ago became a word one used to address a prisoner. Polite words for Mr. and Mrs. (Gospodin, Gospozha) or the more lordly Sir and Madam (Sudar and Sudarina) seem like they belong in a Tolstoy novel.

Dark Linguistic Hole

And few Russians these days seem to come from the world of Tolstoy. The result is a linguistic edginess that mirrors the fast, combative, often unpleasant, daily life of Russia itself.

Increasingly, street language is explosive—unprintable in its excess of profanities and its lack of modulation. "We have fallen into a very dark hole linguistically," said Yevgeny N. Shiryaev, deputy director of the Russian Academy of Sciences Institute of Russian language and an expert on the evolution of common speech. "Obviously speech reflects society and this is, at the moment, not a polite society. What you hear on the street is dangerously rude. I don't mean to be a prude. I think language should change and I am glad that ours is adapting to the needs of a new society. But when a country cannot even produce an accepted way of addressing a woman that isn't an insult, I think that is a significant problem."

SEMANTIC REACTIONS					
PURPOSE:	To examine your own semantic reactions to terms and enable you to see how each of us experiences semantic noise.				
PROCEDURE:	Following is a list of 27 terms. Beside each term place the number which corresponds to your **immediate** reaction to that word according to the scale indicated. Remember that the intent of the activity is to allow you to examine your semantic reactions, so be as honest in marking your reaction as you can. Your immediate reaction is usually the most reliable.				
Reaction	Highly Positive +2	Slightly Positive +1	Neutral or No Reaction 0	Slightly Negative -1	Highly Negative -2
1. patriotism					
2. breast					
3. fuck					
4. asshole					
5. pusilanimous					
6. love					
7. communism					
8. caucasian					
9. mexican					
10. bureaucracy					
11. speech					
12. tits					
13. friendship					
14. balls					
15. chauvinist					

Reaction	Highly Positive +2	Slightly Positive +1	Neutral or No Reaction 0	Slightly Negative -1	Highly Negative -2
16. fox					
17. cock					
18. intercourse					
19. cancer					
20. exacerbate					
21. gay					
22. cum laude					
23. shit					
24. nigger					
25. seersucker					
26. chicano					
27. whitey					

DISCUSSION: Now that you have completed the list, you will have a chance to compare your reactions with another member of the class and discuss the following questions:

1. How do you react to the various words?
2. Why do you react as you do? On what is your reaction based?
3. How can reaction to words (semantic reactions) affect communication?
4. With respect to semantic reactions, what suggestions could you make to improve communication?
5. What variables—i.e., sex, race, religion, income, age, influence your responses? ❏

INSTANT WISDOM

PURPOSE: To demonstrate the power of words and to indicate that meanings are in people and not in words.

PROCEDURE:
1. Distribute a 3 × 5 card to each class member.
2. Write one high-level abstraction word on each side of the card. Hint: It is probably better to choose some value term or a word which you feel is important, emotionally charged, or used politically. Examples are *truth, honesty, humanity, freedom, love.*
3. The following patterns or similar ones should be put on the chalkboard. The terms should then be arbitrarily added to the blanks.

a.	If _____ becomes _____ , then _____ and _____ will prevail.
b.	_____ and much _____ are _____ .
c.	When _____ becomes_____ , _____ will result.
d.	This is an age of _____ and _____ .
e.	The _____ of _____ , not _____ , nor _____ , but _____ .

DISCUSSION:	This activity illustrates the ease of combining highly abstract nouns in order to create impressive rhetoric, *wise sayings,* maxims and political platitudes. The group will be surprised and impressed at the *profound meaning* that results.

1.	Do these statements mean anything?
2.	Is it possible that great speakers use a similar device?
3.	Why can words be combined into such apparently meaningful sentences?	❏

HIDDEN ASSUMPTIONS TEST

PURPOSE:	To discover fallacies of thinking based on hidden assumptions and over-generalizations.

PROCEDURE:	1.	This is a timed test. Answer the questions as quickly as possible.
2.	Once you have answered, go on to the next question. **Do not go back to change any answers.**

1. Each country has its own "Independence Day." Do they have a 4th of July in England? _____
2. How many birthdays does the average man have? _____
3. Can a man living in Winston-Salem, North Carolina be buried west of the Mississippi? _____
4. If you only had one match and entered a room in which there was a Kerosene lamp, an oil heater and wood burning stove, which would you light first? _____
5. Some months have 30 days, some have 31. How many have 28? _____
6. If a doctor gave you three pills and told you to take one every half hour, how long would the pills last? _____
7. A house is built so that each side has a southern exposure. If a bear were to wander by the house, most likely the color of the bear would be? _____
8. How far can a dog run into the forest? _____
9. I have in my hand two U.S. coins which total 55 cents in value. One is not a nickel. What are the two coins? _____
10. A farmer has 17 sheep. All but nine died. How many does he have left? _____
11. Two men play chess. They played five games and each man won the same number of games. There were no ties. How can this be? _____
12. Take two apples from three apples and what do you get? _____
13. Divide 30 by one-half and add 10. What is the answer? _____

14. An archaeologist claimed she found gold coins dated 46 B.C. Do you think she did and why? _____

15. An airplane crashed exactly on the U.S.-Mexican border. Where would they bury the survivors? _____

16. How many animals of each species did Moses take aboard the ark with him? _____

17. Is it legal in California for a man to marry his widow's sister? _____

18. How much dirt may be removed from a hole that is 6 ft. deep, 2 ft. wide, and 10 ft. long? _____

19. If your bedroom were pitch dark and you needed a matching pair of socks, how many socks would you need to take out of the bureau drawer if there are 25 white and 25 blue? _____

20. You have four nines (9,9,9,9). Arrange them to total 100. You may use any of the arithmetical processes (addition, subtraction, multiplication, or division). Each nine must be used once. _____

21. If it takes 10 men 10 days to dig a hole, how long will it take five men to dig half a hole? _____

22. Explain the following true boast: "In my bedroom, the nearest lamp that I usually keep turned on is 12 feet away from my bed. Alone in the room, without using any special devices, I can turn out the light on that lamp and get into bed before the room is dark." _____

23. A doctor refuses to operate on a patient who has been injured in an auto accident in which the patient's father was killed. The doctor refuses to operate because the patient is the doctor's son. How can this be? _____

24. There are 12 one-cent stamps in a dozen, but how many two-cent stamps are there in a dozen? _____

25. What four words appear on every denomination of U.S. coin and currency? _____

26. Which is correct: 7 and 8 are 13, or 7 and 8 is 13? _____

27. If 3 cats kill 3 rats in 3 minutes, how long will it take for 100 cats to kill 100 rats? _____

DISCUSSION:
1. Were you surprised at how many questions you could not answer?
2. Were you surprised at how many questions you answered correctly/incorrectly?
3. What did this test tell you about the assumptions you make? ❑

THE UNCRITICAL INFERENCE TEST

William V. Haney

PURPOSE: To demonstrate the assumptions and inferences we make upon hearing or reading words.

PROCEDURE: This test is designed to determine your ability to think *accurately* and *carefully*. Since it is very probable that you have never taken *this type* of test before, failure to read the instructions **extremely carefully** may lower your score.

1. You will read a brief story. Assume that all of the information presented in the story is definitely *accurate* and *true*. Read the story carefully. You may refer back to the story whenever you wish.

2. You will then read statements about the story. Answer them in numerical order. **Do not go back** to fill in answers or to change answers. This will only distort your test score.

3. After you read carefully each statement, determine whether the statement is:

   a. "T"—meaning: on the basis of the *information presented in the story the statement is* **definitely true**.

   b. "F"—meaning: On the basis of the *information presented in the story the statement is* **definitely false**.

   c. "?"—meaning: The statement may be true (or false) but on the basis of the *information presented in the story you* cannot be *definitely certain*. (If any part of the statement is doubtful, mark the statement "?".)

4. Indicate your answer by circling either "T" or "F" or "?" opposite the statement.

SAMPLE TEST

Sample Story

The only car parked in front of 619 Oak Street is a black one. The words "James M. Curley, M.D." are spelled in small gold letters across the left front door of that car.

Statements about the story

1. The color of the car in front of 619 Oak Street is black.   T   F   ?
2. There is no lettering on the left front door of the car parked in front of 619 Oak Street.   T   F   ?
3. Someone is ill at 619 Oak Street.   T   F   ?
4. The black car parked in front of 619 Oak Street belongs to James M. Curley.   T   F   ?

Remember: Answer **only** on the basis of the information presented in the story. Refrain from answering as you think it **might** have happened. Answer each statement in numerical order. Do not go back to fill in or to change answers.

Story A

Babe Smith has been killed. Police have rounded up six suspects, all of whom are known gangsters. All of them are known to have been near the scene of the killing at the approximate time that it occurred. All had substantial motives for wanting Smith killed. However, one of these suspected gangsters, Slinky Sam, has positively been cleared of guilt.

Statements about Story A

1. Slinky Sam is known to have been near the scene of the killing of Babe Smith.   T   F   ?
2. All six of the rounded-up gangsters were known to have been near the scene of the murder.   T   F   ?
3. Only Slinky Sam has been cleared of guilt.   T   F   ?

By permission, William V. Haney, *Communication and Organizational Behavior,* 3rd edition, Homewood, Ill. Richard D. Irwin, Inc.

4. All six of the rounded-up suspects were near the scene of Smith's killing at the approximate time that it took place.   T F ?
5. The police do not know who killed Smith.   T F ?
6. All six suspects are known to have been near the scene of the foul deed.   T F ?
7. Smith's murderer did not confess of his own free will.   T F ?
8. Slinky Sam was not cleared of guilt.   T F ?
9. It is known that the six suspects were in the vicinity of the cold-blooded assassination.   T F ?

Story B

A business man had just turned off the lights in the store when a man appeared and demanded money. The owner opened a cash register. The contents of the cash register were scooped up and the man sped away. A member of the police force was notified promptly.

Statements about Story B
1. A man appeared after the owner had turned off his store lights.   T F ?
2. The robber was a *man*.   T F ?
3. The man who appeared did not demand money.   T F ?
4. The man who opened the cash register was the owner.   T F ?
5. The store-owner scooped up the contents of the cash register and ran away.   T F ?
6. Someone opened a cash register.   T F ?
7. After the man, who demanded the money, scooped up the contents of the cash register, he ran away.   T F ?
8. While the cash register contained money, the story does *not* state *how much*.   T F ?
9. The robber demanded money of the owner.   T F ?
10. The robber opened the cash register.   T F ?
11. After the store lights were turned off a man appeared.   T F ?
12. The robber did not take the money with him.   T F ?
13. The robber did not demand money of the owner.   T F ?
14. The owner opened a cash register.   T F ?
15. The age of the store-owner was not revealed in the story.   T F ?
16. Taking the contents of the cash register with him, the man ran out of the store.   T F ?
17. The story concerns a series of events in which only three persons are referred to: the owner of the store, a man who demanded money and a member of the police force.   T F ?
18. The following events were included in the story: someone demanded money, a cash register was opened, its contents were scooped up, and a man dashed out of the store.   T F ?

DISCUSSION:
1. Were you surprised at the number of assumptions and inferences you made?
2. Did certain types of words cause you to believe you understood their meaning?
3. What are the implications to your everyday language?   ❑

Facts do not cease to exist because they are ignored. —A. Huxley

POLARIZATION

PURPOSE: To demonstrate that language forces us to speak and think in a polarized manner.

PROCEDURE: Fill in the opposites for the words below. Then try to find an in-between word for the opposites and write the words in the middle column.

WORD	IN-BETWEEN	OPPOSITE
tall	_____	_____
heavy	_____	_____
strong	_____	_____
happy	_____	_____
legal	_____	_____
leader	_____	_____
success	_____	_____
wealthy	_____	_____
woman	_____	_____
beautiful	_____	_____
black	_____	_____
easy	_____	_____
teacher	_____	_____

DISCUSSION:
1. Which is harder to find, an opposite word or an in-between word?
2. Which words are more descriptive—the polar opposites or the in-between words?
3. Is our language structured to make us think in polar opposites? ❏

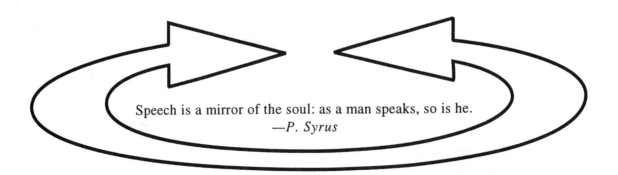

Speech is a mirror of the soul: as a man speaks, so is he.
—*P. Syrus*

OWNING MY COMMUNICATION: A SEMANTIC TASK ———

PURPOSE: To demonstrate responsibility for one's own words.

             To demonstrate how language helps us distort things.

             To demonstrate how language influences thought.

PROCEDURE: Read the following word/phrase substitutes and attempt to use them in
             your everyday language.

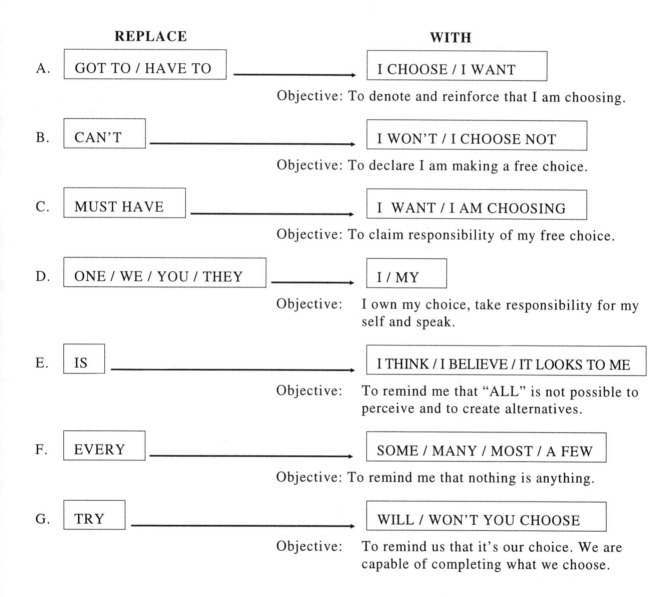

REPLACE   **WITH**

A. GOT TO / HAVE TO ⟶ I CHOOSE / I WANT

Objective: To denote and reinforce that I am choosing.

B. CAN'T ⟶ I WON'T / I CHOOSE NOT

Objective: To declare I am making a free choice.

C. MUST HAVE ⟶ I WANT / I AM CHOOSING

Objective: To claim responsibility of my free choice.

D. ONE / WE / YOU / THEY ⟶ I / MY

Objective: I own my choice, take responsibility for my
              self and speak.

E. IS ⟶ I THINK / I BELIEVE / IT LOOKS TO ME

Objective: To remind me that "ALL" is not possible to
              perceive and to create alternatives.

F. EVERY ⟶ SOME / MANY / MOST / A FEW

Objective: To remind me that nothing is anything.

G. TRY ⟶ WILL / WON'T YOU CHOOSE

Objective: To remind us that it's our choice. We are
              capable of completing what we choose.

DISCUSSION: 1.   Are the suggested replacements more realistic?
               2.   Can you see how language helps you distort things?
               3.   Do these semantic replacements allow you to think more realistically? ❏

E-PRIME

PURPOSE: To practice a more descriptive use of the English language in order to control unintentional evaluations and language inaccuracy.

PROCEDURE:
1. In the sentence below, there is an identity problem.
2. Rewrite the sentences, replacing the verb "to be" (is, are, was, am, etc.) with a process word or more exact phrase. Such a change will comprise what we will call a transformation to **E-Prime,** English without the verb to be. The following are some examples:
    a. Identity statement: "We hold these truths to be self-evident, that all men are created equal, that they are endowed by their creator with certain inalienable rights, that among these are life, liberty, and the pursuit of happiness."
    b. E-Prime: We make the following assumptions: All citizens have equal political rights. All citizens simply by virtue of their existence have certain inalienable rights, including life, liberty, and the pursuit of happiness.
    c. Identity statement: "I am a(n) _____ ."(your occupation)
    d. E-Prime: "People call me _____ ."(your occupation)
3. Now you can give it a try. Rewrite the following identity statements using the **E-Prime** system.

Identity statement: "I am a student."

E-Prime:

Identity statement: "I am not good in biology."

E-Prime:

Identity statement: "This subject is boring."

E-Prime:

Identity statement: "Sauerkraut is not good."

E-Prime:

Identity statement: "Henry is ugly."

E-Prime:

DISCUSSION:
1. The structure of our language encourages us to talk as if (and think as if) "qualities" exist in things. It obscures the role of the observer.
2. The word *is* used in this way is sometimes called the "is of projection" because we use it to project our reactions on the world out there.
3. Consider how this simple exercise has demonstrated how language influences the way we think.
4. Even if you don't continue to use this system, at least assess how such an awareness might be helpful to you in your communication attempts. ❏

STREET TALK TEST

PURPOSE: To examine the way words mean different things to different people

PROCEDURE: Circle the letter for the correct answer of each street term

1. "STALL IT OUT" means:
   a. Stealing a car
   b. Taking a battery out of a car
   c. Stop doing what you're doing
   d. Taking a horse out of the stall

2. "LET'S BAIL" is a term used to denote:
   a. Bailing a client out of custody
   b. A boating term used in boat racing
   c. A term used to say you're ready to leave

3. What is meant by the statement "MAKING BANK"?
   a. A construction term used in building
   b. The process of obtaining money
   c. Bank of America's code for instant credit account

4. The term "WHAT'S UP" means:
   a. What's going on
   b. Let's fight
   c. To look up

5. An East Coast freak haircut is:
   a. Punk rock type
   b. Neat close cropped hair cut
   c. Perm style
   d. Braids

6. The term "HOMEBOY" means
   a. Lazy person
   b. Immature person
   c. Fellow gang member
   d. A gang member who stays home

7. To "SQUAB" means:
   a. To fight
   b. To set territory aside
   c. How pigeons mate

8. "HOLDING IT DOWN" means
   a. Stop using PCP
   b. Throwing your hand sign downwards
   c. Gang members protecting their territory
   d. Holding a "sherm head" down

9. "I'M JUST KICKING IT" means:
   a. A good soccer move
   b. Killing somebody with your feet
   c. Relaxing or passing the time

10. I have a "DEUCE-DEUCE" and a "TRAY EIGHT" means:
    a. Number in dice game
    b. .22 cal. and .38 cal. guns
    c. Two gang members talking about the street they live on

11. What is a "SHERM HEAD"?
    a. History major in school
    b. An Uncle Tom
    c. A cool dude
    d. Chronic user of PCP

12. "TAKE HIM OUT THE BOX" means:
    a. Trouble at a funeral
    b. Killing a rival gang member
    c. Running out of a house you burglarized

13. A "WATER" dealer is:
    a. A Sparkletts man
    b. Radiator mechanic

14. To "BUMP SOMEONE'S HEAD" means:
    a. Street robbery
    b. To lie to someone
    c. Gang initiation
    d. Martial arts kick

By permission, Senior Investigator, Ken Bell, Los Angeles District Attorney's Office.

15. What is a "MUDDUCK"?
    a. Rival gang member
    b. Water fowl
    c. Ugly girl
    d. Ragged car

16. "I don't have any 'SNAP'" means:
    a. I don't have any cookies
    b. I don't have any money
    c. I don't have any weapons
    d. I don't have any burglary tools

17. If someone is ON THE "PIPE," it means:
    a. They are an avid pipe smoker
    b. They are free basing (cocaine)
    c. Slang for homosexual activity

18. If someone told you he has a "GLASS-HOUSE," it means
    a. A person into serious gardening
    b. A new modern house
    c. A 1977–78 "Chevy"
    d. A house that's been shot up before

19. Let's do a "GHOST" means:
    a. A magic trick
    b. To leave your present location
    c. Shoot and run
    d. Beat up a "white" person

20. If someone told you "JAMES HAS A BUCKET," it means:
    a. An ugly girlfriend
    b. A new style hat
    c. An old ragged car
    d. James is a janitor

21. If a person is described as "EASTLY," it
    a. They have an East Coast haircut
    b. They are very ugly
    c. They are an unreliable gang member

22. If someone is "TALKING HEAD" to you, it means
    a. Sign language for deaf and dumb
    b. Silent gang symbols with hands
    c. That they want to fight you

23. What is a "BASE HEAD"?
    a. A person hooked on cocaine
    b. The best tuba player in the band
    c. The leader of the gang

24. A "PRIMO" is:
    a. The best shooter in the gang
    b. A marijuana joint laced with cocaine
    c. The primary target in a gang retaliation

25. What is a "JIM JONES"?
    a. The craziest guy in the gang
    b. A marijuana joint laced with cocaine and dipped in PCP
    c. A rival gang member marked for certain death

DISCUSSION:
1. Were you surprised at the number of questions you had to guess at?
2. What causes words like "Mark" and "Ghost" to change meaning?
3. Why don't words assume a meaning and keep it?
4. Have you used words in a manner that was different than what the dictionary said? Which ones? Why? ❏

THE INS AND OUTS OF SLANG

Cathy Lawhon

Slang separates the fly-fishermen from the rock turkeys, the cyclists from the Freds, the crocks from the live ones.

Don't bother scrambling for a dictionary. You've just discovered the function of slang: If you don't get it, you're not supposed to.

"Slang has a twofold purpose," said Angela Della Volpe, linguistics professor at California State University, Fullerton. "First, it provides identity for a group; it shows you belong. And the other purpose, which is a kind of reversal of the first, is that it's used to exclude those who are not part of the group.

"In Vietnam, the military had its own slang, words that reflected the environment, and it was an 'in' thing that was necessary to keep people who were not privy to the experience out of the interaction," Della Volpe said.

That's how a bombing raid became a "protective reaction strike."

Teenagers use slang to define their cliques, and to close out all non-conforming peers and, of course, parents. The insatiable adolescent appetite for new slang is stimulated by the enormous need for peer identification within an "in" group.

"With kids, slang words stay around only as long as they serve a need," said Dr. Raymond Gibbs, associate professor of psychology at the University of California, Santa Cruz who specializes in psycholinguistics. "And that need is to communicate the things they want to talk about in the way they want to communicate them.

"The main function of slang is not just to transmit information, but show that you have a certain flair," Gibbs said. "It shows you're a member of a social group and that you know how to go about talking about things."

Slang terms are usually coined around everyday ideas or activities within the group. And they are imbued heavily with attitude.

"That's one of the beauties of slang," Gibbs said. "You not only communicate certain information, but your attitude about it as well. It's a way of showing you're hip. If you can use it correctly and appropriately and innovatively, it shows you have a creative sense and puts you at a higher status in some groups. And with children, especially, that is very important."

Slang changes very quickly in teen circles because it becomes passe as soon as parents, teachers or even peers outside the "in" group begin to understand the meaning.

To a lesser degree, members of professions, sporting teams or activities, even members of the opposite sex, use slang to exclude those who don't belong.

"Any kind of jargon or colloquialism is used in that way," Gibbs said. "Reporters, psychologists, we all have our own lingo. I'm not saying that we as academic psychologists have a conspiracy going so no one can understand us, but we all do, in fact, use slang as a private code."

Businessmen exclude businesswomen from their conversations by using sports metaphors in their speech, Della Volpe said.

Colleagues within a job or profession develop their own lingo, which lets them communicate while baffling those on the outside. Participants in sports close out the neophytes with their use of jargon.

And while English purists bemoan the proliferation of slang, Della Volpe said it's the life-support system for language.

"People talk in metaphoric terms," she said. "They use the frame of reference they are most familiar with. Since computers are so wide-

Reprinted from the February 2, 1988 *Orange County Register*

spread, for example, we hear a lot of computer jargon."

Consider the noun turned verb "interface." It was once a point or means of interaction between two electronic systems. It has become a synonym for personal interaction. Or, 10 years ago, one might have said he didn't feel "up to par" (golf slang) without a morning cup of coffee. These days, he's not "on line."

"That's what keeps language alive," Della Volpe said. "Language has to reflect and evolve parallel with the society. If it doesn't, we can't communicate."

Gibbs said he believes in "linguistic anarchy."

"There are people out there who think slang is definitely a terrible thing. They say the language is deteriorating. Well, the thing to note is that the ancient Greeks said the same thing. I believe there is no one correct way of speaking. Language is there to be created and exploited," Gibbs said.

How slang is created is tough to track.

Slang enters the English language in one of two ways, Della Volpe said. An old word takes on a new meaning (relics of the 1960s remember when "fuzz" meant police as well as something on a peach) or a new word is coined by blending words and meaning. Slang words are created by anyone with enough creativity and imagination to come up with a clever turn of phrase.

To the uninitiated, slang sounds like gibberish. But a little linguistic fieldwork can reveal the wealth of meaning behind the most colorful slang.

The following are some examples of what's being spoken out there on the Orange County slang front, gathered by a volunteer corps of high school students, sports enthusiasts and workers in a variety of jobs.

Agro: *adj.* Excited, aggressive, aggravated. "Don't get all agro."

Bogus: *adj.* Fake or unnatural. "Those are bogus eyelashes." Also, a bummer. "That exam was bogus."

Bug-out: *n.* A strange or unusual person. "She's a bug-out."

Chill out: *v.* Relax, calm down. "Hey, chill out, dude."

Fresh: *adj.* Cool, worthy of note. "That outfit is fresh."

Full: *adj.* Very; in the fullest sense. "She's a full bug-out."

Killer: *adj.* Very impressive. "Oh, that's killer."

Lack of oxygen: A phrase used in response to someone who is spacey or absent-minded. "It must be lack of oxygen."

Panic: *n.* A person who is nuts or crazy. "You're a panic."

Put music to it: A phrase used in comeback to anyone who is overly whiny or always complaining. "Aw, come on. Put music to it."

Shape: *n.* A person who doesn't quite fit into any clique. "You're a shape."

Sketch: *n.* Anyone who's not quite all there. Usually used with full as in, "That teacher's a full sketch."

Take a pill: Cool it or cool off. "That guy needs to take a pill."

This junior-high slang report lags about six months—or more—behind the older in slang.

Awesome: *adj.* Outrageously good. "That movie was awesome."

Bad: *adj.* Synonym for good. "Hey, that skateboard is bad."

Cool: *adj.* Hip or bad. "What a cool T-shirt."

Far out: *adj.* Neat, fun. "That class is far out."

Gnarly: *adj.* See awesome, above. "Wow, gnarly."

Rad: *adj.* Short for radical, a surfing term for on the edge, exciting. "Oh, rad." Also, raddest. "He has the raddest bike."

From Dr. Daniel Marcus of El Toro comes the bicycling report:

Fred: *n.* A new or neophyte cyclist. "He's a real Fred."

Wheel sucker: *n.* A person who insists on drafting or getting down low behind the lead biker and letting him block the wind. "Get back, you wheel sucker."

Hook: *v.* To lock the rear wheel hub and bump into another biker's spokes in an attempt to knock him over. "Stop sucking my wheel or I'll hook you."

Spin: *v.* To pedal very fast in a low gear. "I was spinning."

Jack Lynde, vice president of Orange County Musician's Association Local No. 7 reports from the music business:

Not too tightly wrapped: *adj.* Dumb; not much going on upstairs. Usually used in reference to a backstage groupie. "She's not too tightly wrapped."

Short: *n.* A car. "He lit out of his short on the avenue."

Vine: *n.* Suit of clothes. "That's a fine vine."

The fly-fishing slang report comes from Steven Feldman, a Laguna Niguel attorney:

Hardware man: *n.* A fisherman (not a fly-fisherman) who uses spoons (or lures) to catch fish. "He's a hardware man."

Purist: *n.* A fly-fisherman who won't use wet flies (flies designed to go in or under the water.) "Give the dry flies to the purist."

Rock turkeys: *n.* A bait fisherman, particularly one who stands on rocks at the side of a stream with a fishing rod in one hand and a beer in the other. "Look out for the rock turkeys over there."

Ernie Holliday, manager of Adler Shoes in Montclair, reports on slang in the shoe business:

Crock: *n.* A customer who can't make up her mind. "Here comes that crock again."

Dog: *n.* A bad shoe that doesn't sell. "That pump was a dog."

Department 13: *n.* The restroom. "I'll be in department 13."

Drag: *n.* Shoes a salesman left out on the floor from a previous customer. "Pick up your drag.

Duck: *n.* A flat, spread-out foot, or a person with such a foot. "He's got a duck."

Elephant: *n.* A very wide foot, or a person with such a foot. "Who is going to take the elephant?"

Live one: *n.* The salesman's dream. A person who, with a little wining and dining, will buy multiple pairs of shoes. "She's a live one."

Shoe dog: *n.* A career shoe salesman who travels from shoe store to shoe store taking jobs and causing trouble. "The guy is a shoe dog."

Spaghetti: *n.* A very narrow foot or a person with such a foot. "She's spaghetti."

Stiffs: *n.* The extras—shoe trees, shoe polish, etc.—that are sold with shoes. "Don't forget to push the stiffs."

Grant Brittain, photo editor of *Transworld Skateboarding Magazine,* supplies slang from skateboarding (or skating):

Betty: *n.* A tongue-in-cheek expression for girl. "There is an awesome betty."

Bio: *adj.* Particularly impressive. Similar to rad only without the element of danger that rad implies. "That was bio, dude."

Flow: *v.* To give or bequeath. "Flow me some bucks."

Grind: *n.* A cool maneuver that consists of scraping the truck (axle) along the ridge of a banked wall. "Hey, gnarly grind."

Sketchy: *adj.* Term used to describe a skater who always looks as though he's about to fall, but doesn't. "He pulled off a sketchy aerial."

Slam: *v.* To fall accidentally and hard. "That was a bad slam."

Zine: *n.* A skateboard magazine, especially one of the one-man, underground publications with extremely limited distribution. "Have you seen the latest zine?"

The surf report comes from Jim Pinkerton at *Surfing* magazine:

Amped: *adj.* Psyched up to surf. Ready to go. "I'm amped."

Bail: *v.* To exit a wave by jumping away or diving off the board. Terminology borrowed from the aviation term "bail out." "I gotta bail, man."

Grind: *v.* To eat a lot of food very quickly. "Let's go grind."

Schralp: *v.* To surf violently on a wave. Synonym for shred, rip and lacerate. "I just schralped that wave."

Stick: *n.* Surfboard. "Got your stick?"

Stoked: *adj.* The adjective that refuses to die. Happy.

Sgt. Jeri Van Duzen of the community relations office at El Toro Marine Corps Air Station gives the military slang report:

Bird: *n.* Aircraft. "Report to your bird."

Boot: *n.* A new recruit. "Here comes a boot."

Deuce: *adj.* Synonym for field, used to describe field gear. "Pick up your deuce gear."

Grunt: *n.* Infantryman. "He's just a grunt."

Gee dunk: *n.* Snack bar. "I'm headed over to the gee dunk."

Irish pennant: *n.* A hanging thread or loose button on a uniform. "Make sure you don't have any Irish pennants on inspection day."

Roach coach: *n.* Catering truck. "Want anything from the roach coach?"

Unsat: *adj.* Anything that is not right; short for unsatisfactory. "That shoeshine job is unsat."

ESSENTIALLY MORE B.S. ⎯⎯⎯⎯⎯⎯⎯⎯⎯⎯⎯⎯⎯⎯⎯

PURPOSE: To demonstrate the power of words and how people can use words to make themselves appear more intelligent.

PROCEDURE: This technical writing kit is based on the Simplified Integrated Modular Prose (SIMP) writing system. Using this kit, anyone who can count up to 10 can write as many as 40,000 discrete, well-balanced, grammatically correct sentences packed with EMBS terms and pedagogic gobbledygook.

To put SIMP to work, arrange the modules in A-B-C-D order. Take any four numbers, 7162 for example, and read Phrase 7 off Table A, Phrase 1 off Table B, etc. The result is a SIMP sentence. After you have mastered the basic technique you can realize the full potential of SIMP by arranging the modules in D-B-C-A order. In these advanced configurations some additional commas may be required.

SIMP TABLE A

1. A systematized basis upon which to evaluate competencies and outcomes
2. Initiation and maintenance of a comprehensive, flexible syllabus
3. A curricular formation of meaningful conceptual patterns
4. A ramification of commensurate behavioral objectives
5. A rational entailing subtopic analyses of psychomotor, cognitive and affective domains
6. A noncimitant insight into undergirded knowledge transfer
7. The thrust of instructional objectives which preclude assumed
8. Any reasonably consistent doctrinal guide for curricular innovation
9. The identification of functional modes that equate with educational outcomes
10. A clarifying technique reformulated by the component group

SIMP TABLE B

1. According to EMBS procedures
2. Technically speaking
3. Based on integral exponential considerations
4. As a resultant implication
5. In respect to specific goals
6. In this regard
7. Relative to the needs assessment program
8. On the other hand
9. Definitively stated
10. In essence then

SIMP TABLE C

1. Must be based upon developmental conditions and standards with
2. Is further compounded by noncreative concept formulation for
3. Adds vertical organization in complex orientation interplay with
4. Presents extremely interesting subinterval controls to
5. Recognizes and enhances the maximization of individual potential for
6. Effects a significant implementation to functional performance criteria and
7. Neccssitates correlative expertise in specialized areas of
8. Adds dimensional increments to the relevance of theory acquisition for
9. Predicates a viable analysis of multiphasic maturation studies to
10. Postulates that the degree of requisite content mastery is directly proportional to

SIMP TABLE D

1. The philosophy of affective taxonomy formulated by Krathwohl and others
2. Any interpretive assimilation of the correlative mode
3. The minimum essentials of valid behavioral objectives
4. The scope and focus of all pertinent socioeconomic factors
5. The componential perceptions affecting an integrative approach
6. The transitory utilization of polarized value judgments
7. Any conformation of preestablished divergent assumptions
8. The impetus of value indicators restructured through diverse areas of the continuum
9. Humanistic techniques of career orientation modeled after the Harmin-Simon approach
10. All nonsupportive and immediate response situations derived from key result areas

DISCUSSION:
1. Do you know anyone who uses language that is similar to this? If so, who?
2. What causes people to use EMBS?
3. Does this type of language affect society? If so, in what ways? ❏

REACTIONS

Answer the question assigned by your instructor. Remember, openness and honesty are the first steps to being a more effective communicator.

1. Select one of the language barriers to communication that you have experienced in your own communication. Describe the barrier and indicate how it interfered with your communication. What skill will you use in the future to overcome the barrier?

2. In what ways does our reaction to words (semantic reactions) affect our communication?

3. What suggestions would you make to improve communication with respect to semantic reactions?

4. From the very beginning of the day, how long did it take you to slip and use a label or stereotype someone? What was it? What should you have done?

5. If words have power, how is it that "words don't mean; people mean"?

6. Give a recent example of how you reacted to a word because of its connotative impact rather than denotative.

7. Give a recent example of sexism in your language. How might you rid your language behaviors of this barrier?

UNDERSTANDING SELF | 7

Definitions ──────────────────

Self-Image

Definition: How we describe, picture, view ourselves. It is objective, describable, measurable and checkable.

Example: "I am a black female, 24 years old, weighing 123 pounds, 5 feet 6 inches tall." Self-image changes slowly because we develop physically gradually and over extended periods of time.

Self-Esteem

Definition: The value, worth or importance that we put on what our self-image is. It is very subjective.

Example: "I like being black and female. I wish I were a bit older. I would like to lose 10 pounds. I like my height."

Self-Concept

Definition: Our total or world view of ourselves. The complete picture including both our self-image and self-esteem.

Example: "I'm an attractive human being who is intelligent, relates well to others and is generally successful in things I try." Our self-concept changes as our self-image or self-esteem is modified.

Role

Definition: A part we are expected to play in our society.

Examples: Student, mother, brother, worker, athlete, consumer, woman/man, husband, girlfriend, citizen. We are expected to play hundreds of roles in our lives—the more complex our lives, the more roles we are expected to play.

Role Expectations

Definition: The parameters or boundaries of the roles we are playing.

Performance Role

Definition: A role where we are paid (or receive some sort of remuneration) for meeting the role expectations as prescribed by the person or agency that "pays" us.

Example: As a student we meet the specifications set by our teacher. If we do so, we receive knowledge, grade, credit, etc. As a worker we do what our boss tells us (often even dressing as directed)—in return, we get a paycheck.

Personality Role

Definition: A role where we have the right to determine the parameters of the role we are playing.

Example: Friend, brother, sex partner, woman, et al. A son or daughter living at home with mom and dad paying the bills is in a performance role since the person is being "paid" her physical upkeep and therefore meets parents' expectations in doing chores around the house or being in at a certain time. However, when son or daughter moves out and begins paying his/her own bills, then son/daughter becomes a personality role.

Self-Disclosure

Definition: The process of communicating to others verbally and nonverbally our thoughts, feelings, attitudes, beliefs and values. It is taking our masks off and revealing to another person our "real" self

---

THE IMPORTANCE OF UNDERSTANDING SELF

Who am I?
How do I feel about myself?
Do I like (or dislike) parts of my personality or physical appearance?
Am I comfortable with myself?
How can I improve my communication both with myself and with others?

These questions are asked by everyone at some time in life. Many of us are confused over the issues of who we really are and the roles we are expected to play to gain societal or peer acceptance. We are frustrated by the demands of people around us who want us to behave according to their expectations of us and our own expectations of who we are and what we want to be.

Is it possible to know and like who we are, to get in touch with the "real me" buried underneath all the roles we are expected to play in order to be a functioning part of our culture? If it is possible, do we really want to know ourselves? To know and to let others truly know us demands taking risks and being vulnerable. Is it "safer" to live our lives meeting others' expectations and keeping the "real" us hidden from view?

And what does all of this have to do with communication? This, after all, is a book about communication—not psychology.

Here are some things to think about—from people much wiser than the authors of this book.

Honore De Balsac, the great French philosopher-historian, wrote, "Nothing is a greater impediment to being on good terms with others than being ill at ease with yourself."

With regard to meeting the expectations of others, Rabbi Mendel of Kotzk wrote:

> *If I am because I am I,*
> *And you are you because you are you,*
> *Then I am, and you are*
> *But if I am I because you are you,*
> *And you are you because I am I,*
> *Then I am not, and you are not.*

Eleanor Roosevelt, one of the greatest women in American history who survived a lifetime of people attempting to "put her down," wrote, "No one can make you feel inferior without your consent."

Some things to think about? We hope this chapter will give you some answers to the questions we have asked above—and the encouragement to find out and let others know who you really are.

BARRIERS TO UNDERSTANDING SELF

There are real barriers put in place by others and ourselves to our getting to know, accept and like ourselves. Some of them are:

Our confusion between the types of roles we play—those personality roles where we have the right to determine the way the role is played and those performance roles where others have the right to define some of the parameters.

Our fear of risking letting others know what we are truly thinking and feeling because if we do "they" might not like us anymore.

Our willingness to change. Even if where we are hurts we sometimes view change as worse than the pain and loneliness we are currently feeling.

Our practice of comparing ourselves with others—not recognizing that when we do that, we automatically make ourselves into losers.

Our problems with accepting ourselves as we are—zits and all—learning that there are some things about ourselves that we cannot change. And that we might just as well learn to accept those things (and maybe like and use them!).

Our false modesty that does not allow us to rejoice in our own uniqueness and to define, refine and emphasize our strong qualities and attributes.

Our failure to prescribe and follow plans which help us to change those things about ourselves that we can change and want to change.

I open myself up to you,
   so you may see inside:
   the past scars
   and present pains.

I place myself before you
   with nothing left to hide:
   no secrets
   or hidden remains.

I present myself to you,
   a package deal:
   the good and strong—
   the weak.

I ask you to accept me,
   for being real:
   your understanding nod
   is all I seek.

By permission, Denelle Hobbs

LET'S FACE IT: DO WE NEED OUR MASKS?

Leo F. Buscaglia

I have saved a letter sent to me some years ago that was signed "Anonymous." It expresses something that most of us have experienced at one time or another.

It was about the disguises and masks we wear when trying to be like someone else—someone we think others will like more than the "real" us. It was about pretending to be what we're not and hating ourselves for it. The person wrote:

"I'm not even sure who the real me is anymore. I always give the impression that I've got it all together, that I'm in control, that I don't need anyone. But it's only a facade. I see this not only in myself but in others as well. Why can't we take off the masks and really get to know one another?"

After reading the letter I figured that anyone could have written it. These were not the desperate words of an individual without hope. Rather, it was someone seeking the basic human assurances that he is worth something and that others will value him once the mask has fallen; that they will accept and understand him because they are wrestling with similar doubts and fears.

Some of us feel we must always appear to be in control. We disguise confusion and loneliness, dreading the thought that someone might discover the real us and expose our well-guarded weaknesses. At one time or another we have all felt deeply afraid that we will not be loved or taken seriously or, worse, that we'll be laughed at.

To play it safe, we slip into disguises and act out roles. Perhaps your role is to appear nonchalant and sophisticated, airs you hope will shield you from those who take the time to look more deeply.

But if we're honest with ourselves, we will realize that what we need most is for someone to see through the pretense and discover the real us. We need each other's sensitivity, sympathy and understanding to help us overcome our panic and uncertainty. Given a chance, there are many who would be happy to listen and help—and proud of the fact that they were trusted enough to be consulted. What a wonderful discovery it is to find that love is stronger than walls and locked doors.

We don't need masks when we are with people whose love we are sure of: We know they'll love us in spite of our weaknesses. It's the rest of the world we're unsure of and feel we must fool.

Funny thing is, the person we are trying to cover up is exactly the person others want to know. The real person is far better than anything we can concoct. What a tragedy that so many withhold their most precious gift—the unique, undiluted self.

We learn, however, that those self-protective walls we erect become less and less a barrier in the presence of people who try to know us as we really are. And for our part, we must be willing to take a chance on people we hold at arm's length. We must be willing to rip off our masks with determination and say, "Here I am. This is the real me, flaws and all." As Emerson once wrote, "Insist on yourself." Only then can you be the person you are and the person you hope to be.

By permission, Leo F. Buscaglia

SELF-RESPECT AT ROOT OF RELATIONSHIPS

Leo F. Buscaglia

Acclaimed French writer Georges Bernanos wrote, "The supreme grace would be to love ourselves."

Strange how this powerful statement causes many people to take exception. We think of loving ourselves as an immature, egotistical state, hardly one of grace. We seldom consider that only those who have a secure knowledge of self and a sense of personal dignity can share with others, fight the good fight or dare to love.

A letter I received recently represented a sad example of what a negative self-image can do to a person. The writer, a man in his 40s, explained that he had nothing to live for, let alone celebrate.

"I've never been much good," he wrote. "My parents always told me I wouldn't amount to much. Here I am, 40 years old, a nothing." That is heavy baggage to carry around for a lifetime.

I read recently that before the average child finishes elementary school he or she has heard thousands of *nos, can'ts, nevers, you're stupids* and *shut ups*. No wonder some of us grow up thinking of the world as a forbidding place.

Respect for self is like a delicate plant—it requires careful nurturing to grow. Because none of us are sure of ourselves all the time, we need the support of others who affirm our self-worth and who bring out our best.

A little love, the assurance that we are cared for, the knowledge that we are accepted for our imperfect selves—these are the things we need for a secure, healthy self-image. To know that we have the support of others gives us the courage to risk.

In addition, we need a sense of our own importance, to feel that we have worth and are not simply another statistic to be counted and then overlooked.

We feel our uniqueness when people spend the time to listen and are careful not to minimize our feelings and our ideas. It is necessary to feel that we are important to others, a priority in their lives, not merely a convenience. A friend once confided that she often felt that her husband could get what he required from her

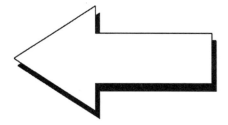 Everyone is a moon and has a dark side which he never shows to anybody.
—*M. Twain*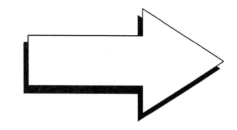

by hiring a part-time housekeeper and an occasional companion.

We learn how to value ourselves from role models—others who believe in themselves and what they have to offer. They help us to see and better understand our own value and the need to share it with others.

I have a friend who is always exciting to be with. Her joy in life and respect for others is contagious. It is amazing to see how others respond to her positive nature. She leaves people smiling or laughing and generally feeling better about themselves. She goes out of her way to compliment someone because she knows how good it makes them feel. "It only takes a moment," she says.

People with low self-esteem feel that they are alone in their misery—the only ones who are unloved or unsupported. It helps to realize that no one is free from suffering, disappointment or failure. It will help if they can understand that pain and disappointment often trigger opportunities for growth. Our greatest survivors admit to histories of failures, tears, fears and uncertainties, but they can also relate how they rose above them.

There are times when no one seems to see any good in us and we accept their verdict, forgetting that we need our own reassurances when others do not supply them. A list of the positive qualities about ourselves might be helpful at such a time. We're often surprised, and maybe even impressed, to see how long the list is. We may also discover how regularly we fail to give ourselves due credit.

We can only give to others what we ourselves have. If we wish to spread joy, understanding, acceptance and love, we must have them first.

To love oneself is the best foundation. After all, there is so much to love. Each of us is unique. Each of us is needed. We have the power to make the world a better place. There is so much we have to offer. There is so much about ourselves to love.

LEADING A GOOD LIFE NOT A CONTEST FOR POPULARITY

Leo F. Buscaglia

I was recently a guest on a national television talk show that encouraged audience participation. A woman in the audience impatiently awaited her opportunity to comment. When it was her turn to speak, she stood and ventilated her not-so-favorable feelings toward me.

"I don't believe you're for real," she said. "People aren't the way you say they are. Anyone who talks about love and goodness all the time is stupid or phony."

Some in the audience were vocal in their opposition to her statement, some were in agreement. It did not matter. I told her that I long ago gave up the notion that I could (or should want to) please everyone. I've learned to be comfortable with the idea that not everyone will like me or believe in what I do.

There are those who spend years agonizing over the fact that another person may not like us or is offended by something we said or did. Some of us even become what we think others want us to be in order not to offend. We tailor our personalities, our conversation, our behavior to suit others. There are those who make such a studied effort to do this that they begin to lose sight of who they are.

Acting the way you believe others would like you to behave does not win friends. We become indifferent to someone who wants to please all the people all the time. (I would prefer to have someone dislike me rather than be indifferent to me.) Sometimes we have to put ourselves on the line at the risk of alienating others. In the end it is better than the possibility of being alienated from ourselves.

Don't confuse others' disapproval of us with dislike. People are often more accepting and forgiving than we give them credit for. Those who like us and love us for who we are will give us the latitude to have different opinions and even be a real pain once in awhile. No friendship can be based on the assumption that "as long as you agree with me you are my friend." That is enslavement, not friendship.

We all like to make good impressions and have people like us, but why do we take rejection, no matter how mild, so seriously? Perhaps it is based on the false idea that someone else has the power to deprive us of love. Actually, that is something only we can do to ourselves. If artists and musicians and writers worried about being accepted or loved by everyone, they would cease to create.

It is enough that they are appreciated and that they feel the love and acceptance of some people. Whether we care to admit it, most of us respect individuals who say, "This is what I feel and I'd like to share it with you. If you like it I'm pleased, but even if you don't, I must continue to express these feelings."

I am not suggesting that we take a "who cares" attitude or be oblivious to how others feel about us. Such individuals are on one end of the scale and those who try to please everybody are at the other extreme. In between these two groups of individuals there is a healthy medium. We have a right and responsibility to be ourselves without worrying whether we are winning friends or influencing people.

THE TWELVE YEAR PUT-DOWN

One of the great challenges faced by teachers of college freshmen and sophomores is the large number of these students who feel that they are inadequate human beings. It is not difficult to understand why so many of our students feel this way, when you stop to realize that they have been taught to feel exactly so for twelve long years.

The tragedy of American education is that even our best students usually receive an essentially remedial education. In most U.S. classrooms, at whatever level of schooling, the student is perceived to be in a state of ignorance which must be remedied. By exposing young people in our society to a mandatory twelve years of being thus perceived, we assure the creation of an inferior citizenry. For whatever else our young people learn in this system, they tend to learn to perceive themselves as inferior.

Put yourself in the college freshman's shoes: "For twelve years you have gone to school to be told what you do wrong! Your grades were determined by your errors. A low grade resulted whenever your errors were abundant. A high grade resulted from a notable lack of error. After twelve years in a system which has assumed your ignorance and emphasized your errors, you now probably feel quite inferior. By essentially assuming your incompetence for twelve years, the education system has gone a long way toward assuring your incompetence, because you have formed your self-image from those images of your self which have been most persistently communicated to you by the system in which you operate. Twelve years in a system of negative reinforcement have tended to make you a master of the art of feeling inferior."

By permission, Noel McInnis; © Environment for Learning, 1970, Aspen, CO, 81611

If . . .

If a child lives with criticism, he learns to condemn.
If a child lives with hostility, he learns to fight.
If a child lives with fears, he learns to be apprehensive.
If a child lives with pity, he learns to feel sorry for himself.
If a child lives with jealousy, he learns to feel guilty.
If a child lives with encouragement, he learns to be confident.
If a child lives with tolerance, he learns to be patient.
If a child lives with praise, he learns to be appreciative.
If a child lives with acceptance, he learns to love.
If a child lives with approval, he learns to like himself.
If a child lives with recognition, he learns to have a goal.
If a child lives with fairness, he learns what justice is.
If a child lives with honesty, he learns what truth is.
If a child lives with security, he learns to have faith in himself and in those about him.
If a child lives with friendliness, he learns that the world is a good place in which to live.

The Watchman-Examiner
By permission, Harper & Row, Publishers, *The Treasure Chest, The Watchman-Examiner*

ON BEING PERSUADED WHO YOU ARE

Based on a Talk at Fullerton State College in 1973 Which He Sent to the Newsletter on the Day He Died

Sidney M. Jourard

Introduction

Man is a mystery, not a problem. The proper stance before a mystery is to open oneself respectfully to its disclosure. A problem is only to be solved. Man is not a problem to be solved, though there are those who view him as such.

A mystery is indefinable. So is man. But there are those who seek to define and describe man's "essence." The peculiarity of man is that, whatever his "essence" might be, it does not determine what he can do with it. Human beings stand before their own substance in the way an artist encounters his paint and canvas—it is up to him to create something of original beauty, or of banality, out of the material at hand. A person will make of his situation what he *believes* is possible.

Belief is the outcome of having been convinced that something is the case. Human beings believe they can and cannot do, can and cannot overcome, can and cannot become, what *someone* has persuaded them is their nature.

On Being Shaped to Conform to an Image

When we come into the world we are the embodiment of incredible possibilities. The various "agencies of socialization," family, school, mass media, shape our growth and development, so that at any given moment in time, like right now, each of us is involved in a repertoire of social roles—sex, age, family and occupational roles—which fits the social system. Spokesmen for the ruling minority try to persuade the majority into believing that they are living in a utopia. This utopia, this good society, this best of all possible societies in the history of mankind, the one in which we are living right now, is not seen as a utopia by blacks, nor women, or by young people between the ages of 14 and 22. It turns out to be a utopia primarily for men in positions of power, who have been schooled in the world outlook of Orange County, California, who are over the age of 40. Orange County is a state of mind rather than a geographical site. White South Africa is like that—not a utopia for most of its citizens. How do you persuade the people for whom a place is not a utopia that it is a utopia? There are three techniques—lying or mystification, bribery and threats. I will discuss some of the ways in which these techniques have been used to maintain the status quo.

Organized religion has traditionally functioned to bribe people with promises of a better life in the hereafter, and to somehow persuade them that you render unto Caesar the things that are Caesar's, and that you render unto God the things that are God's. One of the things that you are not supposed to do is to criticize the way your society is organized. Hardly any of the organized Protestant, Catholic or other churches have been at the vanguard in the history of the western world's liberal or revolutionary movements. It's much more common for the churches to be in direct collusion with the power structure, the military and with the large economic interests. I remember in May, in the *Gainesville Sun,* a small town university newspaper, there was a little article explaining that over 300 million dollars of the endowments of the four or five major Protestant churches of the United States were invested in stocks, in prime war industries and nobody

By permission, Sidney M. Jourard; Association for Humanistic Psychology, January, 1975.

seemed to bat an eye. Of course, the Vietnam war was on. As I reviewed the situation, I realized we've got to broaden our conceptions of space and time, and ways to live life.

Billions of dollars are spent every year in the United States for elementary schools, high schools, colleges and universities. These schools exist to induce a respect, a love and a passion for truth, justice and beauty in the people who go through them. But all that happens is that you socialize Americans. There's a difference between a typical product of our school systems and someone who is committed, passionately, to truth, beauty and justice.

If we spend 8 billion dollars on these institutions, considerably more billions are spent on advertising, the aim of which is to get people to be functionally decorticated so that they can't tell the difference between real value and sham. I consider this absurd. It's almost like the scene in *Catch-22* where a patient was encased in plaster; the nurses would pour fluids in at the top and drain them out at the bottom, and then change the bottles around without even recognizing that the man had been dead for some time. Television, radio and movies also mystify us. Even Dick Tracy and Little Orphan Annie tell their readers how to be. We have been *persuaded* to become, and then be, the kind of person we now are.

On Being Persuaded and Convinced

How have you been persuaded to be you? I mentioned two ways. Bribes of affection and material goods from parents and other agents of socialization. And threats: if you don't stay the way you now are, something awful will happen to you—criticism, prison or mental hospital.

Hypnosis is a kind of persuasion. I actually prefer words like persuasion, convincing and rhetoric, because those terms belong in everyday life. Hypnosis is thought to be an esoteric practice, or a highly specialized medical technique. But there is a sense in which conventional medical healing with drugs and surgery is a kind of convincing. All psychotherapies are a kind of persuasion, as are education and socialization. There are obvious and subtle ways of getting you *to be* in the way that *some-*

body thinks you are. And so we push the question right back: Where did you ever get the idea that you are who you now are? How were you persuaded, seduced and bribed to be that way? The subtlest way in which we are convinced of our identity is other people's views of us, the attributions that they make. The descriptions that are laid on you are a very subtle kind of hypnosis. Here is another kind of hypnosis: Your mother says, "Be sure you have one bowel movement a day or else you'll feel sluggish. Be very sure you always put on rubbers when it rains because you know you are vulnerable to colds." You then miss going to the toilet, and feel sluggish. Every time it rains, if you don't wear a scarf and rubbers you come down with a terrible cold. Your physiology has been invented by your mother. There is a sense, then, in which we are *somebody's* invention. It is very illuminating, and sometimes shocking, sometimes hilarious, to reflect on yourself and your situation and raise the question anew: "Where did I ever get the idea that I had to be this way, or that my situation is this way?" You discover that the script for your action and physiology was written by your mother, your father, a school teacher and your younger brother. They defined you, and here you are.

On Being Convinced One Is Sick and/or Crazy

We are who somebody persuaded us to be. If you are persuaded that you are out of your mind, you may begin to believe that you are mentally sick. If you believe you are mentally sick, you feel you must go to an expert on mental sickness. Consider a college student, a young man 20 years old. He discovers his father is a bore and something of a pompous ass. His mother is a silly chatterbox and he decides to spend little time in their company because it's not very rewarding. He learns Transcendental Meditation and begins to practice it. He starts to smoke marijuana in secret with some classmates. His parents say, "You're really acting strangely. Let's take you to the doctor. You haven't had a checkup for quite some time." (Everybody is persuaded that if they do not consult a doctor twice a year, they may have contracted a terminal illness. A child is taken to the pediatrician every two weeks to be weighed; if he's got an ear, nose or throat infection, he's got to get penicillin. He becomes hooked. He becomes a doctor addict, very early, and he gets withdrawal symptoms.) The student is sent to a psychiatrist, who says, "What originally was a schizoid tendency, a tendency to withdraw, has now escalated into a full-blown episode of catatonic schizophrenia. For his own good the lad ought to be taken to a state hospital." He is sent there and given electroshock and thorazine. By the time he comes out, his kidneys are ruined, he has a haircut, he has put on weight, he starts drinking beer again and he no longer sits in that frightening way in his room all alone, silent.

Every perspective other than the one regarded as sane and proper is regarded as sick and crazy. Sanity and propriety in people are defined by people in power. So that, in a sense, if a person does not share the orthodox view of the good society and of how men, women, children ought to be, then he is invalidated, not listened to. Martha Mitchell was possibly one of the most honest persons in direct touch with the Watergate scandals, but an effort was made to regard her as mentally ill in order to discredit her testimony. The perspective or testimony of a child about adults is usually discredited. For a long time the perspective and testimony of blacks about our racism was discredited. The view of women was long discredited. When the discredited people consented to be ignored, the social system did not change because it was a utopia for its leaders.

On Being a Prophet

In the midst of the darkness and suffering which is the experience of the majority of the people and other living creatures around the world, there arise prophets, people who envision another way for the human situation to be. Life itself, in the present and in the times that follow, is the test of prophecy and the prophet. By prophets I don't mean people who foretell the future, but people who see the connections between present ways in which life is lived and society is organized and consequences that everybody agrees are bad, such as war, physi-

cal disease, psychological breakdown, emptiness of existence, suffering, exploitation, destruction of the environment and so on. It takes a prophet to disengage, in order to see the connection between the way life is lived and those consequences. And it then **calls** for imagination—the ability to envision, to break the hypnotic spell of now, in order to be a prophet. I'll mention some people whom I have regarded as prophets, so as to clarify any definitions of the prophetic function. The Old Testament prophets like Moses, Isaiah, Jeremiah, Amos, fit my criteria of a prophet. Karl Marx, Sigmund Freud and Ronald Laing are all prophets. B. F. Skinner is a prophet in so far as he envisioned *Walden Two,* a kind of utopia organized on the principles of operant conditioning. Hugh Hefner, founder of the Playboy empire, is in some ways a prophet. A. H. Maslow was a prophet, as were Jung and Reich. The founders of Black Liberation and Women's Liberation can be regarded as prophets. The founders of Synanon, Alcoholics Anonymous and Weight Watchers likewise have served a prophetic function in modern times. Questions I ask of any prophet are: Does he or she enlighten other people? Does this prophet challenge people to grow, to make the most out of the flexibility that inheres in man and his situation, or do these prophets invite passivity, stupidity, stupefaction and blind faith? Does following the prophet's way increase capacity for dialogue, empathy, love? Is life enhanced in the person and all whom he contacts?

On Getting Out

When man finds his situation intolerable, he seeks ways to alter it. This calls for a perspective which usually is difficult to obtain. So compelling and hypnotic is the present definition of the situation, that for millennia man left his situation, either literally, by a voyage, or metaphorically through assorted disengagement disciplines. Why? In order to get a fresh perspective on the intolerable situation that he left. Throughout history there are many myths that express this way to a new life. One of my favorite myths is the *Odyssey,* which I see as an allegory of personal growth. It is about a situation that was once life-giving but became stifling and stagnant. In order to make it fit to live in; the hero had to leave, open himself up, enlarge his awareness of human possibilities and possibilities of the world, and then to return. It is most peculiar that in this society, to transcend one's situation, to get out of one's situation, is one of the worst crimes against the status quo; everything is done to prevent it. When people do disengage, they frequently become terrified. A role affects not only your action, but also your experience. And in order to feel like a son, a mother, or a father, you have to repress most of your possibilities of imagining, thinking, remembering, feeling and perceiving. To disengage from the role is to unrepress those possibilities of experiencing. If you have been led to believe that deeply buried in every man is a sewer of filth, rape and murder, that is exactly what you will find when you unrepress.

Powerful pressures prevent a person from getting out, but there are other ways. A voyage is a good way to disengage from your roles in your situation. Yoga and all of the other meditative disciplines are likewise ways of disengagement. In order to truly get *into* meditation, you've got to get *out* of your roles. You can't get into a Hatha yoga posture until you can disengage and uncommit your musculature from the way it has been committed to allow you to be in your usual roles in your daily situations.

Religious ritual, when it is authentic, is a way to disengage a person from his secular roles and activities in order to transform consciousness. The way *of being* that is described in the Old Testament and to some extent in the New Testament, and the way of the Buddha are all "ways out." If a person lives in those ways, he will indeed change his consciousness of his situation, and he will change his body, because to get *into* those ways means getting *out* of your usual roles. An encounter with death, to realize that you are finite, can yield new ways to see one's situation. Professor Bill Soskin believes that John the Baptist nearly drowned those whom he submerged; the encounter with death made it possible for his disciples to feel reborn. Psychotherapy can be away out. It can invite a person out of his roles into new experience which can be both enthralling and se-

ductive. There are some people who never leave psychotherapy. And it is also terrifying for many; for a good psychotherapist invites a person, at his own pace, to disengage from his usual ways of being himself. And as I say, it's exhilarating or seductive. Encounter groups at growth centers where for a weekend, a week or a month you are bombarded with honesty, but more important, acceptance, can make a person get out of his usual roles in a way that is almost exhilarating. It produces a "high" that is astonishing. And, then, so there are people who go to growth centers and they never leave. And I suspect that something of the same sort has happened in eastern ashrams where you go and you never want to leave, for your way of being there seems so much more safe, meaningful, lifegiving and enlivening than your life back home. But I'm biased; I take that to be undialectical, a kind of idolatry. Anything that is idolatrously pursued is destructive of life. To hang on to a high is destructive. Trying to stay out is destructive, just as trying to stay in is destructive. Idolatry of the status quo is destructive. Then comes the hard part; the hard part is the return.

The Return

Personal growth, and fulfillment of lifegiving possibilities in the human situation, calls for new, more viable visions of the good world, the good society and the good life. This fulfillment of the possibilities in the human situation requires a *return* to what one takes to be his home, to make it fit for life. Where is home? Home is not only a piece of geography; it is the roles that you have left. On returning home changed, a voyager may find himself invited to be the person he was when he left. The others may refuse to accept and confirm the changes. To accept this invitation is to invalidate one's growth. Odysseus returned to Ithaca and, to make his home fit for him, he slaughtered his wife's suitors and buried his father. He married off his son and established dominion over his kingdom. This is an allegorical way of saying he had grown. He was a bit bloody, but he had grown larger. The return is hardly ever easy.

Some Techniques That Can Help You . . .
TURN A DRAWBACK INTO A STRENGTH

Dr. Joyce Brothers

Do you feel that you would like life—and yourself—better if you changed some of your ways? For example, would you prefer not to be late for appointments? Or to be neater and better organized? Or not to swear? Then change! You can.

The tools I am about to give you will help you make small improvements in how you respond to others and how you feel about yourself. Do not plan on a major transformation.

Most people are far better than they believe. Their discontent with themselves usually is provoked by a psychological "splinter"—a self-defeating behavior or attitude—or two. Like the pain of a festering splinter in your foot, such a behavior claims your attention until it's removed and the infection is treated.

The rewards can be great for your efforts to heal and change. But be assured: Such alteration won't cause upheaval. Your everyday life will remain on an even keel and will be protected from extremes. There is a natural tendency that works to pull you toward that middle ground—between excess and deficit—where health and happiness reign. This point differs for each of us, so try to find your own middle ground and do not try to conform to an arbitrary norm.

Here are some psychological diagnostic and behavior-modification techniques to help you. Together with the Ripple Effect and the Halo Effect—psychological phenomena that accompany change—they form a Psychological Tool Kit you can use for the rest of your life.

Let's start the healing/changing process:

List Techniques. To change an undesirable trait, you must zero in on *exactly* what it is you need to change. My "List Techniques" will help you. They have led people to discover that traits they'd considered faults were not faults at all. Sometimes they found that they did not even *have* traits they'd been told (and believed) they had!

That happens because much of how you see yourself is made up of perceptions—often faulty—that others have of you. As a youngster, you may have been told that you were shy or thoughtless or selfish. Repeatedly hearing these "truths," you now *believe* them, even though you may be just the opposite. Words can be as abusive as physical blows—and their effect can last a lifetime.

The tools I offer are designed to help you cut away such false perceptions and uncover the real you, with all your actual qualities—best and worst. Your "scalpel" is the Basic Diagnostic List. It yields a thumbnail psychological profile of the *real* you. All you need is pencil and paper. Only you will see it, so be completely truthful.

Basic Diagnostic List

1. Best qualities
2. Worst qualities
3. Goals

Make your list at about the same time and day each week for three consecutive weeks. Always fill in all three categories. Finish the list at the end of the week. Put it away. Don't look at the list again till the fourth week, then compare all three. Were there changes from week to week, either in your goals or the qualities you listed—or in how you positioned them? This happens as new insight is gained. Analyze the changes.

The weekly intervals for the lists are important: Daily, both your conscious and your unconscious will be at work, questioning: *Is* honesty your best quality? *Are* you pushy? Is it really *your* goal to be a space pioneer?

On the fourth week, work on your Master List—a synthesis of your first three lists. Study your lists. Write down your qualities (strongest first) and your goals in order of their importance.

Give most weight to your third-week list—it probably is closest to the real you. Are your qualities and goals compatible with how you are and how you want to be? Even a "best" quality can be self-defeating. For example, you might list "to win elective office" as your goal and "willingness to speak my mind" among your best qualities. Savvy politicians will tell you that, at times, silence is wisdom for them.

How Josie did it. You should easily be able to identify self-defeating traits. Josie did. The production chief at a factory, she was one of the few women—and the only female executive—in the company. The CEO was considering firing Josie because of her abrasive manner and nasty temper.

Josie told me she was neither angry nor abrasive: "I just act that way, because these guys are bone-lazy." But she agreed to do the diagnostic lists. Josie's Third-Week Diagnostic List Worst qualities:

1) Hot temper
2) Bossy
3) Worrier

Josie's Fourth-Week Master List

Best qualities:
1) Work hard
2) Efficient
3) Plan ahead

Goals:
1) Marriage
2) More money
3) Promotion

Her top two faults were related, and that allowed her to tackle them both at once. Josie confessed shock at finding that a hair-trigger temper *was* her worst quality. She came to realize how often she lost her temper because, she said, she found herself thinking about her lists daily, searching for accuracy in diagnosing her best and worst qualities and how they affected her goals.

"Josie, your best qualities are fine assets for an executive," I said. "They should help you get the money and promotion you want. In your worst qualities, you list 'worrier.' But worrying is one aspect of planning. And you list your ability to 'plan ahead' as one of your best traits. And it *is* valuable if not carried to extremes.

"In terms of your job—or any human relationship—your quick temper and bossiness are self-defeating," I continued. "But if reined in, they have positive aspects. Take bossiness: If you can direct people, deal with them fairly and consistently, and get the desired results, your bossiness becomes an asset. But being brusque and using anger to spur them, as you do, is self-defeating. Accurately, you place your hot temper at the head of your list of worst qualities. It *is* the leading problem.

"An occasional, well-controlled, well-chosen show of anger can be a true management asset. But choose the time and place carefully, and know what you want to accomplish.

"Josie," I added, "your top-ranked goal is marriage. But you did not list a single quality conducive to an intimate relationship: Who wants a bossy, hot-tempered, worrywart wife? Where are warmth, understanding and humor? They are as important to your career as to an intimate relationship."

Josie used the psychological tools I gave her and, with the aid of the Ripple Effect and the Halo Effect, turned her self-defeating temper into an asset.

The Ripple Effect describes how one small change in behavior or attitude sets ripples into action, radiating out further and further until even a minor change affects every aspect of your life. It is a very powerful mechanism of gradual change. It took Josie's peers and subordinates a while to alter their view of her, but when they saw that she was reining in her temper, they be came more receptive and less resentful.

"I explode every now and then," Josie says. "But I've thought it out first. I know what I want to achieve."

The Halo Effect refers to the disproportionate effect of first impressions—bad or good. If people meeting women or men for the first time consider them beautiful or handsome or charming (or the opposite), that's how they will see them in future meetings. The Halo Effect doesn't come from looks only. It also can come from the first impression made by your telephone voice, stationery, the car you drive. If people know that you know the President of the United States, a positive Halo Effect for you is established, sight unseen. A positive Halo Effect gets you off on the right foot. *If you measure up* to that first good impression, you are on the way to reaching your goal, whatever it is.

There can be a negative Halo Effect too. If, say, the attractive woman they found charming and witty at first later impresses them as dull, those same admirers will begin to see her as even *less* intelligent than she really is.

A negative Halo Effect can be erased, but it takes time. Studies show that it takes seven or eight subsequent meetings to undo a bad first impression.

Using the List Techniques, Josie managed to identify and alter her self-defeating traits and to overcome their resultant negative Halo Effect. With the aid of the Ripple Effect, she got promoted, got more money and, when I saw her last, was getting nearer to building an intimate relationship.

Reinforcement Techniques. Reinforcement—reward and punishment—helps you fine-tune your life.

- *Positive reinforcement*—reward—encourages a behavior. In *huge doses,* it is good medicine for changing your own behavior.

It's a fact: If you try to change a behavior, you will feel a loss. It's vital to replace that negative with a positive—to give yourself a pat on the back every time you get through a day without doing whatever you are trying not to do: nagging, swearing, biting your nails. Paste a gold star on the calendar and set aside money for tickets to the theater or to a big game.

- *Negative reinforcement*—punishment—is a short-term technique, usually physical, that *discourages* a behavior (chiefly your own). When you lapse into a self-defeating trait while trying to modify it, remind yourself that you want to change. Do so by pinching yourself or wearing a loose rubber band that snaps stingingly at your inner wrist if you pull it. Administer the pinch or sting the *instant* you realize that you've fallen into the old habit. (Maybe you've just dropped clothing on a chair instead of hanging it neatly in the closet, or you've cussed though you want to stop swearing.) The pinch or sting punishes the bad behavior and helps you to reaffirm your goal.

The Reinforcement List. This is your final reinforcement aid. On it, write the whens, whys and effects of your self-defeating trait. Use a notebook that tucks easily into purse or pocket.

1. *Daily record.* Jot down *every time* the unwanted trait or attitude that you are trying to modify crops up. Write the time and the circumstances in your notebook. Entries should be brief.
2. *End-of-day evaluation.* Write answers to the questions that apply:
   a. Did I gain anything when I did this? If so, what?
   b. Did I lose anything when I did this? If so, what?
   c. Could I have handled the situation another way? If so, how?
   d. How did it make me feel?
   e. How might it make others feel?

Evaluate your progress weekly to see what patterns emerge. Nightly, after you have written your evaluations, read them aloud.

3. *Give yourself a dose of positive reinforcement before you go to sleep.* Tell yourself. "I've made real progress in the last two days." Or: "I know I'm going to reach my goal." (Say whatever is positive and encouraging.)

Stand before a mirror and look yourself in the eye when you administer that dose of positive reinforcement.

4. *Look for a pattern.* Your Reinforcement List will reveal a pattern to when the self-defeating trait crops up. It might get the better of you at certain times. Once you have discovered this, you will find that altering the behavior will be easier.

Maintain your Reinforcement List for at least two months. If the unwanted behavior crops up again later, get out your notebook and work on your Reinforcement List for another month.

Rehearsal Techniques. *Acting As If* and *Previsualization* show you how to turn wishes into reality.

- *Acting As If* is self descriptive: Frightened? Act *as if* you are brave. Feel unattractive? Act *as if* you are beautiful or handsome. Eventually, your behavior will affect your feelings. Never fear: Your inner core will not change. You simply want to tweak your behavior, so it won't be a barrier between you and the world.

- *Previsualization* is a kind of mental rehearsal that can make *Acting As If* easier. You visualize doing exactly what you wish to do and *how* you do it—succeeding despite some obstacles. This paves the way for when you *actually* do it—and succeed.

Note: Dr. Mark Rogers is the anesthesiologist who in 1987 led the team that performed the first successful surgical separation of Siamese twins joined at the head. He later said he had visualized *every step* of the 22-hour operation for five months to prepare himself.

At bedtime tonight, visualize coping with some task or situation, using the behavior you'd *like* to have. The desired behavior seems to become established while you sleep.

First, relax. Then visualize the situation that concerns you. Nervous about giving a speech? Visualize yourself actually giving it. See each detail. Walk to the podium and shake hands with the person who introduces you, all the while *acting as if* you are filled with confidence and skill. Look out at the audience. Say your words. Hear the rousing applause. Smile. Bow.

Repeat the process as if you were viewing a film starring yourself. Don't omit a single step. Now, go to sleep. Let your unconscious work for you.

Remember: You are not trying to stamp out that trait or behavior. You are just trying to rein it in so that it is no longer a roadblock keeping you from happiness and success.

A FUZZY TALE

Claude M. Steiner, Ph.D.

Once upon a time, a long time ago, there lived two very happy people called Tim and Maggie with two children called John and Lucy. To understand how happy they were, you have to understand how things were in those days. You see, in those days everyone was given at birth a small, soft, Fuzzy Bag. Anytime a person reached into this bag he was able to pull out a Warm Fuzzy. Warm Fuzzies were very much in demand because whenever somebody was given a Warm Fuzzy it made him feel warm and fuzzy all over. People who didn't get Warm Fuzzies regularly were in danger of developing a sickness in their back which caused them to shrivel up and die.

In those days it was very easy to get Warm Fuzzies. Anytime that somebody felt like it, he might walk up to you and say, "I'd like to have a Warm Fuzzy." You would then reach into your bag and pull out a Fuzzy the size of a little girl's hand. As soon as the Fuzzy saw the light of day it would smile and blossom into a large, shaggy, Warm Fuzzy. You then would lay it on the person's shoulder or head or lap and it would snuggle up and melt right against their skin and make them feel good all over. People were always asking each other for Warm Fuzzies, and since they were always given freely, getting enough of them was never a problem. There were always plenty to go around, and as a consequence everyone was happy and felt warm and fuzzy most of the time.

One day a bad witch became angry because everyone was so happy and no one was buying potions and salves. The witch was very clever and devised a wicked plan. One beautiful morning the witch crept up to Tim while Maggie was playing with their daughter and whispered in his ear, "See here, Tim, look at all the Fuzzies that Maggie is giving to Lucy. You know, if she keeps it up, eventually she is going to run out and then there won't be any left for you!"

Tim was astonished. He turned to the witch and said, "Do you mean to tell me that there isn't a Warm Fuzzy in our bag every time we reach into it?"

And the witch said, "No, absolutely not, and once you run out, that's it. You don't have any more." With this the witch flew away on a broom, laughing and cackling all the way.

Tim took this to heart and began to notice every time Maggie gave up a Warm Fuzzy to somebody else. Eventually he got very worried and upset because he liked Maggie's Warm Fuzzies very much and did not want to give them up. He certainly did not think it was right for Maggie to be spending all her warm Fuzzies on the children and on other people. He began to complain every time he saw Maggie giving a Warm Fuzzy to somebody else, and because Maggie liked him very much, she stopped giving Warm Fuzzies to other people as often, and reserved them for him.

The children watched this and soon began to get the idea that it was wrong to give up Warm Fuzzies any time you were asked or felt like it. They too became very careful. They would watch their parents closely and whenever they felt that one of their parents was giving too many Warm Fuzzies to others, they also began to object. They began to feel worried whenever they gave away too many Warm Fuzzies. Even though they found a Warm Fuzzy every time they reached into their bag, they reached in less and less and became more and more stingy. Soon people began to notice the lack of Warm Fuzzies, and they began to feel less warm and less fuzzy. They began to shrivel up and, occasionally, people would die from lack of Warm Fuzzies. More and more people went to the witch to buy potions and salves even though they didn't seem to work.

Well, the situation was getting very serious indeed. The bad witch who had been watching all of this didn't really want the people to die (since dead people couldn't buy his salves and potions), so a new plan was devised. Everyone was given a bag that was very similar to the Fuzzy Bag except that this one was cold while the Fuzzy Bag was warm. Inside of the witch's bag were Cold Pricklies. These Cold Pricklies did not make people feel warm and fuzzy, but made them feel cold and prickly instead. But, they did prevent peoples' backs from shriveling up. So, from then on, every time somebody said, "I want a Warm Fuzzy," people who were worried about depleting their supply would say, "I can't give you a Warm Fuzzy, but would you like a Cold Prickly?" Sometimes, two people would walk up to each other, thinking they could get a Warm Fuzzy, but one or the other of them would change their mind and they would wind up giving each other Cold Pricklies. So, the end result was that while very few people were dying, a lot of people were still unhappy and feeling very cold and prickly.

The situation got very complicated because, since the coming of the witch, there were less and less Warm Fuzzies around; so Warm Fuzzies, which used to be thought of as free as air, became extremely valuable. This caused people to do all sorts of things in order to obtain them. Before the witch had appeared, people used to gather in groups of three or four or five, never caring too much who was giving Warm Fuzzies to whom. After the coming of the witch, people began to pair off and to reserve all their Warm Fuzzies for each other exclusively. People who forgot themselves and gave a Warm Fuzzy to someone else would immediately feel guilty about it because they knew that their partner would probably resent the loss of a Warm Fuzzy. People who could not find a generous partner had to buy their Warm Fuzzies and had to work long hours to earn the money.

Some people somehow became "Popular" and got a lot of Warm Fuzzies without having to return them. These people would then sell these Warm Fuzzies to people who were "unpopular" and needed them to survive.

Another thing which happened was that some people would take Cold Pricklies—which were limitless and freely available—coat them white and fluffy and pass them on as Warm Fuzzies. These counterfeit Warm Fuzzies were really Plastic Fuzzies, and they caused additional difficulties. For instance, two people would get together and freely exchange Plastic Fuzzies, which presumably should have made them feel good, but they came away feeling bad instead. Since they thought they had been exchanging Warm Fuzzies, people grew very confused about this, never realizing that their cold prickly feelings were really the result of the fact they had been given a lot of Plastic Fuzzies.

So the situation was very, very dismal and it all started because of the coming of the witch who made people believe that some day, when least expected, they might reach into their Warm Fuzzy Bag and find no more.

Not long ago, a young woman with big hips born under the Sign of Aquarius came to this unhappy land. She seemed not to have heard about the bad witch and was not worried about running out of Warm Fuzzies. She gave them out freely, even when not asked. They called her the Hip Woman and disapproved of her because she was giving the children the idea that they should not worry about running out of Warm Fuzzies. The children liked her very much because they felt good around her and they began to give out Warm Fuzzies whenever they felt like it.

The grown-ups became concerned and decided to pass a law to protect the children from depleting their supplies of Warm Fuzzies. The law made it a criminal offense to give out Warm Fuzzies in a reckless manner, without a license. Many children, however, seemed not to care; and in spite of the law they continued to give each other Warm Fuzzies whenever they felt like it and always when asked. Because there were many, many children, almost as many as grown-ups, it began to look as if maybe they would have their way.

As of now it is hard to say what will happen. Will the grown-up forces of law and order stop the recklessness of the children? Are the grown-ups going to join with the Hip Woman and the children in taking a chance that there will always be as many Warm Fuzzies as needed? Will they remember the days their children are trying to bring back when Warm Fuzzies were abundant because people gave them away freely?

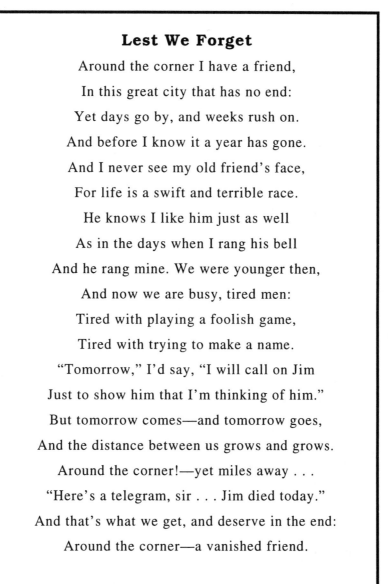

Lest We Forget

Around the corner I have a friend,

In this great city that has no end:

Yet days go by, and weeks rush on.

And before I know it a year has gone.

And I never see my old friend's face,

For life is a swift and terrible race.

He knows I like him just as well

As in the days when I rang his bell

And he rang mine. We were younger then,

And now we are busy, tired men:

Tired with playing a foolish game,

Tired with trying to make a name.

"Tomorrow," I'd say, "I will call on Jim

Just to show him that I'm thinking of him."

But tomorrow comes—and tomorrow goes,

And the distance between us grows and grows.

Around the corner!—yet miles away . . .

"Here's a telegram, sir . . . Jim died today."

And that's what we get, and deserve in the end:

Around the corner—a vanished friend.

—Charles Hanson Towne, quoted in *Wisconsin Odd Fellow*

WARM FUZZIES

PURPOSE: To learn how to give compliments or do something nice for other people and to record their reactions.

PROCEDURE: For this assignment, you are to give at least 10 warm fuzzies (compliments or actions) to 10 different people. Below, list the person you addressed, what you said or did and the reaction of the person receiving the warm fuzzy.

Person:
Warm Fuzzy:
Reaction:

Person:
Warm Fuzzy:
Reaction:

Person:
Warm Fuzzy:
Reaction:

Person:
Warm Fuzzy:
Reaction:

Person:
Warm Fuzzy:
Reaction:

Person:
Warm Fuzzy:
Reaction:

Person:
Warm Fuzzy:
Reaction:

Person:
Warm Fuzzy:
Reaction:

Person:
Warm Fuzzy:
Reaction:

Person:
Warm Fuzzy:
Reaction: ❑

WARM FUZZY BOMBARDMENT ————————

PURPOSE: To see how people respond to compliments.

PROCEDURE:
1. Divide into groups of five or six people.
2. Select a recorder—a person who will write down everything that is said to a particular individual.
3. Starting anywhere in the circle, one person will be focused upon. Once selected, the group will then start giving compliments to the "focused" person. The best way to do this is to simply go around the circle a few times.
4. After the person has received at least 10 compliments the recorder will hand them the written account of what just transpired. Then another person is selected to be the focus individual. This process will continue until everyone has been focused upon.

DISCUSSION:
1. How did you feel when you were the focus person?
2. Did you find it difficult to give compliments to other people?
3. Is giving compliments to other people a motivational skill?
4. In what aspects of your life can you employ what you did in this group? ❏

"Who Are You?"

"Who are you?" said the caterpillar. Alice replied rather shyly, "I-I hardly know, sir, just at present—at least I know who I was when I got up this morning, but I must have changed several times since then."

Lewis Carroll

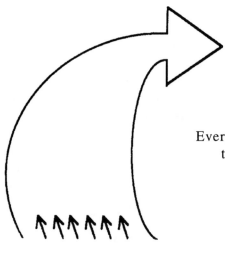

Everything that irritates us about others can lead us to an understanding of ourselves. —*C. Jung*

THE WAY WE SEE ME

PURPOSE: To compare the way you see yourself with the way others see you.

PROCEDURE: 1. Give copies of the questionnaire on the next pages to some of your relatives or friends.
               2. Answer The Way We See Me Questionnaire as the items apply to you.
               3. Take time to compare your questionnaire with each person who answered one.

DISCUSSION: 1. What similarities did you notice among all questionnaire responses? Why?
               2. What differences did you notice among all questionnaire responses? Why?
               3. What did you learn about yourself from this activity?
               4. What effect do our various perceptions of one another have on interpersonal communication? ❑

THE WAY WE SEE ME QUESTIONNAIRE

As part of a class assignment, I am distributing this questionnaire to some of my relatives and friends. It is designed to give me your impressions of my personality. I am attempting to compare the way other people see me with the way I see myself. While it may be difficult for you to express your impressions exactly, I would appreciate as frank a rating as you can give me.

This questionnaire should not take long to complete. First, try to construct an overall view of your impressions about my personality before answering the specific questions. Consider each item briefly and indicate the first choice that occurs to you. If you come to an item which you feel unable to answer with certainty, place a question mark, instead of a check, in one of the spaces to indicate a guess. However, please do answer every question. If you have comments that will help explain any of your answers, please use the space provided or write in the margins. Explanatory comments will be appreciated.

Please begin by considering my main strengths and weaknesses. Describe each as carefully as you can in the spaces below:

Main Strengths:

Main Weaknesses:

How well do the following words apply to me?

	Not at all	Slightly	Moderately	Rather well	Extremely well
Self-confident	( )	( )	( )	( )	( )
Tactful	( )	( )	( )	( )	( )
Irritable	( )	( )	( )	( )	( )
Quiet	( )	( )	( )	( )	( )
Emotionally variable	( )	( )	( )	( )	( )
Serious	( )	( )	( )	( )	( )
Energetic	( )	( )	( )	( )	( )
Well-adjusted	( )	( )	( )	( )	( )
Cooperative	( )	( )	( )	( )	( )
Prejudiced	( )	( )	( )	( )	( )
Unpredictable	( )	( )	( )	( )	( )
Selfish	( )	( )	( )	( )	( )
Leader	( )	( )	( )	( )	( )
Considerate of others	( )	( )	( )	( )	( )

	Not at all	Slightly	Moderately	Rather well	Extremely well
Good natured	( )	( )	( )	( )	( )
Tense	( )	( )	( )	( )	( )
Accepts criticism	( )	( )	( )	( )	( )
Aggressive	( )	( )	( )	( )	( )
Easy to get to know	( )	( )	( )	( )	( )
Imaginative	( )	( )	( )	( )	( )
Sense of humor	( )	( )	( )	( )	( )
Friendly	( )	( )	( )	( )	( )
Dogmatic	( )	( )	( )	( )	( )
Responsible	( )	( )	( )	( )	( )
Ambitious	( )	( )	( )	( )	( )
Physically attractive	( )	( )	( )	( )	( )
Sexually attractive	( )	( )	( )	( )	( )
Mature	( )	( )	( )	( )	( )
Trusting of others	( )	( )	( )	( )	( )
Open	( )	( )	( )	( )	( )

How accurately do these answers reflect your impressions of me?

How well do you feel you know me?

Additional Comments:

Respondent:

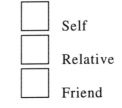

Self

Relative

Friend

THE WAY WE SEE ME QUESTIONNAIRE

As part of a class assignment, I am distributing this questionnaire to some of my relatives and friends. It is designed to give me your impressions of my personality. I am attempting to compare the way other people see me with the way I see myself. While it may be difficult for you to express your impressions exactly, I would appreciate as frank a rating as you can give me.

This questionnaire should not take long to complete. First, try to construct an overall view of your impressions about my personality before answering the specific questions. Consider each item briefly and indicate the first choice that occurs to you. If you come to an item which you feel unable to answer with certainty, place a question mark, instead of a check, in one of the spaces to indicate a guess. However, please do answer every question. If you have comments that will help explain any of your answers, please use the space provided or write in the margins. Explanatory comments will be appreciated.

Please begin by considering my main strengths and weaknesses. Describe each as carefully as you can in the spaces below:

Main Strengths:

Main Weaknesses:

How well do the following words apply to me?

	Not at all	Slightly	Moderately	Rather well	Extremely well
Self-confident	( )	( )	( )	( )	( )
Tactful	( )	( )	( )	( )	( )
Irritable	( )	( )	( )	( )	( )
Quiet	( )	( )	( )	( )	( )
Emotionally variable	( )	( )	( )	( )	( )
Serious	( )	( )	( )	( )	( )
Energetic	( )	( )	( )	( )	( )
Well-adjusted	( )	( )	( )	( )	( )
Cooperative	( )	( )	( )	( )	( )
Prejudiced	( )	( )	( )	( )	( )
Unpredictable	( )	( )	( )	( )	( )
Selfish	( )	( )	( )	( )	( )
Leader	( )	( )	( )	( )	( )
Considerate of others	( )	( )	( )	( )	( )

	Not at all	Slightly	Moderately	Rather well	Extremely well
Good natured	( )	( )	( )	( )	( )
Tense	( )	( )	( )	( )	( )
Accepts criticism	( )	( )	( )	( )	( )
Aggressive	( )	( )	( )	( )	( )
Easy to get to know	( )	( )	( )	( )	( )
Imaginative	( )	( )	( )	( )	( )
Sense of humor	( )	( )	( )	( )	( )
Friendly	( )	( )	( )	( )	( )
Dogmatic	( )	( )	( )	( )	( )
Responsible	( )	( )	( )	( )	( )
Ambitious	( )	( )	( )	( )	( )
Physically attractive	( )	( )	( )	( )	( )
Sexually attractive	( )	( )	( )	( )	( )
Mature	( )	( )	( )	( )	( )
Trusting of others	( )	( )	( )	( )	( )
Open	( )	( )	( )	( )	( )

How accurately do these answers reflect your impressions of me?

How well do you feel you know me?

Additional Comments:

Respondent:

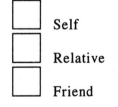

Self

Relative

Friend

THE WAY WE SEE ME QUESTIONNAIRE

As part of a class assignment, I am distributing this questionnaire to some of my relatives and friends. It is designed to give me your impressions of my personality. I am attempting to compare the way other people see me with the way I see myself. While it may be difficult for you to express your impressions exactly, I would appreciate as frank a rating as you can give me.

This questionnaire should not take long to complete. First, try to construct an overall view of your impressions about my personality before answering the specific questions. Consider each item briefly and indicate the first choice that occurs to you. If you come to an item which you feel unable to answer with certainty, place a question mark, instead of a check, in one of the spaces to indicate a guess. However, please do answer every question. If you have comments that will help explain any of your answers, please use the space provided or write in the margins. Explanatory comments will be appreciated.

Please begin by considering my main strengths and weaknesses. Describe each as carefully as you can in the spaces below:

Main Strengths:

Main Weaknesses:

How well do the following words apply to me?

	Not at all	Slightly	Moderately	Rather well	Extremely well
Self-confident	( )	( )	( )	( )	( )
Tactful	( )	( )	( )	( )	( )
Irritable	( )	( )	( )	( )	( )
Quiet	( )	( )	( )	( )	( )
Emotionally variable	( )	( )	( )	( )	( )
Serious	( )	( )	( )	( )	( )
Energetic	( )	( )	( )	( )	( )
Well-adjusted	( )	( )	( )	( )	( )
Cooperative	( )	( )	( )	( )	( )
Prejudiced	( )	( )	( )	( )	( )
Unpredictable	( )	( )	( )	( )	( )
Selfish	( )	( )	( )	( )	( )
Leader	( )	( )	( )	( )	( )
Considerate of others	( )	( )	( )	( )	( )

	Not at all	Slightly	Moderately	Rather well	Extremely well
Good natured	( )	( )	( )	( )	( )
Tense	( )	( )	( )	( )	( )
Accepts criticism	( )	( )	( )	( )	( )
Aggressive	( )	( )	( )	( )	( )
Easy to get to know	( )	( )	( )	( )	( )
Imaginative	( )	( )	( )	( )	( )
Sense of humor	( )	( )	( )	( )	( )
Friendly	( )	( )	( )	( )	( )
Dogmatic	( )	( )	( )	( )	( )
Responsible	( )	( )	( )	( )	( )
Ambitious	( )	( )	( )	( )	( )
Physically attractive	( )	( )	( )	( )	( )
Sexually attractive	( )	( )	( )	( )	( )
Mature	( )	( )	( )	( )	( )
Trusting of others	( )	( )	( )	( )	( )
Open	( )	( )	( )	( )	( )

How accurately do these answers reflect your impressions of me?

How well do you feel you know me?

Additional Comments:

Respondent:

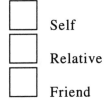

Self

Relative

Friend

YOUNIVERSE

PURPOSE: To examine significant things in your past, present and future which affect your self-concept.

PROCEDURE:
1. In the star labeled *Childhood Past,* list/draw the most significant people, events or ideas which have influenced your self-concept from that period of your life.
2. For *Near Past, Present, Near Future* and *Distant Future* do the same as above.

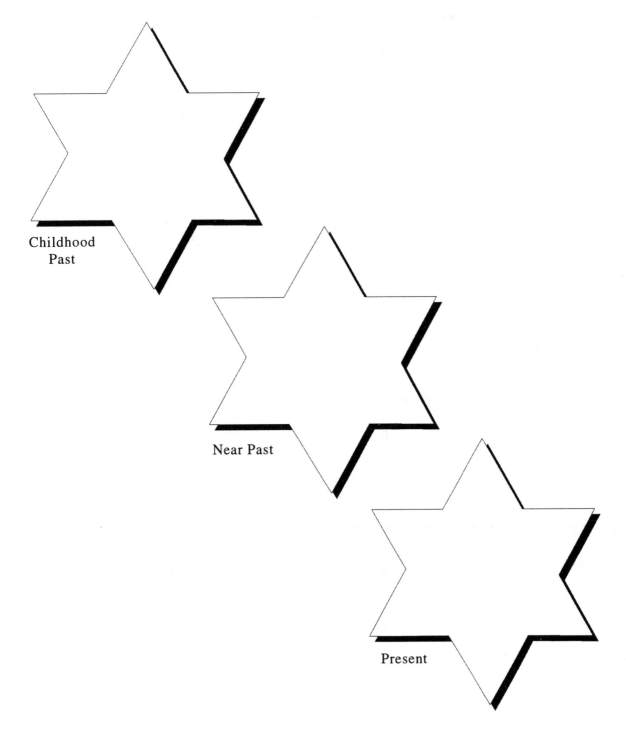

Childhood
Past

Near Past

Present

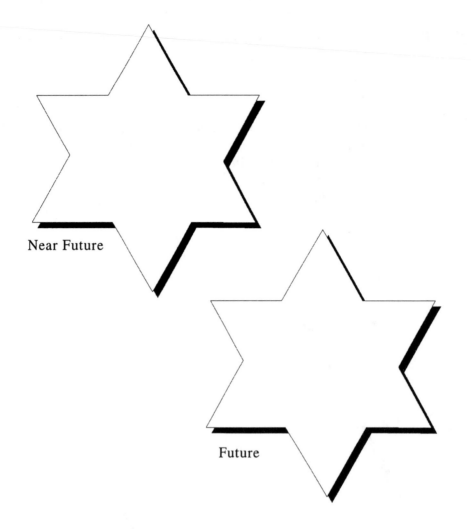

Near Future

Future

DISCUSSION: 1.   How strong a part does your past play in Youniverse?
2.   What past experiences would you eliminate, if you could?
3.   How is your present influenced by your past?
4.   What part do your past and present play in your future?
5.   What effect do your past, present and future have on your self-concept?
6.   How do people, events, ideas and places in your Youniverse affect your intra/interpersonal communication?   ❑

TURNING POINTS IN MY LIFE

PURPOSE: To identify events in your life which have affected you and your intra/interpersonal communication.

PROCEDURE: 1.   In the space below, list at least 10 events in your life which could be said to have been turning points—i.e., travel experiences, school experiences, births, deaths, embarrassments, milestones, etc.
    a.
    b.
    c.

　　　　　　　　　　　d.
　　　　　　　　　　　e.
　　　　　　　　　　　f.
　　　　　　　　　　　g.
　　　　　　　　　　　h.
　　　　　　　　　　　i.
　　　　　　　　　　　j.

2. Briefly state how each of these affected you and your intra/interpersonal communication.
3. Once you have completed these, form small groups and discuss what each has written. Also, discuss the following questions.

DISCUSSION:
1. Specifically, how have these events related to your own intra/interpersonal communication?
2. How might these events relate to the self-fulfilling prophecy which states that people tend to become what they are told they are or think they are?
3. Are there any similar events which have affected people in your group? Discuss.
4. Do people of other cultures react differently than you do to your turning points? How/why?　　　　　　　　　　　　　　　❏

THE TWO ME'S

PURPOSE:
To compare your *actual* characteristics with your *ideal* characteristics.
To see if it is possible to work towards ideal characteristics.

PROCEDURE:
1. List five adjectives that describe you as you see yourself and list under *actual characteristics* below.
2. List five adjectives that describe you as you would like to be and list under *ideal characteristics* below.
3. Get a partner. List your partner's actual and ideal characteristics as you see them. Share 1 and 2 above, discussing the other person's perception of you as compared with your own.

Actual Characteristics	Ideal Characteristics
a.	a.
b.	b.
c.	c.
d.	d.
e.	e.

DISCUSSION:
1. How much did your perception of yourself vary from theirs?
2. According to you, were the other person's perceptions of you accurate?
3. How far were your ideal characteristics from the actual ones?
4. How can you come closer to your ideal characteristics?
5. In conclusion, are you the person you want to be? Discuss.　　❏

FEELINGS, WO, WO, WO, FEELINGS —————

PURPOSE: To identify the feelings that each person is comfortable with and can express.

PROCEDURE: First, complete the "feelings" survey below. Circle the number which expresses how well you deal with each feeling listed.

1. Can express completely in any situation
2. Can express 75% of the time
3. Can express 50% of the time—with difficulty
4. Express only 25% of the time—with reservation
5. Do not express except on a very rare occasion

caring	1 2 3 4 5	displeasure	1 2 3 4 5
sharing	1 2 3 4 5	tension	1 2 3 4 5
love	1 2 3 4 5	hurt	1 2 3 4 5
liking	1 2 3 4 5	disappointment	1 2 3 4 5
concern	1 2 3 4 5	disgust	1 2 3 4 5
sadness	1 2 3 4 5	joy	1 2 3 4 5
depression	1 2 3 4 5	excitement	1 2 3 4 5
fear	1 2 3 4 5	pride	1 2 3 4 5
anger	1 2 3 4 5	patriotism	1 2 3 4 5

Complete the sentences below:

a. I am disgusted when _____

b. I get angry when _____

c. The thing that frightens me most is _____

d. Love is a feeling _____

e. To like someone is _____

f. I am disappointed with _____

g. I take pride in _____

h. I feel tense _____

i. I am concerned about _____

j. The last time I felt real joy was _____

k. I am excited about _____

l. The thing that hurts me most is _____

m. The thing which depresses me most frequently _____

n. I very much care about _____

o. I enjoy sharing _____

p. I feel _____

q. Patriotism _____

r. I am displeased with _____

Form dyads and discuss your answers from the above.

DISCUSSION:
1. What part do feelings play in verbal communication? In nonverbal communication?
2. Is there a feeling that you absolutely cannot deal with? If so, what?
3. How important are feelings to you?
4. How can you work on dealing more effectively with your feelings?
5. Which feeling do you think you deal with most successfully?
6. How do feelings affect your perception? ❏

HOW SENSITIVE ARE YOU?

PURPOSE: To help you realize sensitivity determines how a person will perceive and communicate.

PROCEDURE:
1. Get into small groups and define sensitivity.
2. Individually, answer the Self-Report Device.

SENSITIVITY SELF-REPORT DEVICE

Rating Scale:

1 . . . Very Highly Sensitive to—very important—could change your actions
2 . . . Sensitive to—matters—but won't impede action—may modify
3 . . . Aware of—will take into consideration—but will not let it affect actions at all
4 . . . Not Very Aware of—don't really pay much attention to—of little importance
5 . . . Not Aware of—does not matter one way or the other

Self:

How Sensitive Are You Towards	Circle Appropriate Response				
1. Your appearance	1	2	3	4	5
2. Your mental attitude	1	2	3	4	5
3. Tension	1	2	3	4	5
4. Your physical health	1	2	3	4	5
5. Bodily symptoms	1	2	3	4	5

6.	Your creativity and assets	1	2	3	4	5
7.	Your awareness	1	2	3	4	5
8.	Alertness	1	2	3	4	5
9.	Motivation	1	2	3	4	5
10.	Fatigue	1	2	3	4	5
11.	Your failures	1	2	3	4	5
12.	Your successes	1	2	3	4	5
13.	Your fears	1	2	3	4	5
14.	Your personal problems	1	2	3	4	5
15.	Decisions you must make	1	2	3	4	5
16.	Your opinions of others	1	2	3	4	5
17.	Your behavior towards others	1	2	3	4	5
18.	Your verbal communication	1	2	3	4	5
19.	Your body language	1	2	3	4	5
20.	Your shortcomings	1	2	3	4	5
21.	Personality	1	2	3	4	5
22.	Handicaps	1	2	3	4	5
23.	Position and status	1	2	3	4	5
24.	Intrapersonal competition	1	2	3	4	5
25.	Aptitude	1	2	3	4	5

Other People:

1.	Your family's problems	1	2	3	4	5
2.	Your spouse's feelings and needs	1	2	3	4	5
3.	Your job requirements	1	2	3	4	5
4.	Fellow employees' opinions of you	1	2	3	4	5
5.	Criticism of you	1	2	3	4	5
6.	Criticism of things you do	1	2	3	4	5
7.	Society's ills	1	2	3	4	5
8.	Mass movement	1	2	3	4	5
9.	Fads	1	2	3	4	5
10.	Smoking	1	2	3	4	5
11.	Drinking	1	2	3	4	5
12.	Obnoxious behavior	1	2	3	4	5
13.	Changes in plan	1	2	3	4	5
14.	Appearances	1	2	3	4	5
15.	Personalities	1	2	3	4	5
16.	Strong points (assets)	1	2	3	4	5
17.	Shortcomings	1	2	3	4	5

18.	Handicaps	1	2	3	4	5
19.	Educational level	1	2	3	4	5
20.	Position and status	1	2	3	4	5
21.	Achievements	1	2	3	4	5
22.	Competing with you	1	2	3	4	5
23.	Judgment of you	1	2	3	4	5
24.	Compliments of you	1	2	3	4	5
25.	Advice to you	1	2	3	4	5

Other Variables:

1.	Parties	1	2	3	4	5
2.	Politics	1	2	3	4	5
3.	Environment	1	2	3	4	5
4.	Money issues	1	2	3	4	5
5.	The weather	1	2	3	4	5
6.	The sunshine	1	2	3	4	5
7.	Crowded places	1	2	3	4	5
8.	Arguments	1	2	3	4	5
9.	Meetings	1	2	3	4	5
10.	School counselors	1	2	3	4	5
11.	Colors	1	2	3	4	5
12.	Smells	1	2	3	4	5
13.	Visual stimulation	1	2	3	4	5
14.	Smog	1	2	3	4	5
15.	Disappointment	1	2	3	4	5
16.	Change of plans	1	2	3	4	5
17.	The media	1	2	3	4	5
18.	Poverty	1	2	3	4	5
19.	Art forms	1	2	3	4	5
20.	Religion	1	2	3	4	5
21.	Music	1	2	3	4	5
22.	Death	1	2	3	4	5
23.	Sex	1	2	3	4	5
24.	Television	1	2	3	4	5
25.	Newspapers	1	2	3	4	5

3. Individually, add your scores for each of the three areas. The area in which you earn the lowest score is the area in which you are the most sensitive.

4. Join a small group and discuss your answers. Focus on the following questions.
   a. Are you basically a "sensitive" person?
   b. Are you more sensitive to yourself or to others?
   c. What part does perception play in sensitivity?
   d. Do you see any way in which your sensitivity hampers you?
   e. How does your sensitivity help you?
   f. How do you feel about your overall "sensitiveness?"
   g. Is there any area you'd like to increase your sensitivity in?

5. Self-evaluation: Based on the activity and analysis place a yes or no next to the following statements.

   _____ I am very aware of myself.
   _____ I am sensitive to others.
   _____ I need positive reinforcement from others.
   _____ Others' opinion of me really makes a difference.
   _____ I don't care what others think of me, but I am sensitive to their needs and how I might help them.
   _____ I am basically an individualist.
   _____ I do not "rock the boat."
   _____ My appearance is important to me for my own sake.
   _____ My physical health is more important to me than my physical appearance.

DISCUSSION:
1. What are the implications of the following statements on sensitivity?
   a. My physical environment can affect my personality and motivation.
   b. I care about helping others more than helping myself.
   c. I would sacrifice being sensitive to certain needs and goals of my own to obtain acceptance of others.
   d. I have tunnel vision and am not aware of other variables.
2. What are the perceptual qualifications of a sensitive communicator? ❑

RATE YOUR SELF-CONFIDENCE ————————————

PURPOSE: To determine the nature of self-confidence and how to increase it.

PROCEDURE: Next to each situation, rate how strong your self-confidence is, based on the rating scale.

Rating Scale:

1 ... Feel completely self-confident and capable
2 ... Feel capable, but have some feelings of self-consciousness
3 ... Feel very self-conscious, but do an adequate job
4 ... Feel inferior to the point that it hampers my ambition, willingness to try, for fear of failure
5 ... Complete fear of failure—no self-confidence—will not try at all—don't get in these kinds of situations

_____ 1. In front of a group—acting as the leader

_____ 2. In sports (tennis, basketball, etc.)

_____ 3. In scholastic competition

_____ 4. In my looks

_____ 5. My ability to communicate

_____ 6. My ability to do my job

_____ 7. Taking on added responsibilities

_____ 8. Organizing a big program

_____ 9. As a husband/wife/boy friend/girl friend

_____ 10. Acting as the stabilizing factor

_____ 11. As a parent or a future parent

_____ 12. Artistic/creative abilities

_____ 13. Carry on a conversation

_____ 14. Going on an interview

_____ 15. Volunteering for demonstration

_____ 16. Entering a new situation—new group of people

_____ 17. Speaking out in a group of strangers

_____ 18. Ability to begin a task and carry it through

_____ 19. Risk-taking

_____ 20. Trusting others

DISCUSSION:
1. Will your self-confidence affect your future success? If so, how?
2. Will it affect your interpersonal relationships? How? ❏

PYRAMID POWER: THE Q SORT KEY TO YOUR PERSONALITY —

PURPOSE: To compare your real personality with your ideal personality.

PROCEDURE: *Part I: How You Are Now*

1. Use the 32 items below to describe yourself *as you usually are*. If an item is very much like you, write its number in the How You Are Now Pyramid, above numbers 8 or 9, on the bottom line or in one of the spaces above.
2. If the item is very unlike you, write its number on the bottom line or in one of the spaces above numbers 1 or 2. This is your present personality.
3. Do this for all 32 characteristics.

1.	I give in easily.	17.	I am disorganized.
2.	I am intelligent.	18.	I am tolerant.
3.	I feel insecure.	19.	I am apathetic.
4.	I like to meet people.	20.	I assert myself with others.
5.	I can't make up my mind.	21.	I am afraid to disagree.
6.	I am ambitious.	22.	I am attractive to others.
7.	I am shy.	23.	I am unreliable.
8.	I am likeable.	24.	I am an interesting person.
9.	I feel tense.	25.	I don't trust my feelings.
10.	I express emotions easily.	26.	I am optimistic.
11.	I tend to be suspicious.	27.	I rationalize a lot.
12.	I feel basically contented.	28.	I feel relaxed.
13.	I lose my temper easily.	29.	I avoid facing things.
14.	I am friendly.	30.	I am flexible.
15.	I usually feel confused.	31.	I expect things to go wrong.
16.	I am emotionally mature.	32.	I am unique.

How You Are Now

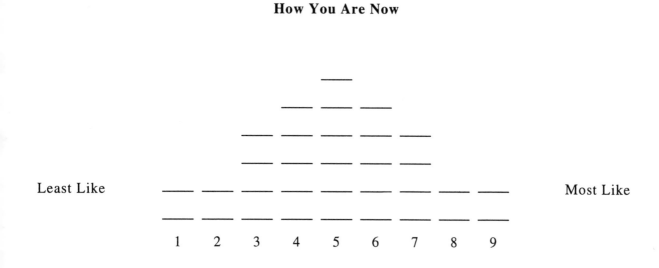

Least Like .... Most Like

1   2   3   4   5   6   7   8   9

Part II: *How You Would Like to Be*

1. Using the same list, describe yourself as you would *like* to be. If an item is very much like the way you want to be, write its number above numbers 8 or 9, on the bottom line or in one of the spaces above.
2. If the item is not at all the way you want to be, write its number on the bottom line or in one of the spaces above numbers 1 and 2. This is your ideal personality.
3. Do this for all 32 characteristics.

How You Would Like to Be

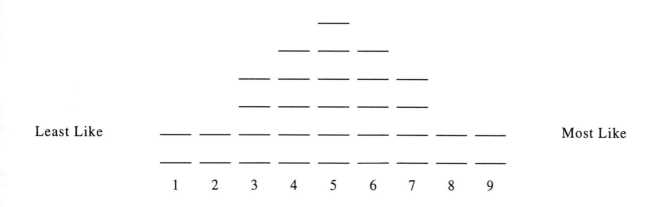

Least Like .... Most Like

1   2   3   4   5   6   7   8   9

Part III: *Scoring*

1. Using the score page, enter the score values (1–9) for both the "real" and "ideal" sorts for each of the 32 items.
2. Find the difference between the scaled values for each item and enter that difference in the third column on the score page. Note: it does not matter whether the difference has a positive or negative sign.
3. There are two variations for completing the scoring.

a. *Variation A*:

   (1) Rank the item numbers in order from those which had the greatest score difference to those with the least score difference.

   (2) This ranked list then tells you the things you want to change about yourself and the order in which you want to change them.

   (3) You may wish to have someone else you know well complete both the "real" and "ideal" sorts on you and compare your results with the results they have for you.

b. *Variation B*:

   (1) Square the difference between the two scores for each characteristic and enter this number in the fourth column.

   (2) Calculate the sum of all these squared differences by adding up all the numbers in column four.

   (3) Divide this sum by 284.

   (4) Subtract this number from 1.

   (5) The answer should be a decimal fraction. This is your Q score and may be evaluated on the following scale:

.50–.84	Generally OK feelings
.36–.50	Mixed feelings
.35 and below	Generally not OK feelings

$$Q = 1 - (\text{difference}^2 \div 284)$$

SCORE PAGE FOR PYRAMID POWER

Items	Real Score	Ideal Score	Difference Real-Ideal	Difference^2
1.				
2.				
3.				
4.				
5.				
6.				
7.				
8.				
9.				
10.				
11.				
12.				
13.				
14.				
15.				
16.				
17.				
18.				
19.				
20.				
21.				
22.				
23.				
24.				
25.				
26.				
27.				
28.				
29.				
30.				
31.				
32.				

Score_____

DISCUSSION: 1. What are some of the significant ways in which your Real Pyramid
                  differed from your Ideal Pyramid?
              2. Were you surprised with your evaluation? Why? Why not?
              3. What can you do to be more like your Ideal Pyramid?
              4. How might the differences between your Real Pyramid and your Ideal
                  Pyramid affect your intra/interpersonal communication?   ❑

I care not what others think of what I do,
but I care very much about what I think of
what I do: that is character! —*T. Roosevelt*

INTERPERSONAL CONFIDENCE WALK

PURPOSE: To examine the ways in which you gain interpersonal confidence or trust.

PROCEDURE: 1. Your instructor will assign you a partner.
              2. Have your partner blindfold you. She will take you around the room,
                  building, or campus.
              3. When the blindfolded partner has developed a high degree of confi-
                  dence or trust, switch places and continue your walk.

RULES FOR TRUST WALK

1. Walk—**Don't run**.
2. Remain in body contact with your partner from the instant the blind-
    fold goes on.
3. Talk to your partner. Share **thoughts** and **feelings**.
4. Remove blindfold and return to the classroom if any of the following
    happens:
    a. Your partner says she cannot continue.
    b. Your partner violates your trust in **any way**.
    c. Your partner becomes frightened, dizzy or disoriented.
5. Follow the prescribed route.
6. After you have reversed roles, and both persons have been on the trust
    walk, thank each other and talk about your experience.

DISCUSSION: 1. How long did it take you to develop confidence in your partner?
              2. How was this confidence developed? Be specific.
              3. Describe the communication between you and your partner during
                  your walk.   ❑

ROLE ANALYSIS

PURPOSE: To examine more closely the roles you play and how these roles affect aspects of communication.

PROCEDURE: Answer the following questions individually and then we will discuss the responses as a class.

1. Try to list five of the roles which you commonly play, making each role separate and distinct from the others—i.e., student, mother, wife, etc.
2. How are each of the following altered by each of the above roles?
   a. Language
   b. Appearance
   c. Attitude
   d. Values
   e. Quantity and quality of communication
3. What major role expectations do you have for each of the following roles?

   a. Teacher
   b. Student
   c. Wife
   d. Husband
   e. Boy friend
   f. Girl friend
   g. Mother
   h. Father
   i. Son
   j. Daughter

   k. Clergyman
   l. Parishioner
   m. Doctor
   n. Patient
   o. Policeman
   p. Citizen
   q. Employer
   r. Employee
   s. Clerk
   t. Customer

4. Analyze the following situations according to how different people might deal with them.
   a. What questions might each person ask?
   b. What factors would determine their reaction to each situation?

How would a . . .	deal with . . .
mother	buying a car
father	selecting a college
fashion model	seeing a ball game
preacher	going on vacation
boy friend	selling a boat
girl friend	stealing an orange
cab driver	punishing a small child
salesperson	getting a speeding ticket
police officer	going to the dentist
rich student	paying a fine
poor student	using leisure time

DISCUSSION:
1. How do roles affect interpersonal communication?
2. Discuss role playing as a means of solving problems which occur in interpersonal communication situations. ❏

HOW A WOMAN CAN BE MORE LIKE A MAN

Laura Saari

"Why can't a woman be more like a man?" laments Henry Higgins in the musical, "My Fair Lady."

A woman can be more like a man, says Dr. Gail Reisman, a specialist in male-female differences and relationships.

In her new consulting business in Anaheim Hills, Reisman helps people adjust to changing roles of women in the workplace. She works with women who want to communicate more like men—and men who want to communicate more like women.

Reisman's clients are women who are joining the executive ranks and want to know how to talk to their male colleagues. They're men in sales and educational positions who want to speak and behave more like women. Reisman has coached a man who had a sex-change operation and wanted a woman's speech patterns and gestures to go along with his new woman's body.

Reisman, who spoke last week at Rancho Santiago College in Santa Ana, believes there are distinct differences in the ways men and women communicate. Becoming aware of the differences, she said, can make you more effective in business and social situations—and at home.

This world of sexual differences in language and behavior is subtle. A smile is not just a smile.

When a man stares at a woman, people often perceive it as a sexual overture, according to Reisman. A woman who stares, however, is perceived simply as friendly.

But if that woman should flash a smile at the same man, Reisman said, the gesture may be interpreted as "a come on."

Using the man's first name or putting her hand on his shoulder also can be interpreted as sexual, although the same behavior isn't judged as sexual from men.

Sexual differences in communication, Reisman said, have to do with the way you're brought up—and with the structure of your brain.

A professor of human development at Cal State Fullerton, with a doctorate in adult learning and development, Reisman said she spent more than seven years studying sexual differences. In some of the language studies, she said, microphones were placed in people's offices, kitchens, even bedrooms, to catalog language differences between the sexes.

Reisman said men's brains are more specialized—with the left side of the brain handling verbal tasks and the right side handling spatial. The tissue between the left and right side, she said, is thicker in women—allowing for "faster crossover." A man who has had a stroke that affects the left side of the brain often will lose more of his language ability than a woman, who has better language capacities in both sides of the brain, according to Reisman.

The communication differences start with the way men and women perceive the world.

Women are more attuned to taste and touch in all parts of the body, she said. They're less tolerant of noise and repetitive sounds. Women have better memories, particularly for detail. Women also get the best grades in manual dexterity. They process information faster.

Men are more attentive to things and more likely to be distracted by novel objects. Women are better at perceiving subliminal messages.

By permission, *Orange County Register*.

Women are more socially responsive, more empathetic. Those are traits that make successful salespeople, according to Reisman. Women pick up nonverbal clues faster.

Reisman said the sexes also think differently.

Men are more analytical, she said. They think more abstractly. They have a better knack for taking a situation out of its context to analyze it. Women have a more complex thought process. They are more observant of the context around an issue or experience. Their thoughts are multi-dimensional. They can take in more information, particularly about the reactions of people around them.

"Women are often accused of not getting to the point," she said. "But for women, there is no point to get to. There are no blacks and whites for women. There are only grays."

When they're in a group situation, Reisman said, men seek closure. They like answers. They expect direct communication. Women are more comfortable with leaving conversations open-ended and with complexity. They expect men to pick up on nonverbal clues, to know what they're thinking after they've been in a long-term relationship with a man.

Differences in thought and perception lead to differences in the way women and men communicate, according to Reisman.

"Culturally, women are open to a lot more influences," she said. "They're very sensitive to the feelings and opinions of everyone around them. They're overly concerned that everyone like them. So they set themselves up to be contradicted and persuaded."

Women, more than men, she said, open their conversations with such hedging statements as: "I may be wrong, but . . ." or "I'm no expert, but . . ." Or they end their statements with questions: "The weather is hot, isn't it?"

"There's a lot more pressure, now even more than a few years ago, against women who are assertive," said Reisman. Women sometimes respond to this pressure, which Reisman defines as a backlash against feminism, by weakening their statements.

Men have difficulties communicating sadness, Reisman said. Women have a hard time expressing anger.

"We tell women in office situations, *do not cry,*" she said. "If you have to dig your fingernails into your hand, if you have to stop and take a glass of water, do it. Men do not know how to deal with tears."

Men speak in commands, she said. Women often ask for what they want with questions—or plead.

"At home, the man will say, 'Johnny, bring me my glasses,'" she said. "The woman will say, 'Johnny, at the next commercial, do me a favor. I'm so tired. Please go upstairs and bring me my glasses?'"

Reisman favors the male style—stating directly what you want—as a more effective form of communication.

In group settings, people who keep their distance, who sit in a less symmetrical position, who take up more space, are judged to have more power, Reisman said.

"But women are taught that the less space they take up the more feminine, the more attractive they are," she said. "So they tend to fold their arms and keep their legs together." They use smaller gestures—fingers instead of hands—and nod and smile more often, which Reisman defines as "low-status gestures."

"When we speak with women and smaller men, we suggest they swing their arms more, take large strides and use open gestures," she said. "Use gestures below the neck. Give the appearance of being taller. Stick your chest out. Wear heels. Use a podium if you're speaking. Distance yourself from your audience." Steepling—forming a steeple with the hands—is a high-status gesture, she said. The more a person covers his face, the more power he is judged to have, according to Reisman.

"People think women talk more than men, but every study has shown this is not the case," said Reisman. "Men speak longer and interrupt more often." She said studies performed in high schools show that boys out-talk girls, 3-to-1. The perception that men talk less, she said, may be related to the fact that women talk more about detail; men want a synopsis.

Reisman's analysis of how women and men are perceived suggests gross inequalities in the power structure.

Men interrupt conversations more often than women, according to Reisman. She said that studies show men account for 90 percent of the interruptions in conversations. Mothers and fathers interrupted their daughters more than they interrupted their sons.

"Interruptions are a good indication of status," she said. "Doctors interrupt their patients. Lawyers interrupt their clients."

When men introduced a topic to a group, she said, the topic was picked up 96 percent of the time. For women, the topic was picked up 36 percent of the time. Women on the average must make three to six attempts when they are trying to get the members of a group to listen to them, she said. Men, she said, are accepted on the first try.

Although behavioral scientists are beginning to study the differences in the way men and women communicate, people have a lot of work to do to accept those differences and embrace them, according to Reisman.

"We have to start accepting what people have to say," she said, "and allow them to do it in their own style, because if we don't, we're missing out on what half the population has to offer."

How do women and men differ?

The differences between men and women in how they speak and view the world are dramatic, according to research by Gail Reisman of California State University, Fullerton. These are some major examples:

Women are:
   More sensitive to taste and touch.
   Less tolerant of noise and repeated sounds.
   Better at receiving subliminal messages.
   Better at remembering details.
   More observant of the context of an issue or event.
   Less able to express anger.
   More likely to ask or plead.

Men are:
   More attentive to objects.
   More likely to be distracted by new objects.
   More analytical.
   More abstract thinkers.
   Less able to express sadness.
   More likely to speak in commands.

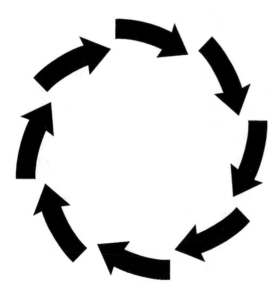

All the world is a stage, And all the men and women, merely players. They have their exits and their entrances, And one man in time plays many parts. —*W. Shakespeare*

four portraits of women

hang
    before
the world's equal rights
amendment
     wearing
horn-rimmed
mental frames.

figure one is
    innocent
freezer paper,
as simple as
    a box
folder on the tomatoe
conveyor belt
of campbell's soup.

number two is painted
hot coal,
aborting many
corset
   loves,
only to prove
devotion in america's
welfare.

the next frame
   clicks
buttons in stock
x changes,
lights fires on stimulating
nights
with
   the gas log
of her
fireplace—
being shrewdly convinced
that one, two
and four
must certainly have
castrated
minds.

and what of portrait
four?
   well, it's blank
textured
rice paper
because I haven't been
levered by pushers
or red sylvania light bulbs;
all women feel right
at home sitting on my
intelligence seat,
especially when i can
paint
self-portraits to new
amendments
   with notes
for timing one final rhyme
just for
   them:
"you say i'm a monkey
so i'll stand on my head
and wait for you to laugh
your three selves to
death."

four portraits of women
hang
   before
the world's equal rights
amendment
    wearing
horn-rimmed
mental frames that all
could use
   a mortifying
intestinal
mud pack.

S-Grace

205

THE CHILDLESS COUPLE

KFI Editorial

There is nothing sadder than the childless couple. It breaks the heart to see them stretched out relaxing around swimming pools in Florida, sitting all suntanned and miserable on the decks of their boat—trotting off to Europe like lonesome fools. It's an empty life. There's nothing but money to spend, more time to enjoy and a whole lot less to worry about.
. . .

The poor childless couple gets so selfish and wrapped up in their own concerns that you have to feel sorry for them. They don't fight over the child's discipline, they don't blame each other for the child's most nauseous characteristics, and they miss half the fun of doing without things for the child's sake. They go along in their own dull way, doing what they want, buying what they want and liking each other. It's a pretty pathetic picture.

Everyone should have children. No one should be allowed to escape the wonderful experience attached to each stage in the development of the young. The happy memories of the baby days, the alert nights, coughing spells, debts, diaper rash, "dipso" baby sitters, saturated mattresses, spilled food, tantrums, emergencies and never ending crises.

Then comes the real fulfillment as the child grows like a little acorn into a real nut. The wonder of watching your overweight ballerina make a fool of herself in a leotard. The warm smile of the small lad with the sun glittering on 500 bucks worth of braces ruined on peanut brittle. The rollicking, merry, carefree voices of hordes of hysterical kiddies, gently massaging potato chips into the rug at the birthday party.

How dismal is the peaceful home without the constant childish problems that make for a well-rounded life and an early breakdown; the tender thoughtful discussions when the report card reveals the progeny to be one step below a moron; the end of the day reunions with all the joyful happenings related like well-placed blows to the temple.

Children are worth it all. Every moment of anxiety, every sacrifice, every complete collapse pays off as a fine sturdy adolescence is reached. The feeling of reward the first time you took the baby hunting; he didn't mean to shoot you; the boy was excited; remember how he cried? How sorry he was? How much better you felt after the blood transfusion? These are the times with a growing son that a man treasures. . . . These memories that are captured forever in the heart and the limp. . . .

Think back to the night of romantic adventure when your budding daughter eloped with the village idiot. What childless couple ever shared in the stark realism of that drama? Aren't you a better man for having lived richly, fully, and acquiring that tic in your left eye? Could a woman without children touch the strength and heroism of your wife as she tried to fling herself out of the bedroom window? The climax when you two became really close in the realization that, after all, your baby girl was a woman with the mind of a pygmy?

The childless couple live in a vacuum. They fill their lonely days with golf, vacation trips, dinner dates, civic affairs, tranquility, leisure and money. There is a terrifying emptiness without children, and the childless couple is too comfortable to know it. You just have to look at them to see what the years have done: he looks boyish, unlined and rested; she's slim, well-groomed and youthful. It isn't natural. If they had had kids, they'd look like the rest of us—tired and gray, wrinkled and sagging. In other words, Normal. . . .

By permission, KFI Radio, Los Angeles, CA.

CHILDLESS WOMEN: RESEARCHER CONFOUNDS STEREOTYPES

Robert Ferrigno

"The correct term is 'voluntarily childless,'" smiles Deborah Hendlin, Ph.D., settling back into the leather armchair of her office. Hendlin, a clinical psychologist in private practice in Irvine, Calif., specializes in counseling women who have chosen not to have children.

Hendlin, who has been practicing for five years, says that current estimates are that 3 percent of the childless women between the ages of 35–44 are childless by choice, a percentage that could double in the future. When the woman is married, in three out of four cases, the decision to make it a voluntarily childless relationship is determined by the woman.

According to Hendlin's research, a voluntarily childless woman would probably be described as intellectually bright, career-oriented, first-born, with an advanced degree and no formal religious affiliation. "There has not been any evidence that there's a gene or a hormone linked to this decision not to have children," says Hendlin, with the same small smile.

Hendlin's interest in this subject was the basis for her doctoral thesis, "Femininity and Nurturance in Voluntarily Childless Women," a study of the emotional differences between three selected groups of women—the voluntarily childless, mothers who planned the number and spacing of their children and lesbians.

While the popular idea of voluntarily childless women is that they are cold and unemotional, hard-driving career women who are too selfish to have children, the results of Hendlin's study dispute that image and came as some surprise to Hendlin herself.

"The survey (of 60 women, 20 in each group) found that there was no difference in the degree of femininity between the three groups: all of their perceptions of themselves as feminine were similar. I did not predict that."

Hendlin makes the point that "femininity," as used psychologically, can be measured by a standardized test, the "Bem Sex-role Inventory," in which 60 items (20 feminine, 20 masculine, 20 neutral) are rated from 1–7 by the person taking the test. Another psychological test, the Edwards Personal Preference Schedule, measures the degree of nurturance by asking women to rate themselves (on a scale of 1–5) in stereotypical traits usually identified as feminine: soft, caring, loves children, etc.

"The survey also found no difference in nurturance between the three groups," says Hendlin, "which goes against the common idea of childless women as materialistic and very into themselves, as being cold and withdrawn, not loving or open. That's the preconception, but the picture that emerged from my research is that there are no differences in these areas between the women who choose to have children and the women who choose not to."

One area in which voluntarily childless women did differ from planned mothers was in their degree of androgyny—defined by psychologists as the balance of typically male attitudes (ambitiousness, aggressiveness) with typically female attitudes (caring, harmonizing). Both voluntarily childless women and lesbians had a greater degree of androgyny, which Hendlin says indicates being in touch with the full range of their human potential.

Hendlin found that women in voluntarily childless marriages happily reported that romance was a high priority in their relationship and that their

By permission, *Orange County Register*.

marriages avoided the sexual stereotyping more common in families with children.

"These women indicated that they felt more equal with their husbands," says Hendlin, than women who were mothers. "They have similar incomes to their husbands, they're out in the world and independent. Voluntarily childless women said they valued the fact that their mate might cook or clean and not make a big deal of it, and they wouldn't think anything of taking care of the cars or the lawn."

Another aspect of Hendlin's study was the finding that differences between individual women are more the result of the degree of education and income level, rather than their decision to have children.

"I can't stress enough," says Hendlin, "that the degree of education and income makes the difference between these women."

While motherhood, or the rejection of it, may make no difference in a woman's femininity or her ability to nurture, the way each group is treated by the rest of society can make a difference in their lives.

One of the main difficulties voluntarily childless women have is the expectations of family and friends, and the sense that they are out of step with a society that has decided once again that having babies is chic.

"Pro-natalism has remained constant throughout history," says Hendlin, "but it does have its ebbs and flows. During the 1960s and 1970s, having children was not emphasized, but now it's back in style. The voluntarily childless women that I hear feel that others are judging them, that the old stereotypes are prevalent. It's like being in the army: they feel that people question whether they are shirking their biological duty.

"Some of these women are asking if there's something wrong with them as women—'Do I have a flaw?' 'Am I mentally ill?' They question their ability to love and nurture, their ability to be selfless and giving.

"Most childless women, once they work this through, don't question it further—it's others questioning it. These issues are not inner-directed, they come from outside—someone says something to them that precipitates it. Most voluntarily childless women seem very confident of their femininity, in fact most of them say they feel more feminine, more sexy than women with children, more erotic. They say, 'I nurture my husband' or 'I nurture the children I teach,' but it's a different thing; it can be turned off and allow other parts of myself to come out.

"Child- and family-centered holidays are particularly difficult, even for women who are very comfortable with the decision—they have to deal with family expectations, and the encounter with extended relatives makes it painfully obvious to these women that they are out of it. When they buy gifts for children, they complain that they were more involved in the holidays before, but now they have to take a back seat to children—the new generation is a source of both delight and resentment."

For her study, Hendlin deliberately chose women between the ages of 35–40, women who were at the end of their childbearing years, because she felt these were women who were dealing with the realities of the decision, not merely postponing the choice.

"Many of the women I see do worry about being lonely in their old age," says Hendlin. "They're concerned that they will be isolated from their peers and out of touch.

"Children have the ability to buffer our sense of mortality, and when women don't have children they feel their mortality in a more direct way.

"Also, in a marriage, a child can take the edge off of a bad relationship. By the same token, a child can blunt a good relationship, so you see a lot of the middle-ground with children. Marriages without children often show both extremes. Good childless marriages stay together, bad ones break apart.

Because being a mother is such an important part of the personal identity of a woman (whereas fatherhood is not an important part of a man's identity), Hendlin says that a voluntarily childless woman has to go through a period of "grieving" over the loss of that part of her psyche that no longer exists as a possibility.

However, once this grieving is complete, Hendlin says that the result is an acceptance of self, and a greater awareness of all the other opportunities open to the woman by her decision not to have children.

ROLE BANDS

PURPOSE: To give you an opportunity to see the effect of roles on your communication behavior.

PROCEDURE:
1. Join a small group and choose a controversial topic for discussion.
2. As a group, set specific goals to be reached by your group.
3. While your group is involved in discussion, your instructor will stick a label on each group member's forehead. Other members of your group will be able to see the role that they will put you in and you will see theirs. However, no group member will be able to see her own *role band*.
4. Continue discussion as you observe and react to one another's *role bands*.
5. Your instructor will call time.

DISCUSSION:
1. What feelings did you have about your particular assigned roles?
2. Were there any similarities/differences between your assigned *role band* and your *real life* roles?
3. Did you observe any self-defeating roles during your discussion?
4. What effect did the assigned roles have on your communication? ❑

HOONHORNS, SELF-CONCEPT AND DISCRIMINATION

PURPOSE: To demonstrate that discrimination is a common behavior. To discuss the various ways people discriminate.

PROCEDURE:
1. Divide into three equal groups: Hoonhorns, Grelfs and Fudds.
2. The Hoonhorns are the first group to be the victims of discriminatory behavior by other group members. Put them in front of the class.
3. Other class members may order the Hoonhorns around, ask them to do anything, insult them, put them down or whatever they feel like because it is accepted in a larger group that they are inferior and unequal. Hoonhorns must obey commands. Take 15 minutes for this step.
4. Do the same with the Grelfs and the Fudds.

DISCUSSION:
1. How do you feel when you are being discriminated against? When you are doing the discriminating?
2. How did your self-image change as you went from one group to another?
3. What kinds of discrimination occur here at school?
4. Why do people discriminate?
5. How does discrimination affect communication? ❑

DISCRIMINATION BEHAVIORS

PURPOSE: To allow individuals to experience discrimination.

PROCEDURE:
1. Four people volunteer to be discriminated against. They are to do exactly as they are told and can't rebel or resist. (Group 1)
2. Two people volunteer to discriminate against the first group.
3. The first group leaves the room.
4. The two people plan to role play as one of the following: racial bigots, prison guards, etc.
5. The first group returns to the room and the second group begins discriminating and role playing.
6. Stop whenever the participants have obviously become distressed or upset, or when the activity has obviously demonstrated its message.

DISCUSSION:
1. How does the first group feel?
2. How does the second group feel?
3. Specifically, what people or groups of people in our society discriminate, and which are discriminated against? How do you think they feel? How might their feelings be manifested?
4. What do you feel is the basic cause of discrimination? ❏

I'M THE GREATEST!

PURPOSE: In our society it is not acceptable to brag; in fact, we are so conscious of this that we go to the other extreme and, in the name of modesty, belittle ourselves by putting ourselves down. Many of us are masters at this. Thus, for the next few minutes, reverse this usual practice and share some positive things about yourself.

PROCEDURE:
1. Get into a circle.
2. Starting at one point, proceed to your right. In turn, each person should give three brags about himself. (For example, I have never received a failing grade in school; I've lost ten pounds and feel great; I have nice, curly hair, I told my best friend how much he meant to me, etc.) Remember that these are our brags; you should think of your own. They can be about little or big things, as long as they have importance to you.
3. If you can't think of three brags when it's your turn, there's a penalty. You must sit and listen without protesting while the rest of us give you compliments. In other words, if you can't say good things about yourself, others will do it for you.
4. Remember, all communication is to be positive. Keep it informal.

DISCUSSION: In our society it's considered a virtue to put yourself down in the name of humility, to say negative things about yourself; conversely, it's considered immodest to talk about your good points. Does this really make sense? ❏

JOHARI WINDOW

The Johari Window provides a way to look at the self. There are things you know about yourself and things you don't know. There are things other people know about yourself and things they don't know. These four aspects represent the various areas of the self.

Area 1 (I know, others know) represents your public self. The information is common knowledge and you feel free about sharing that information with others.

Area 2, blind area (others know, I don't know) includes information others have about you, but that you do not have. This, for example, is the way you look to other people.

Area 3, the hidden area (I know, others don't know) represents the things that you know about yourself, but have been unwilling to share with others. This area includes your secrets and things you are ashamed of.

Area 4, the unknown area (I don't know, others don't know) represents those things about yourself which you don't understand. This is the area of needs, expectations and desires that you have which you cannot understand.

The four areas are interdependent, that is, a change in the size of one area affects the size of the other areas. By self-disclosing, an individual increases the free area and decreases the size of the hidden area. As a result of the hidden area being decreased, the unknown area is likewise decreased. Such disclosing on the part of an individual makes feedback easier by others and, therefore, the blind area and unknown area are also reduced in size.

Self-disclosure can then be seen as a means to aiding an individual in learning more about the self.

The Johari Window

Free Self	Blind Self
Hidden Self	Unknown Self

THE JOHARI WINDOW EXERCISE

PURPOSE: To examine the degree of overall "openness" of your communication.

                               To provide insight into the hidden areas of your personality.

                               To demonstrate self-disclosure as a situational variable.

PROCEDURE: Draw your Johari Window for each of the following environments: speech class, close family, friendship group, spouse, boy friend/girl friend.

❑

INTERPERSONAL SECRETS

PURPOSE: To provide the opportunity to share a private part of the personality in self-disclosure, without fear of judgment. To demonstrate how we all hide similar fears, experiences and expectations.

PROCEDURE:
1. Get into a circle.
2. On a white piece of paper (to insure anonymity), write something truthful about your inner self that you have shared with very few people, if anyone—i.e., thoughts, feelings, behaviors, failures, sexual tendencies, hatreds, prejudices, etc.
3. Fold the paper into fourths and throw it in the middle of the circle.
4. After all secrets are in the middle, redistribute the secrets throughout the group, making sure no person receives his/her own.
5. Read secrets aloud.
6. Give opportunity for any individual to disclose or discuss her secret. Comments should *not* be judgmental or evaluative in any way.

DISCUSSION:
1. To what extent was there a high or low self-disclosure level? Why?
2. Were there any common themes in the secrets? What were they?
3. Why or why didn't you disclose your secret? Are you happy you did or didn't? Why?
4. What are the values and dangers of self-disclosure?   ❑

MASLOW ACTIVITY

PURPOSE: To help you understand and explore Maslow's theory of human motivation and how it relates to communication.

PROCEDURE:
1. Read the following story and determine the order in which you would make your requests.
2. Form a small group and reach a group consensus on the order of the request.
3. After the groups have reached consensus, compare the groups' ranking with Maslow's hierarchy.

SITUATION

You are the sole survivor of your wrecked ship. You have been rescued by a wealthy and eccentric recluse who lives on a uncharted island somewhere in the South Pacific with a small group of his followers. Because the island is uncharted, there is no hope of rescue. Your host, who discovered the island years earlier with his small band of followers, has indicated that you are welcome and all your needs and wants will be satisfied—all you have to do is ask. Below are five requests which you may make. Place them in the order in which you would make them.

Individual	Group	
———	———	companionship of others
———	———	the ability to determine your goals and strive to achieve them
———	———	food, drink, shelter, sex
———	———	recognition and attention from others
———	———	a set of guidelines describing how life on the island is structured

DISCUSSION:
1. How does your ranking and that of your group compare with Maslow's hierarchy?
2. Do you agree or disagree with Maslow's theory? Why?
3. Why do you think Maslow felt most Americans were at level 4?
4. Is there anything about our society which may keep a person from meeting their esteem needs?
5. How does a self-actualized person behave?
6. What role does communication play in meeting needs at each level?
7. What kind of communicator is a self-actualized person?
8. Using communication, how can you help a person move from level 4 to level 5? ❏

MASLOW'S HIERARCHY OF NEEDS

Maslow has classified the basic needs of man into five broad categories:

1. PHYSIOLOGICAL NEEDS—these are necessary for survival. They include the need for food, drink, shelter, sex, avoidance of injury, pain, discomfort, disease, or fatigue, and the need for sensory stimulation. If physiological needs are not satisfied, they are stronger in their motivation than any higher needs.
2. SAFETY NEEDS—these focus on the creation of order and predictableness in one's environment. They include preference for orderliness and routine over disorder, preference for the familiar over the unfamiliar.
3. LOVE NEEDS—are of two types: love and affection between husband and wife, parents and children and close friends; and the need for belonging—identifying the larger groups (church, club, work, organization, etc.). When these needs are not met, feelings of rejection and isolation result with subsequent feelings of mistrust and suspicion toward others.
4. ESTEEM NEEDS—refer to the desire for reputation, prestige, recognition, attention, achievement and confidence. Some sociologists believe that esteem needs are powerful motivators in America.
5. SELF-ACTUALIZATION—the fulfillment of one's capabilities and potentialities. Self-actualization needs take on strong motivating power only when other more basic needs have been fulfilled.

According to Maslow, higher needs act as motivating forces only when those preceding them on the hierarchy have been satisfied.

If you aspire to the highest place,
it is no disgrace to stop at the second or even the third.
—*M. Cicero*

REACTIONS

1. Is it possible to know and like who we are?

2. What does knowing who we are have to do with our communication skills?

3. Are the risks of revealing our "real selves" to others worth it? Why or why not?

4. What harm does role playing do to the communication process? When is it appropriate to play roles?

5. Is it true that we have to know and love ourselves before we can know and love others? Why or why not?

6. Are there any cautions to be observed when we are trying to be open and honest in our communication? If so, what are they?

TRANSACTIONAL ANALYSIS | 8

Definitions

Transactional analysis (TA) is a system of analyzing and diagramming what goes on when people communicate. Transactional analysis provides practical applications which are designed to open communication between people which will be supportive, cooperative and honest.

A conversation consists of a series of interpersonal transactions linked together. A transaction may be either an angry or friendly exchange between two people in their Parent, Adult or Child ego states. In order to understand and apply the basic elements of TA it is necessary to define the most basic forms.

Adult

An ego state that is the part of you that figures things out in an analytical, rational and objective way. It processes data and computes probabilities for dealing with the outside world.

Child

An ego state that consists of feelings and natural impulses. The Child can be "natural," that is, act on his own or the Child will do what parents want him to do.

Critical Parent

An ego state that is fault finding, prejudicial and critical.

Ego State

Everyone has three parts, or persons, within himself—a Parent, an Adult and a Child.

Game

A series of predictable and repetitious patterns of behavior. When your message to another person is "ulterior" or has some hidden purpose, you are playing a psychological game.

Life Position

Everyone has a life position which your Child decided upon in early life, and your life dramas are based on your sense of self worth.

Natural Child

A form of Child ego state that is impulsive, spontaneous, self-centered, pleasure-loving, expressive and often rebellious.

Nurturing Parent

An ego state that is helping and sympathetic.

Parent

An ego state that feels and behaves in the same ways that your mother, father, or parent substitute feels, behaves or does. Your parent can be critical, or helping, or both.

Script

A personal life plan, which your Child decided upon in your early years. Your script is either a healthy one or an unhealthy one, depending on your basic position.

Stroke

A form of positive or negative recognition, conditional or unconditional.

Stamp

The good and bad feelings a person collects from positive and negative strokes.

Transaction

The basic unit of human communication which may be complementary, crossed or ulterior.

IMPORTANCE OF TRANSACTIONAL ANALYSIS

Transactional analysis is the process of understanding what goes on when people communicate. Our transactions can be analyzed in terms of the roles we play. Transactional analysis is designed to develop open communication between people. With this system of diagramming and analysis, we can become more aware of the structure of personality, how messages are transferred from one to another, the games that are played and scripts that are acted out. Such insight enables persons to view themselves with understanding and create a willingness to bring about changes in their lives.

When you read *Transactional Analysis* by Lyman K. Randall, you will have a better appreciation for the importance of TA.

BARRIERS TO TRANSACTIONAL ANALYSIS

Locked in Past Experiences

When people come into this world, they are born okay. However, people can get locked into negative past practices. Fortunately, they can make changes that will free them from the negative influences of the past.

Crossed Transactions

Crossed transactions create breakdowns in communication. The lines get crossed and we receive responses we don't expect.

Games

Ulterior transactions have hidden agendas or secret messages. We must not rely upon just the surface messages. We must also look for the psychological level to make some sense out of the game. Games are programmed to get strokes and deal with not okay feelings.

TRANSACTIONAL ANALYSIS

Lyman K. Randall

1. Knock, Knock, Who's There?

When reality knocks at your door, who answers? A whining, complaining, little boy or girl? A stern, scolding parent? Or a calm, alert adult? For example, suppose your boss tells you that he wants you to work overtime tonight and you have been planning for several weeks to meet some old friends for dinner immediately after work. Do you (a) Turn to one of your colleagues and say, "Why do these things always happen to me, anyway? What's the use in making plans around here? He could just as easily have picked on somebody else." (b) Jump up from your chair and say to your boss, "That's not fair! You have no right to expect me to change my personal plans for this evening when you give me such short notice!" (c) Reply to your boss, "That's going to cause a problem for me. You see, I've been planning for several weeks to meet some old friends tonight whom I haven't seen in three years. Is it possible to get someone else to work late tonight? Or perhaps, I can come in early tomorrow morning. What do you think?"

Perhaps you can remember reacting to similar situations in each of these three different modes of behavior. They're called the Parent ego state, the Adult ego state, and the Child ego state. To simplify things, from now on we'll refer to these ego states as Parent, Adult, and Child with capital letters to distinguish them from actual parents, adults and children.

Recognizing your own Parent, Adult, and Child (or P—A—C for short) is the first step. But what are they? Where do they come from? How do you know one from the other when you see it?

In his book, *I'm OK, You're OK,* Dr. Tom Harris describes the experiments of Dr. Wilder Penfield, a Canadian neurosurgeon. Dr. Penfield, using an electrical stimulus, was able to trigger recorded speech and feelings that were stored like tape recordings in the patient's brain. Not only was the memory of an event recalled, but the whole experience was relived by the individual. For example, one individual recalled an early experience and reported actually smelling the aroma of freshly baked bread. The development of the three ego state concepts was, in part, based on these experiments. The Parent and the Child are permanent recordings in the brain. These tapes are never erased. They can, however, be updated by the Adult.

The Child: C

First, let's take a look at the Child. The child in you is that body of data, recorded and stored in your brain when you were little. It comes from how you responded internally to what you saw and heard in the external world at that time. These recordings are primarily feelings and conclusions about yourself based on these feelings. They include feelings of frustration, inadequacy, and helplessness that were an inevitable part of your childhood. In addition, they contain the early recordings of joy, curiosity, imagination, spontaneity and the excitement born from new discoveries which were also part of your childhood. For these reasons, the Child is often called the "felt concept of life."

In the example above, it was your Child who answered the knock of reality by pouting and sulking away from your boss after he asked you to work overtime. Your Child can be "hooked" by an event that generates strong feelings. You can spot your Child when you find yourself whining, sulking, throwing a tantrum, or abandoning yourself to the joy of a pleasurable new experience.

The Parent: P

Your Parent is that body of data, also recorded and stored in your brain, that comes from your observations about the way your mother and father (or other important "Big People" in your early life) behaved. It is based on external events that occurred essentially in the first five or six years of your life. It is a mosaic of learnings which you constructed as a little person that is captioned. "This is the way the world out there really is!" Because of your smallness and dependency as a little person in a world of "giants," your overriding assumption was that *they* were right. For these reasons, the Parent is often referred to as the "taught concept of life."

Your Parent was the part of you that responded to your boss by lecturing to him about what is or is not a fair and proper way to treat you. Your Parent lectures, moralizes, points its finger righteously or accusingly, teaches and "lays down the law." You'll know your Parent is in charge when you find your scolding finger pointing, hear yourself lecturing about what's wrong (or right) about today's youth, or discover yourself correcting somebody's grammar or manners.

The Adult: A

Your Adult is that part of you that figures things out by collecting and looking at facts. You may find it helpful to think of your Adult as your computer which you use to estimate probabilities and to make decisions based on facts. Everyone, even little children, has an Adult which is capable of making assessments about outside reality. For this reason, the Adult is sometimes called the "thought concept of life."

When you told your boss why working overtime would create a problem for you and suggested some alternatives for him to consider, your Adult had taken charge. Since everyone has three ego states, once you learn to identify your own P—A—C it will be easy for you to recognize the P—A—C in others.

In some ways, our P—A—C's are like three different voices inside us. Our Parent is the voice that says things like: "You must . . . You ought to . . . You shouldn't . . . Don't ever . . ." Our Parent tape plays back such old familiar recordings as: "If you want something done right, do it yourself . . . Big boys never cry . . . Idleness is the devil's playmate . . . A penny saved is a penny earned . . . etc."

Any time you find yourself talking to yourself (either out loud or under your breath) and using the word YOU, your parent is very likely addressing your Child. For example, when you say to yourself. "That was a dumb thing for YOU to do," your Parent is scolding your Child.

Our Child is the voice that says: "I want what I want when I want it . . . Try and make me! . . . Wow! Great! . . . Drop dead! . . . etc." Any time you are experiencing feelings or emotions (happiness, sadness, fear, etc.) your Child is participating in the experience in some way.

Our Adult operates on facts based on what's true today. It is the voice within us which says things like: "What's going on here? Now I see why this happened the way it did . . . What part of me came on just a few seconds ago—my Parent? Adult? or Child? . . . Why did I react just the way I did? . . . etc."

You can become acquainted with your own P—A—C by listening to these three different voices inside yourself. You may not always hear distinct words. Sometimes you will be able to decipher messages from the feelings bubbling up inside you. Naturally, you cannot hear the voices or directly experience the feelings occurring within other people. You can, however, become skilled in spotting the P—A—C in others (and yourself) by watching for the kinds of cues (shown in the chart). The examples in this chart are only a few of the cues to watch for.

As you become more skilled in spotting these P—A—C cues in others, you will also become more aware of some of them in yourself. You can also get some cues from others about how you come across to them by identifying how they react to you. For example, suppose a customer reacts to something you have just said with, "Well, I was only trying to find out where I was supposed to catch my plane!" You might learn something about yourself by replaying what was said (or how you said it) immediately prior to the customer's hurting-complaining response. Possibly the customer thought you were putting him down or scolding him in some way. It is important to stress that everyone has P—A—C ego states operating. The goal of learning TA is to strengthen the Adult in each of us so that we can not only ask, but also answer questions like: "What part of me is coming on? Are these data true, appropriate and reasonable for today's reality?" To put it another way, TA provides us with a means of putting our Adult in the living room of today, ready to respond to the problems of daily living that knock on our "front door of life." This does not mean that we are to do away with our Parent and Child. It would be a dull world without them. It does mean, however, that we want to be free enough to be able to examine these two data tapes.

To the extent that our Parent and Child tapes are archaic and unexamined, we will be dominated by the past. To the extent, however, we are able to learn the truth about how we behave, we will be free. Perhaps this is one of the meanings behind the old saying, "Know the truth, and the truth will make you free."

2. Coming on Straight, Crossed and Crooked

Scene #1

Stewardess: "May I see your boarding pass?"
Passenger: (In angry tone) "I've already given my ticket to the man in the terminal!"

Scene #2

Employee: "I really would like to get your help in solving my lost time problem."
Supervisor: "OK. Why don't you get a thorough medical examination?"
Employee: "I've thought of that, but I don't have the money now."
Supervisor: "Why don't you try to get more sleep each night?"
Employee: "I've tried that, but my neighbors are too noisy." (etc.)

How many times have you found yourself in situations like the two scenes above? It is common for communication wires between people to get crossed in daily conversations. But why? How do these breakdowns in communication occur? And what can you do to untangle them? TA may have some ideas to help you.

In TA a transaction is an exchange of words and related behavior between two people. For example, when you say, "Good morning, Jim" and he says, "Good morning" back to you, you and Jim have completed a bit of social business which we have defined as a transaction.

When we see each person involved in the exchange as having a Parent, Adult and Child, we are able to draw an accurate diagram of what happens in the transaction (thus the term, transactional analysis). The Parent, Adult or Child in one person will always be answering the Parent, Adult, or Child in the other person. Any conversation is a series of transactions, one exchange after another. Transactions can be Adult to Adult, Adult to Parent, Adult to Child, Parent to Parent, Parent to Adult, Parent to Child, Child to Parent, etc.

Examples #1 and #2 following are simple transactions. The arrows indicate who is saying what to whom. In each of these examples, the lines are parallel or uncrossed. As long as the lines in a transaction remain uncrossed, the conversation can go on indefinitely with no breakdown in communication. For this reason this type of exchange is called complementary transaction.

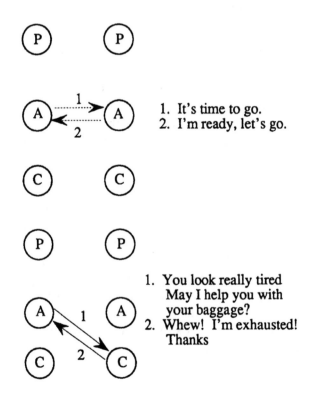

1. It's time to go.
2. I'm ready, let's go.

1. You look really tired May I help you with your baggage?
2. Whew! I'm exhausted! Thanks

221

Scene #1 is an example of a crossed transaction. When we diagram it, the transaction looks like this:

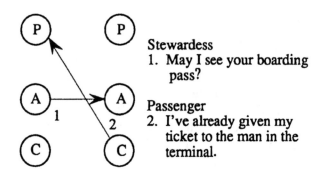

Stewardess
1. May I see your boarding pass?

Passenger
2. I've already given my ticket to the man in the terminal.

In this example the stewardess is using her Adult to ask the Adult of the passenger, "May I see your boarding pass?" Instead of responding with his Adult with something like "Yes, here it is," the passenger responds angrily with his Child, "I've already given my ticket to the man in the terminal." The passenger has reacted as if the stewardess has made an unreasonable demand on him from her Parent when in reality she has not. The communication about the passenger giving the stewardess his boarding pass has broken down. The transaction has become crossed. A second rule of communication is: Whenever the subject is abruptly diverted (rather than simply completed), look **for a crossed transaction**.

In this situation the stewardess has a choice of response to this crossed transaction. She could scold the passenger with her Parent for being so gruff with her. Or she could react with her Child showing anger or hurt feelings. Or she could use her Adult again and give more information to the Adult of the passenger: "Yes, I'm certain you did, sir. However, the man inside gave you a blue or white piece of paper with your seat number written on it. That's your boarding pass which I'd like to see now." It is probable that the customer will respond with his Adult to this last stewardess comment. Thus the transaction is uncrossed and the business of showing the boarding pass can be completed.

Scene #2 is an example of an ulterior transaction. When we diagram it, the transaction looks like this:

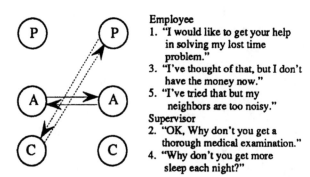

Employee
1. "I would like to get your help in solving my lost time problem."
3. "I've thought of that, but I don't have the money now."
5. "I've tried that but my neighbors are too noisy."

Supervisor
2. "OK, Why don't you get a thorough medical examination."
4. "Why don't you get more sleep each night?"

On the surface this series of transactions appears to involve an employee asking with his Adult for suggestions from his supervisor. And the supervisor in turn, appears to be replying with ideas from his Adult. There is, however, a second, or hidden, psychological level of communication occurring. At this hidden psychological level the employee is saying, "I'm helpless to solve my own problems so I need a wise person (Parent) like you to solve them for me." The supervisor, in turn, responds on the psychological level with, "Yes, I recognize my wisdom and will be happy to give you advice." But then in the 3rd and 5th parts of the transaction, the employee rejects the advice that he appeared to be asking for.

If we look only at the surface or social level of this transaction, it won't make sense to us. It appears contradictory. If, however, we look at the hidden psychological level, we can begin to see that the basic purpose of the transaction was to reject advice rather than to receive it. By rejecting the ideas of the supervisor, the employee is able "to prove" his superiority over the boss in an underhanded or crooked way. This type of transaction is called an ulterior-transaction because it involves two levels of communication, an apparent social level and a hidden psychological level. Ulterior transactions are commonly called games. . . .

222

	Parent Ego State	Adult Ego State	Child Ego State
Voice tones	Condescending, putting down, criticizing, or accusing	Matter-of-fact	Full of feeling
Words Used	Everyone knows that . . . You should never . . .	How, what, when, why, who, probable	I'm mad at you! . . . Hey, great (. . . or any words that have a high feeling level connected with them)
Posture	Puffed-up, super-correct, very proper	Attentive, eye-to-eye contact, listening and looking for maximum data	Slouching, playful, beat-down or burdened, self-conscious
Facial Expressions	Frowns, worried or disapproving looks, chin jutted out	Alert eyes, paying close attention	Excitement, surprise, downcast eyes, quivering lip or chin, moist eyes
Body Gestures	Hands on hips, pointing finger in accusation, arms folded across chest	Leaning forward in chair toward other person, moving closer to hear and see better	Spontaneous activity, wringing hands, pacing, withdrawing into corner or moving away from, laughter, raising hand for permission

3. Work Is Not the Only Thing That Occurs at Work

How many times have you heard, "You're expected to put in 8 hours of work in exchange for 8 hours of pay!" Work, however, is not the only thing that occurs on the job. People have six different ways to structure their time. Whether they are on the job or off makes little difference. These six time-structuring methods apply to all situations. They include (1) withdrawal, (2) rituals, (3) activities or "work," (4) pastimes, (5) games, and (6) authenticity or intimacy. Each of these approaches is related to the life position which you have taken.

The least risky way in which you can fill your time is withdrawal. You withdraw from people and situations when you are physically present by mentally putting yourself in another place or situation. Withdrawal is programmed by your Child as an escape from a boring or threatening present situation. It can also be a way of getting imaginary strokes from imaginary people through daydreams.

Rituals are the next safest way to fill your time and to get strokes. They are fixed ways of behaving towards other people which are programmed by your Parent. Rituals are closely related to good manners or "the proper thing to do when you're with others." For example, when you meet someone you know, usually you will say, "Hi! How are you today?" And the other person will likely say in return,

"Fine. How are you?" This is a greeting ritual in which you give your friend several work strokes in return for several similar strokes from him. If you have good manners, you will probably be a good stroker because you can be depended on to go through with rituals.

A third way you can fill your time is through activities which are often called work tasks. Activities are aimed at getting something done. For example, writing an airline ticket, painting a house, writing a letter, or fixing or serving dinner are all activities. Since work is often done with or for other people, it is also a common way of getting or "earning" strokes. Play and recreation are also activities.

Pastimes are a fourth way you can fill your time. Some pastimes are programmed by your Adult to get more information about another person. A common example of this is, "What kind of work do you do?" Other pastimes are programmed by your Parent or your Child to get strokes from others. Examples of these include, "What did you think of the President's speech last night?" and "Have you heard the story about the drunk who . . .?" If you have a deficiency of pastimes, you will often feel like a wallflower in social gatherings. Everyone else will be getting lots of strokes and getting to know people without getting too close to them.

Interpersonal games are a fifth way you can fill your time. Nearly all people play interpersonal games (not to be confused with recreational games) even though they really aren't much fun. Games are programmed by our Not OK Child to help it get strokes and deal with its Not OK feelings. . . .

Authenticity or intimacy is the sixth way you can fill your time with other people.

Authenticity is programmed by your Adult and occurs when you are in the "I'm OK—You're OK" life position. It is a warm, caring, straight (nongame playing) series of transactions with another person. Authenticity is a means by which people really come together whereas the other five ways of filling time keep you at safe distances from others. In authenticity you are the most vulnerable because you are giving more of yourself away than at any other time.

Your own experience probably tells you that all six of these methods for filling time occur on the job as well as off. The more time you spend with an individual, the more likely you will use all six time-structuring methods. For example, a ticket salesman will probably use only rituals and activities with a customer since he spends so little time with him. On the other hand, a stewardess on a five hour nonstop flight may find that she is engaged in all six time-structuring methods with her passengers.

You can use your job in all six time-structuring ways described above. You can withdraw from relationships by losing yourself in your job. Work can provide you with many opportunities for stroke-exchanging rituals. All jobs are primarily focused on activities designed to get certain things done. Your job also provides you with frequent opportunities for pastimes that help you get to know other people better and exchange recognitions with them. Your job can also serve as a playing field for games. And finally your job can provide you with opportunities for authentic relationships with colleagues and sometimes even customers. Work, therefore, is not the only thing that occurs at work. . . .

LIFE POSITIONS

People may view themselves as: I'm bright; I'm not very intelligent; I make a mess out of everything; I'm mister wonderful; I'm the lowest form of humanity.

People may view others as: People are real junk; People are a joy to me; Everyone is out to take advantage of you; I get along so well with people.

These are but a few examples of the four life positions or life scripts.

The First Position
1. I'm OK; You're not OK
   This person is a blamer, and you aren't worth the gun powder to blow you away.

The Second Position

    2. I'm not OK; You're OK

    This person feels inferior and as a result either withdraws from life or competes ferociously in an attempt to feel OK.

The Third Position

    3. I'm not OK; You're not OK

    This person is not an active member of society. Life isn't worth living. When you lose interest in everything, you just want to die.

The Fourth Position

    4. I'm OK; You're OK

    This person has a good sense of self worth and a positive view of the world. This is the most desirable life position. Life is well worth living.

WHICH EGO STATE IS IN CONTROL? ——————

PURPOSE: To demonstrate that everyone has three persons, or ego states, within himself, and discover which part of you is usually in control.

PROCEDURE: Self-analysis to determine which ego state dominates the way you speak and act, by answering the following questions.

    1. Describe your individual behavior.
        a. How do you sit, stand, or walk? _____

        b. How do you speak? What is your choice of words? _____

    Words like cute, marvelous, awful, childish, filthy are usually Parent words. Suitable, practical and correct are usually Adult words. Words like far out, wow, won't and can't are common Child words.

    2. How do you get along with people?
        a. Is the Parent in you bossy? _____
        b. Does the Parent think she knows it all? _____
        c. Do you often upset the Child in other people? _____
        d. Is the Child in you fun loving and happy? _____

        e. Does the Child in others enjoy being around you and have fun with you? _____

        f. Do people behave as an Adult around you? _____
    3. Check your early childhood years.
        a. Do you find that sometimes you talk exactly the same way you used to when you were a child? _____
        b. Do you sometimes hear yourself say things the way your mother or father did? _____
    4. Check your own feelings.
        a. Which ego state do you actually feel is active in you at any given time, as you transact with others? _____

1. Is your Parent critical or helping?
    2. Does your Adult help you figure things out?
    3. Does your Child act on his own, or does he act so as to please your internal parent? ❏

TA ROLE PLAYING

PURPOSE: To explore both the verbal and nonverbal communication aspects of crossed, complementary and ulterior transactions. To recognize that the outcome of the ulterior transaction will be determined on the psychological level rather than the social level, and this causes people to play games.

PROCEDURE: 1. Form groups of four or five.
    2. Using the information on both verbal and nonverbal aspects of the three ego states, develop a three-act role playing skit.
    3. Role play the first act demonstrating a crossed transaction both verbally and nonverbally.
    4. Role play the second act demonstrating the same situation using both verbal and nonverbal communication to create a complementary transaction.
    5. Role play the third act demonstrating the same situation, using verbal and nonverbal communication to send both the psychological and social messages in a duplex transaction.

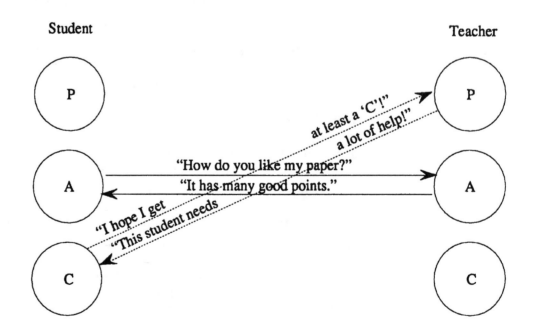

VERBAL	NONVERBAL
Rate	Facial Expressions
Duration	Posture
Pause	Gestures
Loudness	Touch
Emphasis	Body Movements
Pitch	
Tone	
Sentence Structure	
Word Selection	
Slips of the Tongue	

PSYCHOLOGICAL MESSAGE	EXAMPLE
Posture: (Standing with feet spread apart and hands on hips)	"I want you to all relax and feel free to disagree with my point of view."
Gestures: (With neck extended, lips pursed and looking down upon her students)	"I don't like to make judgments about people."
Facial Expressions: (serious)	"You bet I can take a joke."
Rate: (Said slowly in a nasal halting voice)	"I'm not angry; take all the time in the world."
Emphasis: (Loudness)	"Why can't you be like your *sister?*

DISCUSSION:
1. Which transaction is the most emotional in its approach?
2. Which transaction is the most rational in its approach?
3. How important is it to analyze your P—A—C position before communicating with someone else?
4. Do you believe that an ulterior transaction is dishonest?
5. Which transactions create communication breakdowns and why? ❏

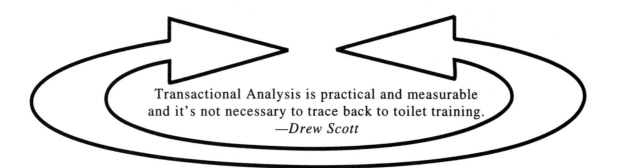

Transactional Analysis is practical and measurable and it's not necessary to trace back to toilet training.
—Drew Scott

EVERYONE NEEDS STROKES

Everyone needs some kind of stroking which may be pleasant or unpleasant. We hunger for recognition which may take the form of a word or a pat on the back. A stroke that helps you to feel that you are OK is called a positive stroke. One that tells you that you are not OK is a negative stroke.

Without strokes, infants suffer mentally and physically and may die because their urge to live decreases. Positive strokes are necessary for physical and mental well-being.

A child's behavior is shaped by the kinds of strokes received, and this behavior is carried over into adulthood. A negative stroke is better than no stroke at all. We go on seeking in adulthood the same strokes we received in our early lives. People play games to receive strokes.

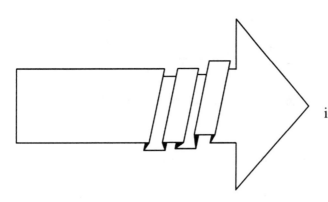

Though past scripting may have molded the individual, with awareness he or she is able to write a new script. —*Corey*

GAMES DON'T SOLVE PROBLEMS

People play games to give or receive strokes, and games have negative pay-offs. A game has an ulterior transaction which is the secret reason for playing the game. A game has a "pay-off" which is the feeling the player gets at the end of the game. The game *Now I've Got You* ends with a feeling of beating the other player. The game *Kick Me* ends with the feeling of being wronged. A Child may want to feel wronged to end an intimate relationship.

When you become aware that you are playing the game, a good way to stop is to refuse the pay-off, which is the feeling that usually results from the game. You can stop the game by not exaggerating your weaknesses or the weaknesses of others. Give and receive positive strokes. You can also refuse to play the games of your Child or Parent.

A FEW GAMES

HARRIED EXECUTIVE: Buries herself in work to keep people from getting too close.

CORNERED: "I'm between a rock and a hard place."

BLEMISH: "You have written a fine composition except for a few minor problems—spelling, grammatical construction, word choice, etc., which just makes a mess out of the Queen's English."

BEAR TRAPPER: Baits the victim, then lets the trap fall.

I'M ONLY TRYING TO HELP YOU: "Haven't I always been right? Just rely on me, the way you always have. I have always had your best interest in mind. It isn't necessary for you to deal with your problems as long as I'm around."

WOODEN LEG: "What can I expect with two strikes against me? e.g., wrong race, no education, wrong side of town, etc."

RAPO: A sexual base that is set up, taken away, then the victim is smashed.

SEE HOW HARD I TRIED: "I'm not responsible for how it all turned out. God knows I've tried."

UPROAR: "I'm right. You're wrong. No, you're wrong and I'm right." Yes! No! No! Yes!

NOW I'VE GOT YOU, YOU S.O.B.: "You're the guilty one and now you are going to pay."

YES BUT: Someone asks for advice and then argues all of the reasons why it is stupid advice. "That's a good idea but. . . ."

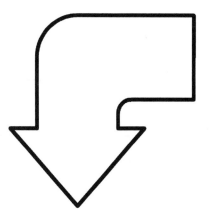

In every real man a child is hidden who wants to play. —F. Nietzche

THE HIDDEN ULTERIOR MESSAGE GAME
OR NOW I'VE GOT YOU

PURPOSE: To evaluate ulterior messages.

PROCEDURE: Read the situation and dialog below. Then in groups answer the discussion questions.

   Tom and a group of friends are watching a championship fight on TV. Tom notices that the only person not enjoying the fight is Jim, who in his opinion is a creep. When the fight is over, and everyone except Jim is paying off wagers, and saying how exciting it was, Tom speaks to Jim:

TOM: Did you like the way the fight turned out? (He already knows that he didn't like it.)
JIM: No, and I don't know how you guys can be entertained by something so barbarous.
TOM: It's weird that you're the only one who had any trouble with it. You have a real problem here.
JIM: (angry) You know what you can do. . . .
TOM: Why are you losing your cool? You're the weirdo, not me.

DISCUSSION: 1. Could Jim have refused to answer Tom's question, or have said something like, "I don't mind your liking it," and letting it go at that?
                    2. Why do we spend so much time playing games when it is such a destructive way of dealing with people?
                    3. How may we stop playing games?
                    4. How may we respond to people who play games?

STROKE ANALYSIS

PURPOSE: To become aware that everyone needs some kind of stroking, pleasant or unpleasant, because strokes are necessary for physical and mental health.

PROCEDURE: With the worksheet below develop a list of verbal and nonverbal strokes that you have received at work, at home, in class, or in your social contacts.

POSITIVE   NEGATIVE

1. _____   1. _____

2. _____   2. _____

3. _____   3. _____

4. _____   4. _____

5. _____   5. _____

DISCUSSION: 1. If a stroke is given to you for what you do rather than for what you are, it is a conditional stroke. There are strings attached because you have to do "good things."
                    2. How many of the positive strokes in the above were conditional?
                    3. What kinds of strokes do you make sure you get?
                    4. How do you make sure you get these strokes?
                    5. What games do you play to get strokes?   ❑

TA WORKSHEET

PURPOSE: To demonstrate your ability in understanding transactional analysis.

PROCEDURE:
1. Draw your P—A—C circles.
2. Circle your life position.
   I'm OK; You're Not OK
   I'm Not OK; You're OK
   I'm Not OK; You're Not OK
   I'm OK; You're OK
3. Circle the stamps you collect:

   Red—anger   Yellow—fear
   Brown—poor me's   Purple—aha's
   Blue—depression   White—blandness
   Gray—boredom   Pink Paisley—stupid
   Black—guilt   Gold—a free happy

4. Circle the game you play:
   Victim games (Payoffs are feelings of inadequacy from an I'm Not OK position)
   If It Weren't for You
   Stupid
   Look How Hard I Try
   Kick Me
   Why Does This Always Happen To Me?
   Persecutor games (Payoffs are feelings of anger from a You're Not OK position)
   I Told You So
   Now I've Got You, You S.O.B.
   Uproar
   Rapo
   Rescuer Games (Payoffs are feelings of blamelessness from a You're Not OK position)
   I'm Only Trying to Help
   Let Me Do It for You

DISCUSSION:
1. Are all of your circles of equal size? Why/why not?
2. Did you circle "I'm OK; YOU're OK?" If not, why not? What does this say about your life script?
3. Did you circle positive stamps or negative stamps? Discuss.
4. What predominant game(s) do you play in your life script?
5. When are games dishonest?
6. Why is it that games keep us from facing up to what we fear, such as responsibility, competition, and how others view us?
7. How important is it to realize that games help you get negative strokes?
8. Why would any Child want to feel not-OK?   ❑

REACTIONS

1. Are you satisfied with the ego state that dominates the way you speak and act? Why or why not?

2. Would you like to have more Parent and Adult and less Child, more Child and less Parent? Why or why not?

3. What can you do to bring about a change in your thinking and behavior to function in your preferred ego state?

4. Explain the difference between the psychological and social messages in an ulterior transaction.

5. What can you do to stop playing games?

6. Recall and explain the kinds of strokes you received as a child.

VALUES | 9

Values—A Working Definition

Valuing is one of our most precious personal rights. Yet, it seems increasingly clear that all too few humans do indeed have clear values. This chapter describes the process of "valuing" and helps participants to not only clarify their values, but ascertain the relationship of these values to the attitudes and behaviors that they exhibit. Do you always understand why you are making a decision? On what principle it stands? Is your behavior consistent or inconsistent with what you say? Are you consistent in how you apply standards, expectations or judgments from one person to the next?

In order to understand the relationship of values to behavior, attitudes and perception, we first need to look at some basic definitions inherent to the discussion of values.

Valuing

When something satisfies all seven of the criteria noted below, it is called a value:

1. Choosing freely

2. Choosing from all known alternatives

3. Choosing after thoughtful consideration of the consequences of all alternatives

4. Prizing, cherishing and being happy with the choice

5. Being willing to affirm the choice publicly

6. Acting, doing something with the choice

7. Repeating the action in some portion of life

Attributes

Those characteristics that define something—that by which it can be described and put into perspective against other things.

Example: Height, gender, personality, intelligence

Consequences

The possible outcomes of any given action(s).

Example: Break the law—pay the price

Choosing

The act of placing in a higher priority one thing over another—the act of selection, picking, using discretion to select among alternatives.

Example: Selecting a life partner

Preferences

Those things which we place a higher priority on than on others; if we had our way and were free to choose—we would go with these things.

Example: All children will be safe and cared for

Decision-Making

The process of:

1. Clarifying the problem or choice

2. Gathering pertinent data

3. Identifying possible alternatives

4. Verifying the consequence of alternatives

5. Choosing one alternative over the other

Judging

The process of evaluating someone, an action or outcome, on the basis of self-established criteria—the discrimination between options; the imposing of values on someone else; the process of estimating, awarding, reviewing, critiquing and reporting the conclusion thereof.

Attitudes

Our views about things which usually give direction to our behaviors.

Behaviors

The acting out of our desires, fears, decisions; the process of making our body take some action in one direction or another—following up on our intentions—with action; to proceed with, discharge, enact, play one's part, conduct oneself

---

THE IMPORTANCE OF VALUES

Values are not just important in their own right. They serve as a base for decisions, actions and judgments and are crucial to making decisions. In those instances when an individual (or group) either knows or is able to explain their values related to the problem, she can use those values directly, deliberately and openly in making the decision. In those instances in which the individual is unaware of her values, those values act at a subconscious level. That is, a plausible solution is that making the decision may be highly frustrating because there are competing values acting on the individual but she is unaware of the source of conflict and thereby unable to respond to the real issue.

It is the purpose of this chapter to present information and exercises that will enable you, by the end of the chapter, to answer the following questions:

1. What is a value?
2. How do values relate to my everyday life?
3. How do values affect the decision making process?
4. How are values formulated?
5. How do values affect my interpersonal communication?
6. What are factors that alter the existence of values in your life?
7. How does "information" affect the valuing/decision making process?

BARRIERS TO VALUING

In our information and highly technological society today, we are constantly being bombarded by conflicting opinions, views, beliefs and desires of other people, groups, family, friends and general public opinion. This information, and the influence with which it is displayed to us, presents many potential barriers to actually developing clear values for ourselves.

Confusion often exists between what we were taught to believe as youngsters and **what we believe as adults**.

Think for a moment about what opinions and values you borrowed from your parents; about those aspects of your current lifestyle that are similar or very different from those of your family members. Think back on those cliches or traditions that you participated in and/or heard as a child that have affected you today.

All of us receive some of our values initially from our families and sometimes those values are based in our religion, nationality, race, socioeconomic status and political upbringing. As we grow older, we sometimes re-examine the values that we "absorbed"—usually because a behavior facing us comes into conflict with our belief system.

Lack of Accurate Information

Ignorance for some is bliss . . . and it can allow us to not see the total picture. When we don't have as much relevant information as possible—when we have only seen one side versus all sides, and when certain key and relevant facts, perspectives, are not known to us—we choose from what is known and the choice may, in the larger context, be inappropriate.

Personal Biases of Others Which Have No Bearing in the Rational World

If we care about or admire someone, we tend to give their thoughts and feelings more credence and priority. Sometimes, because we do not want to offend people we care about, are close to, or are related to, we do not take the risk of offending them by "owning" values different than theirs.

Peer—Family—Work Pressure

All of us are subject to pressures from all of those around us. All of the avenues within which we function—family, work, social—have organizational cultures which reflect values. This culture, both directly and subtly, forces us to confront its values. The threats of noncompliance, rejection and ostracism are usually present. And some of us are not comfortable with "being in the minority" in our thought—of not conforming and being part of whatever "normative" culture we are a part of.

Conflicting Values

At one time or another, we are all faced with alternatives to the decision process that are based on values that seem to conflict. For example, a person who has a priority on stability and security—who values his house and wants to stay there—may be faced with a job promotion that requires him to move somewhere else. Upward mobility and success may also be a high priority. But when placed against the security and stability of a house, which one will prevail?

Lack of Empowerment

People with self-confidence usually do not have any problem being able to articulate their values. They may change their values—but they feel empowered—they feel able to be in charge of the changes. A lack of this feeling—knowing that you are and have a right to be in control—can be a barrier in that you may not be able to exercise the control to identify for yourself and be comfortable with your choice.

Consistency

As choices emerge, in a variety of circumstances, especially if they include passing judgment on ourselves, vs. others, we sometimes have the tendency to be inconsistent in what values guide(s) our decisions. But, if something is truly a value for us, should or shouldn't it apply to all circumstances?

Changing Circumstances

As circumstances and events change, so does pertinence of our decisions. We all must re-evaluate from time to time our choices based on emerging circumstances. And these can pose a challenge to our value system. If we value something because it has certain attributes—and the attributes change—what happens to how we feel about the value?

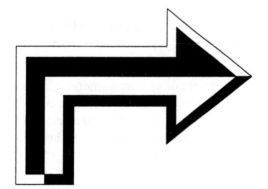

The greatest discovery of my generation is that a human being can alter his life by altering his attitude.
—W. James

the cavity

above green clean shaven lawns
and archaic springing fountains of youth
wavering buildings
raging like the towers of quivering babel
stagger through the heavens
seeking to secure inspirational decay
form the guilded gods
of the swelling golden calf

inside men with silk ties
and suits
nest behind marble desks
settled softly
on rich threads

ladies wearing sleak stirring dresses
wavingly swirve from room to room
delivering bacon and tomatoe sandwiches
and the latest of the bank president
and his flash
with his worn secretary

meanwhile
a block away
shrieks from the hungry seagull
pierce the smoggy mat glazed sky
as he hovers futily over the cluttered dump
below
crushed cylinder cans
and smashed wine bottles
lie crumpled in the infested garbage pit

lunging down
he finds his wanted food eaten
by diseased red-veined faces
and stringy whores of skid row
who crawl through the garbage
fingering
damp green bread
trying to survive
until another bottle
or the capture of another bitch's eye

leads them into their private hell
after several more dives
his warm white feathered body
once like clouds
absorbs remnants of melted butter
now rancid from the heat

approaching his last target
the weight of the seagull's yellow
gummed body collapses
above his scummed feet
and falls
into the pit

and the bank president
lazily passes in comfort
to his white waste
just in time
for a five o'clock martini

S-Grace

MY WORLD NOW: LIFE IN A NURSING HOME, FROM THE INSIDE

Anna Mae Halgrim Seaver

This is my world now. It's all I have left. You see, I'm old. And, I'm not as healthy as I used to be. I'm not necessarily happy with it but I accept it. Occasionally, a member of my family will stop in to see me. He or she will bring me some flowers or a little present, maybe a set of slippers—I've got 8 pair. We'll visit for awhile and then they will return to the outside world and I'll be alone again.

Oh, there are other people here in the nursing home. Residents, we're called. The majority are about my age. I'm 84. Many are in wheelchairs. The lucky ones are passing through—a broken hip, a diseased heart, something has brought them here for rehabilitation. When they're well they'll be going home.

Most of us are aware of our plight—some are not. Varying stages of Alzheimer's have robbed several of their mental capacities. We listen to endlessly repeated stories and questions. We meet them anew daily, hourly or more often. We smile and nod gracefully each time we hear a retelling. They seldom listen to my stories, so I've stopped trying.

The help here is basically pretty good, although there's a large turnover. Just when I get comfortable with someone he or she moves on to another job. I understand that. This is not the best job to have.

I don't much like some of the physical things that happen to us. I don't care much for a diaper. I seem to have lost the control acquired so diligently as a child. The difference is that I'm aware and embarrassed but I can't do anything about it. I've had 3 children and I know it isn't pleasant to clean another's diaper. My husband used to wear a gas mask when he changed the kids. I wish I had one now.

Why do you think the staff insists on talking baby talk when speaking to me? I understand English. I have a degree in music and am a certified teacher. Now I hear a lot of words that end in "y." Is this how my kids felt? My hearing aid works fine. There is little need for anyone to position their face directly in front of mine and raise their voice with those "y" words. Sometimes it takes longer for a meaning to sink in; sometimes my mind wanders when I am bored. But there's no need to shout.

I tried once or twice to make my feelings known. I even shouted once. That gained me a reputation of being "crotchety." Imagine me, crotchety. My children never heard me raise my voice. I surprised myself. After I've asked for help more than a dozen times and received nothing more than a dozen condescending smiles and a "Yes, deary, I'm working on it," something begins to break. That time I wanted to be taken to a bathroom.

I'd love to go out for a meal, to travel again. I'd love to go to my own church, sing with my own choir. I'd love to visit my friends. Most of them are gone now or else they are in different "homes" of their children's choosing. I'd love to play a good game of bridge but no one here seems to concentrate very well.

My children put me here for my own good. They said they would be able to visit me frequently. But they have their own lives to lead. That sounds normal. I don't want to be a burden. They know that. But I would like to see them more. One of them is here in town. He visits as much as he can.

Something else I've learned to accept is loss of privacy. Quite often I'll close my door when my roommate—imagine having a roommate at my age—is in the TV room. I do appreciate some time to myself and believe that I have earned at least that courtesy. As I sit thinking or writing, one of the aides invariably opens the door unannounced and walks in as if I'm not there. Sometimes she even opens my drawers and begins rummaging around. Am I invisible? Have I lost my right to respect and dignity? What would happen if the roles were reversed? I am still a human being. I would like to be treated as one.

The meals are not what I would choose for myself. We get variety but we don't get a choice. I am one of the fortunate ones who can still handle utensils. I remember eating off such cheap utensils in the Great Depression. I worked hard so I would not have to ever use them again. But here I am.

Did you ever sit in a wheelchair over an extended period of time? It's not comfortable. The seat squeezes you into the middle and applies constant pressure on your hips. The armrests are too narrow and my arms slip off. I am luckier than some. Others are strapped into their chairs and abandoned in front of the TV. Captive prisoners of daytime television; soap operas, talk shows and commercials.

One of the residents died today. He was a loner who, at one time, started a business and developed a multimillion-dollar company. His children moved him here when he could no longer control his bowels. He didn't talk to most of us. He often snapped at the aides as though they were his employees. But he just gave up; willed his own demise. The staff has made up his room and another man has moved in.

A typical day. Awakened by the woman in the next bed wheezing—a former chain smoker with asthma. Call an aide to wash me and place me in my wheelchair to wait for breakfast. Only 67 minutes until breakfast. I'll wait. Breakfast in the dining area. Most of the residents are in wheelchairs. Others use canes or walkers. Some sit and wonder what they are waiting for. First meal of the day. Only 3 hours and 26 minutes until lunch. Maybe I'll sit around and wait for it. What is today? One day blends into the next until day and date mean nothing.

Let's watch a little TV. Oprah and Phil and Geraldo and who cares if some transvestite is having trouble picking a color-coordinated wardrobe from his husband's girlfriend's mother's collection. Lunch. Can't wait. Dried something with puréed peas and coconut pudding. No wonder I'm losing weight.

Back to my semiprivate room for a little semiprivacy or a nap. I do need my beauty rest, company may come today. What is today, again? The afternoon drags into early evening. This used to be my favorite time of the day. Things would wind down. I would kick off my shoes. Put my feet up on the coffee table. Pop open a bottle of Chablis and enjoy the fruits of my day's labor with my husband. He's gone. So is my health. *This* is my world.

Seaver, who lived in Wauwatosa, Wis., died in March. Her son found these notes in her room after her death.

70,800,000 JOB MARKETS IN THE UNITED STATES (THAT'S THE TOTAL
NUMBER OF NON-FARM PAYROLLS), including 19,400,000 Manufacturers'
Job Markets. • You narrow this down by deciding just what area, city •
or county you want to work in. This leaves you with however many
thousands or millions of job markets there are in that area or city. •
You narrow this down by identifying your Strongest Skills, on
their highest level that you can legitimately claim, and then
thru research deciding what field you want to work in, above
all. This leaves you with all the hundreds of businesses/
community organizations/agencies/schools/hospitals/
projects/associations/foundations/institutions/firms
or government agencies there are in that area and
in the field you have chosen. • You narrow this
down by getting acquainted with the economy
in the area through personal interviews with
various contacts; and supplementing this
with study of journals in your field, in
order that you can pinpoint the
places that interest you the most.
This leaves a manageable number of markets for you to do
some study on. You now
narrow this down by ask-
ing yourself, can I be
happy in this place,
and, do they have
the kind of prob-
lems which my
strongest skills
can help solve
for them? This
leaves you with
the companies
or organizations
which you will
now carefully
plan how to
approach . . .

One cannot have wisdom without living life. —*D. McCall*

VALUES MODEL

PURPOSE: To examine the basis for the things that we believe.

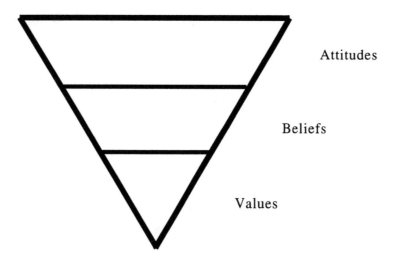

PROCEDURE: Form groups of 5–6 and answer the discussion questions below. Have one member record your group responses.

DISCUSSION:
1. Define
   a. Value
   b. Belief
   c. Attitude
2. Why is the smallest segment of the model on the bottom?
3. Is it possible to have a **belief** about something that is not supported by a **value**? How? Example?
4. Consider your feelings about taking an elective class in Music Appreciation. Trace those feelings from the attitude you have to the **belief** and ultimately the **value.** Can you do the same thing with your attitude about next Saturday's plans? Or your position on abortion?
5. Can we change our **values?** How? What effect would changing a **value** have on the rest of your life? ❑

VALUES IN A CHANGING SOCIETY

Introduction

The values present in a society in any given period are time and culturally bound. This chart illustrates the contrast between the values an individual holds as she progresses through her environments from decade to decade.

Time Factor	Environmental Setting	Resulting Values
Present Age- 70 Years *Value Processing period-1920s	Close Family-WWI "Model T" Flappers	Security-Economic Materialism Team Effort
Present Age- 60 Years *Value Processing period-1930s	Depression	Work Ethic
Present Age- 50 Years *Value Processing period-1940s	WWII Family Decay Mobility	Traditionalism Puritanism
Present Age- 40 Years *Value Processing period-1950s	Affluence Permissiveness T.V.-Jets-Technology Change-"Rock" Music	Change Acceptance Experience Individualism
Present Age- 30 Years *Value Processing period-1960s	Civil Rights Individual Freedoms War	Self-expression Equality Sensualism
Present Age- 20 Years *Value Processing period-1970s	Distrust/Tension Turmoil-Emotional/Social "Me" generation Computers	Emotional Security Experimentation Participation
Present Age- 10 Years *Value processing period-1980s	Affluence Crime/Drugs Peace	Materialism? Conservatism? Emotional Security?

Age-Born in the '90s

A STUDY OF AMERICAN YOUTH

Some contrasting highlights of student attitudes and values appear below:

1960	Early 1970s	Early 1990s
Campus rebellion in full flower.	Campus rebellion dead.	Student awareness/change within the rules.
New life-styles and radical politics appear linked: commune living, pot smoking and long hair, student protest marches.	Almost total divorce between radical politics and new life-styles.	Acceptance/tolerance of divergent lifestyles.
Campus search for self-fulfillment *in place* of conventional career.	Campus search for self-fulfillment *within* a conventional career.	Movement towards financial security, interest in career secondary to its potential for material gain.
Growing criticism of our "sick society."	Lessening of such criticism.	Constructive criticism, active, informed opinions.
Women's movement has little impact on youth values and attitudes.	Wide and deep penetration of women's lib ideas.	Concept of equality accepted by significant numbers of students.
Violence on campus condoned, romanticized.	Violence-free campus, violence rejected.	Violence continues to be rejected.
Value of Education severely questioned.	Value of Education strongly endorsed.	Value of Education seen as requirement for success.
Widening gap in values, morals and outlook between young people and their parents, especially college youth.	Younger generation and older mainstream America moving closer in values, morals and outlook.	Students aware of and interested in what parents and middle America believes.
Sharp split in social and moral values found within youth generation and between college students and the noncollege majority. Gap *within* generation proves to be larger and more severe than gap *between* generations.	Gap within generation narrows: noncollege youth virtually caught up with college students in new social and moral norms.	Gap between generations very narrow, gap between economic groups (college students vs. disenfranchised) becoming quite large.
Challenge to traditional work ethic confined to campus.	Work ethic strengthened on campus; growing weaker among noncollege youth.	Work ethic continues to grow weaker.

Adapted from *The New Morality* by Daniel Yankelovich

1960	Early 1970s	Early 1990s
New code of sexual morality, centering on greater acceptance of casual premarital sex, abortion, homosexuality and extramarital relations confined to minority of college students.	New sexual morality spreads to mainstream of both colleges and working class youth.	Sexual morality significantly affected by sexually transmitted diseases.
Harsh criticisms of major institutions, political parties, big business, military almost wholly confined to college students.	Criticism of some major institutions tempered on campus, taken up by working class youth.	Criticism reflects more enlightened mature judgments.
Campus is main focus of youthful discontent—non-college students quiet.	Campuses are quiet. Many signs of latent discontent and dissatisfaction among working class youth.	Campuses reflect growing political/social involvement but within the law.
Much youthful energy and idealism devoted to concern with minorities. Blacks considered most oppressed.	Concern with minorities lower. American Indians considered most oppressed.	Minority awareness very high on campus, even leading to political action.
Political interest of college youth left or liberal.	No clear-cut political center; pressures from both right and left. New left and radicals decline.	Significant swing to conservative values and ideals.
Law and order anathema to campus.	Campus shows greater acceptance of law and order.	Law and order on campus is norm. Disorder is abnormal behavior.

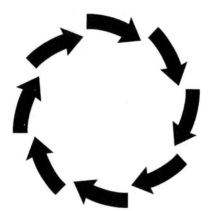

There must be more to life than having everything.
—M. Sendak

Gallup Poll: Four generations say what's gone wrong

Americans believe the nation is in a serious decline, but four key age groups differ on how to get the country back on track

MOST AMERICANS ARE DISCOURAGED, BUT SEE RAYS OF HOPE

American decline: Percent who think the U.S. is in an economic, moral and spiritual or military decline

Economic 79%
Moral 65%
Military 19%

Gloom about the future: Are you satisfied with the opportunity for the next generation to live better than its parents?

Don't know 4%
Satisfied 28%
Dissatisfied 68%

Hard work pays off: Are you satisfied with Americans' willingness to work hard to better themselves?

Dissatisfied 4%
Don't know 41%
Satisfied 55%

BABY BUSTERS: IDEALISTIC BUT CAUTIOUS

(18-31 yrs. old)

Don't favor big change: Percent who said it will take fundamental change to improve the economy

18-31 yrs. 40%
32-49 yrs. 59%
50-67 yrs. 63%
68 and over 50%

Want to help the needy: Percent who said government should spend more on the most needy, even if others get less

18-31 yrs. 42%
32-49 yrs. 36%
50-67 yrs. 39%
68 and over 34%

Want to solve social problems: Percent who want defense savings spent on education, poverty and other social needs instead of the deficit

18-31 yrs. 74%
32-49 yrs. 63%
50-67 yrs. 55%
68 and over 48%

MIDDLE AGERS: LITTLE TRUST IN GOVERNMENT

(32-49 yrs. old)

Think taxes favor rich: Percent who believe if they pay more taxes, they can count on the government to make the wealthy pay their share

18-31 yrs. 12%
32-49 yrs. 6%
50-67 yrs. 14%
68 and over 19%

Look to the private sector: Percent who want to give tax incentives to business and industry to encourage job creation

18-31 yrs. 46%
32-49 yrs. 53%
50-67 yrs. 47%
68 and over 41%

Concern for their children: Percent who say the next generation will be able to live better than their parents

18-31 yrs. 30%
32-49 yrs. 23%
50-67 yrs. 30%
68 and over 27%

SILENT GENERATION: DOWNBEAT AND DISILLUSIONED

(50-67 yrs. old)

Worry about losing ground: Percent who said their standard of living is going down

18-31 yrs. 24%
32-49 yrs. 32%
50-67 yrs. 35%
68 and over 30%

Feel the economy is sliding: Percent who think the country has lost ground with the economy and jobs

18-31 yrs. 59%
32-49 yrs. 66%
50-67 yrs. 76%
68 and over 62%

Fear U.S. can't compete: Percent who are satisfied with America's success at competing economically with other countries

18-31 yrs. 41%
32-49 yrs. 32%
50-67 yrs. 23%
68 and over 28%

DEPRESSION ERA: KEEPING THE FAITH

(68 yrs. and over)

Trust Social Security: Percent who say they can count on Social Security and Medicare when they grow old

18-31 yrs. 30%
32-49 yrs. 21%
50-67 yrs. 43%
68 and over 72%

Trust government more: Percent who think they can trust the government to do what is right most of the time

18-31 yrs. 13%
32-49 yrs. 13%
50-67 yrs. 11%
68 and over 23%

Doubts about work ethic: Percent who are satisfied with America's willingness to work hard to better themselves

18-31 yrs. 59%
32-49 yrs. 57%
50-67 yrs. 52%
68 and over 47%

SOURCE: A Gallup Poll of 1387 adults taken Aug. 31-Sept. 2, 1992; margin of error 3 percent for full sample, 6 percent for generation samples

VALUE VARIABLES ——————————————

PURPOSE: To gain an understanding of the impact of social issues to different people.

PROCEDURE: 1. Working quickly, place each issue from one of the columns in a box on the next page that best represents how strong your opinion is about the issue.
2. What you believe about the issue doesn't matter. How intense your feelings are is our goal.
3. Compare your decisions to others in the class, then answer the discussion questions.

I	II	III
Gun Control	Abortion	Welfare
Illegal Aliens	George Bush	Your Job
Marriage	Birth Control	Sunny Weather
Academy Awards	Snow Skiing	Pollution
Ice Cream	Basketball	Marijuana
Child Abuse	Bilingual Education	Sororities-Fraternities
Football	Alcoholism	Inflation
Energy Crisis	Police	Money
Hunting	Land Developers	Charles and Diana
Career Education	Tuition	Prostitution
Refugees	Premarital Sex	Communication
Sensitivity Training	Nudist Camps	Art Festivals
Bach-Beethoven	Final Exams	Income Taxes
Eddie Murphy	Property Values	Political Science
Student Center	Drug Pushers	Going to the Beach

DISCUSSION: 1. List some of the variables that were behind your choices.
2. Make a master list of these characteristics.
3. How do your choices relate to your values?   ❏

Very Strong Opinion

1	2	3	4
5	6	7	8
9	10	11	12
13	14	15	16

Couldn't Care Less

VALUES AND MUSIC ――――――――――――――――――

PURPOSE: To demonstrate that music is an important form of communication to many people, and reflects what is valued in our society.

PROCEDURE:
1. Bring a recording to class which you like. The recording can be old or new. The only requirement is that, for some reason, you like it.
2. On a volunteer basis, each person should play his/her recording for the class.
3. After the recording has been played, survey the class to see what messages they got from it. Then, volunteer why it is important to you. Allow for any additional questions and comments from the class.

DISCUSSION:
1. To what extent does music form our values? Give examples.
2. To what extent does music reflect our values? Give examples.
3. Name three songs that you can identify with and explain. ❏

All you need is love. —*The Beatles*

COLLAGE

PURPOSE:

To display, through pictures and words, a composite of your values, both abstract and concrete.

PROCEDURE:

1. Using magazines, scissors and glue, cut and paste words and pictures that describe your values and interests. Glue them on a poster board in the format you desire. This may take several class periods or may be done as an out-of-class project.
2. Display all finished collages and assign numbers to each one.
3. Each student will choose one collage and write what they think the person is like by inferring what the collage visually is communicating.
4. These reports will be attached to the collage with a paper clip.
5. When everyone is done, each author will read his/her collage report aloud to the class. They may guess who the person is or he/she may reveal him/herself and comment as to the accuracy of the report if so desired.

DISCUSSION:

1. Was it easy or hard to infer what your individual valued? Explain.
2. Did you find yourself turning pictures or words that describe action into value indicators?
3. Was this person's collage accurate according to her opinion of herself? According to your impression of the person? ❑

GIFT BOX

PURPOSE:

To enable you to identify the material and nonmaterial things you value.

PROCEDURE:

1. Answer the following questions with material items by filling in the blanks:
   a. If you came home today and found a gift box on your door step or in your front yard, what would you like to be in it?

   _____

   _____

   b. What material thing would you want for the person you feel closest to? (Specify person.)

   _____

   _____

   c. What is the smallest material thing you would want for yourself?

   _____

   _____

d. What is the largest material thing you would want for yourself?

_____

_____

Why? _____

_____

e. What would you not want to be in the gift box?

_____

2. Now answer these questions again, responding with nonmaterial answers.

a. _____

b. _____

c. _____

d. _____

e. _____

3. What would you be willing to give up for each of these things, both material and nonmaterial?

1. a. _____

b. _____

c. _____

d. _____

e. _____

2. a. _____

b. _____

c. _____

d. _____

e. _____

DISCUSSION:
1. How important are gifts to you?
2. What values do your material choices indicate?
3. What values can be inferred from your nonmaterial gift wishes?
4. Which values are more important to you, the material or nonmaterial? Discuss.
5. Are you basically a materialistic person? Explain your answer.
6. How important is money to you? ❏

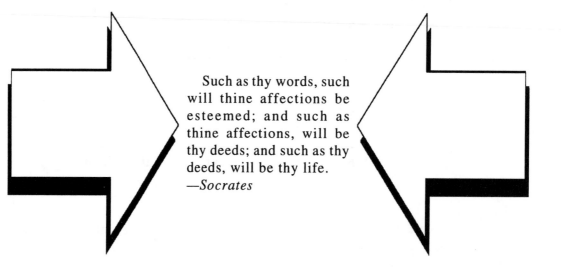

Such as thy words, such will thine affections be esteemed; and such as thine affections, will be thy deeds; and such as thy deeds, will be thy life.
—*Socrates*

IT WAS BECAUSE. . . .

PURPOSE: To examine your position in moral maturity according to the Kohlberg scale.

PROCEDURE:
1. Write down the last time you did something you **knew** was wrong. The more significant the issue, the more meaningful this lesson will be. Try to choose something that you had to **think** about. **Everybody** exceeds the speed limit. We often do it without any guilt at all, so pick something of **consequence.**
2. The issue may be one of ethics, morals, legality or conduct.
3. You may be 100 percent honest. This assignment will **not** be turned in or shared with anyone else.
4. Identify (as close as you can) the reason(s) that best represents your justification to do the above mentioned wrong. (check all that apply)
   - 2 A. "I was asked to, and I told 'em I would, so I went ahead and did it."
   - 3 B. "My decision was really best for everyone involved."
   - ___ C. "I know better than those who say 'It's wrong'."
   - 2 D. "It was a deal, I had to keep my word."
   - 1 E. "Hey, I was told to do it. I had to do it."
   - 4 F. "I was just doing my duty."
   - 4 G. "Well, I could have gotten into trouble if I hadn't done it."
   - 3 H. "Everybody else was doing it."
   - 2 I. "I had a job to do and I did what I was supposed to do."
   - 3 J. "I didn't want to disappoint anybody."
   - 6 ✓ K. "My rules take precedence over other rules."
5. Your instructor will explain the concepts behind Moral Development and show you what level each item above corresponds to. Remember, this brief exercise is only an indication of your level, only **you** can accurately place yourself on the scale.

DISCUSSION:
1. Does Kohlberg's scale fairly reflect Moral Development?
2. Do you agree with your "position" on the scale based on the exercise? Why?
3. What value to you as a communicator is this knowledge of your position?
4. What can you do to advance on Kohlberg's scale? ❏

THE
LAWRENCE KOHLBERG
MORAL DEVELOPMENT SCALE

The Scale:

1 — Is universal, consistent, and unchanging—the world over!
2 — Is inflexibly sequentially upwards (a person may be halfway in one stage and "spill over" in the neighboring two).
3 — Focuses on *why* (the reason) a decision is made, not *what* the decision is (two people at differing stages on the scale can make the same decision—but for different reasons).
4 — Is dependent on conflict (either direct or empathic) for upward growth.
5 — Upper levels (5–6) demand high cognitive development (high intelligence, well educated).

Scale Level	Description	Behavioral Reasoning
1	Deference to Authority	"I did it because told me to."
2	Sense of satisfaction of own needs	"I did it because I wanted to."
3	Seeking approval through being "good" or "nice"	"I did it because _____ will approve of (like) me for making that choice."
4	Respect for Law & Order	"The rules are. . . . The law is. . . . The book says. . . ."
5	Societal Needs	"What is the greatest good for the greatest number?" "Considering everybody involved, what is the best decision?"
6	Universal Ethical Principle	"I make my moral decisions based on a carefully thought out, personally chosen ethical standard that emphasizes the worth and dignity of life."

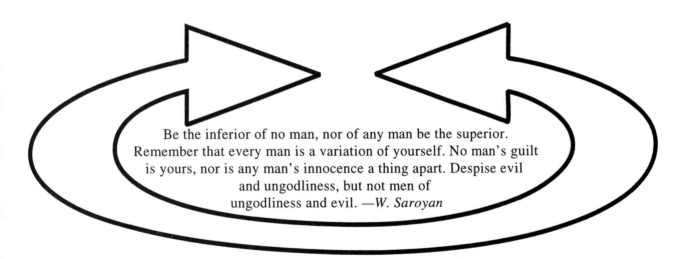

Be the inferior of no man, nor of any man be the superior. Remember that every man is a variation of yourself. No man's guilt is yours, nor is any man's innocence a thing apart. Despise evil and ungodliness, but not men of ungodliness and evil. —*W. Saroyan*

COMPLETE THE THOUGHT

PURPOSE: To engage in free association and inductive reasoning in determining values you have.

PROCEDURE:
1. Complete the following thoughts in the various sections.
2. Pair off and discuss your responses, letting someone else read yours first.
3. Discuss with your partner the "I" thoughts you like most and why.
4. Resume in a large group to share responses and answer discussion questions.

In General

1. On Saturday nights, I like most to . . .
2. When it rains, I . . .
3. Cold weather. . .
4. Crowded, bustling places make me feel . . .
5. In my spare time, I . . .
6. Materialistic things . . .
7. Emotional people . . .
8. The Viet Nam War . . .
9. Abortion is . . .
10. Woman's lib really . . .
11. Childless couples should . . .
12. Sex before marriage . . .
13. As a societal institution, marriage . . .
14. I think homosexuals . . .
15. Richard Nixon was . . .
16. The economic state of our country . . .
17. Education, in terms of my perspective . . .
18. I think that marijuana . . .
19. Minority groups in this country . . .
20. To me, money . . .

Personal Thoughts

1. I cry when . . .

2. I feel most comfortable in a small group when . . .

3. People bother me when . . .

4. _____ makes me feel very self-conscious.

5. I am warm and sincere . . .

6. I get ticked off . . .

7. Religion is something . . .

254

8. The out of doors makes me feel . . .

9. The mountains make me aware . . .

10. Ocean waves remind me of . . .

11. The beach is a place that . . .

12. If I had 6 months to live, I would . . .

13. My mother . . .

14. My father . . .

15. The quiet activity I enjoy most is . . .

16. The sport that interests me the most is . . .

17. _____ has been the most influential person in my life.

18. I respect _____ more than anyone else.

19. The single most motivational *factor* or event in my life was . . .

20. If I could change one thing about myself, I would . . .

21. The thing I like most about myself is _____ .

22. I feel very inferior when . . .

23. The situation I feel most secure in is . . .

24. Of all the many faces of myself, I like the role of _____ .

25. Game-playing is something that . . .

26. Most of all, I want to _____ .

27. _____ is what I like least about myself.

28. The physical characteristic about me that I like most is _____ .

29. Intellectually, I _____ .

30. I make myself laugh when I _____ .

DISCUSSION: 1. What, if anything, did you learn about yourself?
                      2. What values did you become aware of or reaffirm?
                      3. Are you a very social person, or private?
                      4. Did you find this hard to do? Why/why not? ❏

MY OBITUARY-EULOGY ———————————————

PURPOSE: To help you get in touch with your feelings about death and the various things you hope to accomplish before it occurs.

PROCEDURE: In the space below, write the following things: your birth date; the year you think you will die (taking into account your family's longevity and that men live an average of 70 years and women 75 years); personal data (marriage, children, etc.); social, education, and professional accomplishments you hope to attain before your death. Add anything else you would like to have said about you and the things you did.

DISCUSSION: 1. Why did you pick the date of death?
             2. What roadblocks do you envision in achieving the ideals you listed?
             3. Were you uncomfortable with this exercise? Why/Why not? What are your feelings about death? Where did these feelings originate?   ❏

THE ALLIGATOR RIVER STORY ———————————————

PURPOSE: To demonstrate the evaluative process in compromising values.

PROCEDURE: 1. Read the following story.
             2. Rank the five characters from one to five, one being the person you feel is the best person, and five being the person you feel is the worst.
             3. Get into small groups and discuss your ranking.

There once was a woman named Abigail who was in love with a man named Gregory. Gregory lived on the shore of a river. Abigail lived on the opposite shore of the river. The river which separated the two lovers was teeming with man-eating alligators. Abigail wanted to cross the river to be with Gregory. Unfortunately, the bridge had been washed out. So she went to ask Sinbad, the river boat captain, to take her across. He said he would be glad to if she would go to bed with him. She promptly refused and went to a friend named Ivan to explain her plight. Ivan said he did not want to be involved at all in the situation. Abigail felt her only alternative was to accept Sinbad's terms. She went to bed with him and he then fulfilled his promise and took her across the river to Gregory.

When she told Gregory about her agreement with Sinbad, Gregory cast her aside. Heartsick and dejected, Abigail turned to Slug with her tale of woe. Slug, feeling compassion for Abigail, sought out Gregory and beat him brutally. Abigail was pleased to see Gregory getting beaten up, and as the sun sets on the horizon, we hear Abigail laughing at Gregory.

DISCUSSION: 1. How did you rank the five characters? Why?
              2. Did you have to compromise one value for another? If so, explain.
              3. After discussing the rankings in your small groups, would you change your ranking? If so, why?
              4. What might these characters reflect about our society's values?   ❑

THE NUCLEAR WAR

PURPOSE: To reveal how prejudices and values influence decisions. To introduce participants to the myths in our society.

PROCEDURE: 1. Form small groups.
              2. Assume the following story to be true.
                  The United States has been involved in a nuclear war. Eight people find themselves in a shelter capable of supporting only five people for the year of necessary confinement. There are no other known shelters which survived the attack. Your problem is to evict three people so that the remaining five may survive. After your group has come to a decision, place a plus (+) in front of the names of those individuals the group has decided may live in the shelter and a zero (0) in front of the names of those the group has decided to evict.
              3. Your instructor will give your group a list of names and information on the people in the bomb shelter.

DISCUSSION: 1. What values governed your decisions?
              2. Why was a group decision difficult?   ❑

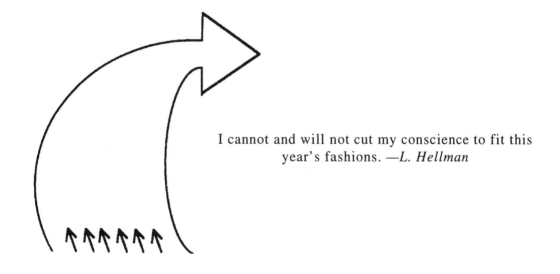

I cannot and will not cut my conscience to fit this year's fashions. —L. Hellman

PERSONAL ASSESSMENT

PURPOSE: To become aware of

—Personal preferences which may affect skill development and decision-making.

—Human relations profile in terms of getting along with people.

—Life-style variables to consider in selecting occupations.

PROCEDURE:
1. Utilize Personal Assessment sheet results on next two pages. Divide class into 4–5 groups and have them consider the following questions: As a result of my self-assessment, if I am successful in selecting a career which suits my personal preferences, the job would have the following characteristics.
2. Once this is completed, have the group brainstorm five possible jobs which require some college education which can meet the requirements for each individual.
3. Next have each person assess where he/she would now place him/herselves on a leadership scale of 1–10, with 10 being a dynamic, resourceful leader. Have him/her then indicate where on the scale he/she would like to be in two years. You may wish to discuss shifts, up and down, and possible strategies to achieve goals. Also highlight the Career Planning Center as a good source of information in matching jobs with personal preferences.
4. Now, utilizing same group or changing composition, have each group brainstorm all the factors which they would consider before selecting a job. Once completed, list all responses on the board; then, have each group rank the top five factors to be considered.

DISCUSSION:
1. How do your personal preferences affect your skills and abilities?
2. Are there any areas in your personal relationships with others that need some attention?
3. What goals can you set for yourself which would help you in getting along better with others? ❏

PERSONAL ASSESSMENT A

Every job demands some skills. Our personal preferences often affect our skills and abilities because we usually do well in those things we like or prefer and often return to the tasks we enjoy. Our personal preferences also affect the decisions we make. Read the items below, considering carefully how each applies to you as a unique person. For each item, please mark the column (X) that best answers the question.

I prefer to do things that require me to:	Very Much or Usually	Sometimes	Seldom or Not at All
1. read and study			
2. get outdoors often			
3. use and work with mathematics			
4. use physical strength			
5. sell to the public			
6. supervise others			
7. meet the public			
8. travel			
9. work with animals			
10. work with groups of young children			
11. follow directions from others			
12. plan events and activities			
13. think rapidly and creatively			
14. be in clean, quiet surroundings			
15. handle and repair equipment			
16. manage and handle money			
17. express myself through writing			
18. order merchandise			
19. judge the merit of other workers			
20. work by myself			
21. fix things			
22. keep accurate and complete records			
23. use my artistic ability			
24. plan and organize my own work			
25. make my own decisions			

Which three of the above that you rated "Very Much or Usually" would be the most important to you personally?

1. _____

2. _____

3. _____

Which three of the above you rated "Seldom or Not at All" would be the *least* desirable?

1. _____

2. _____

3. _____

PERSONAL ASSESSMENT B

In continuing to assess the important "who am I?" and "what am I?" questions relating to occupational choice, consider how you get along with others. Attempt to rate yourself as honestly as possible for each item by marking the column (X) that best answers the questions below.

When I am with other people I:	Usually or Often	Sometimes	Seldom or Not at All
1. am selected to be their leader	_____	_____	_____
2. listen quietly and comment little	_____	_____	_____
3. try to follow the rules of the group	_____	_____	_____
4. volunteer if help is needed	_____	_____	_____
5. get asked to do important jobs	_____	_____	_____
6. talk when others are talking	_____	_____	_____
7. am very social and make others feel comfortable	_____	_____	_____
8. participate in discussions	_____	_____	_____
9. back off when the group decides to do something I am not interested in	_____	_____	_____
10. show respect for those who are older	_____	_____	_____
11. resent being asked for help	_____	_____	_____
12. try to stay out of trouble	_____	_____	_____
13. try to get my ideas accepted	_____	_____	_____
14. criticize others to see if they really know what they want	_____	_____	_____
15. like being the "center" of action	_____	_____	_____

From the questions above, which three do you think occur with the greatest frequency; which three from the "Usually or Often" column happen most often?

1. _____

2. _____

3. _____

Which three occur with the least frequency; which three from the "Seldom or Not at All" column rarely happen?

1. _____

2. _____

3. _____

What can you conclude from A and B? Is there a characteristic pattern in A and B? Are there any apparent contradictions?

_____

_____

_____

SELF-AWARENESS INVENTORY ———————————

PURPOSE: To analyze some ways in which you may want to grow in order to de-
                velop a greater self-awareness.

PROCEDURE: For each of the statements below, underline the number that best identi-
                fies your place on the scale. Next, draw a diamond around the number
                that expresses where you would like to be.

SELF-AWARENESS INVENTORY

   On the basis of this form, you may analyze some ways in which you may want to grow in order
to develop a greater self-awareness. For each of the statements below, underline the number that
best identifies your place on the scale. Next draw a diamond around the number that best expresses
where you would like to be.

1. Ability to clearly know what I like and dislike.
    Not at all able 1 2 3 4 5 6 7 8 9 Completely able

2. Accurate perception of my own strengths and weaknesses.
    Completely inaccurate 1 2 3 4 5 6 7 8 9 Completely accurate

3. Understanding of what I do and why.
    No understanding 1 2 3 4 5 6 7 8 9 Full understanding

4. Awareness of my real feelings about other people.
    Completely unaware 1 2 3 4 5 6 7 8 9 Completely aware

5. Willingness to recognize both positive and negative feelings in myself (e.g., affection,
    warmth, anger, antagonism).
    Totally unwilling 1 2 3 4 5 6 7 8 9 Totally willing

6. Acceptance of responsibility for my own behavior.
    Completely unaccepting 1 2 3 4 5 6 7 8 9 Completely accepting

7. Awareness of a clear and reasonably realistic self-image.
    Completely unaware 1 2 3 4 5 6 7 8 9 Completely aware

8. Awareness of many different aspects and facets of my personality (freedom from self-
    stereotyping and categorizing).
    Completely unaware 1 2 3 4 5 6 7 8 9 Completely aware

9. Awareness of my feelings about my immediate surroundings (place-environment).
    Completely unaware 1 2 3 4 5 6 7 8 9 Completely aware

10. Ability to be myself and behave accordingly (freedom from single role concept or behavior
    pattern)
    Not at all able 1 2 3 4 5 6 7 8 9 Completely able

11. Awareness of what I want and why.
    Completely unaware 1 2 3 4 5 6 7 8 9 Completely aware

12. Awareness of how I relate to and affect other people.
Completely unaware 1 2 3 4 5 6 7 8 9 Completely aware

13. Ability to fully experience the present as opposed to living predominantly in the past or the future.
Not at all able 1 2 3 4 5 6 7 8 9 Completely able

14. Ability to make clear-cut choices and decisions.
Completely unable 1 2 3 4 5 6 7 8 9 Completely able

15. Freedom from rationalizing, projecting and repressing feelings and behavior.
Not at all free 1 2 3 4 5 6 7 8 9 Totally free

DISCUSSION: After completing this form, discuss with your group the following:

    a.   Why do we have trouble "tuning-in" to ourselves and becoming self-aware?
    b.   What values do you have that are related to behavior you are pleased with?
    c.   What values do you have that cause you to behave in less than satisfactory ways?
    d.   Can any of your "scores" be turned into personal goals? How?   ❏

LIFE STYLE CHOICES

PURPOSE: To understand what life questions you are most earnestly seeking answers to.

To understand your *tropisms*—the things you instinctively (or otherwise) *go toward,* and the things that you instinctively go away from?

To determine which values hold the most attraction for you.

PROCEDURE: Take a moment and review one list—indicating with a check if the value would be a *tropism* or deterrent for you.

Physical

physical requirements of the job
stress or other effects on the body
opportunities for exercise
requirements and opportunities to use physical skills
danger or risk of physical harm

Material

income
financial security
job security
costs for education, training, or other preparation
opportunities for pay advancement

fringe benefits

physical surroundings at work (scenery, freedom of movement, indoors-outdoors, etc.)

entry level vs. alternate goal level characteristics of the job

ease of changing job or careers if opportunities or interests change

cost of living

pollution of the environment

opportunities for housing and transportation

Self-Intrapersonal

requirements and opportunities to be alone or reflect

requirements and opportunities to learn about oneself or grow

requirements and opportunities to develop skills or personal attributes

requirements and opportunities for self-management

requirements and opportunities for formal training responsibility of the job

requirements and opportunities for self expression in personal attributes (manner, dress, hours, etc.)

requirements and opportunities for freedom in choosing working conditions (hours, assignments, etc.)

Intellectual—Creative

requirements and opportunities for continued learning-education

challenge of the work

requirements and opportunities for reading

requirements and opportunities to experiment with own ideas

requirements and opportunities to develop new programs, objects, or ideas

intellectual difficulty of the work

preciseness or tediousness of the work

requirements and opportunities to organize or put things in order

amount of variety-stability-monotony on the job

importance and number of decisions to make

specific intellectual *content* interests—list yours (literature, biology, art, psychology, math, physics, history, philosophy, etc.)

Interpersonal Community

requirements and opportunities to organize or lead others

requirements and opportunities to get help or support from others

requirements and opportunities to work independently

requirements and opportunities to be assertive

requirements and opportunities to meet new people

requirements and opportunities to sell

requirements and opportunities to deal with interpersonal conflict

requirements and opportunities to get well acquainted with others

requirements and opportunities to help others

requirements and opportunities to be honest with others

requirements and opportunities to be in a group of peers

requirements and opportunities to be with members of the opposite sex

requirements and opportunities to be with persons of very different or similar backgrounds

requirements and opportunities to be with older or younger persons

requirements and opportunities for status, recognition, or attention

requirements and opportunities to speak to a group

requirements and opportunities to laugh with others
requirements and opportunities to develop interpersonal skills
requirements and opportunities for making good friends
requirements and opportunities for entertaining business acquaintances or others

Recreational

places to go sightseeing
opportunities for participating in sports (list specific sports)
opportunities for concerts, theater, etc.
opportunities for dining, dancing, etc.

Family

opportunities for being with family
opportunities for your spouse (her career, interests, etc.)
opportunities for your children (education, peers, environment, etc.)

Location

frequency of moving
commuting distance
amount of travel
climate
distance from family
urban-rural
opportunities for cultural enhancement
type of country-scenery
social-ethnic composition of the population

Other

amount of time for vacation
working hours
amount of thinking/worrying about the job while not on the job

DISCUSSION: Which values will you look for in a career choice and which will you avoid?   ❑

SELF-APPRAISAL

PURPOSE: To look at the ways you relate to others and the values behind your behavior. The form was originally developed by Edgar Schein, Bernard Bass and James Vaughan. On the basis of this form you may analyze the way in which your values affect the manner in which you relate to others.

PROCEDURE: For each of the statements below, underline the number that best describes your place on the scale. Next draw a diamond around the number which best expresses where you would like to be.

1. Ability to listen to others in an understanding way.
   Not at all able 1 2 3 4 5 6 7 8 9 10 Completely able

2. Willingness to discuss feelings with others.
   Not at all willing 1 2 3 4 5 6 7 8 9 10 Completely willing

3. Awareness of feelings of others.
   Not at all aware 1 2 3 4 5 6 7 8 9 10 Completely aware

4. Understanding why I do what I do.
   No understanding 1 2 3 4 5 6 7 8 9 10 Complete understanding

5. Tolerance of conflict and antagonism.
   Not at all tolerant 1 2 3 4 5 6 7 8 9 10 Completely tolerant

6. Acceptance of expressions of affection and warmth among others.
   Uncomfortable 1 2 3 4 5 6 7 8 9 10 Readily

7. Acceptance of comments about my behavior from others.
   Rejecting 1 2 3 4 5 6 7 8 9 10 Welcoming

8. Willingness to trust others.
   Completely suspicious 1 2 3 4 5 6 7 8 9 10 Completely trusting

9. Ability to influence others.
   Completely unable 1 2 3 4 5 6 7 8 9 10 Completely able

10. Relations with peers.
    Wholly competitive 1 2 3 4 5 6 7 8 9 10 Completely able

DISCUSSION: 1. Identify which area you plan to concentrate on first to improve your communication.
2. How must your change improve your communication?   ❏

HOW STRONGLY DO YOU FEEL?

PURPOSE: To enable you to evaluate your opinions on certain issues in a group setting.

PROCEDURE:
1. The facilitator will, one at a time, describe a series of stances or current controversial issues.
2. All students will move to the part of the room which most accurately reflects their choice.
   strongly agree
   mostly agree
   mostly disagree
   strongly disagree
3. One at a time—the facilitator will call on representatives from each "opinion group" to explain why they feel the way they do.
4. At any time members of any group may leave and go into another group.

DISCUSSION:
1. Is it easy changing groups? Why?
2. What made some people more persuasive than others?
3. Was it easier to be persuasive when you felt strongly about the issue? Why? ❑

LOST IN A LIFEBOAT

PURPOSE: To employ decision making techniques using values to guide your choices.

PROCEDURE: You are aboard a luxury liner that is in the middle of the Pacific Ocean. As dusk approaches, you hear the alert signal to abandon ship. Passengers pour onto the lifeboats, but many do not clear the ship before a bomb explodes and kills hundreds, completely destroying everything on the ship. The remainder of the ship sinks. You are in a lifeboat with 15 people; your boat is equipped to transport eight. You only have enough water for 10 people for three days, but you decide to try to carry all 15. To plan ahead, you feel the group should rank the persons from 1–15, with one being the most necessary person to stay and 15 being the first to go.

Your task: With the description given below and information provided in the story, rank the persons as instructed, first by yourself and then in a small group.

YD	GD		
____	____	1.	Minister, age 25, single, male.
____	____	2.	Electrical Engineer, 40s, female.
____	____	3.	Olympic Swimmer, 40s, male.
____	____	4.	Doctor, female, married, with 3 children at home, age 35.
____	____	5.	Artist, male, 60, widowed.
____	____	6.	Navy Captain, retired, age 70, male, divorced.
____	____	7.	Nurse, married, with no children, female, age 30.
____	____	8.	Pregnant lady, unmarried, age 27.
____	____	9.	Teenage boy, 14, epileptic.
____	____	10.	A rabbi, male, age 40.
____	____	11.	A campus militant, age 21, female.
____	____	12.	Scientist, male, married with 2 kids, 36 years old.
____	____	13.	Youngster, male, 7 years old, only child.
____	____	14.	45-year-old housewife, married, 2 children, can't swim.
____	____	15.	31-year-old ex-con, armed robbery, male, unmarried, 2 children.

DISCUSSION:
1. On what values were your decisions based? Your group's decision?
2. Did your values remain the same throughout, or did they change under peer pressure?
3. What further implications does this activity have for you in the real world? ❏

REACTIONS

1. List three reasons why an understanding of values can help you be a more effective communicator.

   a.

   b.

   c.

2. If values are learned, why are they so difficult to change?

3. Identify the most significant event in your experience that caused you to evaluate a value. What was the outcome of that evaluation? How did it affect your beliefs? Your decisions? Your life?

4. What effect will an understanding of values have the next time you face an ethical decision? Do we always try to do what is "Right"? Why?

DECISION MAKING | 10

Definitions

Most people have no difficulty choosing between A and B if A is a lot better than B. We frequently come face to face, however, with the need to choose between two or more alternatives that appear to be equally good or equally bad. Perhaps one choice gives us what we want at a high cost while another choice gives us only part of what we want at a more affordable cost. Another consideration is that decisions are not made in a vacuum. That is, many decisions that we make involve a string of extensive or complex consequences that may be difficult to determine.

Such choices are difficult. Our success depends not only on making the right choice, but making it in a timely manner. In this chapter, we will look at: 1) why making timely, competent decisions is important; 2) what prevents us from making such decisions; and, 3) how we can become more effective decision makers.

Decision making taxes our intrapersonal communication abilities that are described in the chapter on decision making and often requires considerable interpersonal skill when our decisions involve others.

Decision Making

It is a process that individuals use to select among alternatives to determine the best choice available at that time and in those circumstances. Conceptualizing decision making as a process means that each of us can learn how to use decision making for our benefit as we would learn to use any other tool.

Indecision

An interruption in the decision making process. Many people see indecision as an end result, a stopping point. However, by seeing indecision as merely a step in the process, one can learn how to move to the next step in the process and on to a successful conclusion.

Rational/Analytic Reasoning

A logical, systematic (step by step), linear (follows a path), approach to evaluating the available choices in order to determine which one is the most capable of bringing about the desired results. To be effective decision makers, we must use a rational/analytic approach as a basis for our decision making.

Intuition

The use of one's subjective, subconscious feelings in the decision making process. If you have ever had a "hunch" or a "feeling" about what you should do in a given situation, that has probably been your intuition at work. Many people ridicule intuition; others rely on it entirely. We suggest that intuition be used as a step in the decision making process once the logical/analytic questions have been applied.

Values

Those things to which a person attaches worth. The outcomes that an individual hopes will result from a correct decision are reflective of his values. Our values are usually developed over such a long period of time without our being aware of the changes occurring in us that we may be unaware of their influence in our decision making. Effective decision makers are very clear about their values and apply them in the decision making process.

Irreversibility

The belief, often erroneous, that once we make a decision we cannot change our minds or alter our course. Have you ever said to yourself, "If I buy that and I don't like it, then I'm stuck with it"? Most decisions are not that irrevocable. It may take time or cost some money; we may even have to endure other's attempts to make fun of us for the choice that we made. But we can usually take back a decision that we made. The belief that decisions are irreversible prevents us from making timely decisions.

Disaster Fantasies

A tendency of many people to focus on all the bad things that will happen if they make the wrong decision. As they dwell on these, they generally expand them out of proportion to reality. In making any decision, it is important to accurately estimate the possibility that a negative outcome may occur. But we should look at the possible harms, costs and problems in the same objective way that we estimate the possible profits and pleasure that will occur if the decision turns out the way we want it.

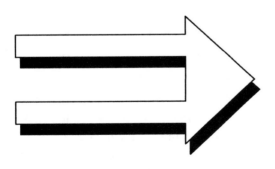

He who never made a mistake
never made anything.

THE IMPORTANCE OF EFFECTIVE DECISION MAKING

One of the major differences between humankind and animals is that animals are controlled by instinct and humans control by making decisions. The ability to make decisions, although not unique to humans, gives us the ability to control our destiny and to change our directions so that yesterday's mistakes do not have to be repeated. On a personal level, it is through our ability to make decisions that we choose our friends, careers, spouses and every other aspect of our lives including how successful we will be.

When you recognize the importance of effective decision making to your future, can you allow yourself to go through life letting decisions "happen"? Let's take a case in point. What if you know that you have a chance for a part-time apprenticeship in your future occupation. If you take the apprenticeship, however, you will have to take a leave of absence from college for the next semester. Rather than make a decision, you "worry and fret" about what to do until the apprenticeship is given to someone else.

How many times have you allowed decisions *about you* to be made by *someone else* because you failed to decide. You can see then that effective decision making really gives you control over your life. In the above situation, perhaps it would have been better for you to have stayed in school and not taken the apprenticeship. But by not deciding yourself, you gave up control over your own life and you lost the chance for some wonderful learning opportunities.

As we go through life, many opportunities will present themselves to us. Some will be financial, professional, social, political, personal, recreational or healthful in nature. The decisions that we make about each of those opportunities will help us to make the next one. Decisions should meet three criteria. They should be: 1) timely, 2) competent, and 3) capable of teaching us lessons about future decisions that we will make. Notice, we did not include in our list that the decision should be "perfect." That is because we cannot always guarantee that we will make the perfect choice. On the other hand, if our choices meet the three criteria listed, we will be successful more times than the odds would predict.

Timeliness

It may seem self-evident to say that a decision needs to be timely because if we delay too long, we may lose the opportunity. On the other hand, we live in a time when we have so much information available to us—such as through computers—that it seems that there is always more time needed to sift through it all to find the answer. Whenever we make a decision, we leap from what we know to what we don't know. Having more information can help us to know more about our chances but it will never completely tell us about the future. At some point, we must risk. Successful decision makers use all of the data that is available within the time limit that is appropriate. Then they decide.

Competency

A competent decision is one about which the decision maker has a good feeling. She believes they carefully determined the outcomes that were desired and evaluated the ability of each alternative to bring about those outcomes. Believing in your ability to make good decisions is important. If you believe that you made a good decision, you will probably work harder to make that decision successful. If you think that you made a poor decision or if someone else made the decision for you, you will not put the energy into making it a success. Each time you use a process for decision making that works for you, you gain confidence in your ability to make decisions and you will, in turn, make even more competent decisions in the future.

Capable of Teaching us Lessons

Even though our decisions are timely and competent, we may still fail to achieve our desired outcomes through no fault of our own. This is where the third criterion of decision making is operative. If we can look back on the process that we used in making the decision and see where we may have improved our system, we will gain insight that will help us in our next decision. When people allow decisions to be made by procrastination or by flipping a coin, they never have a chance to insure that their next decision will be any better than the last one they made. Effective decision makers use a process to make their important decisions. After the decision is made, they ask "how can I do it better the next time?"

To make the kind of decisions that are beneficial to us, we need to understand our values and how they were communicated to us; we need to be effective at processing information at the intrapersonal level; and in many cases, we need to be competent in our interpersonal communication with others.

Effective decision making is an important tool that people today can use to insure that their lives will be as rich and full as they desire. Like any tool, we only become successful when we learn the proper way to use it and practice every chance we get.

BARRIERS TO DECISION MAKING

In this section, we present some of the main reasons why people often fail to make effective decisions.

Fear of Risk

Every time we make a decision, we venture into unknown territory. We have not been there before. We do not know for sure if our choice will produce the results we want. If our decision requires a financial commitment, we may lose our money. If our decision requires that we give someone our word or puts us in a place where we can be personally criticized, we can lose our self-respect. Such losses can be hard to take; none of us likes to lose. When we fear the loss that risk brings, it sometimes feels better to not decide because that way we cannot be blamed. The fact is, if the thing turns out badly, we lose whether we actively or passively decided.

Someone you know is willing to sell you a car that is worth $1,000 for only $500. You think, "hey, I can sell the car by advertising it in the newspaper." You have the $500 needed to purchase the car, plus the money necessary to advertise in the newspaper, but cannot decide whether or not to buy it. There is an obvious risk involved. You could spend $300 advertising the car and then sell it for $600; but if that happens, you would lose $200. On the other hand, if you could only spend $50 for advertising and resell it for $1,000, you could make a fast $450.

Some risks are not worth taking. Others are almost sure things. Some people only focus on the potential for loss so that they are unable to objectively weigh the evidence necessary to make an effective decision.

Unsuccessful Past Decisions

Another reason that people are reluctant to make decisions is because of unsuccessful decisions that they have made in the past. If our past decision making is marred by failure and we have no idea how our decision making led to the failure, we will be very wary of making other decisions that could lead us to failure again. People learn from every experience in life whether they are aware of what they learn or not. When we make a decision and it turns out badly, we may be criticized, demeaned or we may lose something of material value. The next time we are faced with a decision, we remember the consequences of previous decisions and seek to avoid the consequences by avoiding the decision.

Belief that Our Decisions Are Irreversible

Most things in life that we do can be undone. (Even if you squeeze too much toothpaste from the tube, you can save it in a jar until you need it. Perhaps you don't want to keep your extra toothpaste in a jar, but it does allow you a way to compensate for an error that you made.) The same is true if you decide to major in law and decide after a year in law school that you would rather be a marine biologist. You cannot get the year back that you spent in law school.

274

On the other hand, you can leave law school and go to a college that specializes in marine biology. The year in law school could actually help you to increase your commitment to being a marine biologist.

Unfortunately, many people do not realize that they can undo a decision that did not produce the results that they wanted. When people believe that their decisions are irreversible, the fear of failure increases. Imagine how you would feel if you knew you had to get everything correct the first time you tried. it. People who believe in the irreversibility of their decisions apply the same limited thinking to their decisions.

Disaster Fantasies

Disaster fantasies keep many people from effective decision making. Effective decision makers recognize that they may lose some money or prestige if they make the wrong decision. These losses are carefully calculated and weighed against the possible gains from making a good decision. The effective decision maker knows that she can handle the loss.

The ineffective decision maker has no idea how much can be lost. Rather than carefully calculate the potential loss, the ineffective decision maker lets his imagination run wild. Every past real and imaginary frightful experience is free to jump into the mind of one who allows his imagination no limits. Take a minute before you leave home today and imagine all of the terrible things that can happen to you outside of your home. If you applied the same disaster fantasies to all of your decisions, you would freeze into immobility.

Lack of Knowledge of the Decision Making Process

Many people simply do not realize that there are decision making models that can be learned. There are a lot of things that we don't naturally know how to do. If you know how to type, use a computer, or drive a car, you know that you did not do any of those things without learning first how to do them. It is easy to recognize the things that obviously require learning before we can do them. On the other hand, there are many things that we assume that we should know how to do even though we have never been taught. Many people have never been taught how to use a systematic method for effective decision making.

By becoming aware of the barriers to effective decision making, we are able to be alert to our own tendencies to hamper our decision making process. Such recognition is the first step in moving ahead to competent, timely and appropriate decisions.

Wise men admit their mistakes,
foolish men defend them.

THE ELEMENTS OF THE DECISION MAKING PROCESS

Dianne Van Hook, Ed.D.

As human beings, we are confronted on a daily basis with situations that necessitate making decisions. The unique ability to choose and make decisions based upon a sense of memory, knowledge of the past and view of the future separates humans from all other living things. Unfortunately, this decision making ability is not something that is inherited at birth or acquired by simple maturation, but rather it is developed and learned through specific experiences. If decision making skills are not learned and effectively internalized, man will live a less than satisfying "trial and error kind of existence."

In light of the multi-faceted problems and pressures, socioeconomically imposed, that face people today, the ability to choose rationally is one of the most valuable skills a person can develop and exercise on a daily basis. People constantly seek greater freedom in controlling their own destinies, yet many need help in acquiring the skills necessary to "take charge."

PHILOSOPHICAL FOUNDATIONS

The question of how human beings make decisions has been a major concern of psychology for several decades and of philosophy for centuries. Although the field of psychology has supplied many insights into how learning takes place, it has not discovered the final answers as to the nature and conditions of learning and decision making. It is the responsibility of individuals to develop a decision making style based on their values and their philosophy of life that "best fits" them. This involves choosing, problem solving and accepting responsibility for one's own actions.

Unquestionably, decision making is vitally important to normal human functioning and behavior. As Russel Cassel states:

Decision making by man represents one of the most critical and fundamental processes in all human behavior. It is the single vehicle alone by which man incites and directs all psychological locomotion within his lifespace. It is the nucleus from which all personal satisfactions or disappointments and all successes or failures spring.

Historically, this decision making concept has been approached from three distinct points of view. One approach suggests that decision making cannot be understood. The second approach is formal and prescriptive (normative) in nature as exemplified in gene theory, statistics, and Bayesian decision theory. The third approach is descriptive in nature and places emphasis on how a decision is made based on:

1. Antecedent conditions (values).
2. The process itself.
3. The state of the decision maker.
4. The consequences of the process.

In the development of this process, it is important to be aware of the subjective elements that enter into decision making so that one can understand one's self a little better and improve and control these extraneous features, remove them or at least be on guard against their erratic consequences.

The specific process suggested in this chapter is based, in part, on the stages of problem solving set forth by a British political scientist named Graham Wallas, who, in his book entitled *The Art of Thought* (1926) incorporated the following as the stages of the problem solving process:

1. *Preparation:* Clarifying and defining the problem, along with the gathering of pertinent information.
2. *Incubation:* A period of unconscious mental activity assumed to take place while the individual is doing something else.
3. *Inspiration:* The "Aha" or "Eureka" experience that occurs suddenly.
4. *Verification:* The checking of the solution.

There are numerous other schools of thought on the logistics of decision making. Traditionally, most literature dealing with decision making has come from the fields of business and management. However, in recent years, more has been written concerning the *need for* and *development* of decision making skills on the part of students of all ages within the educational system and many models are springing up. In this light, it is important to recognize the difference between decision making and problem solving models. While decision making is problem solving, not all acts of problem solving can be identified as decision making. A comparison of a "creative problem solving process" has been presented by Don Koberg and Jim Bognall (1976) in a self-awareness program they developed. A summary of each appears below:

The Creative Problem Solving Process Contains 7 Steps:

1. Accept the problem.
2. Analyze the situation.
3. Define the overall purpose and objectives to be reached/satisfied.
4. Find alternative solutions of resolving the underlying cause.
5. Measure consequences of each alternative and select the best one.
6. Decide.
7. Evaluate the consequences.

As can be seen, although the differences between the two processes are slight, they are there. Inherent in the decision making process are three major requirements:

1. Examination and recognition of personal values.
2. Knowledge and use of adequate, relevant information.
3. Knowledge and use of an effective strategy for converting the information into action.

The importance of facts and values in this process cannot be overstressed. The factual content of decision making is identifiable, but facts become important to the decision making process as they are assessed through a value frame.

In essence, decision making is *ACTING ON ONE'S OWN VALUES.* When the person has developed a concept of value, identified his/her own values, and developed an ability to integrate their values into actions, their personal decision making skills will become more effective for them.

What's Included in a Good Decision:

1.	Feeling and Facts.	6.	Openness to Failure.
2.	Courage to be your individual self.	7.	Hard Work—clear objectives.
3.	Openness to growth and change.	8.	Good Plan of Action.
4.	Imagination.	9.	Acceptance (Realistic) of your own limitations.
5.	Flexibility.	10.	Responsibility.

OBSERVATION ACTIVITY

PURPOSE: To utilize your observational skills and your increasing knowledge of group dynamics that you may draw valid conclusions regarding a given group's effectiveness.

PROCEDURE:

1. Your assignment is to twice attend a meeting of a group—any group of your choice except family, close friends, job or a group of which you are already a member—observe the proceedings and respond to the questions below.

2. Some groups which have been observed in the past include: city and/or utility board meetings, Alcoholics and/or Parents Anonymous, religious conferences, Parent-Teacher Associations, Weight Watchers, Gay Awareness, therapy and/or sensitivity training groups, etc. It may be necessary to obtain advance permission to attend meetings of your target group. Check with a group representative regarding this.

3. Take the information you have received in class through lectures, films, textbook and participation and apply that information to answering the questions. Explain your answers! Devote at least one paragraph to each question so you may have sufficient space to reflect your thinking.

4. After submitting your written report, get into small groups and be prepared to:
   A. Relate your experiences and observations to other group members;
   B. Discuss whether you felt "competent" decisions were made;
   C. Identify those elements of group interaction that you think either contributed to or interfered with the participants' ability to resolve issues.

DISCUSSION:

1. What gathering did you observe? When/where did you observe?

2. Why do these particular meetings take place? That is, what kinds of decisions are being made? Are they related to therapy? commitment? learning? problem solving? communication? motivation? living skills? crisis/stress management, etc.?

3. How did communication flow? Did it go back and forth evenly, around in a circle, from a facilitator to participants and back to facilitator? Did any member try to dominate? Did the other members allow or block the behavior?

4. How were decisions formulated? Did the participants utilize the 7 step Creative Problem Solving Process described in The Elements of the Decision Making Process article? Did they use a process developed by members? Was each individual allowed to use what ever method s/he chose? How did the other members support or critique the efforts of one individual to decide something?

5. In your opinion, were "competent" decisions made? Why or why not? ❏

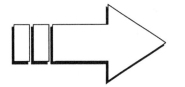

Once to every man and nation comes the moment to decide, in the strife of Truth with Falsehood, for the good or evil side. —*J. R. Lowell*

MCDONNELL DOUGLAS ETHICAL DECISION MAKING CHECK LIST

Kirk Hanson

Analysis

What are the facts?
    Have I defined the problem correctly?
    What decision am I asked to make?
    Who will be affected by the decision?
    What events or actions have led to the situation?
    Do others define the problem the same way I do?
Who is responsible to act?
    What are my formal and informal obligations in this case?
    What role do I play that gives me these responsibilities?
    What general responsibilities do I have which apply?
    To whom are these responsibilities owed?
    Will my decision be understood by others?
    Am I willing for my decision to become a general rule in the company?
Are all parties treated fairly in my proposed decision?
    Are all persons treated the same or can I justify any differential treatment I propose?
    Can I justify the distribution of the benefits and burdens resulting from my solution?
    Are there any groups I have not considered who will believe that they are not being treated fairly?

Implementation

Who should be consulted and informed?
    Do some individuals have a right to be consulted before a decision is made?
    Do some individuals have a right to be notified first?
    Will some persons be harmed if they are not told first?
What actions will assure that my decision achieves its intended outcome?
    What implementation steps are critical to achieving my goals?
    What can interfere with the implementation and what have I done to prevent/hedge against interference?
    With which groups or individuals must I communicate to assure that the decision is carried out?
    What steps must be taken to follow up on the implementation and the effects of the decision?
Implement

Follow up

    Was the decision implemented correctly?
    Did the decision maximize benefits, reduce harms, respect rights and treat all parties fairly?

By permission, Kirk Hanson and McDonnell Douglas.

Select the Optimum Solution

What are the potential consequences of my solutions?
   Who will be affected by my alternative decision and how?
   Are there any second order or unintended effects?
   Does the good I will do outweigh the bad?
Which of the options I have considered does the most to maximize benefits, reduce harm, respect rights and increase fairness?
   Am I satisfied that I have found the best solution possible?
   Can I comfortably explain the decision to my family, my subordinates or my boss?
   Will the decision look as good in time as it does today?
   Will my decision be understood for what it is?
   Am I willing for my decision to become a general rule?
   Does my role give me special responsibilities toward certain individuals or groups?
   Do I have a responsibility to a larger group than is involved here?
What are the consequences of actions (benefit/harm analysis)?
   Who will be affected by my alternate decisions and how?
   Are there any second order effects? unintended effects?
   Does the good I will do outweigh the bad?
What and whose rights are involved (rights/principles analysis)?
   Whose rights may be affected here?
   Are there any civil or basic human rights involved?
   Are there any job or employment rights involved?
   Is there any other type of contract or implied contract?
What is fair treatment in this case (social justice analysis)?
   What individuals or groups deserve equal or balanced treatment?
   Are all persons treated the same or can I justify the differential treatment I propose?
   Can I justify the way the benefits and burdens conferred by my solution are distributed?
   Are there any groups I have not considered who will believe they are not being treated fairly?

Solution Development

What solutions are available to me?
   To reduce harms?
   To maximize benefits?
   To respect rights?
   To be fair to more parties?
Have I considered all of the creative solutions which might permit me to reduce harms, maximize benefits, respect more rights or be fair to more parties?
   Would brainstorming bring better solutions to mind?
   Can I increase the positive effects of the solution?
   Can I decrease the negative effects of the solution?

High office teaches decision making, not substance . . . Most high officials leave office with the perceptions and insights with which they entered. They learn how to make decisions but not what decisions to make. —*H. Kissinger*

DECISION MAKING MODEL

PURPOSE: To help structure the decision making process so that one systematically considers all of the factors necessary for making a competent, timely and appropriate decision.

PROCEDURE:
1. Along the top of the diagram, place the options you have in the decision you are making.
2. Brainstorm to determine the values you wish to have as outcomes to your decision.
3. Rank the values so that you determine which is the most important value that you wish to occur, the second most important value and so on.
4. Give the values a weighting so that the most important value will be counted more heavily than the least important value.
5. List these weighted values along the left side of the diagram.
6. Rate or rank each option according to each weighted value. (For example, if you are ranking each option for Criterion 1, the first choice would receive a score of 5—1 × 5 = 5—and the last choice would receive a score of 20—4 × 5 = 20. The option with the lowest total score would be the "best" choice based on the criteria (values) which you chose.
7. Sum the scores for each option.
8. If the first and second choices are close, sleep on the decision overnight. If you wake up feeling okay about the number one choice, go with it. If you don't feel okay about the number one choice, go with number two. This allows for the use of intuition.

	Option 1	Option 2	Option 3	Option 4
Values (Criteria)				
Criterion (5x the score)				
Criterion 2 (4x the score)				
Criterion 3 (3x the score)				
Criterion 4 (2x the score)				
TOTAL SCORE				

DISCUSSION:
1. How did clarifying your values help you to make your decision?
2. For what kind of decisions would you use this process? Why?
3. For what kinds of decisions would you not use this process? Why not? ❏

REACTIONS

1. Think about a very difficult decision you have had to make. What were some of the psychological/emotional barriers or obstacles that made it so difficult? What was the outcome? Are you still satisfied with the quality (remember the concept of competency?) of your decision? Given the same situation today, would you follow a similar or different process?

2. What are at least four interpersonal elements that affect the "process" of decision making when you attempt to make a decision with someone else? Now that you have done the above, add these four—personality, culture, aggressiveness, expectations—and comment further on what effect they may have.

3. How does one's sense of self-confidence affect decision making behavior? Give an example from your own life where you operated from either high or low self-confidence and explain how it affected your actions.

4. What are at least five sources you can go to for information when you seek to make a "competent" decision?

CONFLICT | 11

Definitions ———————————————————————

Conflict

Definition: The perception of two or more objectives, choices or courses of action which motivates people to resolve the situation. The idea here is based on one generally agreed principle of communication and psychology. That is that humans prefer a state of balance—a consistency within ourselves, our beliefs, our attitudes and our view of the world. Just as we seek to maintain or restore this balance, we seek to avoid or eliminate imbalance.

Example: If I have two good friends who like me and also like each other, I can be said to be in a state of balance in this situation. However, if these two friends suddenly begin to dislike each other, I begin to experience imbalance.

Productive conflict management

Those communication behaviors which lead to positive feelings and results for all parties involved in the conflict.

Destructive conflict management

Those communication behaviors which cause negative feelings and results on the part of any parties involved in the conflict.

Competition

Actions on the part of two or more people to each acquire some scarce resource to the exclusion of the other.

Types of Conflict: Following are the seven types of conflict.

Content Conflict

Definition: Conflicts which arise over perceived differences in facts or information.

Example: If you and I are in a conflict over who won the Super Bowl in a given year, we are experiencing a "content" conflict.

Decisional Conflict

Definition: Conflicts which revolve around decisions that an individual or individuals must face. Sometimes these decisions involve simply ourselves and can therefore be classified as intrapersonal. In this case the conflicts often arise from alternatives which appear equally attractive or unattractive.

Example 1: A decision over which car to buy can confront an individual with equally attractive alternatives.

Example 2: A decision over whether to quit your job and risk unemployment or stay in your job and continue to be dissatisfied would be an example of equally unattractive alternatives.

Material Conflict

Definition: Conflicts are exclusively interpersonal and involve competition for a limited resource, such as money, a job, property, food or any other limited resource. The more of a limited resource which one person gets, the less there is for someone else.

Example: People often find themselves competing for things which are actually not in limited supply. Conflicts over love or esteem are examples of this misinterpretation.

Role Conflict

Definition: This involves disagreements in role expectations between two people or conflicting role expectations in the case of intrapersonal role conflict.

Example: Conflicts between couples over their expectations of one another's behavior are prime examples of role conflicts. Sometimes the intervention of a third party, such as a marriage counselor, is necessary to encourage people to identify their expectations of one another and freely share those expectations with the other person.

Judgmental Conflict

Definition: Judgmental conflicts revolve around conflict value statements as to the worth of something.

Example: Conflicts about whether or not a particular movie, book or political candidate is good or bad.

Expectancy Conflict

It is a natural part of living to make expectations about people and situations but if these expectations are unrealistic, the "reality" can never measure up and we doom ourselves to increasing amounts of dissatisfaction with life.

Ego Conflict

In this type of conflict, the competition is over which person is the better person. Once our ego defense mechanisms come into play, good communication goes out the window and people begin attacking each other.

THE IMPORTANCE OF MANAGING CONFLICT

Many people have believed that seeking conflict was a symptom of mental illness. There was something wrong with an individual if he created a conflict and that person should be helped. Consequently, our parents were told by their parents and we were told by our parents that it is not okay to create or be involved in conflicts. We were probably told to pretend that conflicts don't exist, and then they will go away.

Conflict Doesn't Go Away

But unfortunately, conflict doesn't go away if we turn our backs on it. For example, you and your boyfriend were used to spending a lot of time being together in the evenings. Then he got a new job and had to work five nights a week. Another example is that your girlfriend was elected to a major student body office and is working closely with a very popular guy who is on one of her committees. Perhaps you need to move back home with the family in order to save up some money to get "back on your feet" again. In each of these situations changes occurred between the way it was and the way that it is now. If the conflict that results from the change is ignored, resentment will probably lead to serious problems in the relationship.

Unresolved Conflict Can Lead to Problems

You have probably experienced the emotional reaction to conflict. You feel nervous, upset, anxious, up-tight. Perhaps you can't concentrate on what's happening at school or at work. You may even become physically ill from being "stressed out." Often when we are in conflict, we begin imagining conflict that doesn't even exist or we create new conflict such as kicking the dog when we are upset with our boss.

The way most of us "ignore" a conflict is to pretend that "everything will work out." The fact of the matter is that things don't work themselves out. We have to make them work out. If you fell and broke your arm, would you expect that things will just work out and that your arm will mend all by itself? Probably not. Your arm, however, can mend itself. It will take longer and be more painful than if you had medical assistance and it will probably heal deformed. Many of you think that ignoring a broken arm is too stupid an option to even consider. Yet given "broken relationships" we willingly allow healing to take its own path.

The purpose of this chapter is to help you see that ignoring conflict leads to problems and that confronting the conflict leads to positive results. A second purpose of the chapter is to show that conflict is inevitable in our daily lives.

Conflict Is Inevitable

There are several reasons why conflict is inevitable. We are confronted at home, at work and at play with a limited amount of resources such as money, time, space and availability of people. We have clashes with others over differences of values or interests. Poorly defined responsibilities among members of a group lead to conflict. The different roles that each of us assumes in groups lead to conflict. The aggressive nature of some of those with whom we interact can lead to conflict. Finally, whenever we introduce change, we can have conflict.

Conflict Can Be Beneficial

The skills that are necessary for creative thinking (the process of bringing something new into existence) are derived from the ability to manage controversy. These skills involve discovery of diverse information and viewpoints, handling controversy among persons with diverging ideas and perspectives and maintaining open-mindedness by viewing a problem from various vantage points.

Knowing that it is not good to ignore conflict, and being aware that conflict is inevitable should lead us to be on the look-out for potential conflict and use it for the improvement of our relationships and our lives.

By understanding the nature of conflict, developing a positive outlook about it, learning to recognize the types of conflicts in which we can find ourselves, we can begin to deal with our conflicts in a far more constructive and productive manner. However, it is also necessary to learn to recognize and control the barriers to productive conflict management.

Intelligent discontent is the mainspring of civilization. —E. Debs

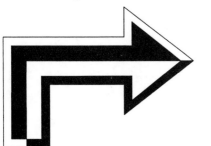

BARRIERS TO CONFLICT MANAGEMENT

Below are some of the barriers to managing conflict in a productive way. It is important to recognize and overcome these barriers in order to manage conflicts productively.

Avoidance

As was mentioned at the outset, people tend to have a negative attitude about conflict and therefore tend to avoid dealing with conflicts once they are perceived, hoping that the conflict will simply go away.

Nonassertiveness

Not being willing to speak your own mind and allow others the same opportunity increases frustration and distorts communication.

Misanalysis

Buying into someone else's conflict or failing to analyze what is actually in conflict causes inappropriate behavior and may cause us to apply the wrong management strategy. Not being able to correctly determine who owns the problem is also an example of misanalysis.

Escalation

Becoming defensive and thereby escalating the situation to an ego conflict produces disastrous effects.

Dirty Fighting

Using strategies associated with nonassertive or aggressive behavior promotes poor communication and leads to escalation.

Competing

Failing to recognize that interpersonal conflict management requires cooperation and good will between the parties generally brings about competition among the individuals involved in a conflict. Rather than cooperatively seeking a "win-win" solution, people go after a "win-lose" answer and ultimately everyone loses.

By understanding the true nature of conflict, developing a positive outlook about it, learning to recognize the types of conflicts in which we find ourselves, avoiding destructive types of conflicts and the barriers to effective conflict management, we can begin to deal with our conflicts in a far more constructive and productive manner. The remainder of this chapter will provide you with opportunities to explore your thoughts and feelings about conflict in more depth. You will have a chance to learn and practice constructive communication and conflict management techniques as well as to avoid destructive types of conflict.

IDENTIFYING CONFLICTS ACTIVITY ————————————

PURPOSE: To help you in identifying the types of conflicts which we encounter in our daily lives.

PROCEDURE: Following is a list of the seven types of conflict discussed at the beginning of this chapter. For each example, write which type you think it is in the space provided.

CONFLICT
TYPES: CONTENT—disagreement over "facts"
DECISIONAL—decision about different courses of action to take
MATERIAL—competition for material goods such as money, job, etc.
ROLE—disagreement over role expectations and/or behavior
JUDGMENTAL—disagreement over the value or worth of something
EXPECTANCY—difference between our expectations of something and the perceived reality
EGO—disagreement over the worth of yourself or someone else

EXAMPLES:

1. You are disagreeing with your boyfriend/girlfriend over which movie to see. _____

2. You are arguing with your brother or sister over who gets use of the family car on Friday night. _____

3. Your boss and you disagree about how you should act around the other employees in your area of responsibility. _____

4. You have had plans for a vacation in Hawaii for several months. You have arrived and now feel upset at how it is turning out. _____

5. You and your father or mother are having an argument over what time you need to be home from a date. _____

6. You are having a disagreement with a friend over who won the Oscar for Best Picture in 1988. _____

7. You are having an argument with a co-worker about the new sick leave policy which has been enacted. _____

8. You have decided to show another player on the team that you are better than him/her. _____

9. You are having a disagreement with your instructor about your study habits.
_____

10. You and another employee are competing for the same promotion. _____

DISCUSSION:
   1. Compare your answers with others in the group.
   2. As you identified these conflict types, what personal examples did you think of? ❑

ANALYZING A DECISION ACTIVITY

PURPOSE: To enable you to apply the basic steps in resolving decisional conflict to a decision in your life.

PROCEDURE:
1. Describe a situation requiring a decision which you are currently thinking about or a recent decision you were faced with. This should be something relatively important and something with at least two alternatives.
2. List and describe each of the alternatives.
3. For each of the alternatives, list the likely outcomes from choosing that alternative.
4. What is the likely outcome if you do not make any decision? (Note—if this is the most desirable outcome, no decision is necessary.)
5. Pick one of the alternatives and role-play that you have made the decision. Describe how you feel.
6. Were you able to feel comfortable with this choice? If not, role-play another choice and again analyze your feelings.

DISCUSSION:
1. How did you feel about the choices before you role-played one?
2. How did you feel about the choice of not making the decision?
3. How can you make use of this decision analysis process in future decisions you face?
4. How many of the decisions you make are irrevocable? What's the worst thing that can happen if you make a decision and it turns out to be wrong for you?   ❏

CONFLICT EXERCISE

PURPOSE: To explore the ways people handle conflict situations.

PROCEDURE:
1. Divide into four groups and move to the four corners of the room so that they may have privacy from the other groups.
2. For five consecutive rounds each group will choose either a plus "+" or a zero "0."
3. The goal is to accumulate positive points. Each round's payoff will be determined based upon the following scoring pattern:

Choices:	Groups score:
+ + + +	Each group gets + 100 points
+ + + 0	Groups voting " + " get -100 points
	Group voting "0" gets + 300 points
+ + 0 0	Groups voting "+" get -200 points
	Groups voting "0" get +200 points
+ 0 0 0	Group voting "+" gets -300 points
	Groups voting "0" get + 100 points
0 0 0 0	Each group gets -100 points

4. In rounds 3 and 5 the scores for that round will be doubled.
5. Prior to the *odd* numbered rounds, the groups will be allowed to negotiate with one another in the center of the room if they wish to do so. Each group should choose a negotiator for this purpose.
6. During negotiations only the negotiators may speak—group members should listen to the negotiations. Groups will be allowed three minutes to discuss their vote after negotiations are completed.
7. For even numbered rounds and any odd numbered rounds when groups do not wish to negotiate, they should decide, within three minutes, among themselves how to vote.
8. Each group's vote should be written on a small piece of paper, collected by the instructor and announced out loud.
9. Groups can record all the scores on the chart below or on a similar chart placed on the board.

Round	Vote	Group 1	Group 2	Group 3	Group 4
2					
3 (x2)					
4					
5 (x2)					

Total Score _____ _____ _____ _____

DISCUSSION:
1. What were the outcomes of this activity? Why?
2. Was there a winner and a loser? Does there always have to be a loser? Why? Why not?
3. What could have happened? How?
4. Was this an example of conflict? Did it have to be a conflict?
5. How do we generally handle conflict situations? Why?   ❏

The man who strikes first admits that his ideas have given out. —*Chinese Proverb*

ATTITUDES ABOUT CONFLICT

PURPOSE: To allow you to explore feelings associated with conflicts.

PROCEDURE: 1.   Complete each statement as openly and honestly as possible, reflecting your feelings about conflict.
  a.   When I win a conflict situation, I feel _____ .
  b.   When I win an argument, I feel _____ .
  c.   When I lose an argument, I feel _____ .
  d.   When I'm in a conflict that is not resolved, I feel

  _____ .

  e.   I get defensive when _____ .
2.   Form a group and discuss your responses.

DISCUSSION: 1.   How did your answers compare to others in your group?
2.   What general conclusions can you make about people's feelings regarding conflict?   ❏

NONPRODUCTIVE CONFLICT STYLES

PURPOSE: To help you explore the nonproductive ways we manage conflict.

PROCEDURE: 1.   Read the following descriptions of nonproductive styles and try to identify those of which you may be guilty.
2.   Form groups and answer the discussion questions below. Indirect conflicts often result in games because the individuals involved do not openly and directly acknowledge the real conflict. These games are called "crazymakers" or "dirty fights" by George Bach and they lead to a worsening of the conflict rather than to a satisfactory solution. There are three basic "crazymakers" styles:

  A.   *The Avoider.* This person denies the conflict by refusing to face up to it directly and assertively.
  Typical Behaviors:
  —pretending there is nothing wrong
  —refusing to fight (falling asleep, leaving, pretending to be busy)
  —changing the subject whenever conversation approaches the area of conflict
  —hinting at the conflict or talking in generalities but never quite coming out and expressing self
  —kidding around when other person wants to be serious thus blocking expression of important feelings
  —attacking other parts of other person's life rather than dealing with real problem

B. *The Manipulator.* This person wants to "win." She attempts, in an indirect way, to get the other person to behave as she wants them to rather than dealing in a direct way.

Typical Behaviors:

—trying to change other person's behavior by making them feel guilty or responsible ("It's OK, don't worry about me . . .")

—going into character analysis by explaining what's wrong with the other person or what the other person really means rather than allowing them to express themself directly

—refusing to allow the relationship to change from what it once was

C. *The Avenger.* This aggressive behavior often results from nonassertive behavior. Because of an unwillingness to deal with the conflict openly and directly, this person attempts to get back at the other person in a number of indirect ways. An especially dirty fighter, he creates fights because he experiences second order conflicts for which he wants to "pay back" or get even.

Typical Behaviors:

—storing up resentment and dumping it all on the other person all at once

—doing things to upset them

—finding fault by blaming other person for things

—bringing up things in an argument that are totally off the subject (other behavior, bad breath, etc.)

—attempting to punish partner by withholding

—encouraging others to ridicule or disregard partner

DISCUSSION:
1. Which of the preceding styles have you been guilty of?
2. What were your feelings when employing any of these styles?
3. What were the results when you used these styles? ❑

DEFENSIVE COMMUNICATION

Jack R. Gibb

One way to understand communication is to view it as a people process rather than as a language process. If one is to make fundamental improvement in communication, he must make changes in interpersonal relationships. One possible type of alteration—and the one with which this paper is concerned—is that of reducing the degree of defensiveness.

Definition and Significance

Defensive behavior is defined as that behavior which occurs when an individual perceives threat or anticipates threat in the group. The person who behaves defensively, even though he also gives some attention to the common task, devotes an appreciable portion of his energy to defending himself. Besides talking about the topic, he thinks about how he appears to others, how he may be seen more favorably and how he may win, dominate, impress, or escape punishment, and/or how he may avoid or mitigate a perceived or an anticipated attack.

Such inner feelings and outward acts tend to create similarly defensive postures in others; and, if unchecked, the ensuing circular response becomes increasingly destructive. Defensive behavior, in short, engenders defensive listening, and this in turn produces postural, facial and verbal cues which raise the defensive level of the original communicator.

Defensive arousal prevents the listener from concentrating upon the message. Not only do defensive communicators send off multiple value, motive and affect cues, but also defensive recipients distort what they receive. As a person becomes more and more defensive, he becomes less and less able to perceive accurately the motives, the values and the emotions of the sender. The writer's analyses of the tape-recorded discussions revealed that increases in defensive behavior were correlated positively with losses in efficiency in communication. Specifically, distortions became greater when defensive states existed in the groups.

Categories of Defensive and Supportive Communication

In working over an eight-hour period with recordings of discussions occurring in varied settings, the writer developed the six pairs of defensive and supportive categories presented in the following table. Behavior which a listener perceives as possessing any of the defensive characteristics listed arouses defensiveness, whereas that which he interprets as having any of the qualities designated as supportive reduces defensive feelings. The degree to which these reactions occur depends upon the personal level of defensiveness and upon the general climate in the group at the time.

Behavior Characteristics of Supportive and Defensive Climates

Defensive Climates
1. Evaluation
2. Control
3. Strategy
4. Neutrality
5. Superiority
6. Certainty

Supportive Climates
1. Description
2. Problem orientation
3. Spontaneity

By permission, Jack R. Gibb, *Journal of Communication,* Vol. 11, No. 3, 1961.

4. Empathy
5. Equality
6. Provisionalism

Evaluation and Description

Speech or other behavior which appears evaluative increases defensiveness. If by expression, manner of speech, tone of voice or verbal content the sender seems to be evaluating or judging the listener, then the receiver goes on guard. Of course, other factors may inhibit the reaction. If the listener thought that the speaker regarded him as an equal and was being open and spontaneous, for example, the evaluativeness in a message would be neutralized and perhaps not even perceived. This same principle applies equally to the other five categories of potentially defense-producing climates. The six sets are interactive.

Because our attitudes toward other persons are frequently, and often necessarily, evaluative, expressions which the defensive person will regard as nonjudgmental are hard to frame. Even the simplest question usually conveys the answer that the sender wishes or implies the receiver would fit into his value system. A mother, for example, immediately following an earth tremor that shook the house, sought for her small son with the question: "Bobby, where are you?" The timid and plaintive "Mommy, I didn't do it" indicated how Bobby's chronic mild defensiveness predisposed him to react with a projection of his own guilt and in the context of his chronic assumption that questions are full of accusation.

Anyone who has attempted to train professionals to use information-seeking speech with neutral affect appreciates how difficult it is to teach a person to say even the simple "who did that?" without being seen as accusing. Speech is so frequently judgmental that there is a reality base for the defensive interpretations which are so common.

When insecure, group members are particularly likely to place blame, to see others as fitting into categories of good or bad, to make moral judgments of their colleagues and to question the value, motive and affect loadings of the speech which they hear. Since value loadings imply a judgment of others, a belief that the standards of the speaker differ from his own causes the listener to become defensive.

Descriptive speech, in contrast to that which is evaluative, tends to arouse a minimum of uneasiness. Speech acts which the listener perceives as genuine requests for information or as material with neutral loadings is descriptive. Specifically, presentations of feelings, events, perceptions, or processes which do not ask or imply that the receiver change behavior or attitude are minimally defense producing. The difficulty in avoiding overtone is illustrated by the problem of news reporters in writing stories about unions, communists, Negroes and religious activities without tipping off the "party" line of the newspaper. One can often tell from the opening words in a news article which side the newspaper's editorial policy favors.

Control and Problem Orientation

Speech which is used to control the listener evokes resistance. In most of our social intercourse someone is trying to do something to someone else—to change an attitude, to influence behavior or to restrict the field of activity. The degree to which attempts to control produce defensiveness depends upon the openness of the effort, for a suspicion that hidden motives exist heightens resistance. For this reason attempts of nondirective therapists and progressive educators to refrain from imposing a set of values, a point of view or a problem solution upon the receivers meet with many barriers. Since the norm is control, noncontrollers must earn the perceptions that their efforts have no hidden motives. A bombardment of persuasive "messages" in the fields of politics, education, special causes, advertising, religion, medicine, industrial relations and guidance has bred cynical and paranoidal responses in listeners.

Implicit in all attempts to alter another person is the assumption by the change agent that the person to be altered is inadequate. That the speaker secretly views the listener as ignorant, unable to make his own decisions, uninformed, immature, unwise or possessed of wrong or inadequate attitudes is a subconscious perception which gives the latter valid base for defensive reactions.

Methods of control are many and varied. Legalistic insistence on detail, restrictive regulations and policies, conformity norms and all laws are among the methods. Gestures, facial expressions, other forms of nonverbal communication and even such simple acts as holding a door open in a particular manner are means of imposing one's will upon another and hence are potential sources of resistance.

Problem orientation, on the other hand, is the antithesis of persuasion. When the sender communicates a desire to collaborate in defining a mutual problem and in seeking its solution, he tends to create the same problem orientation in the listener; and, of greater importance, he implies that he has no predetermined solution, attitude or method to impose. Such behavior is permissive in that it allows the receiver to set his own goals, make his own decisions, and evaluate his own progress—or to share with the sender in doing so. The exact methods of attaining permissiveness are not known, but they must involve a constellation of cues and they certainly go beyond mere verbal assurances that the communicator has no hidden desires to exercise control.

Strategy and Spontaneity

When the sender is perceived as engaged in a stratagem involving ambiguous and multiple motivations, the receiver becomes defensive. No one wishes to be a guinea pig, a role player, or an impressed actor, and no one likes to be the victim of some hidden motivation. That which is concealed, also, may appear larger than it really is with the degree of defensiveness of the listener determining the perceived size of the suppressed element. The intense reaction of the reading audience to the material in the Hidden Persuaders indicates the prevalence of defensive reactions to multiple motivations behind strategy. Group members who are seen as "taking a role," as feigning emotion, as toying with their colleagues, as withholding information, or as having special sources of data are especially resented. One participant once complained that another was "using a listening technique" on him!

A large part of the adverse reaction to much of the so-called human relations training is a feeling against what are perceived as gimmicks and tricks to fool or to "involve" people, to make a person think he is making his own decision, or to make the listener feel that the sender is genuinely interested in him as a person. Particularly violent reactions occur when it appears that someone is trying to make a stratagem appear spontaneous. One person has reported a boss who incurred resentment by habitually using the gimmick of "spontaneously" looking at his watch and saying, "My gosh, look at the time—I must run to an appointment." The belief was that the boss would create less irritation by honestly asking to be excused.

Similarly, the deliberate assumption of guilelessness and natural simplicity is especially resented. Monitoring the tapes of feedback and evaluation sessions in training groups indicates the surprising extent to which members perceive the strategies of their colleagues. This perceptual clarity may be quite shocking to the strategist, who usually feels that he has cleverly hidden the motivational aura around the "gimmick."

This aversion to deceit may account for one's resistance to politicians who are suspected of behind-the-scenes planning to get his vote, to psychologists whose listening apparently is motivated by more than the manifest or content-level interest in his behavior, or to the sophisticated, smooth or clever person whose "oneupmanship" is marked with guile. In training groups the role-flexible person frequently is resented because his changes in behavior are perceived as strategic maneuvers.

In contrast, behavior which appears to be spontaneous and free of deception is defense reductive. If the communicator is seen as having a clean id, as having uncomplicated motivations, as being straightforward and honest, and as behaving spontaneously in response to the situation, he is likely to arouse minimal defense.

Neutrality and Empathy

When neutrality in speech appears to the listener to indicate a lack of concern for his welfare, he becomes defensive. Group members usually desire to be perceived as valued persons, as individuals of special worth and as objects of concern and affection. The clinical, detached, person-is-an-object-of-study attitude on the part of many psychologist-trainers is resented by group members. Speech with low affect that communicates little warmth or caring is in such contrast with the affect-laden speech in social situations that it sometimes communicates rejection.

Communication that conveys empathy for the feelings and respect for the worth of the listener, however, is particularly supportive and defense reductive. Reassurance results when a message indicates that the speaker identifies himself with the listener's problems, shares his feelings and accepts his emotional reactions at face value. Abortive efforts to deny the legitimacy of the receiver's emotions by assuring the receiver that he need not feel bad, that he should not feel rejected, or that he is overly anxious, though often intended as support giving, may impress the listener as lack of acceptance. The combination of understanding and empathizing with the other person's emotions with no accompanying effort to change him apparently is supportive at a high level.

The importance of gestural behavioral cues in communicating empathy should be mentioned. Apparently, spontaneous facial and bodily evidences of concern are often interpreted as especially valid evidence of deep level acceptance.

Superiority and Equality

When a person communicates to another that he feels superior in position, power, wealth, intellectual ability, physical characteristics, or other ways, he arouses defensiveness. Here, as with the other sources of disturbance, whatever arouses feelings of inadequacy causes the listener to center upon the affect loading of the statement rather than upon the cognitive elements. The receiver then reacts by not hearing the message, by forgetting it, by competing with the sender, or by becoming jealous of him.

The person who is perceived as feeling superior communicates that he is not willing to enter into a shared problem-solving relationship, that he probably does not desire feedback, that he does not require help, and/or that he will be likely to try to reduce the power, the status or the worth of the receiver.

Certainty and Provisionalism

The effects of dogmatism in producing defensiveness are well known. Those who seem to know the answers, to require no additional data and to regard themselves as teacher rather than as co-workers tend to put others on guard. Moreover, in the writer's experiment listeners often perceived manifest expressions of certainty as connoting inward feelings of inferiority. They saw the dogmatic individual as needing to be right, as wanting to win an argument rather than solve a problem, and as seeing his ideas as truths to be defended. This kind of behavior often was associated with acts which others regarded as attempts to exercise control. People who were right seemed to have low tolerance for members who were "wrong"— i.e., who did not agree with the sender.

One reduces the defensiveness of the listener when he communicates that he is willing to experiment with his own behavior, attitudes and ideas. The person who appears to be taking provisional attitudes, to be investigating rather than taking sides on them, to be problem solving rather than debating and to be willing to experiment and explore tends to communicate that the listener may have some control over the shared quest or the investigation of the ideas. If a person is genuinely searching for information and data, he does not resent help or company along the way.

Conclusion

The implications of the above material for the parent, the teacher, the manager, the administrator or the therapist are fairly obvious. Arousing defensiveness interferes with communication and thus makes it difficult—and sometimes impossible—for anyone to convey ideas clearly, and to move effectively toward the solution of therapeutic, educational or managerial problems.

Freedom rings where opinions clash —*A. Stevenson*

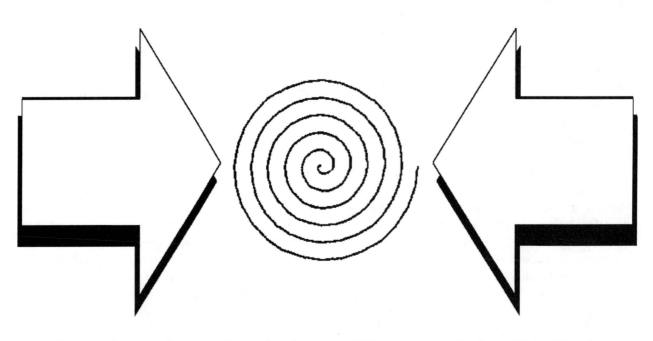

We must learn to live together as brothers or perish together as fools. —*M. L. King Jr.*

NONVERBAL BARRIERS

Nonverbal Symbols Which Increase and Decrease Defensiveness and the
Responding Communicator's Nonverbal Reactions

Sender	**Receiver**	**Sender** (similar for receiver)
Certainty	*(Uncertainty)*	*Provisionalism*
direct eye contact	lack of eye contact	nodding head
crossed arms	turning body away	head tilted to the side
hands on hips	leaning back	eye contact
	jerky body movements	
	shaking head	
	wringing hands	
	body tension	
Superiority	*(Inferiority)*	*Equality*
long eye contact	lack of eye contact	warm colors
hands on hips	hanging head	slower body movements
large desk in office	silence	leaning forward
formal setting	wringing hands	eye contact
higher elevation	body tension	informal setting
		same elevation

By permission, Linda Heun and Richard Heun, *Developing Skills for Human Interaction,* Charles E. Merrill Publishing Company, Columbus, Ohio, 1975.

Evaluation	(Devaluation)	Description
long eye contact	increasing personal distance	slower body movements
pointing	body tension	leaning forward
hands on hips	jerky body movements	eye contact
shaking head	leaning back	
shaking index finger	wringing hands	

Neutrality	(Unconcerned)	Empathy
legs crossed away	lack of eye contact	pleasant background sounds
monotone voice	leaning back	decreasing personal distance
staring somewhere else	legs crossed away	eye contact
cool colors	wringing hands	warm colors
leaning back	body tension	legs crossed toward
body distance of 4 1/2 to 5 feet		nodding head
		personal distance—20–36 inches

Control	(Manipulated)	Problem Orientation
sitting in focal seat	lack of eye contact	decreasing personal distance
hands on hips	turning body away	legs crossed toward
shaking head	wringing hands	leaning forward
long eye contact	body tension	eye contact

Strategy	(Manipulated)	Spontaneity
shaking head	leaning back	leaning forward
long eye contact	lack of eye contact	legs crossed toward
	turning body away	eye contact
	wringing hands	animated natural gestures
	body tension	

HOW TO AVOID DESTRUCTIVE CONFLICT AND ENCOURAGE CONSTRUCTIVE CONFLICT

1. Be wary of communication breakdown. Keep the channels for productive communication open. Avoid comments or other behaviors that might jeopardize the open flow of information. Don't sabotage effective communication.

   Don't interrupt

   Don't discount the other person's statements

   Don't purposely put people on the defensive to see them squirm

   Stay with the subject

2. Recognize "terminological tangles" or arguments about semantics. Remember, there is no ultimately correct or single meaning to most concept words. Don't demand that other people have the same meaning for words that you have. Give the other person specific examples of how you are using disputed words. Ask the other person for examples.

3. When asking questions, avoid all implications (whether in tone or in wording) of skepticism or hostility. Questions should be motivated by curiosity about the speaker's view.

4. Discuss not for victory but for clarification and understanding. If we do so, we shall probably find that ultimately, agreement and disagreement, approval and disapproval, are not so important.

5. Be careful about making assumptions. Don't assume subordinates have understood when you give instructions. Request feedback. Verify their understanding. Also, be careful about making inferences.

6. Train yourself to recognize misunderstandings. Do something about them—as soon as you can. All too often, the fact that misunderstandings exist is not apparent until deeper misunderstandings have already occurred because of the original one.

7. Avoid snap reactions. Pause before responding. Refrain from agreement or disagreement with a speaker, refrain from praise or censure of her views, until you are sure what those views are. Don't be so intent on "shooting down" the other that you are no longer alert for new information.

8. Avoid "allness" thinking. Use sparingly words like *all, always, everybody, everytime, never, nobody.* Consider relative values in your evaluations. Beware of making generalizations about segments of the population.

9. Avoid "either-or" thinking and expressions. Expressing things in polar terms (i.e., good vs. bad, pretty vs. ugly, smart vs. dumb) is part of our conditioning. Committing yourself to one polar position makes compromise difficult. Think of things as being on a continuum. Avoid stereotyping.

10. Practice good listening. Listen unemotionally and with an open mind. Remember, people tend to overstate or overemphasize their points when they feel they are not being listened to with an open mind.

11. Voice your opposition to ideas, not opposition to people.

12. Acknowledge and respect the feelings and experience of others. Don't let personal animosities affect your dealings with others any more than you must.

13. Express your own feelings. Don't make people guess where you're coming from.

14. Stay flexible. Be willing to consider alternate ways of thinking.

15. Don't over commit yourself. Learn to say "no."

16. Avoid "trigger phrases," expressions people may react to in a negative way. Expressions like: "That is a stupid idea" or "You are wrong about that."

17. Give up needing to be right all the time. Let the other person survive.

18. As a group leader, prevent or reduce adversary situations where opposing parties take up firm positions and proceed to bombard each other.

CRAZYMAKERS

What's your conflict style? To give you a better idea of some unproductive ways you may be handling your conflicts, we will describe some typical conflict behaviors that can weaken relationships. In our survey we will follow the fascinating work of Dr. George Bach, a leading authority on conflict and communication.

Bach explains that there are two types of aggression: clean fighting and dirty fighting. Either because they cannot or will not express their feelings openly and constructively, dirty fighters sometimes resort to "crazymaking" techniques to vent their resentments. Instead of openly and caringly expressing their emotions, crazymakers (often unconsciously) use a variety of indirect tricks to get at their opponent. Because these "sneak attacks" don't usually get to the root of the problem, and because of their power to create a great deal of hurt, crazymakers can destroy communication. Let's take a look at them.

The Avoider

The avoider refuses to fight. When a conflict arises, he will leave, fall asleep, pretend to be busy at work, or keep from facing the problem in some other way. This behavior makes it very difficult for the partner to express his feelings of anger, hurt, et cetera because the avoider won't fight back. Arguing with an avoider is like trying to box with a person who won't even put up his gloves.

The Pseudoaccommodator

Not only does the pseudoaccommodator refuse to face up to a conflict, she pretends that there is nothing at all wrong. This really drives the partner, who definitely feels there is a problem, crazy and causes that person to feel both guilt and resentment toward the accommodator.

The Guilt Maker

Instead of saying straight out that he doesn't want or approve of something, the guilt maker tries to change the partner's behavior by making that person feel responsible for causing pain. The guilt maker's favorite line is, "It's o.k., don't worry about me. . . ." accompanied by a big sigh.

The Subject Changer

Really a type of avoider, the subject changer escapes facing up to aggression by shifting the conversation whenever it approaches an area of conflict. Because of these tactics, the subject changer and the partner never have the chance to explore their problem and do something about it.

The Criticizer

Rather than come out and express feelings about the object of her dissatisfaction, the criticizer attacks other parts of the partner's life. Thus, she never has to share what is really on her mind and can avoid dealing with painful parts of relationships.

The Mind Reader

Instead of allowing a partner to honestly express feelings, the mind reader goes into character analysis, explaining what the other person really means or what's wrong with the other person. By behaving this way the mind reader refuses to handle her own feelings and leaves no room for her partner to express himself.

The Trapper

The trapper plays an especially dirty trick by setting up a desired behavior for his partner, and then when it is met, attacking the very thing he requested. An example of this technique is for the trapper to say, "Let's be totally honest with each other," and then when the partner shares his feelings he find himself attacked for having feelings that the trapper doesn't want to accept.

The Crisis Tickler

This person almost brings what is bothering her to the surface, but she never quite comes out and expresses herself. Instead of admitting her concern about the finances she innocently asks, "Gee, how much did that cost?" dropping a rather obvious hint but never really dealing with the crisis.

The Gunnysacker

This person does not respond immediately when he is angry. Instead he puts his resentment into his gunnysack, which after awhile begins to bulge with large and small gripes. Then, when the sack is about to burst, the gunnysacker pours out all his pent-up aggressions on the overwhelmed and unsuspecting victim.

The Trivial Tyrannizer

Instead of honestly sharing his resentments, the trivial tyrannizer does things he know will upset his partner: leaving dirty dishes in the sink, clipping his fingernails in bed, belching out loud, turning up the television too loud and so on.

The Joker

Because she is afraid to face conflicts squarely, the joker kids around when her partner wants to be serious, thus blocking the expression of important feelings.

The Beltliner

Everyone has a psychological "beltline," and below it are subjects too sensitive to be approached without damaging the relationship. Beltlines may have personality traits a person is trying to overcome. In an attempt to "get even" or hurt his partner the beltliner will use his intimate knowledge to hit below the belt, where he knows it will hurt.

The Blamer

The blamer is more interested in finding fault than in solving a conflict. Needless to say, she usually does not blame herself. Blaming behaviors almost never solves a conflict and is an almost surefire way to make the receiver defensive.

The Contract Tyrannizer

This person will not allow his relationship to change from the way it once was. Whatever the agreements the partner had as to roles and responsibilities at one time, they will remain unchanged. "It is your job to . . . feed the baby, wash the dishes, discipline kids, etc."

The Kitchen Sink Fighter

This person is so named because in an argument she brings up things that are totally off the subject ("everything but the kitchen sink"): the way her partner behaved last New Year's Eve, the unbalanced checkbook, bad breath—anything.

The Withholder

Instead of expressing her anger honestly and directly, the withholder punishes her partner by keeping back something—courtesy, affection, good cooking, humor, sex. As you can imagine, this is likely to build up even greater resentments in the relationship.

The Benedict Arnold

This character gets back at his partner by sabotage, by failing to defend her from attackers, and even by encouraging ridicule or disregard from outside the relationship.

SOLVING PROBLEMS WITH PEOPLE ——————————————

PURPOSE: To give you a meaningful way of coping with interpersonal conflicts.

PROCEDURE: This is based on programmed instruction. Simply read and follow each step.

Cover all sections of this page, except 1, with a sheet of paper.

---

1. This program is designed to help improve communication between people. You should be covering all of this page so that only this first instruction is exposed. Each printed instruction is called a frame. A black line, like the one below, means the end of a frame. After you have finished reading this frame, move the cover down to the black line below the next frame, continuing in this manner throughout the program.

---

2. There are several reasons for attempting to improve communication. For one thing, in any close relationship which the partners want to develop, it is inevitable that difficulties will appear between the partners. This session will help you develop a helpful approach to thinking about such interpersonal difficulties.

---

3. Experience has shown that people who successfully resolve interpersonal difficulties typically go through specific stages of thinking. At each state they acquire a broader, more meaningful way of looking at what's going on. This mirrored understanding helps them uncover new approaches to resolving the difficulty. These new approaches come from changes in their awareness, thinking, feeling and doing.

---

4. This is a way of using your own feeling, thinking, and doing to understand and resolve a *particular* difficulty **you now have** with *another person, group, organization.* The more **important** the difficulty is to you, the more **meaningful** will be the learning you get from this technique.) How carefully you follow this technique will depend upon a real decision by you to do something about the difficulty. The chances of your arriving at a meaningful and lasting solution depend on your thinking about your difficulties with persons, groups, or organizations, and your choosing to tackle the most important one **now.**

---

5. Do not move to the next frame until you have chosen a personal problem you want to tackle which has really been bothering you.

---

6. This program presents you with a series of questions about the way you see, and think about, your difficulty. As you answer these questions, you will be following the thinking process which results in increasing or broadening the way in which you look at your problem. You will be going through the stages of effective problem-solving.

---

7. This is not a test of your thinking ability. It is a step-by-step program to help you develop the ability you already have. Our approach will be much like the way a broad jumper teaches himself to jump. We will begin developing your ability to talk with yourself.

---

8. Below, write down a simple statement of your problem. Your first statement is not expected to be very clear or concise. In fact, part of the difficulty in solving a problem is frequently that it is hard to pin down just what the problem is. This technique will help you to identify your problem more clearly.

---

9. Take some time now to write down your first statement of the problem as it looks to you. It will help if you do not struggle with how clearly or grammatically you write it. Try instead to write "off the top of your head."

As I see the problem, it is essentially that . . .

---

10. Now that you've written down your first statement of your problem, compare your words to my example below. If you think of your problem as if **you are not** personally involved in the problem, you are thinking at Level #1. If you do mention that the problem affects you, you are thinking at Level #2.

COMPARE YOUR WORDS TO THESE EXAMPLES

Example at Level #1	Example at Level #2
You do **not** mention yourself.	You **do** mention yourself.
My boss gets angry too easily.	My boss gets angry *at me* too easily.
If your thinking is closer to this example, move to Frame 11. (Your thinking is closer to this Level #1 example, if you **do not** refer to yourself.)	If your statement is closer to this example, move to Frame 12. (Your thinking is closer to this Level #2 example, if you **do** refer to yourself.)

---

11. Your thinking is at Level #1 when you do not think about your problem in words which refer to yourself. You can progress to Level #2 by restating your problem in terms of how you are involved in it. You can probably do this by answering the question, "How is this a problem to **me**?" or "How am I concerned with it?"
If *I were to restate my problem, this time emphasizing how it is a problem to me, I* would say that. . . .

---

12. Now compare your words about your problem to the example below. If you think about how it is a problem to you, but *not* how you **feel and react**, then you are thinking at Level #2. If you also talk about your **feelings and reactions**, you're thinking at Level #3.

COMPARE YOUR WORDS TO THESE EXAMPLES

Level #2

You do **not** mention your feelings and reactions. My boss gets angry at me too easily.

If your thinking is closer to this example, move to Frame 13. (Your thinking is closer to this Level #2 example if you do **not** refer to **your feelings and reactions**)

Level #3

You do mention your feelings and reactions. My boss gets angry at me too easily. This usually *gets me nervous so* I can't work well. His anger also *gets me annoyed at him.*

If your thinking is closer to this example move to Frame 14. (Your thinking is closer to this Level #3 example if you **do** refer **to your feelings and reactions**)

13. You can progress to Level #3 by thinking about your problem again. This time refer to how you **feel and react** in the problem situation.

Focusing on **my feelings and reactions**, I would say that my problem is that . . .

14. Level #4 can be a "break-through" stage in understanding your problem. Now compare your statement with the example below. If your words speak of your feelings and reactions as something **you do yourself**, as in "I get nervous," rather than something or someone else "makes you nervous," then you are Level #4.

COMPARE YOUR WORDS TO THESE EXAMPLES

Level #3

You disown responsibility for your feelings. My boss gets angry at me too easily. This usually gets me nervous so I can't work well. His anger also makes me annoyed at him.

Your words are closer to this Level #3 example if you refer to your feeling and reactions as if they are something done *to* you rather than *by* you. The example says, "My boss's anger gets me nervous." (If you are closer to this example, move to Frame 15.)

Level #4

You own responsibility for your feelings. My boss gets angry at me a lot. When I sense his anger, I get nervous and I don't work well. Then I start getting annoyed at him. If you speak of your feelings and reactions as something *you* do *to* yourself then you are owning them as your own. The example says, "*I* get nervous when my boss gets angry at me." I do not disown my feelings and hold my boss's anger responsible for my feelings. (If your statement is closer to this example and you are confident that you understand the difference between owning and disowning, then move to Frame 18, if not continue with Frame 15.)

15. To check your understanding of the difference between disowning your feelings and owning them, classify the following four examples as either "owning" or "disowning" by the speaker.

   a. "His sloppiness really makes me mad."
   b. "I dislike the way he does his work."
   c. "When you do that, I feel very good."
   d. "You really do make me feel good."

   Which are owning? _____ Which are disowning? _____

16. The answer to Frame 15 is that (a) and (d) are disowning while (b) and (c) are owning.

17. Now, if your statement was not at Level #4, rewrite your problem in words that own your responsibility for your own feelings.

   My problem as I see it now, including my feelings expressed as my own, is that . . .

18. Level #5 can be another "break through" stage in thinking about your problem. Again, compare your statement with the example below. You are at Level #5 if you think about how your ways of thinking, feeling, or doing contribute to the problem. Your contribution may come from things you do or things you do not do.

COMPARE YOUR WORDS WITH THESE EXAMPLES

Level #4	Level #5
You *do not* consider your contribution. My boss gets angry at me a lot. When I sense his anger, I get nervous and I don't work well. Then I start getting annoyed at him. (If you are closer to this Level #4 example, move to Frame 19).	You *do* consider your contribution. My boss gets angry at me a lot. When I sense his anger, I get nervous and I don't work well. Then I start getting annoyed at him. By getting nervous in reaction to his anger, I stay on edge and make more mistakes. My arrogance at him for making me nervous is my reaction to him. He doesn't "make" me nervous; I do it to myself. By not letting him know how I do react to him, though, I also contribute to the problem. (If you are closer to this Level #5 example, move to Frame 20.)

19. If your statement was not at Level #5, rewrite your problem in words that consider **your contribution** to your problem. (It may seem useful if you *think about* the levels of what you are doing as you write.)

My problem as I see it now, also considering my contribution to it, is that . . .

20. When you have gone through Level #1 to #5, you may find that you now have a clearer, more useful way of looking at your problem. You may also find that some of your feelings about the situation have changed or are beginning to change. (This could mean that negative, uncomfortable feelings are becoming less intense or less upsetting. Also, positive *good* feelings may be increasing). In the example, for instance:

Possible feeling change in the example:

I feel less helpless, less angry at my boss, and a kind of relief at realizing that I can do something about trying to do something, but I would rather risk doing something than let things continue as they have.

21. Think for a few minutes about changes in your awareness and your feelings about your situation. What has been going on within you as you have been working on this problem. Write about these changes, if any, in the box below.

As a result of the thinking I have done during this program, the following changes in my **awareness** and in my **feelings** have been taking (or are now taking) place:

22. After thinking through Level #1 to #5, you may become aware of specific changes in your behavior which might be appropriate. (This might mean *doing* something you've never tried before.) For example . . .

Possible action steps in the example:

I could say to my boss, "When you get angry at me, I get so shook up that I even make more mistakes and then I get angry, too. Sometimes I take my anger out on other people."

I could also say to him, "Help me understand what I do that gets you angry. When you get angry, I get so shook up that I can't really concentrate on what you are trying to tell me."

23. Think for a few minutes about specific changes in your behavior which might be appropriate for your problem. Then write about these changes, if any.

Some of the specific things I can do about my problem are:
1.
2.
3.
4.
5.

24. At this point, you need an opportunity to try out the changes in behavior which you have described in Frame 10. In preparation for this, review and picture in your imagination the **specific behavior** you have decided upon. Now think about how **willing** you really are to try out these changes. (How would you rate your willingness to change on a scale of 1 through 9, with 9 being "very willing?")

Rating _____

Remember that the solution of your problem depends at least in part, upon **your** behavior, **your** feelings, **your** attitude, and **your willingness** to change.

25. Talk over your problem and your solution with someone else. For example, go to a friend, talk it over with that friend, and then make a commitment to yourself and to your friend that you will do something **specific**. Your willingness to **do something active** is vital, and having a friend you can consult with can help motivate you to do that something, whatever it is.

Possible reactions of a friend to the action suggested in Frame 19

"If you say those things to your boss, how is he likely to react?" (One of the difficulties may be that my boss could react to my feelings as my problem rather than as a **relationship** problem that involves both of us and requires both of us to think, change, and act.)

26. Without **action** (or your deliberately choosing to defer action and "wait and see"), your thinking is meaningless. **Thinking** about your problem, your **feelings**, and so on, is **not** enough. Begin **now** and **do** something!

27. Now go back through the levels of thinking and list the steps taken.   ❏

STEPS TO NO-LOSE SOLUTIONS

Probably the best description of the no-lose approach is written by Thomas Gordon in his book *Parent Effectiveness Training*. Gordon suggests six steps that you can follow in reaching a no-lose, productive solution to your conflicts:

1. *Identify and define the conflict.* What's the problem as you see it? How does it make you feel? It's important here to use descriptive "I" language and not evaluative "you" language. Make it clear that you want to find a solution that's acceptable to everyone, that you don't just want to argue.

2. *Generate a number of possible solutions.* It's important to have everyone involved contribute as many solutions as they can think of. Don't stop to judge which ones are best in this step; this stifles creativity and can generate bad feelings. You'll pick the best ideas later.

3. *Evaluate the alternative solutions.* This is the time to talk about which solutions will work and which ones won't. It's important that everyone is honest about her feelings and willingness to accept an idea or solution. If a solution is going to work, everyone involved has to support it.

4. *Decide on the best solution.* Now that you've looked at all the alternatives, pick the one that looks best to everyone. It's important to be sure everybody understands the solution and is willing to try it out. Remember, your decision doesn't have to be final, but it should look potentially successful.

5. *Implement the Solution.* Here's where you work out the details of how the solution will operate. If you've decided to set up some sort of schedule, now's the time to work it out and make sure everyone understands it. If money is involved, you need to agree on the amounts involved. The point is to be sure that there are no misunderstandings about how the solution will operate.

6. *Follow up the solution.* You can't be sure a solution will work until you try it out. After you've tested it for a while, it's a good idea to set aside some time to talk over how things are going. You may find that you need to make some changes or even rethink the whole program. The idea is to keep on top of the problem, to keep using your creativity to solve it. It's a good idea to have agreed in advance how long everyone will try out the solution before discussing how well it's working. Set a date in the future to clearly establish a time for this follow-up step.

MANAGING INTERPERSONAL CONFLICTS ———————————

PURPOSE: To summarize the steps in managing interpersonal conflicts productively.

PROCEDURE: 1. Read the following steps to managing interpersonal conflicts.
   a. Identify who "owns" the problem. If it is not yours, avoid advising. Use active listening and help the other person solve his/her problem if you wish. If it is a joint problem then resolution will require cooperation.
   b. Take responsibility for your own feelings (See "Solving Problems With People"). You have a right to think and feel as you do and so does the other person.
   c. Describe your feelings using "I" messages rather than "you" messages. Focus initially on *what* you're feeling rather than on *why* the other person's behavior bothers you.
   d. Communicate your disagreement to others when it occurs rather than storing it up. This tends to reduce hostility. Be specific. Identify the specific behavior, attitude or value which is at issue and talk about it. Here again, "I" messages should be used.
   e. Maintain a supportive climate both verbally and nonverbally (See "Defensive Communication" by Jack Gibb).
   f. Get in touch with the "real" other person by encouraging them to be open. Be sure not to use his/her openness against them later.

Be aware of the other person's nonverbal messages and clarify ambiguous responses.

g. Avoid nonproductive conflict styles and power struggles.

h. Use productive management techniques such as "No-Lose Solutions." *Work* at being a good communicator by giving and requesting feedback.

i. Remember that resolving interpersonal conflicts requires negotiating a "win-win" solution. You will not get everything you want. Solutions require *give and take*.

j. Don't be afraid to re-negotiate if the solution isn't working. A solution is only satisfactory if it works and all parties are content.

k. Learn when you just have to "agree to disagree."

2. Form a dyad and create a role-playing situation to demonstrate how these techniques can be used.

3. Role-play your situation in front of the class and discuss how these steps were utilized in the role-playing.

DISCUSSION:
1. Which steps were most comfortable for you to use?

2. Which ones do you plan to apply to your communication? When? ❏

REACTIONS

1. Write your personal definition of conflict.

2. Describe your own comfort level in conflict situations.

3. Which simple concept from this chapter do you plan to apply first in your next conflict? How?

ASSERTION TRAINING | 12

Definitions

Assertion Training offers us another way of looking at and dealing with sensitive or difficult communication situations.

Assertive Rights

The basic principles/assumptions to which every individual is entitled and on which assertion training rests.

Assertive Behavior

Communicating in a direct, calm, honest, nonmanipulative manner, with a respect for the rights of self and others.

Aggressive Behavior

Communicating in a direct, emotional, threatening, manipulative manner, with a disregard for the rights of others.

Nonassertive Behavior

Behavior which is characterized by an inability or unwillingness to communicate one's true feelings or ideas to others.

Assertion Training Techniques

Those specific communication skills and strategies generally associated with and used by assertive individuals.

THE IMPORTANCE OF ASSERTION TRAINING

How many of us have been placed in the difficult position of being criticized or of having to criticize someone else; of trying to return defective merchandise to a store, only to be accused of breaking it; of having someone try to cut in front of us as we stand in a line? How did we react? Was it with anger, frustration or perhaps we just let the other person have their way?

One very effective method of communication which can be used in these types of situations is Assertion Training. Anyone who has passed by the self-help section of the local bookstore has seen titles like *Creative Aggression, How to Win*, or *Parent Effectiveness Training*. All of these books have their roots in Assertion Training. Many of their primary ideas can be easily traced to the two most popular, as well as influential, books on assertiveness: *Your Perfect Right* by Alberti and *When I Say No, I Feel Guilty* by M. J. Smith.

To understand and appreciate Assertion Training more fully, we need to look at three important areas: the philosophy behind being an assertive person, the three behaviors usually associated with Assertion Training and some valuable techniques that enable us to be more assertive individuals.

Your Rights (and Mine)

To begin with, Assertion Training is based on the assumption that **all** human beings have certain rights. It may be interesting to note that these "rights" have been based on the United Nation's "Bill of Human Rights" and have been modified over time to the list below:

1. I have the right to assert myself as a worthy individual.
2. I have the right to express myself.
3. I have the right to be listened to.
4. I have the right to change my mind.
5. I have the right to express my feelings without always justifying them.
6. I have the right to not always need the goodness of others to survive.
7. I have the right to say, "I don't know."
8. I have the right to say, "I don't understand."
9. I have the right to avoid what I don't want.
10. I have the right to decide whether I want to be responsible for the problems of someone else.
11. I have the right to make mistakes and to accept responsibility for my actions.
12. I have the right, as an assertive person, to decide when and if I want to act assertively, aggressively or nonassertively.

One note of caution before proceeding to our next main area: Assertion Training can lead to too much "I-am-number-one." Many recent books and seminars written and presented under the guise of teaching people how to be assertive are really just teaching people how to get their way—all the time—no matter what. Always remember as you communicate with someone else that just as you have "rights," the other person has those **same** "rights."

Three Behaviors

Now that you understand that you have certain rights as you communicate with others, let's identify the three behaviors generally associated with Assertion Training, one of which will become our preferred focus, with the other two behaviors being the boundaries of that preferred behavior.

Nonassertive Behavior

First, nonassertion is the act of withdrawing from a situation. The emotions, such as fear, anxiety, guilt, depression, fatigue and hurt, are kept within the person.

The nonverbal communication associated with nonassertion is aversion to eye contact, teary eyes, shifting of balance, slumped posture, wringing of hands, biting lips, adjusting clothing, or nervous jitters. As the nonassertive person verbalizes, there are rambling statements, many qualifiers (maybe's, if's), speech fillers (uh's, you-knows), and negatives (don't know's, I don't care's and whatever's).

In general, the nonassertive person denies his own feelings and permits others to act and make decisions. The result is intrapersonal conflict, depression, helplessness, stress, addiction, loneliness and poor self-image.

Aggressive Behavior

Next, let's identify aggression. Aggression is the act of emotionally over-reacting to a situation. The emotions of fear, anxiety, etc. that we mentioned used by this person as a build-up to inappropriate anger, rage, self-righteousness and superiority. (Physiologically, the body temperature is above normal.)

The nonverbal behaviors of aggressiveness are glaring, narrowed eyes, a rigid, forward-leaning posture, clenched fists or pointing fingers and a raised haughty voice. While speaking, there are clipped or interrupted statements, threats (you-betters, watch-outs), name calling, defensiveness, sarcasm, putdowns, judgements (should's, bad's) sexism and racism. In the extreme, aggression is characterized by verbal or physical violence.

Assertive Behavior

Finally, we identify assertion. Assertion is the act of declaring "This is what I am, what I think and feel, and what I want" and doing so as soon as it occurs.

The nonverbal communications associated with assertiveness are eye-contact that isn't uncomfortable for the listener; standing relaxed; hands loose at the sides; steady, firm, clear tone of voice. Assertive statements are concise. Assertive individuals characteristically use words like "I" ("I think/I feel/I want"); cooperative words ("let's resolve this/compromise"); and show openness/willingness ("What do you think/Is this workable").

Aggression - - - Assertion - - - Nonassertion

Some conclusions about assertiveness: Assertive responses are characterized by the use of "I," instead of "you." Assertive responses are usually effective in getting people to change or to reinforce behaviors. Assertive responses run a low risk of hurting a relationship. Assertive responses do not attack the other person's self-esteem or put others on the defensive. Assertion prevents "gunny sacking"—i.e., saving up a lot of bad feelings until you explode.

Assertive Techniques

In terms of possible techniques or verbal strategies, there are various approaches which can be used. The model that is perhaps most widely used in this field comes from M. Smith's *When I Say No, I Feel Guilty,* in which the author presents seven basic techniques. For each technique, we will give a brief explanation and then present a sample situation and dialogue to illustrate their use.

1. Broken Record

Repeat your goal/request over and over without getting distracted and until you wear the other person down.

Situation: You have just received your credit card bill and find charges for purchases you never made—you (Y) contact customer service (S).

Y: You have my transaction on your screen? You see the $39.95 charge for shoes from Shu-World? I never shop at that store and I would like my account credited for that amount, please.
S: Well, we have the receipt and your signature is on it.
Y: You may have something that looks like my signature, but I never shop at that store and I would like my account credited for that amount, please.
S: It is highly unlikely that anyone would forge your signature for $39.95.
Y: I realize that you think it is highly unlikely, but I never shop at that store and I would like my account credited for that amount, please.

Skills for Dealing with Criticism

2. Fogging

Calmly and politely agreeing with your critic that there **may be** **some truth in what they are saying** or telling them that **you can understand why they** *might* **feel that way.** This buys time and puts you in control of the situation.

Situation: At the office, your boss (B) starts complaining that you (Y) are taking too many breaks and using the copier for personal use.

B: Not only do you take too many breaks but now you are using the company copier for your own personal use.
Y: Perhaps I should be more concerned about my break times and use of the copier.

3. Negative Assertion

Openly and honestly admitting your mistakes instead of hiding or lying about them. We all make mistakes.

Situation: At a friend's (F) party, you (Y) knock over a glass, which breaks.

F: That ruins my set which has a lot of sentimental value.
Y: I feel very badly that I broke the glass and I wish I would not have.

4. Negative Inquiry

Asking for more criticism of yourself in order to get rid of criticism that is manipulative. It makes people tell you the truth about why they are angry.

Situation: You (Y) have decided to go away to college and now your closest friend (F) is criticizing your decision.

F: Why did you choose that diploma factory to go to? You won't learn anything there.
Y: I like the school. I don't know why you're so against me going there.
F: I can't believe you don't want to go to a good school.
Y: This is a good school and I still don't understand what you have against me going there.
F: But the students are all rejects from other colleges.
Y: I like this school. I know some of the students who go there and they like it. Are you sure there isn't some other reason you don't want me going to this school?

Conversation Skills

5. Free Information

This is a listening skill. You learn to ask lots of questions about others and their concerns, opinions, etc., rather than talking about yourself too much.

Situation: You (Y) have just started a new job and during lunch break meet another person (P), who mentions that they have just gotten back from vacation.

Y: That sounds great. What did you do during your time off?

6. Self-Disclosure

Admitting openly and honestly your strengths, weaknesses and opinions without apologizing for them.

Situation: Your boss (B) asks you (Y) to do something that you do not know enough about.

B: When you've finished that report, take this software, make the spreadsheet and a graph of it.
Y: I know how to make the spreadsheet, but I'm not sure about the graph.

7. Workable Compromise

This is for two assertive people. For example, when you are both using broken record, you must compromise. This compromise does not have to be **fair**—it only has to **work**. Never use it if you feel that your self-respect will be jeopardized.

Situation: Your boss (B) needs a report by 10 a.m. the next day and asks you (Y) to stay late to finish it.

B: I need you to stay late and finish this report tonight. It must be done for an important meeting I have tomorrow at 10 a.m.
Y: I know this report is important to you, but I have a very important meeting after work.
B: But I **want** this report finished tonight.
Y: O.K. I will stay an extra hour today and if I don't finish, I will come in early tomorrow so that you have it for your 10 o'clock meeting.

BARRIERS TO BEING ASSERTIVE

We Allow Others to Stomp on Us

We can feel helpless and frustrated because we do not speak up. This behavior affects our self-concept/self-image to the extent that we tend to believe that our ideas are not as valuable as others, that we are not as valuable as others.

We Stomp on Others

We sometimes feel the need to dominate others, to "win" at all cost. Consequently, we disregard the "rights" of others. We see ourselves as #1 and turn people off by judging, manipulating and playing dishonest games with them.

We Believe That We Must Always Be Assertive

It is important to remember that assertiveness is a conscious act. Just as we can choose to be assertive, we can also choose to be aggressive or nonassertive. Assertiveness should be viewed as the process of selecting which form of behavior will be the most productive, given the situation in which we are involved.

HOW ASSERTIVE ARE YOU?

PURPOSE: To help you assess your level of assertiveness.

PROCEDURE: 1.   Place an "X" on the following scale indicating generally how assertive you believe yourself to be.

60	120	180	240	300
nonassertive				completely assertive

2.   For each of the statements below, circle the number that best describes you. If an item describes a situation unfamiliar to you, try to imagine what your response would be. Of course, you will not achieve an accurate self-evaluation unless you answer all questions honestly.

1 . . . Never
2 . . . Rarely
3 . . . Sometimes
4 . . . Usually
5 . . . Always

1.	I do my own thinking.	1	2	3	4	5
2.	I can be myself around wealthy, educated or prestigious people.	1	2	3	4	5
3.	I am poised and confident among strangers.	1	2	3	4	5
4.	I freely express my emotions.	1	2	3	4	5
5.	I am friendly and considerate toward others.	1	2	3	4	5

6. I accept compliments and gifts without embarrassment or a sense of obligation.   1   2   3   4   5

7. I freely express my admiration of others' ideas and achievements.   1   2   3   4   5

8. I readily admit my mistakes.   1   2   3   4   5

9. I accept responsibility for my life.   1   2   3   4   5

10. I make my own decisions and accept the consequences.   1   2   3   4   5

11. I take the initiative in personal contacts.   1   2   3   4   5

12. When I have done something well, I tell others.   1   2   3   4   5

13. I am confident when going for job interviews.   1   2   3   4   5

14. When I need help, I ask others to help me.   1   2   3   4   5

15. When at fault, I apologize.   1   2   3   4   5

16. When I like someone very much, I tell them so.   1   2   3   4   5

17. When confused, I ask for clarification.   1   2   3   4   5

18. When someone is annoying me, I ask that person to stop.   1   2   3   4   5

19. When someone cuts in front of me in line, I protest.   1   2   3   4   5

20. When treated unfairly, I object.   1   2   3   4   5

21. If I were underpaid, I would ask for a salary increase.   1   2   3   4   5

22. When I am lonely or depressed, I take action to improve my mental outlook.   1   2   3   4   5

23. When working at a job or task I dislike intensely, I look for ways to improve my situation.   1   2   3   4   5

24. I complain to the management when I have been overcharged or have received poor service.   1   2   3   4   5

25. When something in my house or apartment malfunctions, I see that the landlady repairs it.   1   2   3   4   5

26. When I am disturbed by someone smoking, I say so.   1   2   3   4   5

27. When a friend betrays my confidence, I tell that person how I feel.   1   2   3   4   5

28. I ask my doctor all of the questions for which I want answers.   1   2   3   4   5

29. I ask for directions when I need help finding my way.   1   2   3   4   5

30. When there are problems, I maintain a relationship rather than cutting it off.   1   2   3   4   5

31. I communicate my belief that everyone at home should help with the upkeep rather than doing it all myself.   1   2   3   4   5

32. I make sexual advances toward my husband or sex partner.   1   2   3   4   5

33. When served food at a restaurant that is not prepared the way I ordered it, I express myself.   1   2   3   4   5

34. Even though a clerk goes to a great deal of trouble to show merchandise to me, I am able to say "No."   1   2   3   4   5

35. When I discover that I have purchased defective merchandise, I return it to the store.   1   2   3   4   5

36. When people talk in a theater, lecture or concert, I am able to ask them to be quiet.   1   2   3   4   5

37. I maintain good eye contact in conversations.   1   2   3   4   5

38. I would sit in the front of a large group if the only remaining seats were located there.   1   2   3   4   5

39. I would speak to my neighbors if their dog was keeping me awake with its barking at night.   1   2   3   4   5

40. When interrupted, I comment on the interruption and then finish what I am saying.   1   2   3   4   5

41. When a friend or spouse makes plans for me without my knowledge or consent, I object.   1   2   3   4   5

42. When I miss someone, I express the fact that I want to spend more time with that person.   1   2   3   4   5

43. When a person asks me to lend something and I really do not want to, I refuse.   1   2   3   4   5

44. When a friend invites me to join her and I really don't want to, I turn down the request.   1   2   3   4   5

45. When friends phone and talk too long on the phone, I can terminate the conversation effectively.   1   2   3   4   5

46. When someone criticizes me, I listen to the criticism without being defensive.   1   2   3   4   5

47. When people are discussing a subject and I disagree with their points of view, I express my difference of opinion.   1   2   3   4   5

48. When someone makes demands on me that I don't wish to fulfill, I resist the demands.   1   2   3   4   5

49. I speak up readily in group situations.   1   2   3   4   5

50. I tell my children or family members the things I like about them.   1   2   3   4   5

51. When my family or friends make endless demands on my time and energy, I establish firm notions about the amount of time I am willing to give.   1 2 3 4 5

52. When my husband phones to tell me he is bringing home an unexpected guest for dinner and I've had a hard day at work, I level with him about it and request that he make alternative plans.   1 2 3 4 5

53. When one friend is not meeting all of my needs, I establish meaningful ties with other people.   1 2 3 4 5

54. When my own parents, in-laws or friends freely give advice, I express appreciation for their concern without feeling obligated to follow their advice or suggestions.   1 2 3 4 5

55. When someone completes a task or job for me with which I am dissatisfied, I ask that it be done correctly.   1 2 3 4 5

56. When I object to political practices, I take action rather than blaming politicians.   1 2 3 4 5

57. When I am jealous, I explore the reasons for my feelings, and look for ways to increase my self-confidence and self-esteem.   1 2 3 4 5

58. When a person tells me she envies me, I accept her comments without feeling guilty or apologizing.   1 2 3 4 5

59. When I am feeling insecure, I assess my personal strengths and take action designed to make me feel more secure.   1 2 3 4 5

60. I accept my husband's, wife's or boy/girl friend's interests in other people without feeling I must compete with them.   1 2 3 4 5

Total Score _____

DISCUSSION: 1. How does your initial general rating compare to your actual score? If there is a significant difference, how can you account for it?
2. How important is it to you to be a more assertive person? Why?
3. In what ways can you go about being more assertive?   ❏

FIVE SAMPLE SITUATIONS

PURPOSE: To be able to identify responses as either assertive, nonassertive, or aggressive.

PROCEDURE: Read through each of the following situations and determine which of the three responses is assertive, which is nonassertive and which is aggressive.

1. Cousin Jessie with whom you prefer not to spend much time is on the phone. She says that she is planning to spend the next three weeks with you.

    Responses:
    a. "We'd love to have you come and stay as long as you like."
    b. "We'd be glad to have you come for the weekend, but we cannot invite you for longer. A short visit will be very nice for all of us, and we'll want to see each other again."
    c. "The weather back here has been terrible,"—not true—"so you'd better plan on going elsewhere."

2. You have bought a toaster at Sears that doesn't work properly.

    Responses:
    a. "I bought this toaster and it doesn't work and I would like my money back."
    b. "What right do you have selling me junk like this. . . ."
    c. You put it in the closet and buy another one.

3. One of your workers has been coming in late consistently for the last three or four days.

    Responses:
    a. "I have noticed that for the last few days you have been a little late and I am concerned about it."
    b. "The next time you're late you're fired."
    c. You mumble to yourself and hope he'll be on time tomorrow.

4. You are in a meeting and someone starts smoking, which offends you.

    Responses:
    a. "Hey, man, that smoke is terrible."
    b. You suffer the smoke in silence.
    c. "I would appreciate it if you wouldn't smoke here. I am bothered by it."

5. You are at a lecture with 400 other people. The speaker is not speaking loud enough for all to hear.

    Responses:
    a. You continue straining to hear and end up daydreaming.
    b. You yell out, "Speak up; we can't hear you if you talk to yourself."
    c. You raise your hand and get her attention—"Would you mind speaking a little louder, please."

DISCUSSION: 1.   Was it easy or difficult to distinguish among the three behaviors?
                    2.   Which of the situations were easier to distinguish and why? ❏

ASSERTION TRAINING: PRACTICING BEHAVIORS

PURPOSE: To be able to construct assertive, nonassertive, and aggressive comments in different situations.

PROCEDURE:
1. Form small groups.
2. As a group, take each of the 10 situations and write a nonassertive, aggressive and assertive response for each.
3. As a class, discuss the various responses to each situation.

1. You are in charge of a meeting and Jean walks in somewhat intoxicated.
2. You are talking with some other people and they start talking about Jose. Someone calls him a "wetback," which offends you, because Jose is your friend.
3. You are taking an English class. Your handwriting is the "pits." As a result, your teacher keeps giving you a lower grade, which you feel is unfair.
4. You and a group of friends have decided to go out to dinner. Everyone else wants to go somewhere that you do not like.
5. You want to go out for the weekend with a group of friends. Your parents object. You still want to go.
6. Someone moves into the apartment next to you and you would like to meet them.
7. You are standing in the check-out line at Super Market. Someone keeps pushing their cart into your back.
8. You and a friend are shopping. You see him stealing something, which you feel is wrong.
9. You are wearing a new outfit and someone compliments you on it.
10. Your friend has said she will meet you for lunch at 12:30. She arrives at 1: 15—with no apologies—and you are irritated!

DISCUSSION:
1. Did you find it easier to come up with nonassertive and aggressive comments than with assertive ones? Why?
2. Did you find it harder to come up with assertive comments to some situations as opposed to others? If so, which ones? Why? ❑

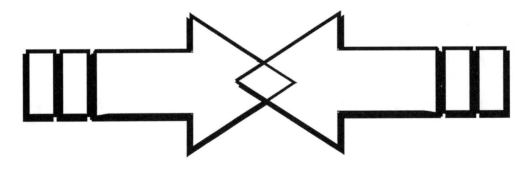

You cannot shake hands with a clenched fist. —*I. Gandhi*

TEN ROLE PLAYING SITUATIONS FOR ASSERTION TRAINING

PURPOSE: To allow you to employ assertive techniques in role playing situations.

PROCEDURE:
1. Divide into pairs.
2. Read over the following situations and choose one that you and your partner would like to act out and decide which part each of you will play.
3. Decide which assertive technique is most appropriate to the situation.
4. Now, act out the situation twice. First demonstrate either a nonassertive or an aggressive reaction. Then, demonstrate assertive behavior using the assertive technique decided on in #3.

1. You just got home from work and somebody wants to go to the show, but you would rather not.
2. A friend who is always borrowing money and never paying you back now asks to borrow $10 more from you.
3. You have bought a tough steak at the market for $5.50 and want to return it.
4. You have booked a flight to Hawaii on Fantasy Airlines. When you get to the airport, you find that your booking has been lost.
5. You have made a mistake on the job. Your supervisor sees it and starts telling you off in front of your fellow workers.
6. A fellow worker is not doing his share of the work, making others fall behind.
7. It is your turn for card club and someone starts nagging about the condition of the cards—bent, sticky, etc.
8. You are at a staff party and someone is standing off to one side of the room not talking to anyone.
9. You are in a group which is discussing a controversial topic and someone says something that you strongly disagree with.
10. You are at a movie and the person in back of you keeps talking.

DISCUSSION:
1. Why did you choose the techniques you did? Was it easy/difficult to select one?
2. How did you feel when the nonassertive/aggressive responses were used?
3. How did you feel when the assertive response was used? ❑

I may disagree with what you say, but I will defend with my life your right to say it. —*Voltaire*

REACTIONS

1. Would you classify yourself as basically nonassertive, assertive or aggressive?

2. List five qualities that place you in that classification.

3. In what kinds of situations do you find it most difficult to be assertive?

4. Why do you find it difficult to be assertive in these situations?

5. Recall and describe a current incident where you reacted either nonassertively or aggressively, when you should have reacted assertively.

6. How do you feel about how you behaved in this situation—i.e., guilty, etc.?

7. How might the situation have changed had you been assertive?

8. Describe a situation where it might be better to react aggressively.

9. Describe a situation where it might be better to be nonassertive.

RELATIONAL COMMUNICATION | 13

Definitions

We share a large part of our lives with other individuals in what we call "relationships." All relationships involve elements of interpersonal communication; however, the study of relational communication focuses specifically on the communication that occurs between two people who are in the process of beginning, continuing or ending a relationship with each other. Although we have many relationships (i.e., with neighbors, our boss, teachers), this chapter will address the intimate communication between family members, close friends or significant love relationships. In order to gain an understanding of the communication process that occurs in these relationships, we will define several terms that will be used in this chapter:

Relational Communication

Definition: Communication that affects our willingness, and that of others, to initiate, continue or terminate our relationships.

Examples: Greeting people, handshakes (initiating), expressing our commitment to the relationship (continuing), telling someone we no longer want to be friends (terminating), etc.

Relational Identity

Definition: The perception of two individuals in a relationship as something different than who they are as individuals.

Examples: We may see ourselves as a "couple," "twosome," or a "duo." We begin to refer to ourselves as "we" or "us" instead of "you and me."

Intimacy

Definition: According to Adler, Rosenfeld and Towne in their book *Interplay,* this can be classified in three areas: intellectual, emotional or physical intimacy. Intimacy is characterized by extended and concentrated communication in any of these areas. It is also not the goal in all relationships.

Examples: We may share our life philosophies with a friend (intellectual), our feelings of love with a parent (emotional), and have a sexual relationship with a girlfriend or boyfriend (physical).

Self-Disclosure

Definition: Sharing information about oneself that the other individual is unlikely to find out by other means.

Examples: Sharing secrets, discoveries, confidential information, past history and experiences or information that we do not commonly express.

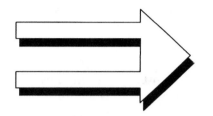

If you judge people, you have not time to love them. —*Mother Teresa*

THE IMPORTANCE OF RELATIONAL COMMUNICATION

Imagine for a moment that you are suddenly alone in the world. You woke up this morning and found that the people you share your home with are gone. You stepped outside and your neighborhood was void of the sounds of people awakening and preparing for a new day—no car engines running or doors closing as other individuals go about their daily routines. You leave for work or school only to find the streets empty. Every store, school or business you see is the same: deserted. As far as you know you are the only person left in the world!

This is not a very pleasant scene but it does allow us to examine how we feel about those who share our lives. Whether it be a parent, a roommate or a spouse, we would sorely miss the company of others if we suddenly found them absent from our lives. The reality is that we are social creatures by nature and our relationships provide the foundation of our daily lives. Understanding how and why we establish these relationships and what barriers we face in successfully maintaining them can help us avoid the "disappearance" of important relationships from our lives. And, most impor-

tantly, the more we understand about how we communicate in these relationships the greater the opportunity we have to make them work well.

Relationships Are Inevitable

Relationships are, fortunately, unavoidable. From business contacts to friendship to intimate love, relationships pervade our lives. We begin by being born into families where we learn the basics of communicating in relationships. Babies learn, through nonverbal communication with their parents, that certain people are more important to their existence than others. Toddlers discover that developing more relationships makes life more interesting. Brothers, sisters, grandparents and more provide social opportunities and stimulation.

Relationships also fulfill basic human needs. Simply communicating with others is not enough. We need to know that significant people share a future with us. We need companionship, love and a sense of belonging. And we don't fulfill these needs in any one relationship. Instead, we often have several or many relationships that serve us differently. We may socialize with one friend and confide in another. And we fulfill others' needs as well. This is the reciprocal nature of relationships. As long as we are both having our needs met we can be quite satisfied with each other. However, as soon as one person starts to expect more than the other person is willing to give or if one person feels she is giving more than she is receiving, then we have a "needs" imbalance and the relationship may suffer as a consequence.

Relationships Develop in Stages

Effective relationships need to be carefully created and constructively maintained. The path a relationship takes does not happen by accident and we can exercise some degree of control by understanding how communication influences the development of relationships. According to researcher Mark Knapp in the book *Interpersonal Communication and Human Relationships*, relationships develop through the following 10 stages:

Initiating—in this stage we want to create the impression that we are an interesting person worth knowing. At the same time we are evaluating the other individual's reaction to us. Initiating is often characterized by communication such as a handshake or "nice to meet you." And if we are really interested in initiating a relationship, we often strategically plan our approach. Being "accidentally" in the same place at the same time, smiling or nodding may gain us the entrance we desire.

Experimenting—at this point we try to find things that we have in common with the other person. We often engage in "small talk." Now, you may be one of those people who find small talk to be superficial and useless but at this early stage of a relationship it serves an important communication function. Besides finding out if we have anything in common, it helps us determine if we want to pursue the next step. For instance, Anthony had wanted to meet Brenda for a long time. When he finally got the courage to introduce himself, he suddenly started telling his life story, including some intimate details. When he asked her out to dinner, she turned him down. Little did he know that she was very uncomfortable with what he had told her. Brenda felt that Anthony was either insecure or moving "too fast!" Small talk would have broken the ice for Anthony and allowed the relationship to develop along a more natural path.

Intensifying—At this point we begin to develop a relationship that will, hopefully, meet our needs. This stage is characterized by informal communication. We start referring to each as "we" rather than "I" or "you." We begin disclosing more about ourselves as the potential for growth becomes obvious. It is here that we find the courage to start expressing our feelings about commitment. Sheri, a college student, stated in class, "I have a friendship that has become very important to me. Yesterday my friend told me that we're going to be friends forever! I can't tell you how nice it is to know I can count on her."

Integrating—In this stage a relational identity is developed. We are recognized by others as a "couple," "partners" or "buddies." We begin interacting with each other based on this new identity called "us." For example, Matthew canceled an appointment so he could go to his girlfriend's company picnic with her. When we integrate, we often take on relational commitments rather than continue to follow our individual schedules.

Bonding—Now we make our commitment known through public rituals. A wedding is an example of such a ritual. Research in psychology indicates that public commitments create in us a stronger desire to make the relationship work. We decide to let the "world" know that we are having a relationship.

Differentiating—We reach a point where the relational identity may be too restricting and we want to re-establish our own identities. Often this is a reaction to conflict in the relationship. For instance, a wife may stop referring to a family automobile as "our car" and start calling it "my car" in an effort to communicate her individuality. This doesn't mean that differentiation cannot have a positive outcome. Recognizing the other person's need for individuality and personal space can strengthen the original commitment to each other.

Circumscribing—Hopefully all relationships will have happy endings. But we all know this is not realistic. At some point what we have with another person begins to deteriorate. The first stage of this disintegration is circumscribing wherein we reduce the quantity or quality of time and energy we put into the relationship. For example, Tony and Sophie became a clear case of a relationship in this stage when they both started spending more time with other friends, avoiding each other's phone calls and responding to each other by saying "you wouldn't be interested" or "it doesn't concern you." The sad part about this is that, while avoiding each other, we often avoid the fact that we are both contributing to the disintegration of what we called "us."

Stagnation—Here we really begin to live life in a rut! The relationship has no novelty or excitement and we react to it in a very routine way. Have you ever had a job that you disliked but you continued to perform? It becomes robotic, repetitive and boring. The same thing happens to a relationship if we allow it to stagnate. We become the stereotypical picture of the old couple living in the same house and never speaking a word to each other.

Avoiding—Stagnation may develop to the point that we cannot handle any contact with each other so we go out of our way to avoid one another. For example, Angela, who dated Mario for 2 months, wanted so badly to avoid him that she dropped out of two classes that they attended together. Avoiding is a clear sign of the death of the relational identity. We no longer talk about "us," rather we communicate in terms "you" or "me."

Terminating—This is, of course, when one or both parties involved end the relationship. It can be brought on by the death of one of the individuals or a decision that staying together is no longer beneficial. This is one of the most difficult stages for it can often be painful to the parties involved. How it occurs often depends on how intimate the relationship was. A casual friendship may end, but a marriage or cutting the ties with a family member may take more negotiation and expressing of feelings.

Most communication researchers agree that all relationships follow a systematic development. However, that doesn't mean that every time we get involved with someone it is destined for termination. What is important is that we discover how to stop the pattern when we've reached a stage where both participants are happy and maintain the relationship at that level.

BARRIERS TO DEVELOPING RELATIONSHIPS

Initiating Relationships

There are many barriers to maintaining good communication in a relationship. However, the first major barrier is how to begin a relationship, how to initiate contact. We have probably all experienced the desire to meet someone and the uncertainty about how to go about communicating with them. Regardless of the kind of relationship we're interested in establishing (we may want a new friend or a new love), we face the barriers of overcoming our own shyness, having our advances rejected and taking the risk of putting ourselves on the line. But if a relationship is going to exist, someone has to make the first move. Arthur Wassmer, in his book *Making Contact,* recommends the SOFTENS Technique to help make the initial contact more productive. He uses each letter of the word "softens" to represent nonverbal behaviors that we can use when breaking the ice with someone new. Taking these nonverbal signals into consideration can help us overcome the fear we often feel on the initial contact. The technique is as follows:

Smiling—genuinely done, helps establish a positive climate

Open posture—communicates interest

Forward lean—communicates involvement

Touching by shaking hands—establishes physical contact

Eye contact—communicates interest, listening and builds rapport

Nodding—communicates listening and can help you focus on what the other person is saying

Space—can promote closeness depending on culture and the kind of relationship you want to encourage

Maintaining a Relationship

The second barrier we face is communicating within the relationship in such a manner that we maintain the relationship. The more intimate the relationship is, the more complex it may become to maintain, whether it is with a family member, a friend or a lover. Intimacy, whether it be physical, emotional or intellectual, can enhance the relationship by allowing two people to bond to each other through this closeness, or it can drive them apart if one or the other is not ready or prepared to maturely deal with the intimacy. Intimacy involves vulnerability and therefore requires trust in each other. If we feel like we are being manipulated or played with, we often find it difficult to be intimate with someone. This can happen when we encounter "control factors." Control factors are any issues in a relationship that cause one or more participants to feel a lack of balance in the relationship. In other words, these factors set things out of control. Several major communication control factors that surface in many relationships are as follows:

Unequal participation—Teresa feels she puts out a lot more effort in the marriage than her husband, Chris. She is feeling very dissatisfied with this imbalance and wants him to contribute his share to the relationship.

Simultaneous Relationships—Rod and Mike have been friends for a long time. Recently, Mike became involved in a club at school and has been spending a lot of time with other people and not much time with Rod. Rod, who has no interest in the club's activities, has made a request for more of Mike's time. Mike feels a tremendous imbalance. He wants to see Rod, but also wants to continue developing his new relationships. He feels like he's doing a juggling act with friends.

Incompatibility—Jennifer and Troy are very attracted to each other. They feel there is a real chemistry between them. However, as they start to spend time together, they find they have little in common. They want to see each other because of the interpersonal attraction, but when together, they have a tendency to argue over opposing viewpoints. They want to resolve this imbalance but don't know how.

Game Playing—Matt feels confused about his relationship with his father. They can be getting along well one day, but the next his dad is putting "some guilt trip on me." He would like to spend more time at home but the emotional "yo-yo" is getting to be more than he can handle.

Control—Jesse is realizing that she is tired of being considered a "little girl" by her parents. Granted, they controlled her life when she was small but she wants to make her own decisions now. She does not want the scales to lean so heavily in her parents' favor.

In each of these situations, the individuals involved feel an imbalance in their relationships. Each one has a choice—they can continue to feel the lack of satisfaction, they can reduce the amount of involvement in the relationship or they can try to resolve the conflict by communicating with their partners about the factor that is causing the problem. This last option is necessary if the relationships are going to be maintained at a positive stage. But this step also requires the willingness to self-disclose feelings in an honest and supportive fashion. If they are willing to take the risk of disclosure then they have the chance to bring balance back to the relationship. But disclosure must be given in appropriate amounts. We can overwhelm another person with our inner feelings and literally chase them away. But if handled sensitively, self-disclosure has two benefits for relationships: it encourages reciprocal disclosure (I will be more motivated to share if you are equally willing) and it can increase the intimacy of the relationship. Lastly, it is important to be aware of the influence self-disclosure has in our lives. It is not only important in maintaining healthy relationships, but it is also one of the first things to diminish as the relationship begins to deteriorate. Relationships that are stagnating are often characterized by a lack of disclosure—the individuals just won't share!

Ending a Relationship

The last barrier we'll address here deals with ending a relationship. For most of us this is one of the most difficult communication situations. Few of us want to play the "bad guy." Yet, if our partner is the one ending the relationship, we may suffer feelings of rejection and a loss of self-esteem. It is very rare to have an outcome where both parties are happy; however, this can happen. For example, Raul was tired of his girlfriend, Janie, playing games and Janie was fed up with Raul continually trying to control her time so they mutually agreed to call it quits and both were happy. Most of us, however, suffer a feeling of loss when we lose relationships whether they be through the death of a family member or the break-up of a love relationship. This is because we are literally in mourning for the relational identity, that element that was composed of ourselves and another. We not only miss the other person but we miss that identity that was "us." As in any mourning situation, acknowledging our grief and allowing it to run its course is one of the best treatments to the pain of an ended relationship.

Knowing why we need relationships in our lives helps us understand the way we communicate within them. We are striving to start and maintain them and, sometimes, find ourselves in one that is ending. Relationships, like life, work in a cycle. And, like life, how much we give them will determine how much we gain from them. The activities in this chapter are designed to help you determine the kind of relationships you want, how to improve the ones you are currently involved in and aid you in acquiring the skills to start new ones. With this information you will, hopefully, never find yourself alone in the world.

ARE YOU MADE FOR LOVE?

Diane Ackerman

A naturalist and prize-winning poet, contributing editor Diane Ackerman holds a Ph.D. from Cornell University. In addition to her four poetry collections, she's the author of five works of nonfiction, including the best-selling "A Natural History of the Senses." This article—an exploration of the biology of love—is adapted from her new book, "A Natural History of Love," published by Random House.

Among the many handicaps that can befall human beings, few are sadder than the inability to feel love. Because we imagine love to be wholly psychological, we don't even have a word for people who are biologically unable to love. But there are some unlucky souls who, through trauma to part of the brain, cannot feel emotion.

Antonio Damasio, a neurologist at the University of Iowa College of Medicine, reports a curious case in which a man we'll call John had been living a normal life as accountant, husband and father. At 35, John had a benign tumor removed from the front of his brain. The operation was a success. But soon afterward his personality changed dramatically. He divorced his wife, became involved with a prostitute, lost one job after another, became penniless—all without feeling anything, not even bewilderment or concern.

Using magnetic resonance imaging to peer inside the brain, Damasio found that a region of John's frontal cortex was damaged. Most likely, this had occurred during the tumor operation, injuring a small portion of gray matter between the eyebrows that seems to be a factory for emotions.

Damasio hooked John up to a machine similar to a lie detector and presented him with emotionally charged slides, sounds and questions. Some were violent, some pornographic. John had no response. A field of flowers registered no differently than a murder.

If the ability to love is something that can be so destroyed, then it has a physical reality, it is matter. But where does love reside in the body?

Throughout history, people have located love in the heart probably because of its loud, safe, regular, comforting beat—that maternal two-step that babies follow from before birth. The image of the heart adorns greeting cards, coffee mugs, bumper stickers and paintings of the crucifixion. A real heart, viewed during open-heart surgery, seems a poor symbol for so much emotion. "In my heart of hearts," we say, making a *matrioshka* doll of it; in the innermost cave in the labyrinth of my feelings. The heart is vital to being alive, the unstated logic runs, and so is love.

Love develops in the neurons of the brain, and the way it grows depends on how those neurons were trained when we were children. Evolution hands out a blueprint for the building of the house of one's life. But, as with a house, much depends on the skill and experience of the builders; the laws and codes of society; the qualities of the materials; not to mention the random effect of landslides or floods or plumbing catastrophes; and the caprices of inspectors or supervisors, of hooligans or neighbors. How we love is a matter of biology. How we love is a matter of experience.

- *The cuddle chemical.* Oxytocin, a hormone that encourages labor and the contractions during childbirth, seems to play an important role in love, especially mother love. The sound of a crying baby makes its mother's body secrete more oxytocin, which in turn erects her nipples and helps the milk to flow. As the baby nurses, even more oxytocin is released, making the mother want to nuzzle and hug the baby. It has been called the "cuddle chemical" by zoologists, who have artificially raised the oxytocin level in animals and produced similar behavior.

Later in life, oxytocin seems to play an equally important role in romantic love, as a sexual arousal hormone that prompts cuddling between lovers and sweetens pleasure during lovemaking. Unlike other hormones, oxytocin flows from either physical or emotional cues—a certain look, voice or gesture is enough—and can be tied to one's personal love history, so a lover's voice alone can trigger more oxytocin. So might a richly woven and redolent sexual fantasy.

This outpouring of hormone may help explain why more women than men prefer to continue cuddling after sex. A woman may yearn to feel close and connected, tightly coiled around the mainspring of the man's heart. In evolutionary terms, she hopes the man will be sticking around for a while—long enough to protect her and the child he just fathered.

- *The infatuation chemical.* When two people find one another attractive, their bodies quiver with a gush of PEA (phenylethylamine), a molecule that speeds up the flow of information between nerve cells. An amphetaminelike chemical, PEA whips the brain into a frenzy of excitement, which is why lovers feel euphoric, rejuvenated, optimistic and energized, happy to sit up talking all night or making love for hours on end. Because amphetamine, or "speed," is addictive—even the body's naturally made speed—some people become what Michael Liebowitz and Donald Klein of the New York State Psychiatric Institute refer to as "attraction junkies," needing a romantic relationship to feel excited by life.

Driven by a chemical hunger, they choose unsuitable partners. Soon the relationship crumbles, or they find themselves rejected. In either case, tortured by lovesick despair, they plummet into a savage depression, which they try to cure by falling in love again. Liebowitz and Klein think this rollercoaster is fueled by

a craving for PEA. When they gave some attraction junkies MAO inhibitors—antidepressants that can subdue PEA and other neurotransmitters—the researchers were amazed to find how quickly their patients improved. No longer craving PEA, they were able to choose partners more calmly and realistically. All this strongly suggests that when we fall in love, the brain drenches itself in PEA, a chemical that makes us feel pleasure, rampant excitement and well-being. A sweet fix, love.

- *The attachment chemical.* While the chemical sleigh ride of infatuation carries one at a fast clip over uneven terrain, lives become blended, people mate and genes mix, and babies are born. Then infatuation subsides and a new group of chemicals takes over—the morphinelike opiates of the mind, which calm and reassure. Being in love is a state of chaotic equilibrium. Its rewards of intimacy, dependability, warmth, empathy and shared experiences trigger the production of that mental comfort food, the endorphins. It's a less steep feeling than falling in love, but it's also steadier and more addictive.

The longer two people have been married, the more likely it is that they'll stay married. Stability, friendship, familiarity and affection are rewards the body clings to. As much as we love being dizzied by infatuation, such a state is stressful. It also feels magnificent to rest, to be free of anxiety or fretting and to enjoy one's life with a devoted companion.

That's a hard tonic to give up, even if the relationship isn't perfect. Shared events (including shared stresses and crises) are rivets that draw couples closer together. Soon they are fastened by so many that it's difficult to pull free.

- *The chemistry of divorce.* Monogamy and adultery are both hallmarks of being human. After the seductive fireworks of infatuation—which may last only a few weeks, or a few years—the body gets bored with easy ecstasy. Then the attachment chemicals roll in their thick cozy carpets of marital serenity. Might as well relax and enjoy the calm and security, some feel. Separated even for a short while, the partners crave the cradle of each other's embrace. Is it a chemical craving? Possibly so, a hunger for the soothing endorphins that flow when they're together.

Other people grow restless and search for novelty. They can't stand the tedium of constancy. So they begin illicit affairs or divorce proceedings.

One way or another, the genes survive, the species prevails. Even when the chemical cycle falters and breaks, it picks itself up and starts again.

TALKING TO PEOPLE IN OUR LIVES

The following five activities are designed to teach you the communication skills of initiating, maintaining and ending a conversation. The activities may be done singly or in a series.

SKILL #1: FIGURING OUT TO WHOM TO TALK ——————

PURPOSE:

To learn to identify nonverbal signals that tell us if a person is willing to have a conversation.

PROCEDURE:

1. For three days observe people you do not know but to whom you are attracted (as a possible friend or love interest).
2. Identify nonverbal signals that communicate to you whether a person is approachable or not (state specifically what the person is doing that makes you feel this way).
3. Describe the communication behavior below.

Not Approachable

1.

2.

3.

4.

5.

6.

7.

Approachable

1.

2.

3.

4.

5.

6.

7.

DISCUSSION:

1. What did the "approachable" people do that made you feel this way? The "unapproachable?"
2. Which person seemed to be the most approachable and why?
3. Which person seemed to be the most unapproachable and why?
4. How approachable do you think other people perceive you and why?
5. How will these observations help you in your future relationships? ❏

SKILL #2: THE ART OF SMALL TALK

PURPOSE: To examine the value of small talk as a way to initiate communication in a new relationship.

PROCEDURE:
1. Select someone you do not know very well and initiate a conversation on one of the following topics: the weather, your favorite foods or hobbies, your jobs, a TV program or movie you've recently seen, a current news event or the surrounding environment.
2. Carry on the conversation for at least 15 minutes, changing subjects if necessary to maintain dialogue.

DISCUSSION:
1. How comfortable/uncomfortable were you using small talk?
2. Did small talk help you find areas of common interest?
3. Did small talk lead to any in-depth conversation? Explain.
4. How can small talk help you start a relationship with someone you're interested in?
5. How can small talk be used in your current significant relationships? ❏

SKILL #3: SHARING YOURSELF— MORE IN-DEPTH CONVERSATIONS

PURPOSE: To explore the value of sharing personal information as a means of encouraging in-depth conversation.

PROCEDURE:
1. Over the next week monitor the conversation you have with family members, friends and in significant love relationships. Select five occasions when you share personal information about yourself with one or more of these people.
2. If you do not normally share personal information, then select five opportunities to do so.
3. For each occasion describe the following:
   a. My partner was:
   b. The information I shared was:
   c. His/her response was:

DISCUSSION:
1. Did the personal information encourage more conversation? Why or why not?
2. How did the person respond? How did you feel about his/her response?
3. How can sharing personal information enhance your relationships? ❏

SKILL #4: ENCOURAGING YOUR PARTNER TO TALK ——————

PURPOSE: To explore the use of open-ended questions (questions that invite a variety of responses rather than a short, specific answer) as a means to maintain a conversation.

PROCEDURE: 1. For each situation below write two open-ended questions that could
keep the conversation going.
2. Divide into dyads.
3. Ask each other the questions you have just written. Take turns role-
playing and responding.

Situation 1: You are out on a blind date. You and your partner are sitting in a nice restaurant and
are looking at the menus. The restaurant overlooks the ocean and it is sunset.

1.

2.

Situation 2: You are visiting a good friend's home for the first time and have just sat down for
lunch. The friend's two young children are playing in the next room.

1.

2.

Situation 3: It's the first meeting of class. You sit down next to a person whom you have been
attracted to for some time but haven't approached before now.

1.

2.

Situation 4: You've just met your fiance's/fiancee's parents for the first time. You are alone with
them in their living room.

1.

2.

DISCUSSION: 1. Was it difficult to come up with your questions and if so, why?
2. Did the open-ended questions encourage conversation between you
and your partner? Why or why not?
3. How might open-ended questions enhance communication in your
relationships?   ❏

SKILL #5: IT'S HARD TO STOP TALKING ———————

PURPOSE: To experience the process of ending a conversation.

PROCEDURE: 1. You will practice the following methods of ending a conversation:
   a. Summary—identifies the main points of the discussion: "I really understand how to organize this surprise party, Mom. I'll get started on the supplies right away."
   b. Value—a supportive statement that points out something that you found useful or are appreciative about: "This talk has helped so much! I really appreciate how much you've listened to my problem."
   c. Future Interest—identifies your desire to meet again: "I would really like to talk further with you about this. Could we get together later today?"
2. For each of the following situations write an example of one of the three preceding methods of ending a conversation. Identify which one you are using:

Situation 1: Disagreement with a parent:

Situation 2: After listening to a close friend who talked about his troubled love life all evening:

Situation 3: After an unenjoyable dinner date:

Situation 4: After having a great date with someone you haven't seen in several years.

DISCUSSION: 1. Do you normally find it difficult to end conversations? Explain.
2. Was it difficult to come up with these endings? Why or why not?
3. How can using specific endings help your communication in your relationships?   ❏

EVERYTHING YOU ALWAYS WANTED TO KNOW
BUT WERE AFRAID TO ASK

PURPOSE: To understand how and why males and females communicate in relationships.

PROCEDURE:
1. Divide the class into two large groups—male and female.
2. Subdivide these groups into smaller groups of five to seven members.
3. Each group will write 10 questions that they want members of the opposite sex to answer. Questions should deal specifically with the way we communicate in relationships.
   Examples: "Why does a woman share what's happening in her relationship with her female friends?" "Why do men resist sharing their inner feelings about the relationship?"
4. Give the instructor the questions and return to the large groups—males on one side of the room and females on the other.
5. The instructor will select questions to ask each side.
6. Volunteers for each side can respond for their group.

DISCUSSION:
1. Did your group have difficulty coming up with questions? Why or why not?
2. What differences/similarities did you notice about the kinds of issues the males were interested in versus the females?
3. Did you learn anything new about the way the opposite sex communicates in relationships? Explain.
4. How would asking questions such as these in your significant relationships improve your understanding of those relationships?   ❏

PRESCRIPTION FOR AILING LOVERS

Linda Zink

Most people, says Irene Kassorla, don't know how to feel good.

If they're feeling too close to another person, they take steps to move away, to protect themselves from being vulnerable or being deserted.

If they feel happy, they do something to spoil it. They say something to start an argument or they bring up unpaid bills—anything to make themselves feel guilty or angry or worried.

People back off from pleasure, Dr. Kassorla believes, because they don't know how to handle it. Nothing in their backgrounds has prepared them for being happy. As a result, they never "enjoy;" they simply keep validating the psychological pain of their childhood and their feelings of being "no good."

"It all began when we were very young, when we were so small, so little, so helpless that we had no equipment to deal with pain. And we were in pain all the time. Only mommy and daddy didn't know we were suffering.

"Everytime someone said 'don't' or 'can't' or 'no' or criticized us, a cash register in our heads went off. But instead of a 'no sale' flag, what popped up was a 'no good' flag. Pretty soon our heads were full of 'no goods.'"

Dr. Kassorla added that the problem with most people is that they've never gotten over being no good. No matter how long our legs or how big our chests, she said, "we all feel we're little kids on the playground," comfortable with pain and uneasy with joy.

Dr. Kassorla, a Ph.D. in psychology who initially earned a reputation for her revolutionary treatment of autistic children, derives much of her philosophy from Freudian psychoanalysis and Gestalt therapy.

But "derive" is where she insists upon drawing the line. "I've tried them all," Dr. Kassorla said, "and I've discarded most of them."

The soundness of her theory aside, Dr. Kassorla does have a certain knack—and a highly profitable one—for being both entertaining and educational. A stodgy, grey-haired professor she's not. This skinny Rhoda Morgenstern turns a lecture into a night club revue and makes psychotherapy appeal to the most skeptical.

Most of the people who were present for Dr. Kassorla's one-day seminar, "Putting it all together—a psychology for lovers," had had experiences with her before, either through her book, *Putting It All Together,* or through televised group therapy sessions. Others had more intimate contact and had worked with her as patients. (Dr. Kassorla likes to be referred to as "doctor" and calls her clients "patients.")

"They're all healthy patients, of course, and very beautiful people," said Dr. Kassorla of the 18 or so people who had volunteered to work in a demonstration therapy session during the morning program.

The day-long seminar, sponsored by UCLA Extension, was billed as an introduction to a five-week course to be offered by Dr. Kassorla during the spring quarter. The ratio of men to women in the sellout crowd of more than 300 people was about 1 to 10. The weaker sex, it would seem, was far more interested than their husbands in "putting it all together"—or in some cases, keeping it together at all.

"No, my husband wouldn't come with me," said a 40ish housewife from Encino who admitted she was bored at home and wanted to do something else with her life. "He knows what she's saying is right, but let's face it, he's a male chauvinist pig from the word go."

Dr. Kassorla's message for the day (aside from telling mothers to "get out of the house, and away from your children" and giving at least one divorcing couple feelings of guilt and inadequacy because they were "throwing their

Reprinted by permission *Long Beach Press Telegram.*

marriage away like Kleenex") was the importance of giving "honest positives."

An "honest positive," Dr. Kassorla explained, is any truthful comment that makes the other person feel good about himself.

For a variety of reasons, Dr. Kassorla said, "even the healthy parent delivers practically no honest positives to his youngster. His folks may be praising him to the sky behind his back, but the kid doesn't know that. Instead, all he gets is the 'nos' and 'don'ts' and criticisms that make the 'no goods' ring up in his head."

Dr. Kassorla came upon the importance of honest positives while doing undergraduate field work in psychology at UCLA Medical Center. After a brief time of watching the autistic children on the ward receive comfort and attention for undesirable behavior, the then-unknown student decided the staff was going about the treatment backwards and as a result was making the parents crazier than they were.

"I'd see a child come in who was a two percent head banger. Because the child was rewarded—or got attention—when he banged his head, he'd be a 1 00 percent head banger by the end of a month. In the meantime, he was ignored when he did something good or normal."

At least one staff member had confidence in her application of positive reinforcement in the treatment of autistic children. She got a patient and a chance and the result was the first recorded therapeutic interaction with an autistic child.

Dr. Kassorla had similar successes with disturbed adults while pursuing her Ph.D. at the University of London. In one instance, she treated a 52-year-old man who had not spoken for 30 years. Within a month she had him talking again.

"In an hour of therapy, I would give the patient about 200 honest positives and about four negatives. And most of my negatives consisted of not saying anything at all."

Later, Dr. Kassorla began using the honest positive approach in her work with healthy adults. According to more than one audience member who had worked with her, the results of the treatment were "fantastic."

"I guess that I've learned to feel good about myself working with the doctor," one woman said.

"She's really a terrific person," remarked another. "And her method makes sense."

According to Dr. Kassorla, the healthy parent or spouse reverses her ratio of 200 honest positives to four negatives. Most people, she said, confuse giving love with giving directions. They nag or punish when they could be getting better results with honest positives.

Dr. Kassorla admitted, however, that learning to give honest positives isn't easy. She warned the audience, "You will make mistakes, you'll fail nine out of 10 times . . . but when you're successful or even when you catch yourself giving a negative instead of a positive, give yourself a kiss on the cheek."

Although a firm believer in being straightforward in her dealings, Dr. Kassorla said she never volunteers negative information. When confronted with a situation where she must be honestly negative, she says she precedes any negative statement with three honest positives and follows it up with yet another honest positive. She suggests the same formula for expressing anger.

"I don't below the belt anyone. If the Hunchback of Notre Dame came up and asked me how I liked his back, I wouldn't tell him, 'Look hunchy, beat it.' I'd tell him I liked his smile and his sense of humor or something and then I'd tell him that I really wasn't too fond of his back."

Dr. Kassorla also touched on the importance of learning to say "I want," especially where sex is concerned. Most people, she believes, are trained out of saying "I want" as children. So instead of being honest, they figured out indirect "dirty manipulations" to get what they want.

"The most dangerous person in the world is a person who doesn't say what he wants," Dr. Kassorla said.

The most important phase of living with a person is respect for that person as an individual. —*M. C. McIntosh*

GOING SHOPPING

PURPOSE: To determine the characteristics we are attracted to in different types of relationships.

PROCEDURE:
1. Divide the class into two groups—males and females.
2. Subdivide these groups into smaller groups of five to seven members.
3. Each group proceeds as follows: imagine that you are going "shopping" for a relationship. For each relationship below write a list of qualities you would be looking for from that person.
4. As a group, select the top 10 qualities from your list and put them in order of importance to you, with #1 being the quality you desire the most, and so on.
5. Each group will be asked to share their "shopping" list with the class.

TYPES OF RELATIONSHIPS

A. A long-term, romantic involvement that could lead to marriage
B. A casual friend—someone to have fun with and date occasionally
C. A "playmate"—a very short-term, "fast and heavy" involvement

DISCUSSION:
1. What do females want in each kind of relationship? Males?
2. What similarities did you notice between the females' and males' lists for each relationship? Differences?
3. How do the similarities between what males want and what females want affect communication? How do the differences affect communication?
4. Do people have their own private "shopping lists" when they want a relationship? How might this affect communication in significant relationships? ❏

THE TYPES OF LOVE

PURPOSE: To understand how we express and are shown different forms of love in our significant relationships.

John Alan Lee studied Americans and Canadians in 1973 and found that they tend to view love relationships in the following categories:

Eros: intense physical and emotional love, not possessive but believes love is more important than anything else in life.

Ludus: treats love as a game that is to be pleasant and fun but not long-term, may tell lies but really doesn't want to cause hurt.

Storage: views love as friendship and the sharing of activities, is not intense but rather relaxed.

Mania: "romantic love," very dramatic and tends toward creating conflict if the partner does not return the intensity and obsessiveness they feel.

Pragma: wants a long-term relationship, avoids emotional extremes that cause problems in relationships, seeks contentment.

Agape: completely giving of self unconditionally, sets no expectations for the other, deeply committed to the other person.

PROCEDURE:
1. In the space following, identify which types of love you have shown to someone else.
2. Identify which types of love have been shown to you.
3. For each type of love you identified, describe the relationship you are thinking of (who was it with, how long it lasted, etc.)
4. Rate your satisfaction with that relationship on the following scale:
   1—completely satisfied
   2—moderately satisfied
   3—neutral
   4—moderately dissatisfied
   5—completely dissatisfied

Type	Received By Me	Description	Rating	Shown To Me	Description	Rating
EROS						
LUDUS						
STORAGE						
MANIA						
PRAGMA						
AGAPE						

DISCUSSION:
1. Were you able to classify the significant relationships in your life according to the above categories?
2. Were you surprised by any of the classifications you used as you began to think about your relationships?
3. Does understanding the categories you used help you understand your level of satisfaction or dissatisfaction with your relationships?
4. How does your communication differ in each of the above categories? Why? ❑

WHEN YOUR EX-LOVER WON'T LET GO

Sheila Anne Feeney

After being dumped by her husband, a woman bought the $150,000 house next door to him. She devoted her days and nights to watching and annoying her ex. When women visited him she would gather the children and loudly admonish them to look. This was easy, because she had also installed mobile spotlights, which she trained on any woman who visited. The man's attorney was hopeful that he could get a court order to unplug the spotlights, but her scrutiny proved unbearable. Eventually, the man gave up and moved.

An American attending veterinary school in Naples, Italy, became frantic when his girlfriend of six years left him and moved back to the United States. Before catching up with her in Seattle, he spent three months wandering from Paris to Miami to Lake Placid, N.Y., to Tacoma, Wash., in search of his departed inamorata. To date, she has ditched him three times and he has found her twice.

The two taut thrillers "Fatal Attraction" and "House of Games" have been drawing box-office crowds who want to see spurned female protagonists get even with men who do not reciprocate their affections.

But while hell hath no fury like a woman scorned, experts say that interpersonal terrorism following a breakup is not the exclusive domain of females. Although expressions of romantic obsession may vary between the sexes (men are more likely to become violent and be direct in their harassment; women are more likely to pen a "poison" letter and act anonymously), both men and women are capable of lashing back at an ex in ways that can range from the self-demeaning to the deadly. The spurned party can vent his rage and de-spair in acts that can make the former lover's life hell.

The emotions that surge to the surface in the wake of a breakup can be powerful and the retaliatory responses devised can be creative and diverse. Spiteful ex-lovers use the courts to file suit after vengeful suit. Message-machine tapes are jammed with endless playings of "our" song. Employers and the Internal Revenue Service may be hounded to fire or audit the dumper. A surveillance campaign might be waged, complete with detectives and telescopes. Irrational letters may be mailed to family and mutual friends.

Harassment is not always hostile: Sometimes the badgering takes the form of repetitive begging and tearful appeals for reconciliation. While scorned wives may trump up endless excuses to call or drop by, ex-husbands often prefer the passive-aggressive standby of being late with child-support or alimony checks.

Statistics are not kept on the various and subtle forms of terrorism a spurned lover may exact, but there is a feeling that such behavior may be on the rise. "Maybe people are more neurotic," says attorney Raoul Lionel Felder. In nearly three decades of practice "I didn't come across it as much before as I have in the past couple of years."

Dr. Robert Jay Lifton, professor of psychology and psychiatry at City University and John Jay College of Criminal Justice in New York, suggests that such behavior may be attributable to an absence of consistent and clear principles to guide social relationships. A person unfairly victimized in a business deal can seek justice in court, but no tribunal exists to hear crimes of the heart.

By permission, Sheila Anne Feeney, *New York Times*.

"We lack a structural set of social arrangements to resolve severe human and sexual conflict," Lifton says. When there is no way for a person to seek the square shake to which he feels entitled, he is more likely to resort to vigilante-type actions.

Other psychiatrists concur that often it is the lover who feels betrayed and emotionally swindled who is most likely to obsessively seek reconciliation or revenge.

Theories differ over why some people are unable to bounce back from the normal "postdepartum" blues that descend after a loved one bails out, but the capacity for vengeful or bizarre behavior lurks in all of us. "Who among us is not guilty of the midnight phone call?" one single woman said. "It's hard to break the habit of talking with and being with that person."

"I've seen well-adjusted people act and do crazy things when they are emotionally distressed about another person with whom they are in a real or imagined relationship," says divorce lawyer Judith Bader-York. Even the most accomplished people, she says, "can engage in unstable behavior."

Other stresses at the time of a breakup can also cause a person to focus excessively on the loss of a love. Any rejection can be amplified by the welter of painful memories of past failures and loss that the experience triggers. All the pain of the past may seem to converge, fueling and accentuating an isolated occasion for sadness.

Yet a wife who has been left bereft and impoverished after years of loyalty may come to grips with her disappointment in a dignified way, while a woman dismissed after a weekend fling might work year-round to make a cad's life hell. Why?

Sharon Nathan, president of the division of women's issues of the New York State Psychological Association, notes that compulsive conduct can occur even when a relationship was lousy or casual. "It has more to do with the symbolic value of the person and what he or she represents" than with the qualities of the person or the relationship, Nathan explains.

Psychologists agree that people rarely are dumped as pre-emptively as they claim to be, or deceived to the degree they perceive themselves to be. Usually, Nathan says, "a careful reconstruction shows that the jilted person's expectations were not well-founded to begin with."

Lifton suggests that lovers who won't let go "are people who are particularly susceptible to the fear of falling apart. One may see the relationship as one's whole life—and the severance of the relationship can become associated with death."

Violence is most likely, Lifton continues, when the person "feels his or her own life threatened in some actual or symbolic way." When feeling worthless and under duress, he says, rage and anger are safer to experience than the "fear of falling apart."

Even hateful communication can be perversely satisfying to someone suffering from love withdrawal. Felder observes that harassment is often a misguided method for an embittered ex who finds hostile communication more rewarding than none at all.

Dr. Edward M. Shelley, assistant professor of clinical psychiatry at Columbia-Presbyterian Medical Center in New York, confirms that even the most venomous phone calls can have a subtext of caring. Futile pursuit can also be a way of denying that the relationship is over, Shelley says. People usually feel depressed and angry when they are jilted. Having been made to feel helpless, the "victim" will try to turn the tables by putting the agent of his or her distress at the mercy of unwelcome interruptions and letters.

The problem, Shelley explains, is that "it gets you nowhere. It doesn't get your lover back and it doesn't solve anything."

While obsessive thinking may not get someone into the overt trouble that compulsive behavior causes, Shelley points out that it is self-defeating. The lovelorn woman whose mind reels with ruminations about her previous sweetheart is not able to fairly evaluate any other candidates for the vacancy.

Someone who feels emotionally short-circuited from an abrupt breakup may believe that the person who pulled the plug owes them an explanation. A polite phone call to the ex requesting a meeting at his or her convenience—and talking things over without recriminative remarks—can often help heal the wounds.

"It's surprising how many times a jilted lover is able to get a good response" with this method, says Shelley. "It's amazing how reasonable people can be when they are treated reasonably."

DIAGNOSING YOUR RELATIONSHIP —————————————

PURPOSE: To identify strengths and weaknesses of a specific relationship that you are in.

PROCEDURE: 1. Select a relationship that is important to you (family, friend or significant love relationship).
                2. For each statement below place an initial on each line as to how it relates to the relationship you have selected.
                3. After completing all statements, review each one and analyze how satisfied you feel using the following scale:

                    S = Satisfactory
                    OK = Acceptable but not exceptional
                    D = Somewhat disappointing

You may have marked an item low on the continuum and like it that way. Or you may have marked an item high but feel uncomfortable about it. One person's intimacy is another's anxiety!

1. *Cooperation*
    A. We identify, define, and solve our problems together. We respect each other's competence.
        Rarely . . . . Often
    B. We work together as a team without competing or putting each other down.
        Rarely . . . . Often
    C. We make decisions together. We make the most of what each of us has to contribute.
        Rarely . . . . Often
    D. We share our opinions, thoughts and ideas without becoming argumentative or defensive.
        Rarely . . . . Often
    E. Overall, I am satisfied with our mutual respect and cooperation in thinking, deciding and working together.
        Rarely . . . . Often

2. *Compatibility*
    A. We accept and work through our differences to find a common life style with regard to our social and public images.
        Rarely . . . . Often
    B. We accept and work through our differences to find common values with regard to religion, morality, social concerns and politics.
        Rarely . . . . Often
    C. We accept and work through our differences with regard to our social life and choice of friends.
        Rarely . . . . Often
    D. We accept and work through our differences so that we are able to share a basic approach to roles and rules.
        Rarely . . . . Often

By permission, Gerald L. Wilson, Alan M. Hantz and Michael S. Hanna, adapted from *Interpersonal Growth Through Communication*, 1989; William C. Brown Publishers.

E. Overall, I am satisfied with the way we deal with our differences, maintain a life style and share values.

Rarely . . . . Often

3 *Intimacy*

A. We often play together. We put fun into what we do together.

Rarely . . . . Often

B. We express our emotions and feelings openly and freely. We say that we are scared, sad, hurting, angry or happy.

Rarely . . . . Often

C. We tell each other what we like and dislike. We ask openly for what we want from each other.

Rarely . . . . Often

D. We "let go" with each other. We play, relax and have fun with each other.

Rarely . . . . Often

E. Overall, I am satisfied with the level of openness and intimacy in our relationship.

Rarely . . . . Often

4. *Emotional Support*

A. We listen, understand and empathize with each other's disappointments, hurts or problems.

Rarely . . . . Often

B. We encourage and support each other when one of us is making basic life changes or trying new behavior.

Rarely . . . . Often

C. We take responsibility for nurturing when either of us is sick or hurting.

Rarely . . . . Often

D. We are emotionally supportive of each other when either of us feels anxious, dependent or in need of care.

Rarely . . . . Often

E. Overall, I am satisfied with the nurturing and support we give to and receive from each other.

Rarely . . . . Often

DISCUSSION:

1. What relationship strengths were you able to identify from this analysis? What weaknesses?

2. What communication areas would you like to work on in this relationship?

3. Overall, how satisfied are you with the information you have discovered about this relationship and why?

4. What have you learned from this analysis that can enhance other significant relationships in your life? ❏

Pain shared is halved. Joy shared is doubled. —*D. Corkille-Briggs*

Ad Inexplorata

As I travel

Baggage becomes heavier

until you offer your hand

guide my belongings with ease

with a smile.

I project a future of smiles,

move toward a long flight

together—side by side yet,

we each have a window seat.

Suddenly, I want nothing

but the view—open space, brightness.

I soar away, ask for blanket,

to place my barriers.

Unknowingly you drift.

The turbulence grows.

Jet engines, the constant roar

of life, work together

toward a flight of success.

We both hear, if we listen

I close the window shade halfway

you float back in

our defenses are down

we engage in the landing.

By permission, *Tracy Schleder*

SELF-DISCLOSURE QUESTIONNAIRE ————————————

PURPOSE: To discover how much of ourselves we disclose to other people.

To realize that different people affect what and how much we disclose of ourselves.

PROCEDURE:
1. The answer sheet on pages 170 and 171 has columns with the headings "Mother," "Father," "Sibling" (brother or sister), "Female Friend," "Male Friend," "Spouse," and "Significant Other."
2. You are to read each item on the questionnaire; then indicate on the answer sheet the extent that you have talked about each item to the person, that is, the extent to which you have made yourself known to that person. Use the rating scale provided.
3. Be sure to think of only one person in each category throughout the entire survey. Do not, for example, skip from one friend to another. Select one person for each category and then answer according to what you have talked about with the person.

SELF-DISCLOSURE RATING SCALE

3   I have talked in full and complete detail about this item to the other person. This person knows me fully in this respect, and could describe me accurately.

2   I have talked specifically to this person, yet have felt hesitant to talk in complete detail. This person knows me well, but not fully in this respect.

1   I have talked in general terms about this item. The other person has only a general idea about this aspect of me.

0   I have told the other person nothing about this aspect of me.

-3   I have lied or misrepresented myself to the other person about this aspect of me.

Attitudes and Opinions

1. What I think and feel about religion, my personal views.
2. My personal opinions and feelings about religious groups other than my own (e.g., Protestants, Catholics, Jews, atheists, etc.).
3. My views on the present government—the president, government, policies, etc.
4. My personal views on sexual morality—how I feel that I and others ought to behave in sexual matters.
5. My views on the question of racial integration in schools, transportation, etc.
6. My views on social movements (e.g., women's rights, gay liberation, ecology action, affirmative action, etc.).

Tastes and Interests

7. My favorite foods, the way I like food prepared and my food dislikes.
8. The kinds of movies that I like to see best, the TV shows that are my favorites.
9. The style of house, and the kinds of furnishings that I like best.

10. The kind of party or social gathering that I like best, and the kind that bore me or that I wouldn't enjoy.
11. My favorite ways of spending spare time (e.g., hunting, reading, cards, sports events, parties, dancing, etc.).
12. To what extent I use alcohol/drugs.

Work (or Studies)

13. What I find to be the worst pressures and strains in my work.
14. What I feel are **my** shortcomings and handicaps that prevent me from working as I'd like to, or that prevent me from getting further ahead in my work.
15. How I feel that my work is appreciated by others (e.g., boss, fellow workers, teacher, husband, etc.).
16. How I feel about the choice of career that I have made, whether or not I am satisfied with it.
17. How I really feel about the people that I work for, or work with.
18. My own strengths and weaknesses as an employee.

Money

19. Whether or not I owe money, if so, how much?
20. All of my present sources of income (e.g., wages, fees, allowances, etc.).
21. My total financial worth, including property, savings bonds, insurance, etc.
22. My most pressing need for money right now (e.g., outstanding bills, some major purchase that is desired or needed).
23. How I budget my money, the proportion that goes to necessities, etc.
24. To what extent money is important to me.

Personality

25. The aspects of my personality that I dislike, worry about, that I regard as a handicap to me.
26. Things in the past or present that I feel ashamed or guilty about.
27. What it takes to get me really worried, anxious and afraid.
28. What it takes to hurt my feelings deeply.
29. The kinds of things that make me especially proud of myself, elated, full of esteem and self-respect.
30. The things about my personality that I would really like to change.

Body

31. How I wish I looked, my ideals for overall appearance.
32. Whether or not I have any long-range worries about health (e.g., cancer).
33. My present physical measurements (e.g., height, weight, waist, etc.).
34. My feelings about my adequacy in sexual behavior, whether or not I feel able to perform adequately in sex-relationships.
35. Whether or not I have any health problems (e.g., allergies, headaches, heart condition, etc.).
36. The physical characteristics I admire about myself.

Behavior

37. What the various roles that I "act out" are.
38. The extent to which I like or dislike these roles.
39. Which role is most like me and why.

40. The extent to which society's stereotyping influences my behavior and interaction with other people.
41. To what extent do I play "games" in order to be socially accepted.
42. To what extent tactile communication (touching) plays in my communication behavior.

Communication

43. To what extent do I say what I am really thinking at the time.
44. To what extent do I use profanity for shock value.
45. To what extent I use nonverbal communication for social gain (e.g., possessions, dress, appearance, cues, etc.).
46. My strengths relative to self-confidence in expressing my opinions.
47. The aspects of my communication I like (e.g., straightforward, clarity, organized, etc.).
48. Whether I am self-conscious about speaking in public or not and why.

SELF-DISCLOSURE: ANSWER SHEET

	Mother	Father	Sibling	Female Friend	Male Friend	Spouse	Significant Other
1							
2							
3							
4							
5							
6							
7							
8							
9							
10							
12							
13							
14							
15							
16							
17							
18							
19							
20							
21							
22							
23							
24							

	Mother	Father	Sibling	Female Friend	Male Friend	Spouse	Significant Other
26							
27							
28							
29							
30							
31							
32							
33							
34							
35							
36							
37							
38							
39							
40							
41							
42							
43							
44							
45							
46							
47							
48							
Totals							

DISCUSSION:
1. Who do you reveal yourself to the most?
2. What is it about these relationships that causes you to reveal yourself?
3. Who do you reveal yourself to the least?
4. Do the roles that you and the other people assume in your daily lives affect your self-disclosure in your relationships with them?
5. What kinds of things do you reveal the most? The least?
6. Does the amount of self-disclosure with each person satisfy you, or should there be more self-disclosure with certain people and less self-disclosure with others?
7. Did the results of the questionnaire surprise you? If so, how/why? ❑

TOO CLOSE FOR COMFORT—A RISING FEAR OF INTIMACY

Cathy Lawhon

Newport Beach psychotherapist Dr. Pat Allen defines intimacy as "being willing to make and keep contracts and commitments." Unfortunately, she and colleague Dr. James Prescott say, fewer and fewer people are willing to make and keep agreements. And those who are trying are struggling.

"People are phobic about intimacy, either physical intimacy, mental intimacy or both," says Allen, a prominent speaker and therapist who describes herself as a blend of feminist Gloria Steinem and Marabelle Morgan of Total Woman fame. "Some people are phobic at the initiation level, where they are not willing to even make the contract. They're the casualties. Then there are people who tentatively make the contract, then pull out of it."

The intimacy outlook wasn't always this grim. But single-parent families, dual-career families bent on acquiring status and possessions, the sexual freedom encouraged by birth control and the repression of sexual pleasure imposed by monotheistic religions have helped to create a society that all too often finds intimacy painful, Allen and Prescott say.

The discomfort with intimacy begins at the physical level and extends to the emotional level.

"Because we don't know how to be physical," Allen says, "we don't know how to be emotional. We are animals first. We have to start with bodies and then work our way up to human."

"A useful model," the Irvine-based Prescott says, "is to go back to a baby and look at the intimacy and spontaneity, joy and happiness that come from that very close physical relationship with the mother and that very basic caring and nurturing and compassion. Those things influence very much the kind of commitments they'll be able to make.

"That's where Shere Hite (in her recently released book *Women and Love)* so misses the boat by dumping on men as being solely responsible for the lack of intimacy," Prescott continues. "She diminishes the very important role of women as mothers."

Children raised without touching and physical intimacy develop an aversion to or an avoidance of intimacy, says Prescott, who experimented with isolation-reared monkeys during his 1966–1980 stint with the National Institute of Child Health and Human Development in Bethesda, Md.

"For monkeys, pleasure becomes pain, affection becomes violence," Prescott says. "Humans experience that to a lesser degree, developing an impairment to experiencing pleasure through intimacy."

Like the monkeys who grew up without mothers, infants in dysfunctional families become adults with a limited capacity for intimacy. Few parents purposely deprive their children of physical intimacy. But pressures of modern society sometimes make it difficult, especially for single parents, to give them adequate attention.

"If you go to a grade school now, 64 percent of the kids are raised in one-parent homes," Allen says. "Every little girl under age 10 who doesn't have tactile closeness to her father is going to be a deprived, hostile female. These abandoned girls are turning into castrating females who are producing castrated males. We're going in circles.

By permission, *Orange County Register*

353

"Little boys have an over-connection with mother. That little boy has an inability to give. If a boy is raised with Dad, he's got his role model, but is disconnected from mother."

Babies who spend eight to 10 hours a day in infant care centers while both parents work grow to distrust intimate relationships too.

"There's no way these kids are getting their emotional needs and basic trust met," Prescott says. "They're lined up in those cribs and they become apathetic and depressed. Infants need to be held and stroked and moved. And they need that intimate connection of breast feeding with the mother."

In Jungian terms, the child growing up with two career people is stuck in a family of two fathers, Allen adds.

"I say that in a healthy family, one of the members has to be responsible for the status and security. In our culture that has been the man. The other member is responsible for the sensuous and sexual needs of the family. In many families, nobody is doing the sensuous and sexual except for the little Mexican lady who's coming in from Tijuana. And she may be an absolute love and may indeed be a life-saver for these kids. But you've still got a real screwed-up deal here."

Is it possible for both mother and father to provide status and security and fill the sensual and sexual needs of the family? Absolutely, Allen responds. It's even OK if the dad fulfills the sensuous and sexual needs. But neither scenario is common. "In our money-grubbing society," she says, "we value money and power more than love."

Ironically, however, sexual freedom for women has also aided the demise of intimacy, Allen says.

"I believe we're still reverberating off the (birth control) pill movement," she says. "When women became capable of casual sex, it immediately lifted sanctions that used to require women to be very, very careful about the reason they had sex. Men and women could both practice casual sex, which negated intimacy. I'm teaching women to know their integrity and what their standards are, then stand by it. You don't go to bed (with a man) until you have longevity, exclusivity and continuity."

While the dearth of intimacy diminishes happiness within marriages and other romantic relationships, on the job and between friends, it also profoundly affects society. Prescott maintains that children who are deprived of intimate, physical contact become violent adults who abuse spouses, children and themselves.

"Studies suggest that during formative periods of brain growth," Prescott says, "certain kinds of sensory deprivation—such as lack of touching and rocking by the mother—result in incomplete or damaged development of the neuronal systems that control affection.

"Since the same systems influence brain centers associated with violence, in a mutually inhibiting mechanism, the deprived infant may have difficulty controlling violent impulses as an adult."

Self-abuse shows up in the addiction to alcohol and drugs, even suicide.

"Children in non-bonding families have what we call ontological insecurity," Allen says. "It's a disbelief in their right to exist. It's the precursor for schizophrenia or depersonalization. It leads to the ability to die without regard."

"And people are drowning their emotional pain in drugs and alcohol," Prescott adds. "They're stuck in the gratification phase, and that's the only way they can get it."

Unfortunately, Allen and Prescott can suggest no quick-fix solutions to becoming a more intimate and less troubled society, short of increasing general awareness. It's a huge task that they try to tackle by sponsoring day-long training sessions for intimacy and affectional bonding. Allen also hosts free group-therapy hours at 7:30 p.m. every Wednesday at a neighborhood community center, where she gets "about 500 people a night asking questions about how to find love."

But a meaningful move toward a more intimate society must begin with providing loving, stable environments for children, they say.

"The only appropriate reason for divorce is violence, or if you're becoming physically, mentally or emotionally ill in the relationship. And I mean certifiably ill as diagnosed by a doctor or therapist," Allen says. "Any other reason is based on some egocentric, prideful decision about what is expected and what is assumed."

Prescott's other suggestions for raising happy, intimate humans include making sure the child is wanted.

"I like to use the foreign-language analogy," Prescott says. "Any newborn can learn any language in the world and speak it like a native if it's exposed to the language in the period of brain development for encoding language. But once you pass a certain point, there is no longer a neural blueprint for that language and the child will always speak it like a foreigner with an accent."

CONNECTIONS

1. Smile! It makes your face light up and your eyes sparkle.

2. Say hello to strangers. It feels good to be acknowledged.

3. Look people in the eye when you are with them. Show them they are your present priority.

4. Remember and use people's names when you speak to them. It makes them feel valued.

5. Focus on the positive. Everyone has something to contribute that is useful.

6. Praise freely—but require a request for criticism.

7. Be tolerant. There are as many opinions and preferences as there are people.

8. Give freely to others. The best reward is knowing you have made a difference.

9. Be enthusiastic. Passion is contagious and magnetic.

10. Have patience. Have you ever had a bad day?

RELATIONSHIP ROLES

PURPOSE: To examine the different purposes that different significant relationships serve in our lives.

PROCEDURE:
1. For each situation below list three people whom you would select to meet the situation.
2. List these people in the order of whom you would call on first, second and third.
3. Explain why you picked each person.

Situation: You are stranded 200 miles from home and need someone to drive your brand new sports car to you. Whom would you ask?

Person: **Reason:**

1.

2.

3.

Situation: You are going out of town for two weeks and need someone to stay at your house and take care of your pets. Whom would you ask?

Person: **Reason:**

1.

2.

3.

Situation: You have been offered another job and feel very uncertain about taking it. Whom would you discuss this with?

Person: **Reason:**

1.

2.

3.

Situation: You just broke up with a person that none of your friends or family likes very well. Whom would you share the news with?

Person: **Reason:**

1.

2.

3.

Situation: You just found out that a very close family member has been killed in a
                        traffic accident. Whom would you tell?

Person: **Reason:**

1.

2.

3.

DISCUSSION: 1.   Was it difficult selecting people for any of the situations? Why or why
                          not?
                     2.   How does the situation change the way we communicate with others?
                     3.   What did you learn about these relationships and the roles they play
                          in your life?   ❏

REACTIONS

1. List three examples of relationships in your life where your communication has been influenced by the stage each relationship is in. Describe how communication is used in these relationships.

2. What kinds of barriers do you encounter that make it difficult to maintain important relationships?

3. How does self-disclosure influence your relationships?

4. How does understanding the role of communication in relationships help you establish and maintain meaningful relationships in your life?

JOB SEARCH SKILLS | 14

Definitions ————————————————————

A perfect time to apply your communication skills is during the job search process. For example, the networking process will afford you an opportunity to use both your verbal and nonverbal skills as you meet people who will give you information about their particular field and perhaps help you join them in that world. Clear and thoughtful writing in your cover letter and resume will attract attention of prospective employers who will invite you to an interview. Finally, the employment interview offers you the opportunity to manage both your verbal and nonverbal communication skills.

Cover Letter

A letter adapted for a particular end which highlights one's background with specific items that most relate to the needs of a prospective employer. You tailor your experiences to the employer's anticipated needs.

Resume

A selective, well-organized synopsis of your education, accomplishments and special skills. The resume is a brief sales device designed to communicate your value as an employee.

Networking

The art of making and using contacts who can help you reach your objective. You identify people who can supply you with important information and resources.

Employment Interviewing

A highly concentrated face-to-face meeting designed to determine the interviewee's qualifications and determine a job "fit."

THE IMPORTANCE OF JOB SEARCH SKILLS

The Bureau of Labor Statistics estimates that the average worker will have six employers in the course of a lifetime. The average worker searches for a job once every three to four years.

Generally, the harder you work at job hunting the quicker you will find employment.

Many people begin the job search process and fail to compete in today's workplace because they are ill equipped without a basic understanding of how to network, write a resume and conduct themselves in an interview.

BARRIERS TO GETTING A JOB

In this section, we will present the major mistakes that prevent job seekers from getting hired.

10- to 12-hour Work Week

For a person who is unemployed, job hunting should be a 40-hour work week. You must not burn out after a few hours to return home to wait for that "phone call." You must talk to people to get leads. Don't be surprised if you meet someone who will change your life.

Failure to Network

Networking is making and using contacts. Job hunters are not always willing to develop and pursue leads from contacts. Friends and acquaintances will give you referrals which are most effective job sources.

Canned or Poor Resumes

You must get an interview to be hired. In order to get an interview you must write a well-prepared resume and a cover letter which is original and well-focused. These items are screening devices for the personnel department. You will be eliminated from consideration as an applicant if they don't indicate you are qualified and would be a good employee. This initial impression is an indication of what can be expected from you after you are hired.

Poor Interview Techniques and/or Preparation

Good physical appearance creates a positive self-image and self-respect. You must reflect a positive attitude. During the interview you must listen attentively and sell yourself by showing enthusiasm. You must communicate that you know and care about the job. Your responses must address the specific needs of the employer. It requires preparation to discover the problems of the person who has the responsibility to pick you for the position in the organization. It is most important to practice interviewing.

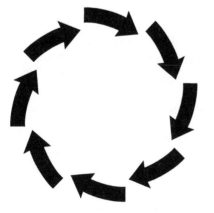

The impossible is often the untried. —*J. Goodwon*

NETWORKING

One key element which promotes professional success is networking. Networking refers to establishing contacts with individuals who can help you succeed in your endeavors. Many jobs are attained through word-of-mouth rather than through classified advertisements. Thus, the more people you know that are in related fields the better chances you have at being successful. How does one network? Four specific ways include colleges and professors, part-time jobs, organizations and volunteering.

Going to college and doing well is important for many career opportunities. When you go to a four-year college or university, you should ideally pick the best college you can for your major field of study. You should distinguish yourself in that program by achieving rank in the top 10 percent of your class. You should also get to know and work with and for your professors and prove your abilities to them so they will be willing to recommend you when you graduate. Remember, these are important people who are well networked. You should also have one or more of these people become your mentor. Mentors are guides who help you make the right moves to be successful. Thus, do not just attend school and go home!

Another suggestion while in college is to become active in campus activities, organizations, athletics, student governments, etc. Many organizations look for these kinds of involvement because they want well-rounded individuals working for them.

Getting a part-time job in the field you want to enter while you are going through college can be a great help in being successful. For example, if you are majoring in accounting, get a job with an accounting firm. The biggest and/or best would be ideal. While there you should become the best part-time employee the company has ever had. For example, arrive at work early; leave late and work hard. Even if your job is a low level one to start you will be distinguishing yourself as a unique person and will advance and quite possibly create a good position for yourself within that company. Per-haps you will also find someone in a position above you who will become a mentor. You should also look for positions the company may not have and create that position which you feel they need and you can fill. Then go sell it to management—many people obtain very good jobs through this method.

Organizations are an excellent way to network, especially if you take leadership positions within them and become known as a "doer" who is committed and successful. Examples of organizations in which you could become active are clubs associated with your major in college. For example, if you are a finance major, join the finance club and become an officer such as the president. Become a very active leader and do things such as bringing onto the campus successful professional people in your field to speak to your group. Get to know these people and impress them. There are also state and national organizations which are affiliated with your major field. For example, future teachers may want to become student members of groups such as the National Education Association and California Teachers Association.

Becoming involved in civic organizations is also a good idea. Examples are Rotary, Lions, Kiwanis, Soroptimist, American Association of University Women and breakfast business networking clubs. In these organizations you are not only networking with successful people, you also have the opportunity to "give back" to your community through service projects.

Volunteering is another way to "give back" to your community as well as get to know other successful people. You may want to volunteer in political campaigns, hospitals, Special Olympics, Red Cross, United Way, for example.

In summary, networking is important to your professional success. Not only do you become acquainted with people, you contribute to your community and expand your social skills and build lasting friendships.

THE 1-2-3'S OF RESUME UPDATE

Dianne Vozoff

Let's face facts: it's the rare professional who likes to while away the hours, pondering the subtleties of an old resume. Once you're comfortable in the right job, basic instinct seems always to point you toward the nearest closet and its highest shelf, where the pitiful thing can be stashed for future use. If you're curious about your own knack for translating career know-how and personal charm onto looseleaf paper, take a few minutes and quiz yourself.

True	False		
_____	_____	1.	The cardinal rule to effective resume writing is: More is Better.
_____	_____	2.	The best resume extensively outlines all your professional achievements.
_____	_____	3.	A career objective at the beginning of your resume is not necessary because the thrust of the entire document should suggest your professional ambitions.
_____	_____	4.	What's in your resume must always take precedence over how it's said.
_____	_____	5.	A good resume is flexible enough to cover various job options within your professional field of interest.
_____	_____	6.	A well-done resume paints a clear sketch of who you are as a person—your height, weight, race, age, sex, marital status and hobbies—so that an employer will know whether or not you're right for the company.
_____	_____	7.	Employers like to see that you're a person concerned with things other than just your job, so always include as much volunteer work, continued education and association involvements as possible.
_____	_____	8.	All resumes should contain the complete names, addresses and telephone numbers of personal and professional references.
_____	_____	9.	Even the best resume tends to get boring, but you can relieve the drudgery by varying visual format and mixing grammatical style.

_____ _____ 10. To help your resume stand out from the hundreds an employer may receive, have it printed on an extra-heavy, tastefully colored paper stock. Consider a distinctive typeface and a unique layout.

_____ _____ 11. Asking friends and professional associates to read and critique your resume is not always a good idea because their input can easily confuse you and cloud essential issues.

_____ _____ 12. Your resume should be accompanied by a cover letter if you're sending it out "cold," but if it's sent in response to a specific ad, the employer will know why you're sending it.

_____ _____ 13. A cover letter is primarily intended to repeat the more pertinent points of your resume.

_____ _____ 14. It may take a lot of hard work, but it's possible to write a resume good enough to secure for you the job you want.

_____ _____ 15. It's necessary to spend the time and money to update your resume only when you're actively seeking a job.

(See answers in article below)

The truth of the matter is that a resume is a resume is a resume, and there's only so much that can be done with anyone's. It's equally true, however, that if you're ever to be a fully active and prepared executive, you need one—and a good one—on hand, all the time. An up-to-date resume not only guarantees you immediate application to any worthwhile career opening that should come your way, it forces you to begin the process that all successful professionals must eventually master: regular assessment of what you've accomplished, what you're doing right now and where you want to head from here.

The most important thing to remember when you're updating is that you're doing just that: updating, not extending. At every step along the way, be prepared to discard items which five years ago were relevant, even brilliant, but no longer help to reinforce your professional profile. Just because you've been involved in a particular field for 17 years, don't assume that you need a page of resume to reflect each 12-month period. Edit. And edit

again. Then type the whole thing and edit some more. That's the key to successfully updating.

In case you're straining at the bit over the results to this little quiz, you should know that the answer to every question is "False." Each illustrates a popular myth in resume lore, and as such, each is a trick question designed to make you doubt what you thought you knew, might have known or just plain guessed to be the case. If you answered "True" to any of the questions, you're heading for a foolhardy move come resume season. And a wrong resume move can produce only a limited number of consequences—all of them unnerving, unsatisfying or simply uneventful.

With such murky terrain ahead, would you care for a pointer or two?

1. The resume rule of thumb is not "More is Better." Quite the contrary, it's "Less is Best." You've undoubtedly heard the rule that resumes should be only one page long, two at the most. Take it to heart.

Don't ramble, don't try to overimpress. No resume should be a three-ring circus enticing, enthralling and entertaining employers beyond the boundaries of human imagination. Be sedate, be professional, be concise. That's what employers look to find. And too, a lot of recruiters won't even get to page two of a resume. So, again, edit until you have one solid, representational page of professionalism.

2. Falling for the misconception that a good resume must extensively outline all professional achievements is how so many people end up with one of the length of Fifth Avenue. A strong resume gets down to basics immediately, and it highlights only those professional achievements which strengthen candidacy for the available position. Although there are exceptions to the rule, those achievements (if you have them under your belt at all) are usually your most recent. You should mention a major career success from, say, 10 years ago only if it can dramatically reinforce an image of progress, dedication and expertise.

Again, remember to edit for professionalism, not ego gratification. Even if the project you managed was outrageously impressive, 14 years ago is a long time. Don't continue to commit it to paper if it doesn't help to pull your resume together today. Be content that you, a few close friends and a grateful former employer know the secret.

3. You should always—repeat, always—state a career objective at the beginning of your resume. If you take nothing else from this simple exercise, remember at least this one fundamental rule. And if the best objective you can think of is "Finding an interesting position with a growing company," go back to your scratch pad and begin again.

A well-written career objective at the beginning of your resume tells any employer that you know what you want from your next job. Employers like that sort of professional focus—provided you make your interests relevant to theirs. Be specific. Your professionalism will be reflected in how articulately you can state your own ambitions.

When you first sit down to update your resume, spend a lot of time on the career objective statement. Keep reworking it until you're satisfied that it does in fact say something and that it accurately reflects your current goals. In essence, if your career objective is clear and tight, all other updating work will fall automatically into place. Each word that follows will be included to support that initially stated career aim. Without this essential element, your resume can only meander through years of 9-to-5. And the people least fooled into thinking you'd be a good addition to a growing company will be those employers you'd like most to impress.

Remember, too, your career objective should change every so often—if for no other reason than that you've theoretically reached the goals you set for yourself five years ago. When you sit down to review your resume and find that, even after all this time, you're no closer to reaching your old goal, it's a good thing you've decided to work on your resume. Because you need a new job.

4. What's in your resume is more important than how it's said. Wrong. Ironically, how you explain what you've done is, in the end, far more important than the achievements themselves. This is not to say that professional achievements are irrelevant. They do, after all, explain why you're presenting a resume in the first place. But you must convey your ability in a way which is meaningful to employers and makes them notice you for what you've accomplished.

Think of it this way: if you've bothered to go through all the effort involved in updating the content of your resume, you might as well go the next step and upgrade the way in which you convey your accomplishments. Action words. That tired old resume phrase must take on a lively meaning now. The more experienced you are, the more powerful your words must be. In updating, make sure your resume uses words that reflect responsibility, management authority, commitment, growth, strength and intelligence.

5. No resume is flexible enough to cover all bases. After years of professional experience, you've no doubt accumulated varied enough knowledge and expertise to confuse even yourself—if you were to read it all in a list.

As you prune your old resume to make room for more pertinent information, categorize professional experience. Chances are, all past positions have afforded growth in several areas. Then you can draft several resumes, each highlighting different areas of experience. In this way, you're likely to discover the need for two, three, maybe even four different resumes, each one supporting different career objectives and relevant to different fields and companies.

A multi-purpose resume is a lazy resume. It says too little to an employer and doesn't help you much in understanding your own professional growth. Instead, keep several up-to-date and specific resumes on file. They will allow you the luxury of career mobility. When you see an ad or arrange for an informal interview, you can choose the best resume from your repertoire and then tailor it further, if necessary, to the specific company.

This approach also has a hidden advantage: if, as you categorize, you see that you've accumulated years of employment but no transferable skill, you're on your way to escaping the dreaded Professional Rut.

6. If you're bothering to tell a prospective employer your weight, height, race, age, marital status and hobbies, you might just as well include your favorite dessert and brand of laundry detergent. People tend to include this sort of information to illustrate how well they'd fit into the employer's corporate image. The problem is obvious: what if you miss the mark? Unless you're absolutely sure that Widget Manufacturing is looking specifically for people into sky diving, don't mention it on your resume. List your credentials and let them call you in for an interview based on those impeccable qualifications.

7. It's not always wise to indicate a lot of volunteer experience, association memberships or even continued education on your resume. When you first start your career, it's crazy not to include it on resume. But as you become more seasoned, more specialized and more professionally sophisticated, employers like to see your resume reflect almost obsessive dedication to your work. Too much volunteer experience or association activity can reflect poorly on your image as a top-flight professional. As you update your work experience and find the need to include more and more career information, delete the "extras" from your resume. This doesn't mean going whole hog and listing nothing at all; it means listing with discretion.

For example, if you're interested strictly in socially oriented work and feel confident that employer interest would be piqued if they knew that you were black, then continue until retirement to list your NAACP membership. Likewise, mention of a prestigious professional association membership couldn't hurt.

8. No resume should contain specific personal or professional references. This is especially true as you develop within your field. If you have reference data on your current resume, get rid of it even before you compose your career objective statement. At the very bottom of your new resume, tag on those immortal last words: "References available upon request." And mean it. When you're called in for an interview, arrive with letters of professional reference or supply the interview executive with phone numbers and addresses. As for personal references, ask yourself this: what recruiter is likely to be swayed by a rave review from your Aunt Helen or your next door neighbor? For all intents and purposes, there is no room on a professional resume for mention of personal references.

9. The only boring resume is one which says nothing. Even if it's laden with impressive experience and the most remarkable design since the wheel, your resume will turn off an employer if it's written with inconsistent verb tenses or poor sentence structure. It should be easy to read, say what must be said, and then end. Period. Mixing style and repeating information is not the solution to a boring resume. Instead, rewrite it and tighten it up until it speaks fluent Actionese. That's what makes a resume exciting. At its hard-nosed core, a resume is a document, not an original work of art.

10. Fancy is foolish. In most cases, you'll be sending your resume to employers because they've run a recruitment classified ad in a daily or professional journal. The other possibility is that you'll leave it behind after an interview arranged through business contacts or friends. In either event, you already have the employer's attention. Vying for extra notice with a gimmick presentation can only inhibit the recruiter from wanting to read what you've written.

Again, updating your resume means increasing its ability to quickly communicate your professional value. If you try to bowl recipients over with scented, cobalt blue parchment that's been embossed with your family's coat of arms and then covered with fancy Gothic type, you'll succeed. They will be bowled over. And your resume will bowl right along with them directly into the nearest wastepaper basket.

11. If you don't feel that you can ask your friends and associates to read and criticize your resume without confusing or clouding issues, then perhaps you've aligned yourself with the wrong people. These are precisely the individuals who know you—perhaps no better than you know yourself, but certainly more objectively. They are the people who understand your field. You've worked with them and shared important achievements with them. If you must, chase them down and corner them in your den with hot coffee until two in the morning. But get them to read your resume and help you update your new composite. If you find their help confusing, then you were already confused. Use their input as a beacon light leading you out of a dark and dangerous fog.

12. You always need to send a cover letter with your resume! Whether you're mailing it "cold" or in response to a specific ad, a cover letter must accompany every resume you send out because most employers will look for it. And they'll be unfavorably impressed if it's missing. Besides, a clear, friendly, professional, sparingly informative letter will reinforce your image of experience, confidence and know-how.

13. Not only is it not the primary purpose of a cover letter to recapitulate your resume, but at no time should it rehash information that's available elsewhere. The cover letter gives you your moment to shine. That's the appropriate place for revealing just a little of your unique personality (you know, the one that's going to be an intelligent addition to the company). If your resume is a formal document—and it should be—think of your cover letter as a short conversation: here you can highlight something of special significance in your resume. If you're at a total loss for words, just say hello and-please-get-back-to-me. But to recapitulate what's already on your resume adds nothing to your chances of getting an interview. It's a waste of time—yours and the employer's.

14. Perhaps the most common career development myth is that a really good resume can secure a worthwhile job. No resume can do that, so don't design or expect yours to accomplish the impossible. Nobody is hired because of their resume, only interviewed. The best professional resume is a sophisticated, modern-day calling card. As such, its sole function is to take you another step toward the personal interview setting. And there, in that one-to-one interaction, you will no doubt enlighten the employer to the indisputable fact that, yes indeed, you are the best candidate for the job.

15. Even if you're happily employed at a company which seems to offer unlimited growth potential, you should still take your resume out once a year, dust it off and read it as if you had just been canned. Could you send it out with only a single date change? If so, you're not growing. The energy you expend updating is never wasted, only stored for wiser, future use.

In professional circles, there is a right and a wrong way of doing just about everything. But there is room for self-expression—provided you express who you are in language which employers understand. Following the suggestions outlined in this article is only a beginning to the long process of updating your resume. As you work and rework your composite, you'll find that rules which at first seemed rigid become magically flexible. That's as it should be. Bend them, twist them, stand them on their heads until they feel right to you. But never be so bold as to break them outright. Unless, of course, you want your career to gather dust just like a useful resume—the one forgotten on your closet shelf.

SCORE BREAK-DOWN

If you answered "False" to all 15 quiz questions, even if you got a couple wrong, consider yourself a whiz kid. If you're currently employed at anything other than book editing for a career development publishing house, you're hiding a needed light under a bushel basket.

10–12   False answers puts you in the Resume Titan category. You're obviously one of the big kids.

7–9   False answers suggest that you're in need of some brush-up reading. But don't feel bad; most of us are only human.

6   False answers or less and you're a sad statistic, a Resume Monkey. Have another banana and hire a professional to write your resume for you.

COVER LETTERS AND RESUMES

PURPOSE: To examine sample cover letters and different types of resumes.

PROCEDURE:
1. Read the resume guidelines and sections listed below.
2. Read and consider the one sample cover letter.
3. Consider and compare the three sample resumes. Bear in mind that the format should match the nature of the job.
4. Correct the one problem cover letter.
5. Correct the one problem resume.

DISCUSSION:
1. What factors influence the choice of a resume format?
2. What is the purpose of a cover letter?
3. How does one decide what to include in the resume? The cover letter?

Note: Always keep a copy of any letter/resume you send. You may want to refer to such information later when you are called for the interview. You may also want to build on either item as a rough draft the next time out.

RESUME PREPARATION GUIDELINES

DO'S

1. Keep to one or two pages (maximum).
2. Use quality paper and type it or print it.
3. Make it succinct, impactful and use "action" words. (It should sound "exciting.")
4. Remember, it is a "sales" tool.
5. Type it very neatly, preferably on an electric typewriter or word processor. Lay it out carefully. Format and readability are important.
6. Keep it in the third person; make it "flow."
7. List career objective, education (if degee'd), experience (with most recent chronological items first), and miscellaneous.
8. Show favorable information.
9. Write in short sentences and in plain English.
10. Proofread it!

DON'TS

1. List salary data/history. (Use separate sheet if requested.)
2. Be too wordy and too long.
3. Use "I," "me," etc.
4. Show information which could be unfavorable.
5. List sex, marriage status, or hobbies.
6. Falsify information. (Think about what is not said.)
7. List references specifically. (After interview, O.K.)
8. Put anything in unless it puts you in a favorable light.
9. List race, number of children, religion-related information.
10. Try to use one resume for a "catch-all" which will suffice for any and all types of jobs.

SECTIONS TO BE INCLUDED IN YOUR RESUME

Personal Information
    Name
    Address
    Phone(s)
    Objective: As specifically as possible describe which position you want to fill

Educational Background (list first only if you have no work experience)
    Schools Attended
    Dates of Attendance
    Degrees Awarded/Major
    Honors Received
    Grade Point Average (If to your advantage)

Work Experience Data (list before education if you have work experience)
    Places of Employment (most recent first)
    Your Job Title (s)
    Work accomplishments (use action verbs)
    Inclusive Dates of Each Employment (year only)

Professional/Honorary Associations in which you hold memberships

Interests and Hobbies (anything you can do well)

COVER LETTERS

A cover letter should accompany a resume. The cover letter is extremely important because it can generate an interest in you as a candidate for a job. You need to be as specific as possible and use appropriate examples of what you have done in order to catch the attention of the reader.

148 East Willow Ave.
Inglewood, CA 90027
April 15, 1994

Personnel Director
The Irvine Company
550 Newport Center Dr.
Newport Beach, CA 92663

Sir:

I wish to express my interest in the position of Personnel Representative which I saw advertised in the <u>L.A. Times</u>. I fulfill all of the basic qualifications listed in the position description. I have two years of experience working in the Personnel Department at Hughes Aircraft. As Assistant to the Director of Human Resources at a large school district, I also had the opportunity to become experienced in the area of training and development. In addition to these skills, I have screened, interviewed, and referred candidates for employment in a wide variety of job classifications.

I currently hold an A.A. Degree in Business Management and will receive my B.A. in June with Personnel Administration as my major. I minored in economics and have a fine mix of academic preparation and practical experience for success in a business-related environment.

My resume details the above mentioned experience as well as other skills I possess that may also be attractive to your company. I look forward to meeting with you to discuss in depth my abilities and your company's needs. I will call you in two weeks.

Thank you for your time and consideration.

_____

Gary B. Swelt

Home Phone: (310) 432-1167
Bus. Phone: (714) 911-7621

Enclosure

SAMPLE RESUME 1

Roberta Tracy
1224 Walnut St.
Long Beach, CA 90808
Home Phone: (310) 498-3775
Work Phone: (310) 597-9086

OBJECTIVE: A professional level position in personnel

EXPERIENCE   Over 17 years of general personnel experience in business and industry
SUMMARY: with specialization in college recruiting.

EXPERIENCE:

1983–Present   <u>Miller-Berger Construction</u>
Employment Representative

Responsible for recruitment, selection and placement of all
company employees as well as new employee orientation.
<u>Accomplishments</u>: Designed college recruitment brochure to attract
college graduates to company management positions. Designed and
implemented new employee orientation.

1979–1983   <u>Long Beach Water and Power</u>
Employment Clerk-Interviewer

Responsible for accepting and screening applications, writing
follow-up correspondence and interviewing clerical personnel.
<u>Accomplishments</u>: Designed interview follow-up letters as well as
interview appraisal sheet. Administered and scheduled typing tests.
Participated in new employee orientation.

1978–1979   <u>St. Theresa's Hospital</u>
Employment Clerk

Responsible for accepting and filing applications and Equal
Employment Opportunity cards as well as preparing and delivering
weekly jobline phone message.
<u>Accomplishments</u>: Developed efficient application filing system.
Designed internal job posting format and system.

EDUCATION: A.A. Speech Communication, Long Beach City College 1993
B.A. Business, California State University (in progress)

MISCELLANEOUS:

Dean's Honor Roll 1992 and 1993
- Officer: Student Speech Communication Association
- Member: Personnel and Industrial Relations Association (PIRA)

SAMPLE RESUME 2

Gary B. Swelt
661 Portray Place
Orange, CA 92633
(714) 499-7621

CAREER OBJECTIVE

Personnel Management

Personnel Administration

- Monitored performance evaluations
- Assisted in wage and salary upgrades
- Supervised clerical staff of three job classifications
- Provided input into department budget
- Conducted panel interviews
- Recruited for various position classifications
- Interviewed and referred candidates for vacant positions
- Coordinated generalist employment functions

Training

- Performed training needs assessment
- Facilitated new employee orientation program
- Conducted in-house workshop for employees on motivation
- Planned in-service training

Employment

Employment Coordinator, Taco Bell, Inc., Irvine, CA 89–Present
Personnel/Training Asst., H.B.U.S.D. Huntington Beach, CA 88–89
Personnel Clerk/Receptionist, Hughes Aircraft, Torrance 86–88
Yeoman, Ship's Office, U.S. Navy, San Diego, CA 84–86

Education

B.A. Personnel Administration, California State Univ. Long Beach, 1993
A.A. Business Management, Orange Coast College 1988

Affiliations

Toastmasters International, Club #233 Newport Beach Chapter
American Society for Personnel Administration

SAMPLE RESUME 3

The following two formats illustrate creative alternatives to the traditional resume. They might work well for someone going into a field where creativity is admired.

COLLAGE FORMAT

Procedure:

1. Form a collage of pictures on a poster board.
2. Take a black and white snapshot of your pasteup.
3. Have the picture printed on the paper of your choice.
4. Personal information can be printed on either the reverse side of the collage or on separate pages to be inserted inside.

Caution: Do some homework before using photographs. It may be considered illegal for a future employer to use it.

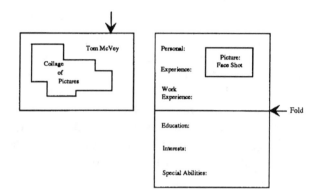

Nothing succeeds like the appearance of success.
—*C. Lasel*

PROBLEM COVER LETTER

January 23, 1994

Mr. Harold E. Spring, President
Product Market, Inc.
123 Anywhere St.
Thistown, California
90865

Dear Mr. Spring,

I am sending you with this letter my own Resume because I saw your add in the Times. I would very much like to have this job. I am working part-time in sells and would really like to move up.

In the past several years, I have worked over 175,000 hours in the sales and marketing of Stayway products.

I am contacting you because your company looks to be in need of a man with my incomparable experience to work on a full time basis. If so you may be interested in some of the things I have done.

For example, during the past year, I have singlehandedly sold over $5,000,000 worth of computer equipment and services throughout the United States. Due to these sales, I have been the number one sales-man for Allied Computers for the last year.

During the last five years, I have been responsible for over $25,000,000 in retail sales for products raging from tools and hard-ware to sophisticated computers.

If this kind of experience would be invaluable to your company, I would love to talk with you.

Fondly,

Harrison L. Smith
7305 Sycamore Street
Anytown, Arizona 92651

Gene A. Allen

RESUME

12098 Wheat Lane	Date of Birth: 7/7/56
Anytown, California	Height: 5′ 11″
90748	Weight: 189
	Health: Very good
	Sex: Male
	Marital Status: Single

EDUCATIONAL EXPERIENCE

High School Diploma (1974)
Seal High School
GPA: 2.0

Bachelor of Arts (1978)
Emory University, New York
Major: Business Administration
GPA: 3.0
Activities: President of AEO Fraternity
Varsity Football

Master of Science (1980)
Emory University, New York
Major: Economics
GPA: 3.0

WORK EXPERIENCE

1980 to 1988   Position: Administrative Assistant
                Place: Vanderbilt University, New York
                Duties: Assisted college president with all his duties.

1988 to Present Position: Executive Director, UNICEF
                Place: Baltimore, Maryland
                Duties: Worked with 480 employees; in charge of in-service
                            training and coordination of 53 field offices
                Supervisor: Dr. M. L. Singe

REFERENCES—will be furnished on request

OUTSIDE INTERESTS—racquetball, astrology, bridge, sailing, skiing, and wood working

BRAINSTORMING FOR RESUMES ———————————

PURPOSE: To brainstorm some ways to create effective resumes.

PROCEDURE:
1. In small groups think up as many possible suggestions for resumes as you can.
2. Brainstorm at least 20 action verbs that can be used for accomplishments. Examples include designed, presented, developed, created.
3. Get back into a large group and present your ideas to the class.

DISCUSSION:
1. What types of resumes were most and least effective? Why?
2. To what extent would it be important in tailoring a specific resume to a specific job?

INTERVIEW PREP KIT

Once you have been notified that you are to have an interview, it makes good sense to prepare. An interview is not a "spontaneous" event. It is a sales experience. You must use your interview time to convince the company that you are the one for the available position. Careful preparation will help you display yourself well.

Your interviewer may have a copy of your resume in advance. For some jobs, usually hourly rated, resumes are not requested. It is useful, however, to have some ready in any case. You will usually fill out an application blank in advance. Take care in filling out applications. Take all the time you need to guarantee precision and accuracy.

Once you enter the interview, pay attention to the amenities. Watch for directions about where to sit. Take the cue from the interviewer about whether you are to exchange names and shake hands. Wait for him to start the interview—do not blurt how eager you are to go to work.

Dress Carefully

Do not convey messages that you do not intend to convey. A great many decisions are made about us based on the way we dress. For example, if we are wearing excessively expensive clothing to an interview, the interviewer may conclude that we tend to live beyond our means. If our clothing is "scudsy," excessively "sexy" or "studlike," the interviewer may get some interesting ideas but they will usually not have anything to do with the job. The best advice is to dress discretely, using quiet, semi-dark or dark colors, with little ornamentation. Keep cleavage to a minimum. Make sure slacks and pants are not too tight. The clothing need not be high fashion, or even new. But it must be neat and clean, appropriate to the occasion.

Prepare Yourself with Information About the Company

Many companies provide a brochure for prospective employees. If your company does, you can get the following information from the brochure. If there is no brochure, check at your local library to find out about the company. If both of these alternatives are unavailable, feel free to ask for information at the interview. You should know the following:

1. Name, location, size of the company and type of business
2. Types of jobs currently available

———————————

By permission, Dr. G. M. Phillips; Penn State University

3. Conditions under which you might work
4. Nature of the training program
5. Opportunities for education and advancement
6. Promotion policies. Whether there is a union.
7. The fiscal history and employment stability record of the company.
8. Turnover rate and prognosis for permanence.
9. Whether travel or relocation is required.
10. Salary offered, job description, qualifications for the position.
11. Nature of the community in which the company is located.
12. Employee benefits.

You should be suspicious of any company that is unwilling to provide this basic information. Be careful in asking about it, however. You do not want to give the impression that #12 is more important than #3 or #5. Consider the impact of the questions on your potential future employer.

Prepare Your Remarks for the Interview

Your interviewer will use the interview to size you up to see if you are qualified, will fit into the company, have the kind of personality they are seeking. Given that you are equally qualified with your competition, whether you are hired or not is at the discretion of the interviewer. Generally, people who are sloppy, inarticulate, excessively heavy, smoke, use drugs or alcohol, act unconcerned, cannot prove what they assert or "lip off" to the interviewer do not get hired. There is no affirmative action procedure for these people. However, heavy people can reduce, sloppy people can dress neatly, inarticulate people can learn speech skills.

There are certain types of questions which are currently illegal. If you are asked these kinds of questions you face a moral problem. You might blow the interview if you do not answer them. If you answer them, you may answer them wrong. You always have the right to protest to the local employment service. Any employer who asks these questions may actually be trying to discriminate, but most likely they are unaware of the specifics of the law. Be careful of the following:

1. Employers cannot ask you what your name was before you changed it.
2. Employers cannot inquire about your birthplace, or the birthplace of any member of your family.
3. Employers cannot ask you to disclose your ancestry or national origin.
4. Employers cannot ask for your age unless, for some reason, it is a bona fide criterion.
5. Employers cannot ask you to name your religion, the church you attend or state the religious holidays you observe. S/he can declare the days of work required, so that you may choose not to accept the job if it violates your religious commitment.
6. Employers cannot ask about the citizenship status of anyone except you. They may ask if you are a citizen or whether you intend to become one.
7. Employers cannot ask any questions at all about your relatives. They may ask you for the name of someone to notify in case of emergency.
8. Employers cannot ask about your national origin or race.
9. Employers cannot ask questions about physical handicaps unless it is specifically relevant to the job. They can require physical examinations.
10. Employers cannot ask you to report times you were charged with felonies or misdemeanors, but they can ask you to report convictions.
11. Employers cannot ask about marital status, children, expectations for children, cohabitation, your spouse, etc. They can assert the conditions of employment and let you choose.
12. Employers cannot ask you to disclose memberships in organizations which would disclose your race, religion or national origin.

13. Questions about sexual preference are not illegal.
14. Employers can question you intensively about your education, job qualifications, work experience and they may require you to take whatever examinations can be justified for the position.
15. Employers can inquire into your character, including use of drugs and alcohol, hobbies, outside activities.

Under the Buckley Amendment, you can get access to your personnel file. If you are having trouble getting employed, you may find this useful. You can discover the kinds of invidious information that might be interfering with your ambitions.

To prepare yourself best, get a one-minute speech prepared on each of the following topics. When you do, you will have an answer to the questions most frequently asked in interviews.

1. My educational achievements in high school and college.
2. What I am interested in.
3. My skills are . . .
4. How I can be motivated to do my best work.
5. The kind of criticism that helps me most.
6. How I have demonstrated leadership.
7. My vocational goals now, five years from now, 10 years from now.
8. I am mature because. . . .
9. My past work experience has been. . . .
10. I am a creative person because . . .
11. How I can help your organization.
12. Why I am interested in your company.
13. My extracurricular activities qualify me because. . . .
14. My volunteer activities qualify me because. . . .
15. What I have learned in the past few years.
16. I have read the following books and they are about . . .
17. I read the following magazines regularly because . . .
18. How I have gotten along with my previous employers.
19. What I have learned on my previous jobs.
20. My school grades do/do not estimate my ability because. . . .
21. The kind of work I am most interested in . . .
22. I can get along well with people because . . .
23. I can demonstrate that I want to get ahead by. . . .
24. How I get along with people from various backgrounds.
25. Why I am your best choice.

Do not talk about how badly you need the job. Do not run down other candidates. Be responsive to the interviewer's questions. If you do not understand a question, ask him/her to restate it. Try to integrate your prepared remarks to meet interviewer questions. Be terse or ignore altogether illegal questions.

Employers will evaluate you on: communication skills, definitive handshake, neatness in appearance and on application and vita, promptness, responsiveness to social cues, good manners, directness in answering, economy of expression, whether you appear organized and have your future planned. They will look for willingness to work, qualifications for the job, courtesy to past employers, interest in and knowledge about the company, desire for permanence, maturity, social awareness, decisiveness, sense of humor. They will reject you for excessive garrulity, nonresponsiveness, flippancy, temper and arrogance, name dropping (never drop the name of a company officer on a personnel interviewer. If the job is a set-up he has already done his work). Any interviewer may reject you for any reason. It is some times wise to ask if you can call or write (in the event you don't get the job) and get some evaluation of your performance in the interview.

After the interview, find out how you will be notified. Do not call the company unless you are asked. If you are told to, call exactly when requested. Companies do not like to be pestered. If the company does not notify you on time, wait a discreet 24 hours and go on with your search. Companies are not always reliable, but it won't help you get a job if you tell them off about it.

JOB INTERVIEWING: DO'S AND DON'TS

DO	DON'T
Have a neat, conservative appearance	Look casual, sloppy
Look interviewer in the eye	Look at other things while talking or listening
Appear calm and relaxed	Fidget with anything or shift in chair
Show interest and enthusiasm	Indicate lack of interest in the company
Be assertive and tactful	Be overbearing or very meek
Use proper English	Use slang or swear words
Speak clearly and loud enough	Mumble to yourself
Have specific professional plans and goals	Appear to be just rambling around
Be willing to compromise	Overemphasize money
Know what salary the job generally pays	If your record is poor, be prepared to explain
Make the most of your scholastic record	Make excuses or evade issues
Be direct and honest	Fool around and show poor manners
Act mature and courteous	Give a limp or aggressive handshake
Give interviewer a firm handshake	Condemn past employers
Treat past employers with respect	Say you loaf during vacations, didn't like school work or indicate in any way that you are lazy
Indicate a strong desire to work	
Show a sense of humor when appropriate	
Know what you're talking about—knowledge of area and job responsibilities—give short clear answers	Act like you're shopping around or only want the job for a short time
Show high moral standards	Be frivolous or cynical
Do your homework—find out all you can about the company	Give vague, indefinite, long-winded answers
Be on time for interview	Indicate low morals, radical views or prejudices
Ask questions and show vitality during the interview. Remember, this is a two-way street.	Indicate that you know nothing about the company and what it does
Show appreciation to interviewer for his/her time	Be late, without a *very* good reason
	Be apathetic or afraid to ask questions
Keep a cool head in answering all questions	Forget to thank the interviewer
	Get frustrated and irritated
Be prepared to answer *all* kinds of questions—rehearse with someone. Use a video tape.	Be unprepared—take it for granted that you've got it made

NEGATIVE FACTORS EVALUATED DURING THE EMPLOYMENT INTERVIEW AND WHICH FREQUENTLY LEAD TO REJECTION OF THE APPLICANT

1. Poor personal appearance
2. Overbearing—overaggressive—conceited "superiority complex" "know it all"
3. Inability to express himself clearly—poor voice, diction, grammar
4. Lack of planning for career, no purpose and goals
5. Lack of interest and enthusiasm—passive indifference
6. Lack of confidence and poise—nervousness—ill at ease
7. Failure to participate in activities
8. Overemphasis on money—interest only in best dollar offer
9. Poor scholastic record—just got by
10. Unwilling to start at the bottom—expect too much too soon
11. Makes excuses—evasiveness—hedges on unfavorable factors in record
12. Lack of tact
13. Lack of maturity
14. Lack of courtesy—ill mannered
15. Condemnation of past employers
16. Lack of social understanding
17. Marked dislike for school work
18. Lack of vitality
19. Fails to look interviewer in the eye
20. Limp, fishy handshake
21. Indecision
22. Loafs during vacations—lakeside pleasures
23. Unhappy married life
24. Friction with parents
25. Sloppy application blank
26. Merely shopping around
27. Wants job only for short time
28. Little sense of humor
29. Lack of knowledge of field of specialization
30. Parents make decisions for him
31. No interest in company or in industry
32. Emphasis on whom he knows
33. Unwillingness to go where we send him
34. Cynical
35. Low moral standards
36. Lazy
37. Intolerant—strong prejudices
38. Narrow interests
39. Spends much time in movies
40. Poor handling of personal finances
41. No interest in community activities
42. Inability to take criticism
43. Lack of appreciation of the value of experience
44. Radical ideas
45. Late to interview without good reason
46. Never heard of company
47. Failure to express appreciation for interviewer's time
48. Asks no questions about the job
49. High pressure type
50. Indefinite response to questions

By permission, *The Northwestern Endicott-Lindquist Report* published by The Placement Center; Northwestern University, Evanston IL.

SAMPLE INTERVIEW QUESTIONS

Dr. Frank S. Endicott

The following list represents those questions most frequently asked by job interviewers.

What are your future vocational plans?

In what school activities have you participated? Why? Which did you enjoy the most?

In what type of position are you most interested?

Why do you think you might like to work for our company?

What jobs have you held? How were they obtained and why did you leave?

What courses did you like best? Least? Why?

Why did you choose your particular field of work?

What percentage of your college expenses did you earn? How?

How did you spend your vacations while in school?

What do you know about our company?

Do you feel that you received a good general training?

What qualifications do you have that make you feel that you will be successful in your field?

What extracurricular offices have you held?

What are your ideas on salary?

If you were starting college all over again, what courses would you take?

How much money do you hope to earn at age 30? 35?

Do you think that your extracurricular activities were worth the time you devoted to them? Why?

What do you think determines a person's progress in a good company?

What personal characteristics are necessary for success in your chosen field?

Why do you think you would like this particular type of job?

Do you prefer working with others or by yourself?

What kind of boss do you prefer?

Are you primarily interested in making money or do you feel that service to humanity is your prime concern?

Can you take instructions without feeling upset?

Tell me a story!

How did previous employers treat you?

What have you learned from some of the jobs you have held?

Can you get recommendations from previous employers?

What interests you about our product or service?

Have you ever changed your major field of interest while in college? Why?

When did you choose your college major?

Do you feel you have done the best scholastic work of which you are capable?

How did you happen to go to college?

What do you know about opportunities in the field in which you are trained?

Which of your college years was the most difficult?

Did you enjoy your four years at this university?

By permission, *The Northwestern Endicott-Lindquist Report* published by The Placement Center; Northwestern University, Evanston IL.

Do you like routine work?
Do you like regular hours?
What size city do you prefer?
What is your major weakness?
Define cooperation. Do you demand attention?
Do you have an analytical mind?
Are you eager to please?
What job in our company would you choose if you were entirely free to do so?
What types of books have you read?
Have you plans for graduate work?
What types of people seem to rub you the wrong way?
Have you ever tutored an underclassman?
What jobs have you enjoyed the most? The least? Why?
What are your own special abilities?
What job in our company do you want to work toward?
Would you prefer a large or small company? Why?
Do you like to travel?
How about overtime work?
What kind of work interests you?
What are the disadvantages of your chosen field?
Are you interested in research?
What have you done which shows initiative and willingness to work?

Note: If you take the time necessary to write out brief answers to each of these questions in the list, it can help you clarify your own thinking and establish ready answers.

CAN'S AND CAN'TS OF INTERVIEWING QUESTIONS ————

PURPOSE: To approach a job interview from the perspective of the person on the other side of the desk in order to successfully anticipate questions and to be knowledgeable about your rights.

Note: Federal and state laws and regulations limit what can be asked in a preemployment interview. While no questions are expressly prohibited, the EEOC (Equal Employment Opportunity Commission) looks with disfavor on direct or indirect questions relating to race, color, religion, sex or national origin. Once the individual is hired the information not permitted to be asked may be obtained if a valid need exists for it, and it does not lead to discrimination.

PROCEDURE: 1. Read through the list of Can's and Can'ts familiarizing yourself with the nature of such data.
2. Then form a dyad and conduct:
    a. an illegal interview
    b. a legal interview
3. Switch roles.
    Note: Be sure to practice tactful ways of dealing with such illegal or inappropriate questions. Remember, you still may want the job even if the interviewer does not follow EEOC guidelines.

Subject	Yes/Can Do or Ask	No/Cannot Do or Ask
Age	Age after hiring. "Are you over 18?"	"How old are you?" Estimate age.
Children	Numbers and ages of children after hiring for insurance purposes.	"Do you have children at home? Who cares for them? Do you plan to have more?"
Criminal Record	If security clearance is necessary can be done prior to employment.	"Have you ever been arrested, convicted or spent time in jail?"
Housing	"If you have no phone how can we reach you?"	"Do you own your own home?" "Do you rent? Do you live in an apartment or house?"
Marital Status	Status after hiring for insurance purposes.	"Are you married? Single? Divorced? Engaged? Living with anyone? Do you see your ex-spouse?"
Military Status	"Are you a veteran? Why didn't you serve? Any job-related experience? "	"What type of discharge do you have? What branch?"
Physical Data	Explain manual labor lifting, other requirements of the job. Show how it is performed. Require a physical exam.	"How tall are you?" "How heavy?"
Sex	Notice appearance.	Make comments or notes about appearance.

DISCUSSION: What are your opinions of being subjected to an illegal interview?

Speech Communication is the most important tool of any profession. —R. West

VERBAL AND NONVERBAL AWARENESS DURING INTERVIEWS

PURPOSE: To sensitize the prospective interviewee to the distracting verbal/nonverbal mannerisms she might exhibit.

(—) Verbal	(—) Nonverbal
"you know"	No eye contact
"like"	fidgeting, wringing hands
"ah"	inappropriate dress
"and um"	poor posture

PROCEDURE:
1. Form a triad.
2. Brainstorm as many such negative verbal and nonverbal mannerisms as you can in five minutes.
3. Practice being an interviewee while an observer or the interviewer tallies your mannerisms.
4. Reverse roles.

(—) Verbal	(—) Nonverbal

DISCUSSION: What positive verbal or nonverbal behaviors might you substitute?

(+) Verbal	(+) Nonverbal

INTERVIEW ROLE PLAYING ——————————————————

PURPOSE: To give you an opportunity to test your interviewing skills.

PROCEDURE:
1. Select one person to be the interviewee and have the interviewee play the actual job situation that he would be interviewed for—i.e., police officer, management trainee, secretary, teacher, etc. Have this person leave the room.
2. Select four people to play the role of interviewers, giving them specific roles—i.e., one who asks personal questions, one who asks academic and educational questions, one who is sympathetic with the person, one who is antagonistic, etc. Interviewer should not know the role these people are playing.
3. Interviewee comes back into the room as if he were entering the act.
4. Interviewers will ask questions—some of which can be taken from the list of "Sample Interview Questions" by Dr. Endicott in this chapter. There should be a 10–20 minute time limit.
5. As interview is taking place, observers should write down the negative and positive behaviors of the interviewee.

DISCUSSION:
1. What are the most and least effective things the interviewee did in it?
2. Give specific suggestions for improvement.

| KISSING UP

Mitchell Schnurman

It may smack of insincerity, but **IT WORKS**

It can be demeaning. It can be obvious. It can be juvenile.

But "kissing up" to the boss still works; maybe that's why so many people do it.

In a business world where layoffs are common and promotions are rare, corporate climbers are looking for any edge. Almost intuitively, they know that kissing up can tilt the tables their way.

And now an academic study confirms what most of us realize by the time we're in kindergarten: Teachers' pets usually get the stars.

"Performance is what matters most when you want to get ahead," says Ron Deluga, a psychology professor who recently studied the subject. "But kissing up can make a real difference. People can be rewarded without it, but it won't be easy—and it won't be as often."

After surveying more than 300 supervisors and subordinates in New England, Deluga concluded that flattering bosses, and agreeing with them most of the time, increases your chances of advancement by about 5 percent.

The most effective stroke you can give: praising the boss to her boss.

Next best: complimenting your supervisor on how he handled a tough project or business meeting.

Most career experts don't recommend such tactics, unless you genuinely believe a compliment is due. Even then, they say, you may need grace and subtlety to pull it off so as not to appear patronizing.

But even obvious ploys have an effect, at least in the short term, Deluga says. Laughing at the boss' jokes, dressing the way he or she does, echoing the boss' intensity about the workplace—they all help, on some level, to separate the "in" group from the "out" group.

"Even when both sides know it's going on, kissing up still works," says Deluga, who teaches at Bryant College in Smithfield, R.I.

"Even executives want to feel good about themselves."

Career experts say they aren't surprised by Deluga's findings. Workers with good people skills—the ones most likely to develop a rapport with supervisors—are also the ones most likely to advance. The study, they say, simply underscores another reality of the workplace: Just doing the job isn't enough.

"Anybody who thinks they can get ahead by just working hard is beyond naive—they're living on another planet," says Fort Worth psychologist Richard Citrin. "Kissing up to the boss, brownnosing, boot-licking—they're all descriptions of how we interact.

"From my experience in organizations, the people who were willing to kiss up also were willing to take on extra projects. They had more energy and enthusiasm. They took the time to develop relationships with their supervisors and peers. They were plugged in, so of course they moved ahead."

As Citrin sees it, there's nothing wrong with kissing up; in fact, it's one key to getting along.

That doesn't mean offering up endless flattery, he says. That will backfire anyway, alienating peers who may undercut you in the future.

The goal, he says, should be to develop strong interpersonal relationships with supervisors and colleagues. Most supervisors want to talk about their lives, too, so take a genuine interest, says Citrin, who works at the Iatreia Institute for the Healing Arts in Fort Worth.

"People who are artful at brown-nosing are doing it in a larger context—they really care about the organization, or a project or even the boss. And it pays off for them in the long run," he says.

To many people, that's called politicking. And even those who don't practice it still recognize its value. But kissing up, to most, represents crossing the line—practically selling your soul to please the boss.

From the Fort Worth Star-Telegram, January 6, 1994. Reprint courtesy of the Fort Worth Star-Telegram.

"What I've seen the most is what I call the 'young puppy' syndrome," says Russ Pate, vice president and general manager of Hill and Knowlton in Dallas. "It's when somebody acts like a young puppy, always wagging his tail and eager to please. No matter what the boss says, he nods in agreement.

"It's transparent to anybody whose eyes are open, but I've seen people build their careers around it. It gets pretty pathetic, though, when you're 40 years old and you're still a young puppy."

Pate recalls a banker who climbed the ranks at a large institution, in part by endlessly praising his supervisor. But that tactic is never a sure thing.

Colleagues often scorn workers who are blatant about kissing up, locking them out of the corporate grapevine. And managers who are most susceptible to it often get stuck on the corporate ladder, experts say.

The issue can create a dilemma for ambitious subordinates: How do they build a rapport with their supervisor and not cross the line?

One rule: Don't fake it.

Too many people will see through false compliments and, rightfully, end up questioning a person's motives.

But it's not always easy to know what's acceptable at the office and what crosses the line. One person's kiss-up may be another's common courtesy.

How an action is perceived often depends on the company's culture and the supervisor's approach.

Paul Lazzaro, who heads a Fort Worth advertising agency that bears his name, doesn't care for flattery or "yes" men. Too obvious, he says.

Yet he has been impressed when employees clipped news articles that recognized the company, or sent notes of congratulations for winning an industry award. He also was moved by an anniversary gift from a worker.

"Everyone appreciates recognition, no matter what stage they're in," says Lazzaro.

The actions also tell him something about the workers: "I think of business as a game, and to get ahead, you have to know how to play it. I'm always interested in people who've figured that out."

One factor many climbers overlook is the importance of cultivating ties with their colleagues.

That usually pays more dividends than kissing up to the boss, says Marilyn Moats Kennedy, who writes and lectures about careers.

"In the end, as you move up the ladder, most people show their leadership qualities with their peers and subordinates, not their supervisors," says Kennedy, who writes the monthly newsletter Career Strategist, in Wilmette, Ill.

Her advice for getting ahead: Focus on achieving things that can be objectively measured, and always deliver what you promise.

Although results still matter most, she also believes that most employees should work on improving their people skills. Start by participating in community groups, trying out leadership techniques.

As you learn to relate to volunteers and motivate them, it will be easy to transfer those skills to the workplace, she says.

But it often takes practice and experience to develop a knack for office politics, and to understand the subtleties.

Consider, for instance, how to deal with a "secret." Sometimes bosses tell workers something they want shared with the rest of the staff, she says. Other times, they don't want it mentioned.

"Not everyone picks up on this magically," Kennedy says. "Don't be afraid to ask for clarification, or to verify what you think you know."

Her suggestion: "Say, 'If this a secret, it goes no further. Is that what you had in mind?'"

Knowing how to relate to people is not only a factor in promotions; it can make a difference in getting a job.

Carolyn Ulrickson, who directs the career placement center at Texas Christian University, tells seniors to follow the school's sports teams—even if they're not fans.

Why?

Because corporate recruiters often read about the teams before they come to campus and mention the subject when the interview begins.

"Sports are always a good icebreaker," says Ulrickson, "You may not give a hoot about how the Horned Frogs did on Saturday, but you don't have to say so. Why start the interview on a negative note?

"That's a dead giveaway about how you deal with people."

REACTIONS

1. Using the questions found in the Interview Prep Kit, prepare yourself with information about a specific company or agency in your city. List that information here.

2. Make a list of friends, relatives and acquaintances to be part of your network.

3. You have met a person at a party. Prepare the answer to either one of these questions: "What type of work do you do?" or "What do you intend to do with your major when you graduate from college?"

4. Make a list of the most impressive things about you.

SELECTED READINGS

—. *Beyond Words: An Introduction to Nonverbal Communication.*
Adler and Towne. *Looking Out/Looking In: Interpersonal Communication.*
Alberti and Emmons. *Stand Up, Speak Out, Talk Back: The Key to Self-Assertive Behavior.*
—. *Your Perfect Right.*
Applbaum and Anatol. *Strategy for Persuasive Communication.*
Applbaum, Jenson and Carroll. *Speech Communication: A Basic Anthology.*
Applbaum and others. *Fundamental Concepts in Human Communication.*
V. Axline. *Dibs: In Search of Self.*
Bach and Deutsch. *Pairing.*
Bach and Goldberg. *Creative Aggression.*
Bach and Wyden. *The Intimate Enemy.*
R. Bach. *Jonathan Livingston Seagull.*
L. L. Barker. *Listening Behavior.*
R. L. Benjamin. *Semantics and Language Analysis.*
D. K. Berlo. *The Process of Communication.*
E. Berne. *Games People Play: The Psychology of Human Relationships.*
—. *What Do You Say After You Say Hello?*
J. S. Bois. *The Art of Awareness.*
K. E. Boulding. *Image: Knowledge in Life and Society.*
D. E. Broadbent. *Perspective and Communication.*
A. Bry. *The TA Printer: Transactional Analysis in Everyday Life.*
C. Castaneda. *Journey to Ixtlan.*
S. Chase. *The Tyranny of Words.*
J. C. Condon. *Semantics of Communication.*
—, and Yousef. *An Introduction to Intercultural Communication.*
J. A. DeVito. *The Interpersonal Communication Book.*
—. *Language: Concepts and Processes.*
W. Dyer. *Your Erroneous Zones.*
Eisenberg and Smith. *Nonverbal Communication.*
P. Farb. *Word Play: What Happens When People Talk.*
J. Fast. *Body Language.*
V. E. Frankl. *Man's Search for Meaning.*
C. Frederick. *EST: Playing the Game the New Way.*
E. Fromm. *Art of Loving: An Inquiry into the Nature of Love.*
Galvin and Book. *Person to Person: An Introduction to Speech Communication.*
Giffin and Patton. *Basic Readings in Interpersonal Communication: Theory and Application.*
—. *Personal Communication in Human Relations.*
E. Goffman. *The Interaction Ritual: Essays on Face-to-Face Behavior.*
—. *The Presentation of Self in Everyday Life.*
T. Gordon. *P.E.T., Parent Effectiveness Training: The Tested New Way to Raise Responsible Children.*
J. H. Griffin. *Black Like Me.*
B. Gunther. *Sense Relaxation Below Your Mind.*
—. *What to Do Until the Messiah Comes.*
E. T. Hall. *Beyond Culture.*
—. *Hidden Dimension.*
—. *The Silent Language.*
W. V. Haney. *Communication and Organizational Behavior.*

T. A. Harris. *I'm OK, You're OK: A Practical Guide to Transactional Analysis.*

S. I. Hayakawa. *Language in Thought and Action.*

—. *The Misuse of Language.*

H. Hesse. *Siddhartha.*

E. Hoffer. *The True Believer.*

K. Horney. *Our Inner Conflicts.*

James and Jongeward. *Born to Win: Transactional Analysis with Gestalt Experiences.*

W. Johnson. *People in Quandaries: The Semantics of Personal Adjustment.*

D. Jongeward. *Transactional Analysis: The OK Boss.*

S.M. Jourard. *The Transparent Self: Self-Disclosure and Well-Being.*

Kahn and Cannel. *The Dynamics of Interviewing.*

J. Kavanaugh. *Celebrate the Sun.*

Keen and Fox. *Telling Your Own Story.*

J. W. Keltner. *Interpersonal Speech Communication.*

M. Knapp. *Nonverbal Communication.*

J. Lair. *I Ain't Much Baby—But I'm All I've Got.*

I. Lee (ed.). *Language of Wisdom and Folly.*

Lorayne and Lucas. *The Memory Book.*

M. Maltz. *Psychocybernetics.*

B. Marshall. *Experience in Being.*

A. Maslow. *Toward a Psychology of Being.*

Matson and Montagu (eds.). *Human Dialogue.*

R. May. *Love and Will.*

—. *Man's Search for Himself.*

M. Mayeroff. *On Caring.*

A. Mehrebian. *Nonverbal Communication.*

L. Metcalf. *Values Education: Rationale, Strategies and Procedure.*

K. A. Menninger. *Love Against Hate.*

—. *Man Against Himself.*

A. Montagu. *Touching: The Human Significance of the Skin.*

Myers and Myers. *The Dynamics of Human Communication: A Laboratory Approach.*

Newman and Berkowitz. *How to Be Your Own Best Friend.*

Nichols and Stevens. *Are You Listening?*

Nierenberg and Calero. *How to Read a Person Like a Book.*

G. Orwell. *1984.*

Pace and others. Communicating Interpersonally: A Reader.

L. J. Peters. The Peter Plan: A Proposal for Survival.

—, and Hull. *The Peter Principle: Why Things Always Go Wrong.*

J. Powell. *Why Am I Afraid to Tell You Who I Am?*

H. Prather. *Notes to Myself.*

Raths, Harmin and Simon. *Values and Teaching.*

C. Rogers. *On Becoming a Person.*

—, and Stevens. *Person to Person: The Problem of Being Human.*

Samovar and Porter. *Intercultural Communication: A Reader.*

V. Satir. *Peoplemaking.*

W. Schultz. *Joy.*

D. Seabury. *The Art of Selfishness.*

E. L. Shostrom. *Man, the Manipulator: The Inner Journey From Manipulation to Actualization.*

S. Simon. *I Am Loveable and Capable.*

S. Simon and others. *Values Clarification: A Handbook of Practical Strategies for Teacher and Student.*

B. F. Skinner. *Walden Two.*

M. J. Smith. *When I Say No, I Feel Guilty.*

C. M. Steiner. *Scripts People Live: Transactional Analysis of Life Scripts.*

B. Stevens. *Don't Push the River.*

J. O. Stevens. *Awareness: Exploring, Experimenting, Experiencing.*

J. Stewart (ed.). *Bridges Not Walls: A Book About Interpersonal Communication.*

—, and Cash, Jr. *Interviewing: Principles and Practices.*

M. Vernon. *Perception, Attention and Consciousness.*

K. Vonnegut, Jr. *Slaughterhouse 5.*

M. R. Thimpson. *Why Should I Hire You? Seven Proven Steps for Getting the Job You Want.*

K. Thurman. *Semantics.*

A. Toffler. *Future Shock.*

D. Trumbo. *Johnny Got His Gun.*

C. H. Weaver. *Human Listening: Processes and Behavior.*

M. Wentzell and D. K. Holland. *Optricks: A Book of Optical Illusions.*

SELECTED RESOURCES

Chapter 1

Readings

E. Berne. *What Do You Say After You Say Hello.*
W. Schutz. *Joy.*
Keen and Fox. *Telling Your Own Story.*
Newman and Berkowitz. *How to Be Your Own Best Friend.*
L. Zunin, *Contact: The First Four Minutes.*

Chapter 2

Readings

Adler and Towne. *Looking Out/Looking In. Interpersonal Communication.*
Applbaum, Jenson, and Carroll. *Speech Communication A Basic Anthology.*
J. A. DeVito. *The Interpersonal Communication Book.*
Galvin and Book. *Person to Person. An Introduction to Speech Communication.*
J. W. Keltner. *Interpersonal Speech Communication.*
Myers and Myers. *The Dynamics of Human Communication. A Laboratory Approach.*

Films/Videos

"Communication Primer." C22 min.
    Overview of the Communication Process.
"Information Processing." 30 min.
    Introduction to key communication concepts.
"The Communication Process"
    Description of the SMCR Model of Communication. C28 min., 1987.

Chapter 3

Readings

V. Axline. *Dibs: In Search of Self.*
D. Bone. *The Business of Listening: A Practical Guide to Effective Listening.*
L. Barker. *Listening Behavior.*
T. Gordon. *P.E. T., Parent Effectiveness Training The Tested Way to Raise Responsible Children.*
Nichols and Stevens. *Are You Listening?*
C. Rogers. *On Becoming a Person.*
L. Steil, L. Barker, K. Watson. *Effective Listening: Key to Your Success.*
C. Weaver. *Human Listening Processes and Behavior.*

Films/Videos

"Are You Listening?" C20 min.
    Good and bad listening are illustrated through scenes from a family's daily life.
"Introduction to Feedback." C11 min.
    Presents the idea and importance of feedback.

"Process of Communication." BW 48 min.
    Feedback is illustrated in three communication situations.
"Power of Listening." C30 min.
"Listening Beyond Words." C20 min.

Chapter 4

Readings

S. Broadbent. *Perception and Communication.*
C. Castenada. *A Separate Reality; Teaching Don Juan.*
W. B. Key. *Media Sexploitation and Subliminal Seduction.*
M. Vernon. *Perception, Attention and Consciousness.*
Wetzell and Holland. *Optricks: A Book of Optical Illusions.*

Films/Videos

"Information Processing." C35 min.
    Analysis by David Steinberg.
"Perception." C28 min.
"Omega." C13 min.

Chapter 5

Readings

H. Bosmajian. *The Rhetoric of Nonverbal Communication.*
C. Castenada. *Separate Reality.*
Eisenberg and Smith *Nonverbal Communication.*
J. Fast. *Body Language.*
B. Gunther. *Sense Relaxation Below Your Mind.*
E. T. Hall. *Beyond Culture.*
A. Kendon. "Some Functions of Gaze Direction in Sound Interaction," *Acta Psychologica 2b (1967).*
M. Knapp. *Nonverbal Communication.*
A. Mehrabian. *Nonverbal Communication.*
A. Montagu. *Touching. The Human Significance of the Skin.*
Nierenberg and Calero. *How to Read a Person Like a Book.*
H. Prather. *Notes to Myself.*
Reusch and Kees. *Non-verbal Communication: Notes on the Visual Perception of Human Relations.*
Wentzell and Holland. *Optricks: A Book of Optical Illusions.*
L. Zunin. *Contact: The First Four Minutes.*

Films/Videos

"The Critic." C10 min.
    Humorous criticism of abstractions. Narrated by Mel Brooks.
"Louder Than Words." 20 min. ISGS
    Explores various aspects of nonverbal communication.
"Solo." 17 min.
    Serves as a study of silence and communication within the environment.
"Communication: The Nonverbal Agenda." C30 min.
    An overview of nonverbal communication.

"The Tramp" BW28 min. Silent Fim, 1915.
"Making Your Point Without Saying a Word." C27 min., 1990.
"Kinesics and Proxemics" C60 min., 1983.
"Face Value." C38 min., 1988.

Chapter 6

R. L. Benjamin. *Semantics and Language Analysis.*
J. S. Bois. *The Art of Awareness.*
K. Boulding. *Image: Knowledge in Life and Society.*
S. Chase. *The Tyranny of Words.*
J. C. Condon. *Semantics and Communication.*
J. A. Devito. *Language: Concepts and Processes.*
P. Farb. *Word Play: What Happens When People Talk.*
S. I. Hayakawa. *Language in Thought and Action.*
W. Johnson. *People in Quandaries: The Semantics of Personal Adjustment.*
I. Lee (ed.). *Language of Wisdom and Folly.*
G. Orwell. 1984.
K. Thurman. *Semantics.*

Films/Videos

"To Be a Man."
    From the series. "Know What I Mean."
"The Eye of the Storm."
"The Language of Man."
"Profanity as a Second Language."
"Communities of Speech." C29 min., 1981.
    Examinations of American dialects.
"The Shape of Language." C29 min., 1981.
    Definition of language and how humans communicate.
"Men, Women, and Language." C29 min., 1981.
    Biological and cultural origins of the differences between men's and women's use of language.

Chapter 7

Readings

L. Buscaglia. *Living, Loving, and Learning.*
H. Hesse. *Siddhartha.*
K. Horney. *Our Inner Conflicts.*
S. M. Jourard. *The Transparent Self: Self-disclosure and Well-being.*
J. Lair. *I Ain't Much, Baby—But I'm All I've Got.*
M. Maltz. *Psychocybernetics.*
A. Maslow. *Toward a Psychology of Being.*
J. Powell. *The Secret of Staying in Love.*
J. Powell. *Why Am I Afraid to Tell You Who I Am?*
C. R. Rogers. *On Becoming a Person.*
Rogers and Stevens. *Person to Person. The Problem of Being Human.*

Films/Videos

"Adventures of *." C10 min.
  Animated portrayal of human development to adulthood, emphasizing the inability to find happiness.
"Aspects of Behavior." C31 min.
  Dr. A. Maslow's last filmed interview (1971).
"Black History: Lost, Stolen or Strayed." 1 hr.
  Black self-concept.
"Black and White: Uptight." C35 min.
  Explores the ways in which prejudice is perpetuated.
"Eye of the Storm." C25 min.
  Blue Eyes Vs. Brown Eyes.
"Feelings of Rejection." BW21 min.
  Shows effects of not being able to assert oneself in childhood.

Chapter 8

Readings

E. Berne, *Games People Play*.
E. Berne, *Sex in Human Loving*.
E. Berne, *The Structure and Dynamics of Organizations and Groups*.
E. Berne, *What Do You Say After You Say Hello?*
A. Bry, *The TA Primer: Transactional Analysis in Everyday Life*.
T. A. Harris, *I'm OK, You're OK: A Practical Guide to Transactional Analysis*.
James and Jongeward, *Born to Win*.
D. Jongeward, *Transactional Analysis: The OK Boss*.
C. M. Steiner, *Scripts People Live. Transactional Analysis of Life Scripts*.

Films/Videos

"TA" C30 min.
  Overview of Transactional Analysis.

Chapter 9

Readings

Applbaum and Anatol. *Strategies for Persuasive Communication*.
E. Hoffer. *The True Believer*.
S. Simmon and others. *Values Clarification. A Handbook of Practical Strategies for Teachers and Students*.
A. Toffler. *Future Shock*.

Films/Videos

"Duet." C9 min.,
  Two animated puppets show how two neighbors become bitter towards each other when one of them acquires a material object.
"51%." C25 min..
  Women's career options and new range of decisions available.

"Future Shock." C35 min.
   Visual portrayal of social, political, and future changes.
"Is It Always Right To Be Right." C8 min.
   Parable centers on poverty, race, generation gap.
"Moral Development," C30 min.
   Reenactment of Kohlberg's Moral Development scale.
"The Gods Must Be Crazy." Full length feature film, Twentieth Century Fox. Available on videocassette
   Humorous but lesson-filled film about the clash of cultures and the need for understanding
   and tolerance.
"The Star-Spangled Banner." C8 min.
   A moving essay on war.
"You Are What You Are Because Of What You Were When." C32 min.
   Examines values in a timeframe and how these affect strategic thinking decisions.
"You Pack Your Own Chute." C30 min.
   Recognize and overcome unrealistic fears which prohibit action.
"Transcendental Voyeurism."

Chapter 10

Readings

L. Metcalf. *Values Education: Rationale, Strategies, and Procedure.*
Peters and Hull. *The Peter Principle: Why Things Always Go Wrong.*
J. Jongeward. *Born to Win.*
A. Toffler.   *Future Shock.*
               3rd Wave.
D. Yankelovitch. *New Rules.*
G. Sheehy. *Passages.*

Films/Videos

"A Case Study for Critical Thinking: Vietnam." C, 1987.
"Logic." C29, 1988.
   The relationship between sound thinking and common sense.

Chapter 11

Readings

Addeo and Burger. *Ego Speak.*
Alberti and Emmons. *Stand Up, Speak Out, Talk Back: The Key to Self-Assertive Behavior.*
Alberti. *Your Perfect Right.*
Bach. *Creative Aggression.*
—. *Intimate Enemies.*
—. *Pairing.*
Daigon. *Violence.*
Fensterheim. *Don't Say Yes When You Want To Say No.*
Gordon. *Parent Effectiveness Training.*
—. *Teacher Effectiveness Training.*
—. *Leadership Effectiveness Training.*
Korda. *Power; How To Get It and How To Use It.*
Laswell and Lobsenz. *No Fault Marriage.*

O'Neill. *Open Marriage.*
—. *Shifting Gears.*
Ringer. *Winning Through Intimidation.*
Rubin. *Winners Notebook.*
Smith. *When I Say No I Feel Guilty.*

Films/Videos

"Fine Art of Keeping Your Cool." C25 min.
"Responsible Assertion." C20 min.
"When I Say No I Feel Guilty." C30 min.
"Dealing with Conflict and Confrontation." C Vol. 1, 73 min.
                                            C Vol. 2, 57 min.
                                            C Vol. 3, 83 min., 1993.
"The Art of Resolving Conflicts in the Workplace." C37 min., 1992.

Chapter 12

Readings

Alberti and Emmons. *Your Perfect Right.*
Bower, Sharon and Gordon. *Asserting Yourself.*
Smith, M. *When I Say No, I Feel Guilty.*

Films/Videos

"When I Say No, I Feel Guilty." C28 min.
    Overview of assertiveness techniques
"Responsible Assertion." C25 min.
    Introduction to assertiveness principles

Chapter 13

Readings

Adler, Rosenfeld, and Towne, *Interplay.*
H. Bloomfield, *Making Peace With Your Parents.*
Faber and Elaine, *How to Talk So Kids Will Listen and Listen So Kids Will Talk.*
H. Goldberg, *The Hazards of Being Male.*
H. Goldhor-Lemer, *The Dance of Intimacy.*
H. Halpren, *Cutting Loose: An Adult Guide to Coming to Terms With Your Parents.*
Phillips and Wood, *Communication and Human Relationships.*
Wilson, Hantz, and Hanna, *Interpersonal Growth Through Communication.*

Chapter 14

Readings

Blanchard and Johnson, *The One Minute Manager*
Doyle and Strauss, *How To Make Meetings Work*
A. Lakein, *How to Get Control of Your Income and Your Life*
R. Frost, *The Road Less Traveled*

Films/Videos

"You Are What You are Because of What You Were When." C20 min.
"Group Dynamics—Group Think." C25 min.
"Decisions." C27 min.
"Interview Techniques." C25 min., 1992.
"Sell Yourself: Successful Job Interviewing." C23, 1990.

ANSWER GUIDE

Do not read the following materials, unless instructed to do so. It may ruin the activities for you, as well as for the other members of the class. Thank you!

COMMUNICATION QUIZ P. 24

1. F	4. F	7. F	10. T
2. F	5. T	8. F	11. F
3. F	6. F	9. F	12. T

VETERANS/ROOKIES P. 28

1. H	4. I	7. J	10. C
2. E	5. G	8. B	
3. A	6. D	9. F	

LISTENING QUIZ P. 41

1. F	6. F	11. F	16. T	21. F
2. F	7. F	12. T	17. T	22. F
3. F	8. T	13. T	18. F	23. F
4. F	9. F	14. T	19. T	24. T
5. F	10. F	15. T	20. T	25. T

"THE SOUND OF SILENCE" LISTENING ACTIVITY P. 47

a. In the first verse, to whom does the singer say "hello"?—darkness
b. Why does the singer want to talk to his old friend?—a vision softly creeping left its seeds while he was sleeping
c. He walked along streets made of what material?—cobblestone
d. He turned his collar to the_____ and _____?—cold and damp
e. What flashed and stabbed his eyes?—neon light
f. How many people did the singer see?—10,000 maybe more
g. To whom did the people bow and pray?—the neon god they made

PERCEPTION: AGREE/DISAGREE P. 79

1. D	4. A	7. A	10. D
2. D	5. A	8. A	11. A
3. A	6. D	9. D	

QUIZ: COMMON PERCEPTION P. 88

1. Bottom
2. To the right
3. Right
4. Blue, Red, White, Yellow, Black, Gold
5. Q, Z
6. 1,0
7. Left
8. 20
9. Red
10. 88
11. 5
12. Top left to bottom right
13. 12 (no #1)
14. Right
15. Top
16. Clockwise as you look at it
17. Roosevelt
18. 6
19. Left
20. 5
21. 6
22. Bashful
23. 6
24. (Skipped on purpose)
25. Ace of Spades
26. Left
27. ONE
28. *, #
29. 3
30. Counterclockwise

COUNT THE SQUARES P. 92

There are forty squares in the diagram

HIDDEN ASSUMPTIONS TEST P. 142

1. Yes
2. 1
3. No (Living)
4. Match
5. all of them
6. 1 hour
7. White
8. Half-way
9. 5 cents, 50 cents
10. 9
11. Different opponents
12. 2
13. (No question)
14. He didn't know it was B.C.
15. They don't
16. None (Moses?)
17. Impossible
18. None
19. 3
20. 99 9/9
21. Can't
22. Go to bed in daytime
23. Doctor is mother
24. 12
25. U.S. of A.
26. Neither
27. 3 minutes

THE UNCRITICAL INFERENCE TEST P. 143

Story A		Story B	
1. T		1. ?	10. ?
2. ?		2. ?	11. T
3. ?		3. F	12. ?
4. T		4. ?	13. ?
5. ?		5. ?	14. T
6. ?		6. T	15. ?
7. ?		7. ?	16. ?
8. F		8. ?	17. ?
9. ?		9. ?	18. ?

STREET TALK TEST P. 149

1–c, 2–c, 3–b, 4–a, 5–b, 6–c, 7–a, 8–c, 9–c, 10–b, 11–d, 12–b, 13–b, 14–a, 15–c, 16–d, 17–c, 18–c, 19–b, 20–c, 21–a, 22–c, 23–a, 24–b, 25–c.

IT WAS BECAUSE. . . . P. 243

A–2, B–5, C–6, D–2, E–1, F–4, G–4, H–3, I–2, J–3, K–6.

THE NUCLEAR WAR P. 247

Below you will find a list of 10 people—you can either present all 10 or eliminate 2 and just present 8.

Alice, the science professor—She is a brilliant woman who, in addition to teaching, is doing cancer research. She is cold and impersonal, but the group has already recognized her as a good organizer and pacifier.

Jim, the minister—He has a very easy-going manner and has remained calm and optimistic during the hours of waiting for the radio message. He has helped settle several arguments and helped to calm Donna when she cried. His presence seems reassuring to the whole group.

Sally, a nurse—She is a brilliant woman who has completed nurse's training and has returned to college to receive a degree which will allow her to teach nurse's training courses. She is a very fastidious person and the idea of no bath, wearing the same clothes for a month, and sleeping with other people is offensive to her.

Linda, a literature major—She has read extensively and has already had several short stories published. She is a good story teller and has kept the group entertained with some of her stories. She has traveled widely and has had many interesting experiences which she can share. She was in the Peace Corp at one time and has taken a survival course.

Donna, Fred's wife—Ordinarily she has a pleasant personality; but now she is somewhat temperamental and excited, because she is expecting a baby in two months. She had a tearful outburst soon after the group entered the shelter.

Fred, a medical student—He has had two years of medical study and spent four years in the Navy as a medical assistant. He has close association with his father who is a doctor. You know he would be a great aid; but he refuses to stay unless his wife, Donna, is also chosen to stay.

Joe, a repairman—He is the only one without some college education. He has a great deal of practical knowledge and would be able to take care of the air-filtration system. He sneaked a candy from the food supply and seems unaware of the necessity for self-control as far as food and water supply is concerned. He is a rather uninteresting overweight fellow.

John, a basketball player—He is a big, husky, black basketball player, the star center of the team. He is highly respected by everyone on campus. He is physically strong and was the only one able to lift the heavy metal plate that had to be put over the shelter door. He has a wife and a child who may have survived the bomb, if they reached shelter in time.

Tim, a musician—He gets along well with everyone. He has a contagious smile and a good sense of humor. He plays the guitar and has helped improve everyone's mood. He is attentive towards the girls and has already offended Helen who thinks he is being fresh.

Helen, a home economics major—She is studying nutrition and dietetics. Her training makes her efficient (even domineering and bossy) and the first thing she did was to appraise the food supply. She is an imaginative cook and could fix the shelter's food supply in an appealing way. She is also a very sexy, attractive young woman.

FIVE SAMPLE SITUATIONS FOR ASSERTION TRAINING P. 313

1. a. Non-Assertive
   b. Assertive
   c. Aggressive

2. a. Assertive
   b. Aggressive
   c. Non-Assertive

3. a. Assertive
   b. Aggressive
   c. Non-Assertive

4. a. Aggressive
   b. Non-Assertive
   c. Assertive

5. a. Non-Assertive
   b. Aggressive
   c. Assertive